The Gleam of Bayonets

The Battle of Antietam
and the Maryland Campaign of 1862

by James V. Murfin

Maps by James D. Bowlby

Introduction by James I. Robertson, Jr.

BONANZA BOOKS
NEW YORK

DEDICATED TO

THE MEMORY OF

PRIVATE

LEVI MITCHELL SCOTT

(1835 - 1904)

COMPANY D

(SMYTH RIFLE GREYS)

48TH VIRGINIA INFANTRY REGIMENT

JONES' BRIGADE

JACKSON'S DIVISION

JACKSON'S CORPS

ARMY OF NORTHERN VIRGINIA

Foreword

Few battles in which Americans died have left such a mark on history as did Antietam. Few battles have held in their final moments of victory and defeat the vast political, economic, and military implications that did this bloodiest single day of the Civil War. Antietam was the turning point in the history of the Confederacy; it was, diplomatically speaking, one of the decisive battles of the world; on it hinged the very existence of the United States. Seldom have two protagonists engaged in open, deadly conflict with such high stakes resting on the consequence. Never in American history have two army commanders been charged with such grave responsibilities.

On September 4, 1862, General Robert E. Lee began crossing the Potomac River with the Army of Northern Virginia. His sojourn in Maryland lasted only 14 days, but they are 14 days we can ill afford to forget. Lee brought with him the hopes and fears of a newborn nation; an undefeated nation on the verge of foreign recognition and independence. When he returned to Virginia on the night of September 18, he left on record one of the most gallant struggles in military history; a battle which brought neither victory nor defeat, but which opened the door for the ultimate downfall of his government.

Any study of the Battle of Antietam (Sharpsburg) and the Maryland Campaign of 1862, is, in the same sense, a study of Major General George Brinton McClellan, for it is this Civil War campaign which made and ultimately broke his military career. The two are synonymous; the story of one is the story of the other. They are so closely entwined that one cannot fail to note the enormous effect this one man had on the destiny of his nation.

The Maryland Campaign began, not with invasion on September 4, but in the early morning hours of September 2, when Abraham Lincoln called on Maj. Gen. McClellan at his home in Washington and asked him to assume command of the defenses of the city. The relationship between these two men was a strange one. It had started in July of the previous year and had run a rugged course through a winter and spring of inactivity and failure. By the time September 1862 had come, the Union was at its lowest ebb, with three major defeats and not one victory to its credit. Lincoln was faced with a critical moment in his career; he was faced with his greatest dilemma, George B. McClellan.

In order to fully comprehend the true significance of the battle at Sharpsburg, it is first necessary to glance back to those days from July 1861, when McClellan came to Washington to command the Federal Army of the Potomac, to September 1862, when Lee decided to bring his war for Southern independence to Northern soil. These were days of apprehension and frustration for the President of the United States, unending days of fruitless efforts to gain that which he needed so desperately, a victory from the commander of his army.

The conduct of the Maryland Campaign by both Lee and McClellan cannot be explained away with the Dunkard Church, or Bloody Lane, or Burnside Bridge, dramatic as they may be. Lincoln's struggle to effect an efficient military command system, in which Antietam played such an important role, is the struggle between the Chief Executive, Commander-in-Chief of the armed forces, the nation's policy maker, and a man whose lust for military power led the nation to the brink of disaster.

The alternating currents of George B. McClellan's mind, and how, psychologically and militarily, they affected nearly 17 months of the Civil War, are examined in Chapter One of this manuscript; "McClellan—Lincoln's Dilemma." The author in no way attempts to evaluate the complexities of the art of war and how it is applied to or affects this month of crisis; September 1862. It is considered essential, however, that the reader have some interpretation of this relationship between President and General as an introduction to one of the most fascinating phases of American history.

As this manuscript progressed, it became increasingly apparent that it was developing more into a study of General McClellan than the Battle of Antietam. It seemed almost a natural course of events, as if the cards were falling into a predestined position. McClellan's actions affected every move of Lee's army, and Lee, in some way, affected each of McClellan's decisions. One would expect this in war, but never as prevalent as in this campaign. Lee invaded Maryland *in spite of* McClellan; he divided his army in the face of the enemy *because of* McClellan; he stood at Sharpsburg *in defiance of* McClellan. Though Lee's strategy has been questioned and his army was nearly ruined, in every way the Maryland Campaign was his show. He was fighting for survival. McClellan was fighting for his military career. When battle was done, both had lost. The relationship, therefore, between these two generals is as important to the story as that between Lincoln and McClellan. It is the underlying theme of this manuscript.

If the following pages are opinionated, it is because the author comes from an opinionated age; the age of the Civil War Round Table, where a subject is selected, developed, and openly discussed and analyzed. It is through this very manifestation of Civil War interests that this manuscript stems. The Maryland Campaign of 1862 has been carried from one Round Table to another and will always remain a favorite among scholars and historians. This student makes no claims to solving its mysteries, nor will this study quench the thirst of those who seek the "last word." Much work remains to be accomplished. Antietam has been sadly neglected. It remains one of the most decisive battles of the Civil War, yet its fields pass calmly through the years almost unnoticed. Should this work do little more than arouse interest in one of the most beautiful of our historic shrines, then the mission will be fulfilled.

James V. Murfin
Hagerstown, Maryland

Preface

Seldom is a historical study, particularly of the Civil War period, accomplished by one man alone. This manuscript claims no exception. Without the encouragement of a group of dedicated persons who felt that Antietam had been neglected much too long, *The Gleam of Bayonets* would not have been started. Whereas the Civil War Centennial years have conceived and nurtured writings on literally hundreds of phases of the conflict, primarily from new and renewed interests, this work stems from just the opposite; an alarming lack of interest in the "bloodiest single day" of the war. Research notes gathered through the years might well have remained dormant were it not for the realization that Antietam was neither well known or understood. Its Centennial observance, September 17, 1962, clearly illustrated this sad note.

The writing of *The Gleam of Bayonets* began as an assignment for the Civil War Centennial edition of the *Herald-Mail* newspaper in Hagerstown, Maryland, published in August 1962 to commemorate Antietam. When Mr. Thomas Yoseloff suggested expanding this foundation for book publication, the job of coordinating six years of research and writing was launched. His sincere interest in the subject was a major contribution to the manuscript's completion.

For nearly eight years I conferred with dozens of historians and buffs on every aspect of the Maryland Campaign of 1862. There was not always agreement on the decisiveness of the battle nor on McClellan's generalship, the two most argued points. Every effort was made, however, to report historical facts objectively. As research and writing progressed, conclusions were quickly drawn that September 17, 1862, was, in many ways, one of the most fateful days in American history. Documentary evidence further pressed the conclusion that George B. McClellan was responsible for a major Federal military failure and the continuation of the war for three additional years. Although support

11

for these convictions is strong among historians, this student must bear sole responsibility for the conclusions expressed herein.

The Gleam of Bayonets can in no way be considered the last word on Antietam. The mysteries surrounding this campaign will invite students to its study for years to come. Eventually a complete and definitive analyzation will be made. Until such time, it is my hope that this effort will be a contribution of some value to its better understanding.

A deep debt of gratitude is owed a gentleman whose name should appear on the title page; Louis E. Tuckerman. Mr. Tuckerman, a teacher of long standing and respectability in Washington County, Maryland, refuses credit for the accomplishments of his students. In actuality, it was his unwavering faith and patience and a phenomenal knowledge of Antietam that guided this manuscript. Instructor of American History at Hagerstown Junior College, Mr. Tuckerman read, criticized, and advised on nearly every phase of the writing. More often than not, it was his sound judgement and genius for interpreting the military minds of Lee, Lincoln, and McClellan that set my work on the right path.

Sharing an important part of the credit for this manuscript is a young graduate student of history at Rice University, Joseph L. Harsh. Mr. Harsh's interest in Antietam predates his charter membership in the Hagerstown Civil War Round Table during high school. At Gettysburg College, where his senior thesis on the morning phase of the battle received high praise, he demonstrated great promise as a young historian. From a mutual interest in Antietam and a close friendship, developed what we considered the best foundation for writing history; a meeting of the minds or "historical therapy," as it came to be known. Through a series of weekly confrontations at the desk as well as on the battlefield, many problems were solved, questions posed and answered, and theories developed and exploded. Joe Harsh's keen awareness of history and its complexities makes him a likely subject for future Antietam honors.

E. B. Long's name has probably appeared on more Civil War acknowledgement pages than any other; such is the respect accorded his work. His research for Bruce Catton's Civil War Centennial History is a milestone in the field. Through Mr. Long's generosity, several years of Antietam "road-work" in the form of his Centennial History notes were compiled into one package and made available for my use.

These few lines are meager efforts at expressing appreciation to a fine gentleman and good friend. Without his aid, the manuscript would not have been completed.

Dr. Francis A. Lord, whose collection of regimental histories was placed at my disposal, ranks high in esteem by writers throughout the nation, this student included. It was his vast knowledge of the Federal common soldier that aided in locating much of the human interest surrounding Antietam. Through the critical days of this work, his never ending encouragement and willingness to answer questions were valued beyond expression.

My most sincere appreciation to Dr. James I. Robertson, Executive Director, United States Civil War Centennial Commission, who has written the Introduction to this book. Our close relationship throughout the months of work greatly strengthened that much needed morale to face a historical writer's frustrations. I am, indeed, honored by his comments.

The battle maps are the work of James D. Bowlby, Alexandria, Virginia, a long-time Antietam student. Through a series of field surveys over ten years, Mr. Bowlby revised the famous Cope series of time-interval maps, fourteen in all. The original research has been accepted by the Antietam National Battlefield Site as the most accurate interpretation of the Campaign. I am indebted to Mr. Bowlby for his contribution, and to Mr. William Mumma, Mr. Earl Anderson, Mr. Theron Rinehart, and Mr. Charles Koontz of Hagerstown, Maryland, for their assistance in the preparation of the final art.

I would be remiss if I failed to extend special appreciation to Mr. John Knickerbocker, Director of the Civil War Institute, Gettysburg College, Gettysburg, Pennsylvania. The Institute houses one of the finest collections of Civil War books in the country and was opened as my research base for many months. Mr. Knickerbocker's many considerations permitted me to circumvent numerous problems in obtaining inaccessable material. I am indebted also to Mrs. Reba Sponcler, Research Librarian, Washington County Free Library, Hagerstown, Maryland, and to her staff for fulfilling my research needs with such grace and kindness.

In today's Civil War writings, the emphasis is on heretofore unpublished material. Two of the more valuable contributions to the study of the Maryland Campaign of 1862 included in this manuscript fall into this category; the Jefferson Davis "Pennsylvania" document and the Frederick, Maryland, photographs. Mr. Louis H. Manarin, to whom sole credit for research on the "Davis proclamation" must be given, unselfishly granted me permission to use his notes extensively throughout Appendix B. Mr. Manarin is editor of the North Carolina Confederate Commission's monumental Centennial publication, *North Carolina Troops: A Roster, 1861-1865.* His "Davis" discovery was published first in *The North Carolina Historical Review,* April 1964. Mr. Benjamin B. Rosenstock, an Attorney-at-Law in Frederick, Maryland, is a grandson of the owner of the photographs of Union and Confederate troops in that city. The Confederate photograph has never been published and is considered by experts as a rarity; the only known photograph of Confederate troops in formation during a campaign. Although there is no documentation to identify the date or military unit, the Rosenstock family memoires substantiate that it was taken during the Confederate occupation, September 1862. I am indebted to both Mr. Manarin and to Mr. Rosenstock for making their research available.

Members of the Hagerstown Civil War Round Table were a constant source of encouragement and assistance. Specifically, I must mention those who aided me with the loan of books and information concerning everything from ammunition to river fords: Hilten Bennett, Samuel Pruett, R. U. Darby, George Cash, E. Russell Hicks, John Divine, John Frye, Charles E. Petty, Dr. Edward L. Vail, the Rev. John Schildt, and Thomas Germack.

My appreciation to Robert Lagemann and John Bryce, Jr., Historians, and Dwight Stinson, former historian, Antietam National Battlefield Site, for the use of maps and manuscripts and their own studies of Antietam; Robert H. Fowler, Editor, Col. Wilbur S. Nye, Frederic Ray, and Beverly Fowler of *Civil War Times Illustrated* for their support while I was employed by that publication, and for the use of the magazine's files of photographs and articles; Franklin Schurz, Jr., Publisher, Joseph Harp, Editor, and Harry Warner, Staff Writer, Hagerstown *Herald-Mail,* for seeing fit to publish my original Antietam study.

I am indebted to many others who offered valuable assistance in obtaining rare manuscripts, letters, diaries, and photographs. Their names are mentioned here with sincere appreciation: Norman Larson, Raleigh, North Carolina; Jeanne and Reginald Predham, Neptune

City, New Jersey; William Welch, Rochester, New York; Lester Howland, Henrietta, New York; J. Howard Beckenbaugh, Boonsboro, Maryland; Elden Billings, Washington, D. C.; Mr. and Mrs. Hugh B. Okeson, West Richfield, Ohio; Kenneth M. Broughton, Secretary, Confederate Historical Society, London, England; Maxwell H. Herriott, Milwaukee, Wisconsin; Gerald Nelson Hess, Hyattsville, Maryland; Robert Shosteck, Curator, B'nai B'rith Committee on Jewish Americana, Washington, D. C.; Robert Waitt and Betty Bacon, Richmond Civil War Centennial Committee, Richmond, Virginia; George Beck, Sunbury, Pennsylvania; George Markham, Milwaukee, Wisconsin.

William H. Haggard, National Weather Records Center, Ashville, North Carolina; C. E. Dornbusch, Cornwallville, New York; Willard E. Wight, Decatur, Georgia; Harold R. Manakee, Director, Maryland Historical Society, Baltimore, Maryland; J. Harman Smith, Georgia Department of Archives and History, Atlanta; David Estes, Emory University Library, Atlanta; R. S. Wilson and R. L. Duncombe, United States Naval Observatory, Washington; Hal Bridges, History Department, University of Colorado; Dr. David Mearns and Dr. C. Percy Powell, Manuscript Division, and Carl E. Stange, Prints and Photographs Division, Library of Congress; Josephine Cobb, National Archives; Stanley Wagner, Harrisburg, Pennsylvania; Mildred H. Thompson, Takoma Park, Maryland; David B. Sabine, Yonkers, New York; Barbara Harper, Gettysburg, Pennsylvania.

And to the following archives, libraries, historical societies, and private collectors for use of letters, diaries, manuscripts, etc., listed in Bibliography: Union Theological Seminary Library, Richmond; Columbia University Library, New York; Historical Society of Pennsylvania, Philadelphia; Illinois State Historical Library, Springfield; North Carolina Department of Archives and History, Raleigh; Virginia State Library, Richmond; Duke University Library, Durham, North Carolina; Public Record Office, London, England; Brown University Library, Providence, Rhode Island; Henry E. Huntington Library, San Marino, California; Yale University Library, New Haven, Connecticut; Massachusetts Historical Society, Boston; State Historical Society of Wisconsin, Madison; University of North Carolina Library, Chapel Hill; Dr. Francis A. Lord, Rockville, Maryland; Mrs.

Amy Bassett, Bluff Head-Huletts Landing, New York; Walter Wilgus, Falls Church, Virginia.

Special appreciation is extended to Mrs. Thelma Carbaugh, Gettysburg, Pennsylvania, who sacrificed countless lunch-hours and evenings to type various drafts of the manuscript. Her continued interest and masterful interpretation of my notes aided me greatly in meeting deadlines and publisher's specifications.

The ultimate completion of this work, however, is a tribute to the remarkable patience of a devoted family who sacrificed much during its progress. My wife, Nancy, read every word written through a dozen drafts and displayed the courage of a veteran in our joint quest to solve the riddles of Antietam. Her tolerance of long exploratory trips and her keen ability to perceive that which was all too often hidden from me was invaluable. I shall always be in her debt for the assistance and loyalty she gave this work.

Acknowledgments

The author gratefully acknowledges the following permissions to reprint copyrighted material in this work:

From *Basic History of the Confederacy* by Frank Vandiver, copyright © 1962, reprinted by permission of D. Van Nostrand Co., Inc., publisher.

From *Berry Benson's Civil War Book,* edited by Susan Williams Benson, copyright © 1962, by University of Georgia Press, reprinted by permission of the publisher.

From *Bohemian Brigade* by Louis M. Starr, copyright © 1954, by Louis M. Starr, reprinted by permission of Alfred A. Knopf, Inc., publisher.

From *The Civil War: The American Iliad, As Told by Those Who Lived It* by Otto Eisenschiml and Ralph Newman, copyright © 1956, reprinted by permission of the authors.

From *General Edmund Kirby Smith, C.S.A.,* by Joseph H. Parks, copyright © 1954, by Louisiana State University Press, reprinted by permission of the publisher.

From *Gunner With Stonewall* by William Thomas Poague, edited by Monroe F. Cockrell, copyright © 1957, by McCowat-Mercer Press, Inc., reprinted by permission of the publisher.

From *Halleck: Lincoln's Chief of Staff* by Stephen E. Ambrose, copyright © 1962, by Louisiana State University Press, reprinted by permission of the publisher.

From *A History of the South: The Confederate States of America, 1861-1865* by E. Merton Coulter, copyright © 1950, by Louisiana State University Press and the Littlefield Fund for Southern History, The University of Texas, reprinted by permission of Louisiana State University Press.

From *I Rode With Stonewall* by Henry Kyd Douglas, copyright © 1940, by The University of North Carolina Press, reprinted by permission of the publisher.

From *John Dooley, Confederate Soldier,* edited by Joseph T. Dur-

© 1945, by Charles Scribner's Sons, reprinted by permission of the publisher.

From *The Wartime Papers of R. E. Lee* by Clifford Dowdey and Louis H. Manarin, copyright © 1961, by The Commonwealth of Virginia, reprinted by permission of Little, Brown and Co., publisher.

From *Stonewall Jackson and the American Civil War* by Col. G. F. R. Henderson, copyright © 1961, by Longmans, Green and Co., reprinted by permission of David McKay Co., Inc., publisher.

Contents

Maps and Illustrations

Maps

Illustrations appear as a group following page 224.

Introduction

A current and popular pastime is to debate which of the 6,221 engagements fought during the American Civil War was *the* decisive battle. The error of such a diversion is twofold. First, it is impossible to stamp one tragic moment, one horrible event, as the watershed of a four-year war whose impact shook the very foundations of the Western Hemisphere's most powerful nation. Moreover, history is not a listing of stop-and-go, semi-isolated occurrences. Man's past is a continually flowing, undammed stream, fed by the tributaries of yesterday's experiences, and composed of the active molecules of human thoughts and deeds.

Be that as it may, proponents have argued that the war's climactic moment came with the Confederates' shortsighted salvos at Fort Sumert, at the Southern loss of strategic Fort Donelson, on a rise of ground near Gettysburg, or in the battle smoke that shrouded Federal victories at Atlanta or Nashville. Yet an increasing number of students regard still another engagement as the critical conflict of the war, and they have good reason for doing so.

Late in September, 1862, from the village of Sharpsburg, Md., a Wisconsin officer wrote his brother: "We were in the fearful battle at this place on the 17th—it was a great, enormous battle—a great tumbling together of all heaven and earth—the slaughter on both sides was enormous."

Indeed it was. Wesnesday, September 17, 1862, ranks as the bloodiest one day of an incomparably bloody civil war. In and around Sharpsburg, along the banks of a sluggish stream known as Antietam Creek, over 21,000 Americans fell dead or wounded in the course of a single day's fighting. It was war at its worst: bruising, vicious, open combat, devoid of much command leadership. Ralph Waldo Emerson might well have had the participants of this engagement in mind when he stated: "A hero is no braver than an ordinary man, but he is brave five minutes longer."

Antietam had more than its share of such valorous souls. It also contained personalities and decisions that form some of the might-have-beens in American history.

The central figure at Antietam—and consequently in this study— is Major General George Brinton McClellan, who early in September, 1862, resumed command of the twice-defeated but still determined Army of the Potomac. McClellan remains one of the war's more controversial figures, largely because his successes and his shortcomings were so pronounced. He never suffered a stunning defeat; but neither did he ever win a smashing victory. Antietam brought out the best and the worst in the man.

On the one hand, he restored confidence in the Federal army, learned of Lee's exact dispositions through an extraordinary stroke of good luck, and ultimately managed to thwart the most serious Confederate invasion of the North made during the war. But on the other hand, had McClellan at Antietam attacked Lee with the promptness, precision and persistence expected of a commanding general, the Civil War—at least in the East—might well have ended two and a half years sooner.

Tactically, Antietam was a draw. Strategically, politically, diplomatically and morally, it was a Union victory of high magnitude. The Confederates were forced back to the battle-scarred fields of Virginia. Southern morale received a stiff blow. Even worse for the Confederates, the stalemate at Antietam cut short the prospects of foreign intervention at a time when it seemed most likely to materialize in behalf of the South. Lastly, and in many respects most importantly, Lincoln used the springboard of the Antietam "victory" to issue his preliminary Emancipation Proclamation, a document which crystallized liberal opinion around the world in support of the Northern cause.

After September, 1862, the battle line of the Civil War were more clearly defined. Old issues evaporated as the conflict became one of state sovereignty and slavery vs. the Union and human liberty. Because both sides were in essence fighting for freedom—an idea that can never be compromised—the war after that fateful autumn lost its limitations and became one that of necessity had to be fought to the bitter end. Antietam was the catalyst in this transformation.

Here, presented in full for the first time, is an almost blow-by-blow account of the awesome battle fought along Antietam Creek. Nothing has been omitted; both sides receive equal treatment. Mr. Murfin undertook this study as a labor of love. Said labors extended over a period of years and included scores of hours spent tramping over the battlefield. Although he is not by training a professional historian, Mr. Murfin's research has been prodigious. He ably demonstrates a mastery of sources—which is more commendable because he is treating of that most complex of subjects: battle.

The author writes with interest, insight, and understanding. He instills life into the inanimate whole by allowing a host of battle participants to tell their own stories. The result is a skillfully woven narrative of contemporary recollections and modern commentary.

Most of all, the complicated and relatively neglected Battle of Antietam has at last found a worthy historian.

James I. Robertson, Jr.

Dramatis Personae

ABRAHAM LINCOLN, 1809-1865, 16th President of the United States of America. Serving 21st month in office during Maryland Campaign. 53 years of age.

JEFFERSON DAVIS, 1808-1889, President, Confederate States of America. Transylvania University; West Point, 1828. Northwest Frontier; War with Mexico. United States Congress, 1845; United States Senate, 1847; Secretary of War, 1853. Inaugurated President provisional Confederate government, February, 1861; permanent government, February 22, 1862. 54 years of age.

GEORGE BRINTON McCLELLAN, 1826-1885, Major General, United States Army. West Point, 1846. War with Mexico. Resigned, 1857. Vice-President, Illinois Central Railroad. President, Ohio and Mississippi Railroad. Maj. Gen., Ohio Volunteers; Maj. Gen., Regular Army, Department of the Ohio. Western Virginia Campaign. Command of Division of Potomac. Succeeded Winfield Scott as Commander-in-Chief of Federal armies. Peninsula Campaign, Spring, 1862. Commander, Army of the Potomac, Antietam. 36 years of age.

HENRY WAGER HALLECK, 1815-1872, Major General, United States Army. West Point, 1839. War with Mexico. Maj. Gen., August 1861. General-in-Chief of Federal armies, Maryland Campaign. 47 years of age.

AMBROSE EVERETT BURNSIDE, 1824-1881, Major General, United States Army. West Point, 1847. War with Mexico. Resigned, 1853. Manufactured firearms in Rhode Island. Invented breech-loading rifle, 1856. Treasurer, Illinois Central Railroad, 1861. 1st Manassas; coastal installations, North Carolina. Brig. Gen. after 1st Manasses. Commanded IX Corps, Left Wing, Army of the Potomac, Antietam. 38 years of age.

29

JOSEPH HOOKER, 1814-1879, Major General, United States Army. West Point, 1837. Seminole War; War with Mexico. Resigned, 1853. Farmed in far west. Brig. Gen., May 1861. Peninsula Campaign; 2d Manassas. Maj. Gen., May 1862. Commanded I Corps, Army of the Potomac, Antietam. Wounded. 48 years of age.

EDWIN VOSE SUMNER, 1797-1863, Major General, United States Army. Black Hawk War; War with Mexico. Brig. Gen., March 1861. Commanded II Corps, Army of the Potomac, Antietam. 65 years of age.

JOSEPH KING MANSFIELD, 1803-1862, Major General, United States Army. West Point, 1882. War with Mexico. Brig. Gen., May 1861. Maj. Gen., July 1862. Commanded XII Corps, Army of the Potomac, Antietam. Mortally wounded. 59 years of age.

JOHN SEDGWICK, 1813-1864, Major General, United States Army. West Point, 1837. Seminole War; War with Mexico. Brig. Gen., August 1861. Peninsula Campaign. Commanded 2d Division, II Corps, Army of the Potomac, Antietam. Wounded. 49 years of age.

WILLIAM HENRY FRENCH, 1815-1881, Brigadier General, United States Army. West Point, 1837. Seminole War; War with Mexico. Brig. Gen., September 1861. Commanded 3d Division, II Corps, Army of the Potomac, Antietam. 47 years of age.

ISRAEL BUSH RICHARDSON, 1815-1862, Major General, United States Army. West Point, 1841. Seminole War; War with Mexico. Indian scouting; farmed in Michigan. Brig. Gen., May 1861, Maj. Gen., July 1862. Commanded 1st Division, II Corps, Army of the Potomac, Antietam. Mortally wounded. 47 years of age.

WILLIAM BUEL FRANKLIN, 1823-1903, Major General, United States Army. West Point, 1843. War with Mexico. Brig. Gen., May 1861. 1st Manassas; Peninsula Campaign. Commanded VI Corps, Army of the Potomac, Antietam. 39 years of age.

JACOB DOLSON COX, 1828-1900, Brigadier General, United States Army. Oberlin College, 1851. Lawyer; state (N.Y.) Senator. Brig. Gen., May 1861. 2d Manassas. Commanded Kanawha Division, IX Corps, Army of the Potomac, Antietam. 34 years of age.

ROBERT EDWARD LEE, 1807-1870, General, Confederate States Army. West Point, 1829. War with Mexico; Superintendent, West Point, 1852-1855; led army against John Brown, Harpers Ferry. Offered command of Federal armies by Lincoln, April 18, 1861. Resigned U.S.A., April 23, 1861. Military advisor to Jefferson Davis. Peninsula Campaign; 2d Manassas. Commanded Army of Northern Virginia, Antietam. 55 years of age.

THOMAS JONATHAN ("Stonewall") JACKSON, 1824-1863, Major General, Confederate States Army. West Point, 1846. War with Mexico. Resigned U.S.A., 1851. Instructor, Virginia Military Institute. Brig. Gen., C.S.A., June 1861. 1st Manassas; Peninsula Campaign; 2d Manassas. Commanded Jackson's Corps, Antietam. 38 years of age.

JAMES LONGSTREET, 1821-1904, Major General, Confederate States Army. West Point, 1842. War with Mexico. Resigned U.S.A., June 1861. Brig. Gen., C.S.A., June 1861. 1st Manassas; Peninsula Campaign; 2d Manassas. Commanded Longstreet's Corps, Antietam. 41 years of age.

JAMES EWELL BROWN STUART, 1833-1864, Major General, Confederate States Army. West Point, 1854. Cavalry against John Brown, Harpers Ferry. Resigned U.S.A., May 1861. Brig. Gen., C.S.A., September 1861; Maj. Gen., July 1862. Peninsula Campaign; 2d Manassas. Commanded Confederate Cavalry, Antietam. 29 years of age.

DANIEL HARVEY HILL, 1821-1889, Major General, Confederate States Army. West Point, 1842. War with Mexico. Resigned, U.S.A., 1849. Instructor, Washington College; instructor, Davidson College; superintendent, North Carolina Military Institute, 1859. Brig. Gen., C.S.A., July 1861; Maj. Gen., March, 1862. Peninsula Campaign. Commanded D. H. Hill's Division, Jackson's Corps, Antietam 31 years of age.

AMBROSE POWELL HILL, 1825-1865, Major General, Confederate States Army. West Point, 1847. Seminole War; War with Mexico. Resigned, U.S.A., March 1861. Brig. Gen., C.S.A., February 1862; Maj. Gen., May 1862. Peninsula Campaign; 2d Manassas. Commanded "Hill's Light Division," Jackson's Corps, Antietam. 37 years of age.

JOHN G. WALKER, 1822-1893, Brigadier General, Confederate States Army. War with Mexico. Resigned U.S.A., March 1861. Brig. Gen., C.S.A., January 1862. Commanded Walker's Division, Longstreet's Corps, Antietam. 40 years of age.

LAFAYETTE McLAWS, 1821-1897, Major General, Confederate States Army. University of Virginia; West Point, 1842. War with Mexico. Resigned U.S.A., May 1861. Maj. Gen., C.S.A., May 1862. Peninsula Campaign. Commanded McLaws' Division, Longstreet's Corps, Harpers Ferry, Antietam. 41 years of age.

JOHN BELL HOOD, 1831-1879, Brigadier General, Confederate States Army. West Point, 1853. Resigned, U.S.A., April 1861. Brig. Gen., C.S.A., March 1862. Peninsula Campaign; 2d Manassas. Commanded Hood's Division, Longstreet's Corps, Antietam. 31 years of age.

HENRY KYD DOUGLAS, 1840-1903, Lieutenant, Confederate States Army. Franklin and Marshall College, 1859. Lawyer. Assistant Inspector General, Jackson's staff, Antietam. 22 years of age.

The Gleam of Bayonets

In apparent double battle line, the Federals were moving toward us at charge bayonets, common time, and the sunbeams falling on their well-polished guns and bayonets gave a glamour and a show at once fearful and entrancing.

Lt. E. A. Stickley
Stonewall Brigade
Army of Northern Virginia

We had not proceeded far before I discovered that a heavy force of the enemy had taken possesion of a cornfield in my immediate front and from the sun's rays falling on their bayonets projecting above the corn could see that the field was filled with the enemy, with arms in their hands, standing apparently at support arms.

Maj. Gen. Joseph Hooker
First Corps
Army of the Potomac

1

McClellan – Lincoln's Dilemma

Early on the morning of September 2, 1862, two grim-faced men made their way through the streets of Washington. The sky, dark and gloomy, reflected the despair of the nation's capital. Depression lay heavily on the shoulders of the two silent figures. It was a mood of dark forebodings, of troubled minds, and of a troubled nation. One was the Chief Executive of the United States. The other was the General-in-Chief of the armies. Both were on a mission that not only would bring rapid-fire repercussions, but would also have drastic effects on American history.

Washington was in a state of acute anxiety. Three days before, less than 30 miles from the city, the Federal army had suffered its third successive major defeat at the hands of the Confederate army. The remnants of Maj. Gen. John Pope's Army of Virginia—some 30,000 strong—had begun to filter into the streets of the capital from Manassas. Ambulances carrying the wounded were clogging the southern approaches. Stragglers and stalled wagons slowed the city's pace to a standstill. Liquor sales had been suspended. The Treasury Department and the banks were preparing to send their money to New York. Gunboats were anchored at strategic points on the Potomac. At the Navy Yard a fully-manned steamer, with boilers burning and captain's suite ready for the President, was floating with the tide.

In the face of impending crisis, panic gripped Washington. For the second time in less than 14 months, the Confederate army was at the doorstep of the Federal capital. It was firmly believed that another opportunity would not be passed by. Robert E. Lee's next move was as

35

inevitable as was Abraham Lincoln's trip that morning. Lincoln knew, as did his companion, Maj. Gen. Henry W. Halleck, that a storm of protest would be raised at the cabinet meeting that afternoon. His problem was not simple, and his only solution could not have been more complicated. The army was broken. The capital was in danger. The nation was on the brink of disaster. They must talk to the one man, the only man, who could deliver them from ruin.

It was a little over a year ago, as Washington lay in another seige of panic, that George Brinton McClellan, a brilliant thirty-four-year-old major general, fresh from a series of victories in western Virginia, received a telegram from Washington. "Circumstances make your presence here necessary . . . come hither without delay."[1] Five days after the tragedy at Manassas Junction, July 21, 1861, McClellan arrived in Washington. Within forty-eight hours he had assumed command of the Potomac Department of the Federal army.

McClellan was known to the War Department long before Manassas. His military career, although not spectacular, was impressive. He had graduated from West Point with high honors. Shortly thereafter, he served with Robert E. Lee, P. G. T. Beauregard, Joseph E. Johnston, and Winfield Scott in the war with Mexico. Sufficiently impressed with McClellan's record, Secretary of War Jefferson Davis sent the young officer to Europe in 1855 to observe armies and military tactics in the Crimean War. Duty as an engineering instructor at the military academy and later as an engineering officer in the West, led in 1857 to McClellan's appointment as chief engineer with the Illinois Central Railroad. By 1861 he had attained the presidency of the Ohio and Mississippi Railroad and was living in Cincinnati. At the outbreak of hostilities he was appointed a major general of Ohio volunteers; within a matter of weeks he received the same rank in the regular army and was assigned the Department of the Ohio (Illinois, Indiana, Ohio, and parts of Pennsylvania and western Virginia). In seniority he was the highest ranking officer in the army next to the old general-in-chief, Winfield Scott.

The campaign in western Virginia was not really a campaign at all. It was more a series of early contacts with the Confederates which, when reported to Washington, elevated McClellan's stock at the War Department. When the time came, McClellan was the only general with victories. Thus, he seemed the logical choice for command of the army.

With an air of confidence McClellan arrived in Washington and quickly began the almost impossible task of reorganizing the army into a force capable of defending the capital. His job, simply put, was to bring life to a defeated and disorganized army. Soldiers were deserting in wholesale lots. Morale was nonexistent. In one of his first reports, McClellan wrote:

I found no army to command; a mere collection of regiments cowering on the banks of the Potomac, some perfectly raw, others dispirited by the recent defeat. I found no preparations whatever for defence, not even to the extent of putting the troops in military positions. Not a regiment was properly encamped, not a single avenue of approach guarded. All was chaos, and the streets, hotels, and bar-rooms were filled with drunken officers and men absent from their regiments without leave—a perfect pandemonium. A determined attack would doubtless have carried Arlington Heights and placed the city at the mercy of a battery of rifled guns.[2]

The immensity of the situation, compounded by unforseen political problems, was summarized in an amazingly prophetical statement by Edwin M. Stanton, soon to become Secretary of War. "If [McClellan] had the ability of Caesar, Alexander, or Napoleon, what can he accomplish? Will not Scott's jealousy, cabinet intrigues, and Republican interference thwart him at every step?"[3] Any lesser man would have thrown his arms in despair and retreated to the comforts of business administration whence McClellan had come. But those very administrative abilities soon proved to be the panacea that Lincoln was seeking.

McClellan's lights burned long into the night. His perseverance astounded all of Washington. From dawn to sunset he drove himself with a force unlike any seen in the military for many years. Slowly the army began to catch the McClellan fever. Within a matter of weeks a new and exciting drama unfolded along the Potomac. Veterans of Manassas were aligned with new recruits and then organized into provisional brigades. New commanders were chosen as divisions gradually took shape. A new army was born, the name for which McClellan himself chose. "I saw the absolute necessity of giving a name to the mass of troops under my command, in order to inspire them with *esprit de corps;* I therefore proposed to call my command 'The Army of the Potomac.' "[4]

William H. Russell, a London *Times* correspondent who had witnessed the defeat at Manassas, wrote on September 2, 1861: "Never perhaps has a finer body of men in all respects of *physique* been assembled by any power in the world, and there is no reason why their *morale* should not be improved so as to equal that of the best troops in Europe."[5] Russell's statement was no exaggeration. What he had seen was a great transformation, a regeneration of the military forces of the United States. This was a lasting credit to McClellan, one of few he would gain during his military career. He had started with little—"a collection of undisciplined, ill-officered, and uninstructed men, who were, as a rule, much demoralized by defeat and ready to run at the first shot."[6] He ended with the finest army ever seen on the North American continent.

Even Lincoln soon caught the McClellan fever. The President was pleased with what he saw, and it appeared more and more each day that his selection of McClellan as a possible successor to "Old Fuss and Feathers" Scott, General-in-Chief of the armies, was correct. Nicolay and Hay, Lincoln's secretaries, wrote that McClellan "inspired a remarkable affection and regard" to everyone in Washington, from "the President to the humblest orderly who waited at his door."[7] Aside from Maj. Robert Anderson, who so valiantly defended Fort Sumter, McClellan was the Union's only hero. Although his victories in western Virginia were far from examples of military art, they were victories enough to inspire the army and the people. This was what Lincoln needed.

"No one has denied that McClellan was a marvelous organizer," wrote the Comte de Paris, who served for a period as the general's aide-de-camp:

His military bearing breathed a spirit of frankness, benevolence, and firmness. His look was piercing, his voice gentle, his temper equable, his word of command clear and definite. His encouragement was most affectionate, his reprimand couched in terms of perfect politeness. Discreet, as a military or political chief should be, he was slow in bestowing his confidence; but, once given, it was never withdrawn. Himself perfectly loyal to his friends, he knew how to inspire others with an absolute devotion.[8]

McClellan began a love affair with the army that would last throughout the war, though his career would not. The troops called him "Little Mac," and the press dubbed him "The Young Napoleon" because of his stature, manner and drive. He responded with a charm that endeared him to all hearts and he accepted the adulation as well deserved. It was obvious that McClellan had also caught the "fever."

On July 27, 1861, the day he took command, McClellan made an amazing confession to his wife. "I find myself in a new and strange position here: President, cabinet, Gen. Scott, and all deferring to me. By some strange operation of magic, I seem to have become the power of the land." He wrote of becoming the all-powerful leader. "I receive letter after letter, have conversation after conversation, calling on me to save the nation, alluding to the presidency, dictatorship, etc. . . . . I have no such aspiration. I would cheerfully take the dictatorship and agree to lay down my life when the country is saved."[9]

Within a matter of days after his arrival, McClellan wrote: "I have Washington perfectly quiet now. . . . I have restored order very completely already."[10] Though he had accomplished most extraordinary results and had all of Washington, including the Congress, at his feet,[11] the honeymoon did not last long. Soon the signs of strain between army headquarters and the various departments of the government began to show. "Little Mac" obviously wanted Scott's job of commanding all the armies and was determined not to "respect anything that [was] in the way."[12] The old general had had a great deal of respect for McClellan when the war started. Mac had served well with him in the war with Mexico, and Scott had subsequently watched his career carefully. In his first proposals to Lincoln on strategy, Scott had recommended McClellan as the leader of a vast Mississippi expedition to cut off the lifeline of the Confederacy. The picture had now changed, however. With the tenacity with which Napoleon plotted for military power, McClellan worked diligently for military superiority. His rows with General Scott started early and friction grew with each passing day. "The old general always comes in the way," McClellan wrote his wife. "He understands nothing, appreciates nothing. I have to fight my way against him. [He] is the most dangerous antagonist I have."[13]

Scott clearly saw the favoritism being shown McClellan and how, slowly but surely, he was being eased out of position. He began championing Henry W. Halleck, who was making a reputation for himself in the western theatre of operations. The agitation between Scott and McClellan increased until, under pressure from the White House and the War Department, the aged Scott retired from the army. On the first day of November, 1861, McClellan assumed command of all Federal forces and found " 'the army' just about as much disorganized as was the Army of the Potomac . . . no system, no order, perfect chaos."[14]

By this time, however, the pressure was on McClellan. In October, as the first signs of fall appeared, the public began to wonder why the Army of the Potomac had not taken to the field. Here was the man who had written to his wife on August 2: "I handed to the President tonight a carefully considered plan for conducting the war on a large scale. . . . I shall carry this thing on *en grande* and crush the rebels in our campaign . . ."[15] The weather was good and the roads were still dry. The time seemed most appropriate. For the first time since his arrival, McClellan began to show signs of weakness. The press, which only a few weeks before had praised his abilities, began yapping at his heels. "On to Richmond," the public clamored. The North now had a marvelous army of 168,000 well disciplined men, a thirty-mile ring of fortifications around Washington, and a military spirit that was the envy of all foreign observers. But none of these accomplishments brought McClellan any closer to the enemy, then still encamped at Manassas. To his critics McClellan snapped: "Let those who criticise me for the delay in creating an army and its material point out an instance when so much has been done with the same means in so short a time."[16]

In the fall of 1861 the Confederate forces at Manassas numbered, at the most, 41,000 men "capable of going into battle."[17] Allan Pinkerton, head of a private detective agency employed by McClellan, estimated 100,000 Southern troops. McClellan believed Pinkerton and made no attempt to reconnoiter with his own scouts. He thus established for the record one major fault on which historians would dwell for a century. On August 8, the general wrote to Scott: "I am induced to believe that the enemy has at least 100,000 men in front of us . . . with that force at my disposal, I would attack the positions on the other side of the Potomac and at the same time cross the river above the city in force."[18] The Confederates were thinking the same thing. On October 1, General Joseph E. Johnston, in command at Manassas, told Jefferson Davis that had he 19,000 more men as good as the

41,000 on duty, along with the necessary transportation and ammunition, he could "cross the Potomac and carry the war into the enemy's country."[19]

But as the days went by, McClellan's estimate of Confederate strength grew. Later, in October, he wrote to the Secretary of War: "As you are aware, all the information we have from spies, prisoners, etc., agrees in showing that the enemy have a force on the Potomac not less than 150,000 strong, well drilled and equipped, ably commanded, and strongly intrenched."[20]

Exactly why McClellan relied so heavily on Pinkerton's reports can never be adequately explained. Southern prisoners, escaped Federal prisoners, and trapped Northern citizens who were permitted to return to Washington, all confirmed much lower figures for the Confederate army. At least two newspapers,. *Harper's Weekly* and the Washington *National Republican,* reported by the end of September that the Rebel force numbered 60,000 troops. That "the total force of the enemy in Virginia does not exceed 100,000 men," one reporter wrote, "is as certain as it can be made by anything short of an actual count."[21] By this date the Army of the Potomac had at least 85,000 men available for advance into the field.[22]

To McClellan, at least, the Army of the Potomac was outnumbered and the general was being plagued with "a set of men to deal with unscrupulous and false; if possible they will throw whatever blame there is on my shoulders . . . I can't move without more means. . . . the enemy have from three to four times my force; . . . I . . . only wish to save my country, and find the incapables around me will not permit it."[23]

Although the Young Napoleon was growing increasingly weary of Lincoln as his superior ("I am becoming daily more disgusted with this administration—perfectly sick of it."),[24] the Commander-in-Chief seemed to have "absolute confidence" in the general. Lincoln supported McClellan's repeated delays. "You shall have your own way," the President had told McClellan.[25] And in a December message to Congress, Lincoln publicly defended the selection of McClellan to head the armies:

It is a fortunate circumstance that neither in council nor country was there, as far as I know, any difference of opinion as to the proper person to be selected . . . there is . . . hope there will be given him, the confidence, and cordial support thus, by fair implication, promised, and without which, he cannot, with so full efficiency, serve the country.[26]

While defending McClellan publicly, however, Lincoln was privately very disturbed. It had become painfully evident that the general had no plans in the works for any offensive action. "I will hold McClellan's horse if he will only bring us success," said the President.[27] Although he was ever mindful of the importance of defending Washington and was determined not to let it rest unmanned, Lincoln wanted McClellan to take to the field before the bad weather of winter arrived. There was still time if he hurried. Therefore, early in December, Lincoln, more to prod McClellan than anything else, submitted a plan of attack on the Confederate forces at Manassas. The general quickly rejected Mr. Lincoln's ideas and replied that he had "actively turned toward another plan of campaign" that he did not think "at all anticipated by the enemy . . ."[28] He told the President nothing more. This was the first inkling of McClellan's forthcoming Urbana plan, which would place him between the enemy at Manassas and the Confederate capital at Richmond. But while the general still kicked it around in his mind, the rains came and winter compounded his problems. For the first time McClellan had a legitimate excuse for staying in camp. Then he came down with typhoid fever. All military plans in the Eastern theatre came to a complete standstill. Not a single concrete blueprint for action had been proposed since McClellan had come to Washington six months earlier.

On January 27, 1862, Lincoln wrote General War Order No. 1 directing that a general movement of all Federal forces, both army and navy, be made against the Confederates by February 22.[29] The order itself was absurd. Military orders are simply not written a full month in advance of execution with complete disregard for interim events. Lincoln knew this and was severely ridiculed for it, but he had ulterior motives. Pressure on the White House was overwhelming. McClellan was now out of his sickbed, his illness not as severe as Lincoln had imagined. How else could he move McClellan into action without openly breaking his publicly stated confidence?

Maria Lydig Daly, wife of a prominent judge, wrote in her diary on January 29, 1862, that "the rebel army . . . threatens Washington, and still hopes to take it, whilst over three hundred thousand soldiers lie opposite them, idle and well-fed, with full pay, their families supported by public charity, their officers spending their time in reveling, flirting, and drinking." Mrs. Daly recorded the rumors circulating Washington society. "McClellan, they now say, is incapable, and is striving after the Presidency. . . . It will not be worth having soon."[30] Years later McClellan defended these accusations when he wrote:

They committed a grave error in supposing me to be politically ambitious and in thinking that I looked forward to military success as a means of reaching the presidential chair. At the same time they knew that if I achieved marked success my influence would necessarily be very great throughout the country—an influence which I should certainly have used for the good of the whole country, and not for that of any party at the nation's expense.[31]

On January 14, President Lincoln made a most important change in his administration. Simon Cameron, inefficient Secretary of War, was replaced by Edwin M. Stanton, brilliant lawyer of some renown, energetic, outspoken, a man who liked and demanded power, and a Democrat. McClellan, regarded as a prominent member of the Democratic party, would now have at least one friend in the administration, or so he thought. Between Stanton's appointment and his actual occupation of office, he had gone to McClellan's home with a proposition that he would not accept the office unless the general was certain that he could make some valuable contribution to ending the rebellion. McClellan consented, although he was highly perturbed at Lincoln for making the appointment without consulting him first. Exactly why Stanton went to McClellan is unknown, for he embodied precisely what McClellan opposed. Where the general was against any interference into military affairs by civilians, Stanton had an intense dislike for professionally trained soldiers. He would, in ensuing months, become one of McClellan's bitterest enemies. That evening, however, Stanton played one of his best roles. "He said that acceptance would involve very great personal sacrifices on his part, and that the only possible inducement would be that he might have it in his power to aid me in the work of putting down the rebellion; that he was willing to devote all his time, intellect, and energy to my assistance, and that together, we could soon bring the war to an end. If I wished him to accept he would do so, but only on my account . . ."[32]

In late January, McClellan showed the first signs of his Urbana plan to the War Department. Stanton told him to take it direct to the President, which McClellan did. The general advocated an amphibious movement down the Potomac and through the Chesapeake Bay, to Urbana at the mouth of the Rappahannock River, where he would establish a base and from there a direct line into Richmond. This not only would pull the potentially dangerous Confederate army away from the fringes of Washington, but it would employ the easiest possible method of supplying his army, via naval routes, the York River, and then by rail from West Point to Richmond. Lastly, McClellan announced, this plan would "gain a decisive victory which [would] end the war."[33]

Lincoln wasted no time in disapproving the plan. He immediately repeated his order for the Army of the Potomac to move on Manassas not later than the 22d of February. McClellan was panic-stricken at the thought of the overwhelming odds facing him, and he begged Lincoln to reconsider his Urbana scheme. After much soul-searching, and much against his better judgement, the President finally relented. McClellan felt so much better that for the first time in months he had some nice things to say about Lincoln. But the President was obsessed with a fear for the safety of Washington. While McClellan was sailing away on his little adventure (the success of which Lincoln doubted), the Rebels might launch a full-scale attack against the capital. Lincoln had made a serious mistake in not forcing McClellan to attack Manassas and clean out the thorn that was in his side. The more he thought about it, the more it pained him that he had not insisted. Finally, on March 8, the President summoned the general to the White House to discuss "a very ugly matter."[34]

Rumors had been circulating through official Washington that McClellan was deliberately leaving the city to the Rebels, "that my plan of campaign was . . . conceived with the traitorous intent of removing its defenders from Washington, and thus giving over to the enemy the capital and the government, thus left defenceless."[35] Only McClellan's account of his meeting with Lincoln remains. In this he quotes the President as saying that it looked "much like treason" to him. The general was enraged. "I arose, and, in a manner perhaps not altogether decorous towards the chief magistrate, desired that he should retract the expression, telling him that I could permit no one to couple the word treason with my name." Lincoln assured him that it was only rumor and that he himself did not believe it to be an act of treason. Nonetheless, McClellan insisted on proving to the President that there was no basis to the stories by laying out detailed plans for the Richmond campaign, the first time that he had done so. Again the President reluctantly approved;[36] but to put a check on McClellan, he issued an order placing the twelve new divisions of the army into four corps commanded by four senior officers, all of whom outranked McClellan, and several of whom were older and who resented the young commander.[37]

On top of all of McClellan's problems, the Confederates gave him the real setback. The day following his session with the President, the general was informed that the Rebels had evacuated their camp at Manassas and repaired to a position behind the Rappahannock. This forced a cancellation of the Urbana plan. In a rush of blind fury, McClellan ordered an immediate advance and occupation of the enemy's site. In so doing, he nearly ended his career. It not only appeared foolish, moving so rapidly into the evacuated area after months of attack delays, but once there, it was apparent to all that the enemy's forces were far less than everyone had been led to believe. Now the suspicions about "Little Mac" began to gain impetus. It would be recalled that he had done this same thing in western Virginia. Correspondents sent back stories telling of a camp which could not have housed more than 60,000 Confederates, and reports were offered second hand that the Confederates themselves had stated these figures. To hide his embarrassment, McClellan rebuked the papers for trifling "with the reputation of an army" and deluding the country with "gross understatement of the number of the enemy."[38] Rather than question Pinkerton's figures, he remained loyal to the original report. It is significant to note that though McClellan's memoirs were written years later when, in retrospect, the Pinkerton figures appeared ridiculous, he failed through quite obvious intentions to give the true picture. Not once did he alter, even through footnotes, any facts or figures which by that time were contradictive of common knowledge. Nor did the editors, who on several occasions defended the general's statements, attempt to make corrections.

This series of events left Lincoln little choice but to issue his War Order No. 3. "Major General McClellan having personally taken the field at the head of the Army of the Potomac, until otherwise ordered, he is relieved from the command of the other Military departments, he retaining command of the Department of the Potomac."[39] There immediately sprang two schools of thought on the significance of this order. It was obvious that Lincoln had taken about all he could take. The pressure from the War Department to remove the general from command, coupled with his increasing anxieties for some definitive military actions in the east, forced him into a decision that was long overdue. On the other hand, the order had stated "until otherwise ordered," which clearly meant to McClellan supporters (as it did to the general himself) that this was only temporary and that it had been done because McClellan, being in the field with the Army of the Potomac, could not direct overall operations of all the commands. The order itself seemed to have little if any effect on McClellan. He responded with a cordial letter of acceptance to the President and then immediately launched another plan of attack on Richmond, this time between the York and James Rivers on what was known as the Peninsula.

Neither Stanton nor Lincoln was overly enthusiastic about the proposals. Yet, once again the Commander-in-Chief consented, this time with certain conditions. Washington could not be left unguarded, nor could Manassas, now that it was in Federal control. McClellan must see to that before he left. Stanton's message to McClellan struck an impatient cord. "Move the remainder of the force down the Potomac, choosing a new base at Fortress Monroe, or anywhere between here and there; or at all events, move the remainder of the army at once in pursuit of the enemy by some route."[40] Few times in the history of this country has a general taken to the field with such wholesale mistrust from his superiors.

The first regiments of the Army of the Potomac began their amphibious movement from Alexandria on March 17. They would establish their base of supply around April 1 at Fortress Monroe, which was still held by Federal forces. McClellan himself was anxious to get started. He left Alexandria on April 1 after a brief interview with the President, who had come to see him off. The general made no attempt to assure Lincoln that he was following his orders to leave Washington secure. It was not until after he had departed that a message arrived at the War Department indicating the arrangements he had made. McClellan stated that he had left 73,456 men to guard the capital. In this total he had included those troops at Manassas and surrounding areas, some 35,000 which were in the Shenandoah Valley, and those actually scattered along the Potomac and in Washington. He had counted men twice, counted non-existing regiments which he proposed calling up, and counted forces already moved to other areas. After his letter had been deciphered and appraisals made by the War Department, it appeared that only 19,000 men were in a position to actually defend the city.[41] Had McClellan deliberately disobeyed Lincoln's orders? It looked as though he had. Thoughts of treason again entered Lincoln's mind.

At the time this dangerous situation was realized, two corps were still in Alexandria awaiting departure for the Peninsula. Lincoln ordered one, the First Corps under McDowell, to remain, giving the city an additional 30,000 men.[42] McClellan protested, stating that he was beginning to meet the enemy head on and that he needed all of the troops he could get. He was outnumbered again. Lincoln, suppressing his anger and sidestepping pressure from Congress and the War Department to bring McClellan back on charges of treason and conspiracy, wrote the general a kind but firm letter on April 9:

Your dispatches complaining that you are not properly sustained, while they do not offend me, do pain me very much. After you left, I ascertained that less than twenty thousand unorganized men, without a single field battery, were all you designed to be left for the defence of Washington. My explicit order that Washington should . . . be left entirely secure, had been neglected. It was precisely this that drove me to detain McDowell.

The President concluded with a very polite suggestion that the general move at once and without any complaints. It had overtones of irritation and warning.

And, once more let me tell you, it is indispensable to *you* that you strike a blow. I am powerless to help this. You will do me the justice to remember I always insisted that going down the Bay in search of a field, instead of fighting at or near Manassas, was only shifting, and not surmounting, a difficulty—that we would find the same enemy, and the same or equal intrenchments, at either place. The country will not fail to note—is now noting—that the present hesitation to move upon an intrenched enemy, is but the story of Manassas repeated.

I beg to assure you that I have never written you, or spoken to you, in greater kindness of feeling than now, nor with a fuller purpose to sustain you, so far as in my most anxious judgement, I consistently can. *But you must act.*[43]

McClellan's relationship with the White House and the War Department grew steadily worse. The next few months would reveal, as far as the President was concerned, the difference between McClellan the fighting man and McClellan the administrator, and they would clearly show how empty his victories in western Virginia had been, if, indeed, anyone by this time considered them victories at all. McClellan's supporters would later argue that the general had done the best he could on the Peninsula under existing circumstances, but McClellan's best was simply not good enough for the President and his Secretary of War.

Despite his anxiety for a decisive victory and his apprehensions at sending the army so far from Washington, Lincoln continued to suppress a strong anti-McClellan movement in the administration. McClellan failed to recognize this, or perhaps he did not want to recognize it. "This inability to see things as they were," T. Harry Williams has so aptly suggested, "is the key to the whole McClellan problem. He saw everything as he wanted it to be. Almost literally he lived in a world of make-believe . . ."[44] The benevolent, yet firm, attitude with which Lincoln wrote the letter of April 9 completely escaped the general's eye for reality, as had all other sincere attempts to prod him into action. McClellan knew for a fact that Stanton had come to dislike him intensely. Without stopping to consider the opportunities Lincoln had offered him, he blindly assumed the President was also conspiring against him.

On April 11, McClellan wrote of his woes to his beloved wife Ellen:

Don't worry about the wretches [in Washington]; they have done nearly their worst, and can't do much more. I am sure that I will win in the end, in spite of their rascality. History will present a sad record of these traitors who are willing to sacrifice the country and its army for personal spite and personal aims. The people will soon understand the whole matter.[45]

There can be no doubt of McClellan's loyalty to the Union. At the same time there is no doubt of Lincoln's loyalty. The general should have seen this and given the President his due. He should also have known, certainly after six months, that Lincoln was his mentor and the only thin thread binding him to his army. Instead he wrote to his wife:

They [Lincoln and his cabinet] determined to ruin me in any event and by any means: first, by endeavoring to force me into premature movements [Lincoln's insistence on a drive on Manassas], knowing that a failure would end my military career; afterwards by witholding the means necessary to achieve success [Lincoln's withdrawal of McDowell's corps to defend Washington]. They determined that I should not succeed, and carried out their determinations only too well and at a fearful sacrifice of blood, time and treasure.[46]

After he launched the ill-fated Peninsula Campaign, seldom did McClellan speak of the President in anything but disparaging terms. He referred to Lincoln as the "original Gorilla" and added: "What a specimen to be at the head of our affairs now!"[47] A. K. McClure, Lincoln's friend and confident, wrote: "McClellan [did] both himself and Lincoln the gravest injustice. I am quite sure that the two men of all the nation who most desired McClellan's success in the field were Lincoln and McClellan themselves."[48]

But it was with a troubled heart, mindful of enemies, seen and unseen, that McClellan early in April set about his operations on that peninsula of land between the York and James Rivers. General Peter S. Michie, West Point instructor and biographer of McClellan, commented: "General McClellan had now arrived at the most critical point of his career as a commander of an army in the presence of an enemy."[49] He was now facing the enemy again—but for the first time, the real enemy and real war. He could take Yorktown easily with the 50,000 men he had available on landing; yet he must move rapidly, for Johnston would be advancing southward from his position near Culpepper to reinforce the small force under Maj. Gen. John Magruder. However, McClellan did not move fast enough. Magruder had set up a line of about 11,000 men across the Peninsula from Yorktown, behind the Warwick River, to the James, a distance of about 14 miles. McClellan knew, at least at first, that he outnumbered the

Confederates, but Magruder pulled a Confederate stunt that triggered McClellan's old malady. The young Confederate general, fully aware of his weak position (he hardly had enough to man the lines), and knowing that it would be days before reinforcements could arrive, began shifting his units back and forth in full view of Federal pickets. The deception had its intended effect. The Pinkerton boys worked overtime and came up with a report that startled McClellan. Had an attack been inaugurated immediately, the defenses would have been broken, but McClellan was "outnumbered" again. He settled back for a long seige, which was actually what he preferred anyway.

On April 6, Lincoln telegraphed his general: "I think you better break the enemies' line . . . at once."[50] That night McClellan wrote his wife: "I was much tempted to reply that he had better come and do it himself."[51] The seige continued. By the 17th, Johnston had arrived from the north, taken overall command and swelled the ranks to 55,000 men.[52] He wrote to Robert E. Lee, then serving in the capacity of military advisor to Jefferson Davis: "No one but McClellan would have hesitated to attack."[53] It seemed that the Confederates knew McClellan as well, if not better, than did Washington.

During the four-week seige of Yorktown, the Federal forces grew as additional units of the Army of the Potomac arrived by water at Fortress Monroe. At this point, after a full month of build-up, a Federal thrust at Johnston would surely have netted great results; but the Confederates, ever mindful of the odds and not wishing to be caught, pulled back to Williamsburg on May 5. When McClellan marched, he repeated his Manassas "victory." The Rebels had evacuated. Lincoln would be reminded of his message of April 9. He had told the general then that the country would not fail to note "that the present hesitation to move upon an entrenched enemy is but the story of Manassas repeated."[54]

The President and Stanton visited the Peninsula right after the army occupied Yorktown. McClellan could not, or would not, see them. He was busy—busy sizing up the results of the battle at Williamsburg which had inflicted rather serious damages on the Union right wing that had followed Johnston's withdrawal. Although the official party from Washington remained behind the Federal lines for six days, McClellan continued to busy himself with an amphibious movement up the York River from Yorktown to West Point. Lincoln returned to Washington without talking to his general.

By May 25, McClellan was on the Chickahominy River, about seven miles from Richmond, and he was extremely nervous. According to his intelligence, the Confederate forces then numbered 200,000 troops. Exactly how Pinkerton established such a fantastic figure is unknown. He was 130,000 men from the truth. McClellan pleaded with Washington for more troops. Anyone would do, even McDowell, on whom he blamed the withdrawal of the First Corps from his army. Lincoln replied that he would aid the army in every way he could and that he would send McDowell by land to join the forces at Richmond, thus keeping a sizable army between the two capitals and preventing any Confederate surprise thrust at Washington. But McDowell never got under way.

Confederate intelligence was far superior to that of the Union. It was known in Richmond, long before McDowell was scheduled to move, exactly what his plans were. As a diversion, Stonewall Jackson was sent to the Shenandoah Valley. There was no doubt in Confederate minds that any movement in the general direction of Washington, no matter how remote the move might be, would keep McDowell at home. Jackson was most effective. In addition to stirring things up in the Federal capital, he succeeded in playing havoc with three armies, Fremont's Mountain Department, Bank's Department to the Shenandoah, and McDowell's Virginia Department, before he returned to Richmond.

McClellan, of course, was not happy at all with the second detention of McDowell. He could see nothing but disaster in the fact that Lincoln and Stanton were "deliberately" keeping troops from him. He had split his army in such a manner that, without reinforcements, he considered himself in extreme danger. East of Richmond the Chickahominy River ran in a southeasterly direction until it emptied into the James. The river formed a formidable obstacle to McClellan's plans. Believing that Richmond could only be taken from the south, McClellan assigned his Third and Fourth Corps to a position on the south side of the river. The Second, Fifth and Sixth Corps were posted north of the river extending the Union right to meet McDowell if he was sent south. This position was held even after Lincoln informed McClellan that McDowell would not join him.

On May 31, Johnston ordered an assault on the Federal left, an excellent strategic move which would have been successful had it not been for confusion among new recruits in their first battle. The Federal right was kept busy while Johnston sent about 42,000 men against 17,000 troops of the Sixth Corps. Slowly the Federals withdrew, but the attacks came in piecemeal style, thus affording the Third Corps the opportunity to reinforce the lines. By the end of the day, the Confederates faced 40,000 Federals. In an effort to correct the situation, Johnston took personal command on the field, was seriously wounded and taken back to Richmond. Command passed temporarily to Maj. Gen. Gustavus W. Smith.

The next morning Smith attempted to renew the effort but found it impossible. The Federal lines held firm. McClellan called the battle at Seven Pines a great victory. Washington speculation ran high as to what kind of a victory it would have been had the general taken some initiative and pressed the engagement with the troops he held north of the river who had remained relatively inactive. Seven Pines, victory or not, revealed another side of McClellan's character.

Following the battle he wrote: "I am tired of the sickening sight of the battle-field, with its mangled corpses and poor suffering wounded! Victory has no charms for me when purchased at such [high] cost. [Federal casualties had been 5,000.] Every poor fellow that is killed or wounded almost haunts me!"[55] "He loved [his men] so much that he did not want to hurt them," T. Harry Williams has written. "[This quality] made him forget the hard fact that soldiers exist to fight and possibly to die. The trouble with McClellan was that he liked to think of war as bloodless strategy . . ."[56] McClellan had written that Manassas would be "the brightest passage of my life, that I accomplished so much at so small a loss."[57] And he had said in a letter to his friend, Ambrose E. Burnside, that Manassas and Yorktown were his "brightest chaplets."[58]

While repairing the damage to the Third and Fourth Corps, McClellan renewed his call for more troops. Part of McDowell's corps, about 9,000 men, was sent, but this still was not enough for McClellan. On June 8, Lincoln, feeling that the danger to Washington had subsided, ordered McDowell to move up to McClellan's aid. Then, suddenly, McClellan changed his attitude. McDowell's corps had originally been offered to McClellan on the basis of a separate, independent, cooperating command and not as an addition to the Army of the Potomac. McClellan would have none of this. He could not forget his bitterness toward McDowell. Now that he saw that he might get the reinforcements he claimed he needed to take Richmond, he informed Secretary Stanton: "If I cannot fully control all his troops, I want none of them, but would prefer to fight the battle with what I have, and let others be responsible for the results."[59] Any less tolerant man than Lincoln would have relieved his general for this direct insult to the administration. In effect, McClellan was refusing to accept direction from the War Department and stating that should there be failure, the blame would lie at the department's doorstep.

Lincoln once more appeased McClellan by writing a kind letter of apology. He withdrew McDowell's services by saying that the army was in no shape to come anyway. One division, which had tangled with Jackson in the Valley "has got so terribly out of shape, out at elbows, and out at toes, that it will require a long time to get it in again," wrote Lincoln. "I now fear [McDowell] can not get to you either way [by land or water] in time." The President closed with some biting words which completely escaped McClellan. "I believe I would come and see you, were it not that I fear my presence might divert you and the army from more important matters."[60]

The day following Johnston's wounds, command of the Confederate army was given to Robert E. Lee. With this, it became the Army of Northern Virginia, a title, according to Douglas S. Freeman, adopted through popular usage rather than a formal proclamation or order.[61] McClellan and Lee had met before. Both had served on Winfield Scott's staff in Mexico. Scott saw great promise in these two men and on several occasions assigned them together on duties and projects. Although their association was not as close as some during that period, Lee was well aware of McClellan's capabilities and incapabilities. Now facing each other with opposing armies, Lee would carefully analyze the Federal commander through the next months. In nearly every prevailing situation, Lee would analyze him correctly.

As the weeks of June passed, McClellan began his plans for a Richmond offensive. He moved the Second and Fourth Corps from north of the Chickahominy to the south, leaving only the Fifth Corps under

Fitz-John Porter to make contact with any reinforcements who might be joining him by land. Concentrated so near Richmond, McClellan planned to lay an artillery barrage that would level the city. Then he would take it by assault. General James Longstreet wrote: "McClellan's plan . . . was wise enough and it would have been a success if the Confederates had consented to such a programme."[62]

With four of McClellan's five corps south of the Chickahominy, Lee would try Johnston's plan of a few weeks earlier except that this time he would assault the Federal right. To do so at no risk to his own army, he would have Magruder perform some more theatrics in front of McClellan's left. While Lee prepared, Magruder, with 25,000 men, demonstrated his "superior forces" for some 60,000 Federals. Again his deception worked. He was confirming McClellan's intelligence reports. Late in the day on June 26, A. P. Hill struck at the Fifth Corps.

The day before this attack came, McClellan sent Stanton a telegram which, for the first time, broke Lincoln's patience with the general:

The rebel force is stated at two hundred thousand . . . I regret my great inferiority in numbers, but feel that I am in no way responsible for it. . . . if [the army] is destroyed by overwhelming numbers, [I] can at least die with it and share its fate. But if the result of the action, . . . is a disaster, the responsibility cannot be thrown on my shoulders; it must rest where it belongs.[63]

In actuality, Lee had 85,000 men as compared to McClellan's 105,000 troops, but McClellan was reading Pinkerton's reports again.

The President's reply reveals the emotional strain he was under in dealing with McClellan. The day Lee launched his offensive, Lincoln replied:

Your . . . dispatches . . . suggesting the probability of your being overwhelmed by 200,000, and talking of where the responsibility will belong, pains me very much. I give you all I can, and act on the presumption that you will do the best you can with what you have, while you continue, ungenerously I think, to assume that I could give you more if I would. I have omitted and shall omit no opportunity to send you reenforcements whenever I possibly can.[64]

McClellan had no time to reply and probably no inclination to do so. He was busy with his first military conflict with Robert E. Lee.

The following seven days were to reveal much to the military commanders of both sides and to the Union strategists in Washington. It would show, for the first time under fire, McClellan's great fear of superior forces and his unwillingness to take the initiative. Although A. P. Hill's attack on the Fifth Corps gained the Confederates nothing but a retreat by nightfall, McClellan refused to aid his right wing. Once again Magruder's deception was working. Faced with these "overwhelming odds" on his left, and rather than withdraw any troops to aid Porter, McClellan ordered the Fifth Corps to pull back. Late that evening he wired the War Department that it was a great victory.

Lee, too, was not without problems. Jackson, who was to coordinate the attack with Hill, was slow in arriving and left Hill to manage alone. He would do the same thing the next day when Hill pursued Porter to Gaines's Mill. By the afternoon of the 27th, however, Lee had 65,000 men in action and the Federal lines began to break. Only the wise judgment of the commanders of the Second and Sixth Corps, Edwin Sumner and William Franklin respectively, prevented the battle from becoming a complete rout. Without specific instructions from headquarters, they rushed to Porter's aid in time to prevent the Fifth Corps from being driven into the Chickahominy. That night Porter withdrew to the south side of the river.

McClellan acted very strangely during these two days. He made no personal effort to direct his men as did Lee. On the morning of the second day, he was "reposed," meaning he was sleeping, until 10:00 A.M., while orderlies from Porter's corps waited to see him. Despite his jubilant message to Stanton of the 26th ("Victory today complete and against great odds. I almost begin to think we are invincible."),[65] he quickly reverted to his old self by the next day and wired Stanton that he was being "attacked by greatly superior numbers in all directions."[66] His reluctance to leave his left unmanned in order to aid Porter clearly indicated that Pinkerton's figures had become an obsession. But two men saw through Lee's trick. Generals Phillip Kearny and Joseph Hooker of the Third Corps informed McClellan that they were certain only a thin line existed in front of them and that Richmond could be taken without great losses. But it was too late. The general had made up his mind. The Army of the Potomac would withdraw south to the James. Then McClellan launched into another attack on the administration:

I have lost this battle because my force was too small. I have seen too many dead and wounded comrades to feel otherwise than that the government has not sustained this army. If you do not do so now, the game is lost. If I save this army now, I tell you plainly that I owe no thanks to you or to any other persons in Washington. You have done your best to sacrifice this army.[67]

McClellan's actions were inexcusable. Porter's corps had acted with great valor. Lee had suffered badly on the 26th, and his victory on the 27th was not really a victory at all. The Confederates had made mistakes at the beginning and would not fully recover. McClellan could have held, or counterattacked, in view of what Lincoln was planning.

On June 26, an order was issued from the War Department combining the departments of McDowell, Banks, and Fremont, all of which were operating separately in defense of Washington, into one army. It became the Army of Virginia and at its head Lincoln put John Pope, a young man similar to McClellan in many ways, but distinctively different in that he liked to fight. The President's purpose in consolidating these forces was to aid McClellan by sending Pope to Richmond by land, thus forming a gigantic convergence of Federal power around the Confederate capital. The idea was good but it was thwarted before it ever got started. By the time Pope had taken command, McClellan was in retreat.

The Federal withdrawal to the James River base at Harrison's Landing lasted throughout the next five days. On the last day, at Malvern Hill, Lee was repulsed with devastating blows that cost him 5,000 men. McClellan's losses were half that number. Despite superior artillery positions, advantages in numbers, and generals who were willing to fight and had fought well, McClellan did not once consider an offensive. Despite clear-cut advantages throughout the seven days, McClellan was determined that he would not be run over by an army that outnumbered him by two to one. On July 2, he left Malvern Hill for his newly established base on the river—left the field deserted to a dumbfounded Confederate command. Thus ended the Peninsula Campaign.

General George Meade, a friend of McClellan, summed up the Peninsula failure in these words: "McClellan was always waiting to have everything just as he wanted before he would attack, and before he could get things arranged as he wanted them, the enemy pounced on him and thwarted all his plans . . . Such a general will never command success, though he may avoid disaster."[68]

Throughout the Peninsula Campaign, Lincoln had made every attempt possible to comply with McClellan's request for reinforcements and appeased him beyond the tolerance of normal men. His messages to the general were always kind, in most cases gentle to the point of being apologetic. On the third day of the battle he wrote: "Save your Army at all events. Will send re-inforcements as fast as we can." With a sorrowful tone, he continued: "I feel any misfortune to you and your army quite as keenly as you . . . If you have had a drawn battle, or a repulse, it is the price we pay for the enemy not being in Washington. We protected Washington, and the enemy concentrated on you; had we stripped Washington, he would have been upon us before the troops sent could have got to you."[69]

McClellan was relentless. "No one need blush for the Army of the Potomac. I again repeat that I am not responsible for this, and I say it with the earnestness of a general who feels in his heart the loss of every brave man who has been needlessly sacrificed today."[70] Early on the morning of the last day, he telegraphed: "I need 50,000 more men, and with them I will retrieve our fortunes."[71] Lincoln replied: "When you ask for fifty thousand men to be promptly sent you, you surely labor under some gross mistake of fact. . . . I have not, outside your Army, seventy five thousand men East of the mountains. Thus, the idea . . . is simply absurd. I only beg . . . you will not ask impossibilities of me." And then the words of appeasement: "If you think you are not strong enough to take Richmond just now, I do not ask you to try just now."[72]

Lincoln was hurt over McClellan's failure; but master of composure that he was, he remained calm, fighting off radical decisions handed him by various members of the war staff. He thanked McClellan for what he had done. "I am satisfied that yourself, officers and men have done the best you could." And he suggested that if the general at any time felt "able to take the offensive," he was "not restrained from doing so."[73]

McClellan called his withdrawal "unparalleled in the annals of war. . . . we have preserved our trains, our guns, our material, and above all, our honor."[74] He classified a complete retreat in the face of inferior forces as another of his "bright moments." He had been victorious at Manassas, Yorktown, Gaines's Mill and now, as he sat reflecting on the past seven days battle, he was victorious in failure. Lincoln's endurance with the military mind was magnanimous.

Since the removal of McClellan as general-in-chief in May, Lincoln had served in that capacity, directing the movements of all the armies. Now he decided that the position must be filled by a competent military man. By the end of the Peninsula Campaign he had made up his mind that that man would be Henry Wager Halleck. Halleck, who was serving in the West, came to Lincoln highly recommended. The President had made a quick trip to West Point to consult with the old general, Winfield Scott, before he made the appointment. Scott enthusiastically supported Halleck as he had before his retirement. On July 11, orders were issued for Halleck to repair to Washington at once.

Halleck was the first general to land in Washington who failed to cause any kind of a stir. He did not carry the handsome military figure or the exciting personality that seemed to mark McClellan. But he was considered one of the foremost military minds in the country. Lincoln hoped he had made the right selection this time.

Halleck had not made a hit with McClellan either. McClellan talked of resigning when he heard of the appointment. He had once commanded Halleck. How could he now serve under him? Both McClellan and his army considered the appointments of Halleck and Pope as direct insults. It was said that if Stanton, whom McClellan considered as responsible for all his troubles, ever set foot at Harrison's Landing, he might come away "badly abused."[75] Halleck did set foot at McClellan's headquarters shortly after his arrival to assume command of the combined armies. The trip to the James was to determine what should be done with the Army of the Potomac. McClellan still insisted on reinforcements. If he had 30,000 more men, he told Halleck, he could resume his offensive against Richmond. Halleck, skeptical of McClellan's abilities at this point, agreed to send 20,000. But no sooner had

Halleck returned to Washington than McClellan stated that Lee still had 200,000 troops and that he must have at least 40,000 reinforcements before he could advance. This was the same old story Lincoln had heard a dozen times over. He saw no excuse to hear it again. His mind was made up. The Army of the Potomac would be withdrawn from the Peninsula and brought back to Washington. Lincoln went so far as to offer the command to General Ambrose Burnside, thus showing his complete dissatisfaction with McClellan. Burnside declined the offer from the President and urged him to retain McClellan, despite the problems he faced. Whether or not McClellan ever realized it, Burnside saved him from the humiliation of a direct relief of command in the spring of 1862.

To McClellan, however, Halleck's order of August 3 amounted to the same thing. "It is determined to withdraw your army from the Peninsula to Aquia Creek," the order stated.[76] McClellan vigorously protested. "Your telegram of last evening is received," he wrote. "I must confess that it has caused me the greatest pain I ever experienced, for I am convinced that the order to withdraw this army to Aquia Creek will prove disastrous to our cause."[77] Halleck replied, "You cannot regret the order . . . more than I did the necessity of giving it. It will not be rescinded and you will be expected to execute it with all possible promptness." [78]

How wise the decision was to withdraw the army has been debated by historians for a century, and will be argued for years to come. It would be two years before a Federal army would again get as close to Richmond as McClellan did. With this in mind, the proposals to remove McClellan from command and replace him with a fighting general began to show merit. Halleck's theories of uniting the two armies (McClellan's and Pope's) were accepted by the President. Halleck made it clear to Lincoln that, according to the "rules of war," these two armies could not adequately continue the war to victory with a force of 200,000 between them. He had swallowed the overestimated figures his intelligence had given him from the beginning of the campaign and, in so doing, had convinced the President that Lee was an immovable object to be reckoned with only by an irresistible force. The die was cast. The Army of the Potomac began to withdraw.

McClellan's pace in removing his army from the Peninsula was no faster than in advancing. Lee, who had accurately predicted what would happen to McClellan's army, ordered the Army of Northern Virginia to move on the day of the Federal withdrawal. Before the first divisions of the Army of the Potomac made their landing at Aquia Creek, a tributary of the Rappahannock River, Confederate forces had raced north to face Pope, who was now just south of Manassas, and had surrounded him. The fate of the newly organized Army of Virginia would be decided in a matter of days.

General Halleck, who had impressed Lincoln so much with his "textbook" military knowledge, now showed signs of severe nervous strain. He had, more as an inducement for rapid movement to northern Virginia, offered over-all command again to McClellan. It became increasingly evident that he had done so without serious consultation with Lincoln and Stanton, for when McClellan pressed him for a clarification, he deliberately avoided the question. Pope was in trouble. McClellan and his officers, nearly all of whom shared their commander's dislike for Pope, were conveniently finding excuses for not cooperating, and problems in the west were mounting. Halleck was confused and tired. Then suddenly Pope's communications with Washington were cut. Jackson's ride around the Army of Virginia had severed the Federals from the outside world. When Halleck received no word at all from Pope, he went into panic. The chain of command crumbled right in front of Lincoln's eyes. The general-in-chief of the armies directed McClellan, as ranking officer, to do the best he could with the armies in the field, but to remember that any orders to Pope must go through his office. It was clearly time for Lincoln to resume direction of the war effort.

During the late days in August, when Pope came face to face with the Confederate Army of Northern Virginia, McClellan remained in camp at Fredericksburg trying to determine exactly where he stood with Halleck and Lincoln. No one would give him a clear answer and, understandably, he was concerned. But he did not make it any easier for his superiors by some of his actions. After expressing concern for Pope's army and offering his help, he had another of his now famous reversals.

On August 27, at the request of Halleck, McClellan informed his chief that the corps of Sumner and Franklin were ready to move to Pope's aid and had been ordered to do so. Within a matter of several hours, he suddenly found excuses why he could not carry out his own orders. "I have no means of knowing the enemy's force between Pope and ourselves."[79] He said that Franklin had no horses for his artillery and that he could not locate his cavalry. And then he began working on Halleck as he had Lincoln and Stanton. "I am not responsible for the past and cannot be for the future," he wired the general.[80] And he wrote his wife, "I have a terrible task on my hands now—perfect imbecility to correct. No means to act with, no authority, yet determined, if possible, to save the country and the capital. I am heartsick with the folly and ignorance I see around me."[81]

Throughout the next three days, McClellan delivered to his superiors one of the most flagrant examples of insubordination that the Civil War produced. He deliberately refused direct orders from his general-in-chief, orders that were written with good cause, validity, and sincerity. He attempted on almost every occasion to counteract the orders with open defiance, manufactured and unjustified excuses, and suggestions to help Pope's Army of Virginia. Gideon Welles, Secretary of the Navy, commented in his diary: "Personal jealousies and professional rivalries, the bane and curse of all armies, have entered deeply into ours."[82]

Finally, on August 30, the day Lee soundly whipped Pope on the fields at Manassas Junction, McClellan received an order from the War Department that gave him command of all his army which had not been released to Pope. In actuality, this constituted his own staff, about 100 men in his camp, and a handful left at Fortress Monroe. He wrote his wife, "I feel like a fool . . . I am left in command of *nothing* . . ."[83] That night Halleck called for McClellan. "I beg of you to assist me in this crisis with your ability and experience. I am utterly tired out."[84]

Before McClellan arrived in Washington the next morning, Halleck offered Burnside the command of the army for the second time. Again, Burnside turned it down in favor of his friend whom he still claimed as the best man for the job. When McClellan arrived, out of sheer desperation, Halleck "verbally" gave him "command of the defenses [of Washington], expressly limiting [his] jurisdiction to the works and their garrisons, and prohibiting [him] from exercising any control over the troops actively engaged in front under Pope."[85]

As McClellan was reporting to Halleck, Pope was accusing the officers of the Army of the Potomac of refusing to co-operate with him and blaming his defeat on their insubordination. McClellan denied the charges but Lincoln, who by this time was thinking that the general was "a little crazy," ordered him, in firm tones, to wire Porter and the others to support Pope. McClellan consented to the President's demands and then retired to his home.

When Lincoln had brought McClellan to Washington thirteen months before, he had just experienced the first blow of the war, defeat at First Manassas. "Little Mac," the young hero, was to be the answer. He showed great possibilities. Not only would he heal the wounds McDowell had left in Northern morale, but he would organize the finest "marching" army in military history. This he did with ease. But the following months brought the humble Lincoln to exasperation. Nearly seven months of inactivity on the part of the new Army of the Potomac gave the administration its first severe test and the President fought with great patience and forebearance to hold his cabinet from crumbling under pressures from military and political radicals. Against his own better judgement and the advice of dozens of close associates, Lincoln repeatedly defended the bumbling of a general he had chosen as the leader of his army. He suffered irresponsiveness, insubordination, absurd military and political demands, and the unwarranted and unrequested advice of a man who sincerely thought he was the savior of the Union but who had not the fortitude nor the capability to grasp realities, a man who both despised him and needed him. With great passion, Lincoln bore the burdens of his army through defeat, through agonizing days, weeks, and months of waiting for victory, a victory he needed and wanted so badly for his general. The general did not respond.

This was Lincoln's dilemma—George Brinton McClellan. This was the man Lincoln and Halleck would visit on the morning of September 2. This was the man whom the President would ask to salvage the pieces once again.

2

"The Most Propitious Time"

On September 3, 1862, General Robert E. Lee wrote President Jefferson Davis: "The present seems to be the most propitious time since the commencement of the war for the Confederate Army to enter Maryland."[1] (See Appendix E, Document 1.) This was how Davis' former military advisor analyzed the Federal withdrawal to Washington. Much had happened in the three months since Lee had taken command of the Confederate army. He had stepped into the shoes of the victor of First Manassas (Joseph E. Johnston), and had carried the Confederate defensive campaign successfully through McClellan's Peninsula efforts and Pope's offensive at Second Manassas. Richmond had been threatened and was now safe. The North Carolina coast and the Shenandoah Valley, both of which had been occupied by Federal troops, were nearly cleared. With the exception of Winchester, Norfolk, and Fortress Monroe, Virginia was free of any substantial Federal force. Both the Army of the Potomac and the Army of Virginia were broken and in retreat. Washington was in panic while Confederate morale ran high. Although the war for the Confederacy had thus far been defensive, it had been victorious, and all three of the major campaigns in the east had taken place in Virginia. It was clearly time for a reappraisal of Confederate strategy. But whatever decisions would be made, they must be done quickly while the obvious initiative still remained in their hands.

Lee's burden was great during the early days of September. He was left with few alternatives. He could withdraw the army to a position behind the Rappahannock River, set up a defensive line with part of his army while sending the other part off to the west to join the campaign against Federal-held Louisville. This "utilizing of interior lines" had worked successfully twice before—during the Peninsula Campaign when Jackson was sent off to the Valley and again at Second Manassas, when Jackson rode around Pope and cut his communications. Considering the condition of the Federal armies, there was some merit to using the scheme again. But McClellan was once more in command. Although the fighting spirit of the enemy might be broken, the Confederate army remembered the amazing feat of reorganization that took place following First Manassas. This left but one other alternative: invasion. General E. P. Alexander, Lee's "master gunner," wrote that Lee had to take the offensive. "He could not afford to sit down before Washington and await the enemy's pleasure."[2] The decision was made. For the first time since the war began, Lee took the initiative and became the aggressor.

Aside from the need of subsistence, always a basic and compelling reason, Lee had six motives for invasion. First, "The purpose, if discovered, will have the effect of carrying the [war] north of the Potomac."[3] Lee knew he would be discovered and he was well aware of the psychological effect an invasion would have on Washington and the North. Up to this point in history, psychological warfare, in its truest sense, was virtually unknown. Although nowhere in Lee's papers does such a theme run, the invasion of Maryland was a brilliantly calculated move to unnerve the Federal government in a time of crisis. Up to this point the North had not felt the emotional strain of war on its own soil. Its devastating effects would be reflected in the hysteria of Washington during the next three weeks, and the relief with which the North accepted McClellan's empty victory at Antietam. The war at this point was almost like a story told to children—of far away places and legendary figures with red capes and plumed hats. But now Lee was bringing it north. That confidence which had not been broken by Pope's defeat at Second Manassas would be crushed by Lee's invasion.

Secondly, "If it is ever desired to give material aid to Maryland and afford her an opportunity of throwing off the oppression to which she is now subject, this would seem the most favorable."[4] Maryland was a border state in the truest sense. The eastern shore and southern counties, which surrounded Washington. were almost entirely agricultural, maintaining close relationship with Virginia through its traditional colonial ties as well as its annual large tobacco crops. Slavery was still an established institution and the people openly exhibited Southern sympathies. Lee labored under the false impression that the central and western counties, which he had decided to invade, shared these same sentiments. Contrary to his belief, he would be entering a section of the state which, economically and socially, was on the same level as the North. Agriculture had also played an important role in the development of these counties, but old colonial customs were rapidly being pushed aside for industry, better roads, and other social improvements. Slavery had been discarded in favor of skilled labor. They were far from being void of Southern sentiments, however. Hundreds of families were divided, and among these Lee would find friends.

Moreover, during the early days of the war, Maryland had virtually come under a state of martial law. Talk of secession had greatly alarmed Washington. In order to prevent the capital from becoming an isolated island in the Confederacy, the Federal military had taken over the city of Baltimore and had spread its arm of authority into the surrounding counties. Lincoln had suspended the writ of habeas corpus. Wholesale arrests of outspoken Southern sympathizers were made. All secessionist members of the state legislature were taken into custody. By this time Maryland was being referred to in the South as the "weeping maiden, bound and fettered, seeking relief." On December 21, 1861, the Confederate Congress had passed a resolution "that no peace ought to be concluded with the United States, which does not insure to Maryland the opportunity of forming a part of the Confederacy."[5] Lee, remembering the Baltimore riots and the political battles in Annapolis, thought, as deliverer of these "oppressed" people, he would gain their undivided support, add thousands of recruits to the hundreds who had already joined the army from Maryland, and perhaps he would even achieve an effective secession. He was sure to replenish his wagon trains with badly needed food and clothing for his army. Even if Maryland did not succumb to Confederate overtures, this last gave him cause enough to seek greener pastures north of the Potomac.

Thirdly, "We can not afford to be idle, and though weaker than our opponents in men and military equipment, [we] must endeavor to harass, if we can not destroy them. I am aware that the moment is attended with much risk, yet I do not consider success impossible, and shall endeavor to guard it from loss. As long as the army of the enemy are employed on this frontier, I have no fears for the safety of Richmond . . ."[6] Although Confederate intelligence had proven superior in many ways to that of the Federal army, Lee could only guess what move McClellan might make next. Should it be an offensive one, it would undoubtedly be aimed at Richmond—McClellan's goal. If Lee invaded now, McClellan would have to follow and would do so with all his reconcentrated forces, thus forestalling further pressure upon the Confederate capital. Though he felt reasonably certain that Richmond would be safe, General Lee did not hesitate to suggest to Davis that every precautionary measure be taken to insure that the army would not have to be recalled from its march into enemy territory:

I earnestly recommend that advantage be taken of this period of comparative safety to place its defense, both by land and water, in the most perfect condition. A respectable force can be collected to defend its approaches by land, and the steamer *Richmond* [an ironclad modeled after the *Merrimac*], I hope, is now ready to clear the river of hostile vessels.[7]

Lee could rely on McClellan being cautious—he knew him so well now—but his chances of catching him off guard while on the move were far greater than if he was in a strong defensive position. "Harass" the enemy, keep him on the move, but above all, keep him from Richmond. A direct attack on McClellan was not one of Lee's initial plans, or not one which he disclosed in advance of the invasion. In retrospect, however, Lee, in a conversation with a friend in 1868, made a statement which indicated that "attack" was one of his considerations. "Had the Lost Dispatch not been lost," Lee said, "and had McClellan continued his cautious policy for two or three more days longer, I would have had all my troops reconcentrated on [the] Maryland side, stragglers up, men rested and I intended to attack McClellan, hoping the best results from [the] state of my troops and those of [the] enemy."[8]

Fourthly, "Should the results of the expedition justify it, I propose to enter Pennsylvania . . ."[9] As the Mississippi River was to the Confederacy, so the Baltimore and Ohio Railroad and the Pennsylvania Railroad were to the Union. They were not only main lines of supply to the west but vital lines of communication. The B & O, although running on the border, as it were, was solidly controlled by strong Union support. Its vast potential of 4,000 locomotives and cars, and its capabilities of supplying 10,000 troops daily, made it a prime target. Once Lee had crossed the Potomac, B & O traffic could be interrupted. Then, if he was in a strong defensive position, his next target would be the Pennsylvania Railroad. He intended to reach Harrisburg where he would destroy the Susquehanna River bridge. Once this was accomplished, and only then, would he consider any moves on Baltimore and Washington.

Lee's next reason for invasion was of primary importance to the cause for Southern independence. Both England and France were favorably impressed with the Confederacy's progress in the war. Although they had not recognized it as an independent nation, they had given it belligerent rights, ceasing to regard Confederate ships as mere pirates on the open seas. Cotton was extremely important to both nations, a point of diplomatic negotiations the Confederate State Department had not failed to exploit. Also, the ineffectiveness of Lincoln's naval blockade of the South was proving an important advantage for negotiations. The time was ripe for recognition.

If England recognized the Confederacy, France was certain to follow suit. This move would then accomplish one of two things; either bring an immediate stop to hostilities or push the United States dangerously close to international crisis and perhaps global war. In either case, the Richmond government was sure to gain. The Confederate States of America would become a sovereign and independent nation.

The string of Confederate victories to date had almost convinced England that recognition was feasible. Early in September, while Lincoln and Stanton fretted over the defenses of Washington, British Prime Minister, the Viscount Palmerston, and Lord John Russell, the Foreign Minister, agreed to call a cabinet meeting in early October for the purpose of discussing the Confederacy. (See Appendix E, Documents 18, 24, 29, and 30.) Europe's eyes were on Lee's progress and he knew what was at stake.

The sixth reason, as indicated by Lee's dispatch to Jefferson Davis on September 8 (See Appendix E, Document 8.), was his hope to influence the forthcoming Northern Congressional elections. In the election of 1860, the Republican Party had come to power on two main factors—the split in the Democratic Party, which had been transpiring during the Buchanan administration, and the platform on the slavery-freedom issue. To some then, the answer to the South's problems did not lie in secession, but in the acquisition of Northern allies in Congress and in the courts. Lee figured that the needed influence could be bought, not by money and political skulduggery, but by a military victory on Northern soil. If it could be accomplished before election time in the fall, pressure could be brought to bear in the right political circles; a reunited Democratic Party would hold the balance of power, and before another spring had set in, the United States would be ready to negotiate with the Confederate States. By the same token, economic pressures would be brought to bear on Northern business. On July 21, 1862, the Richmond *Examiner,* in one of its many "invasion" editorials, stated that there was "but one method of putting an end to the war, and that is by destroying the Federal credit."[10] "The tone of the Masses, the Press, and the Legislature," wrote Col. J. F. Marshall of South Carolina, "will all change from a thirst for our blood and property to that for peace."[11]

There was a seventh reason for invasion; not Lee's, but one which Jefferson Davis harboured as extremely important to the cause. Davis was both a military man and a public servant. A West Point graduate, he had served in the war with Mexico, in the Senate and the House of Representatives, and as Secretary of War under Franklin Pierce. His career had been long and distinguished and now he was in the midst of the herculean task of organizing and maintaining the loosely knit Confederate states. He was, and has been for a century, the subject of severe criticism for his policies, both political and military. Only recently, in the light of more objective studies, has the real Davis come to light. It is a tribute to modern research that his "national strategy" for the South is now understood.

Defensive warfare was accepted from the beginning of the conflict as the only policy for the South. Frank E. Vandiver has pointed out in his treatise on the Confederate President that "Davis clearly understood the Confederacy did not need to win the War; like the American colonies in the earlier Revolution, the South needed merely to avoid losing. It wanted only to be left alone, to repulse invasion."[12] But with conditions as they were in early September, he revised his strategy and with good reason. In addition to Lee being in Maryland, Generals Braxton Bragg and E. K. Smith were on a concerted drive into the seesaw state of Kentucky. In a political two-pronged maneuver, Davis proposed to carry the Stars and Bars to enemy territory, not as a conquering army, but as bearers of peace. In a long letter to Lee, Bragg, and Smith, the President directed that the people of the Union should be informed, by proclamation, of the Confederate war aims; that their design was not conquest, but self-defense, and that "the responsibility thus rests on the people of [the individual state being entered] of continuing an unjust and aggressive warfare upon the Confederate States . . . and with them . . . the option of preserving the blessings of peace, by the simple abandonment of the design of subjugating a people over whom no right of dominion has been ever conferred either by God or man."[13] Davis' letter was dated after Lee crossed the Potomac, and carried blank spaces for specific state names to be filled in when the appropriate time was reached. It was a noble effort and a fascinating document designed as a strategic political and diplomatic move to follow a show of Confederate strength. Records do not reveal that any of the states involved ever heard Davis' words. (See Appendix B.)

There was an eighth reason for Lee's invasion. Although it can not be considered tantamount to the others, it can be assumed with certainty that public opinion played an important role in the decision. Southern newspapers had been calling for invasion since First Manassas. Jackson's brilliant maneuvers in the Valley and the Confederacy's success on the Peninsula renewed the excitement. On August 11, the Richmond *Dispatch* wrote: "Another 'Manassas letharge' is gradually settling upon us . . . It is fated, it seems, that we are never to reap the fruits of our victory, no matter how decisive."[14] One month later, after Lee had crossed the Potomac, the editor of the *Dispatch* said, "Some of our contemporaries seem to feel doubts not fully expressed however, with regard to the policy of advancing into Maryland. We entertain none whatever." As a matter of fact, he went on to comment, the war would have been over by then if the Confederate army had invaded after First Manassas.[15] On September 6, the Charleston *Mercury* picked up the call.

Our victorious troops in Virginia, reduced though they be in numbers, and shattered in organization, must be led promptly into Maryland, before the enemy can rally the masses of recruits whom he is rapidly and steadily gathering together. When the government of the North shall have fled into Pennsylvania, when the public buildings in Washington shall have been razed to the ground, so as to forbid the hope of their ever again becoming the nest of Yankee despotism, then, at last, may we expect to see the hope of success vanish from the Northern mind, and reap the fruit of our bloody and long continued trials.[16]

With an almost gleeful arrogance that was typical of so many Southern editors, the Richmond *Examiner* declared: "From the ignoble exhibitions which have been already given by the North even at the distant threat of invasion, we may justly anticipate the dismay that will seize her armies, and the agony that will wring the hearts of her selfish people when our troops have once obtained a footing north of the Potomac."[17]

By early September, Southern morale was at its peak. At no time during the war were Confederate prospects for the future so high. Lee was on Lincoln's doorstep and Generals Smith and Bragg were threatening Louisville, Kentucky. G. F. R. Henderson, in his classic study of Stonewall Jackson, wrote: "But for deficiencies in numbers and in *material,* the higher *morale* and the more skillful leading would make ample compensation . . ."[18]

In short, Lee's strategy was to harass the Army of the Potomac by feigning an attack on Washington, thus drawing away any threats to Richmond. At the same time he would seek the support of Maryland. If all went well, he would advance to Pennsylvania, secure a "beachhead" north of the Mason-Dixon line, and most assuredly bring on foreign intervention in one form or another. In any event, the fall election in the North would bring drastic changes advantageous to the Southern cause. Lee developed what today would be called a "wait and see" policy. Though he had certain goals and accomplishments to attain, he would plan his campaign as he marched, basing it on the ofttimes unpredictable actions of the enemy and its general.

Some years after the Civil War, in a conversation with his close friend, Col. William Allan, Lee spoke briefly of his invasion intentions:

Gen. Lee said he had never invaded the North with an eye to holding permanently the hostile portions of it [Allan recorded]. That especially in 1862 his object was not primarily to take Baltimore, or to undertake any very decided offensive movement. It was in the first place to get the enemy away from the Manassas side, next to subsist our own army. He says he could not stay where he was at Manassas, from want of supplies and adequate transportation. He could not go forward for he thought it injudicious to attack the fortifications. To have retired into Loudon was giving the enemy possession of Fairfax and inviting him to flank him towards Richmond.[19]

While Lee was making his plans, all was not quiet on the Potomac. Lincoln and Halleck had arrived at McClellan's residence at 7:30 A.M. on September 2. The general was having breakfast when his guests were shown to the study. The visit was brief and to the point. Lincoln informed him that Pope's army was in full retreat and that 30,000 men were on the roads to the city. According to McClellan, the President expressed the opinion that the troubles now impending could be overcome better by him than anyone else. "He instructed me to take steps at once to stop and collect the stragglers, to place the works in a proper state of defense, and to go out to meet and take command of the army when it approached the vicinity of the works; then to place the troops in the best position—committing everything to my hands."[20] (McClellan had come to Halleck's office the day before to receive a verbal order to this same effect. "Halleck . . . directed me to take charge of Washington and its defences but expressly prohibited me from exercising any control over the active troops under Gen. Pope."[21] Lincoln was now carrying this one step further.)

He then . . . asked me if I would, under the circumstances, as a favor to him, resume command and do the best that could be done. Without one moment's hesitation and without making any conditions whatever, I at once said that I would accept the command and would stake my life that I would save the city. Both the President and Halleck again asserted that it was impossible to save the city, and I repeated my firm conviction that I could and would save it. They then left, the President verbally placing me in entire command of the city and of the troops falling back upon it from the front.[22]

"Pray that God will help me in the great task now imposed upon me," the General wrote. "I assume it reluctantly . . . [and] only consent to take is for my country's sake . . ."[23]

A most interesting sidelight on McClellan's visit to Halleck's office on September 1 does not appear in *McClellan's Own Story* but is included in the collection of McClellan's papers in the Library of Congress. In a letter to his wife, dated 1:00 A.M., September 2, the general reveals an unusual determination and an indication, unverified by other sources, that he had talked with Lincoln before the breakfast meeting.

Last night [wrote McClellan] I had just finished an application for a leave of absence when I received a dispatch from Halleck begging me to help him out of the scrape and take command here . . . of course I could not refuse so I came over this morning, mad as a march hare and had a pretty plain talk with him and Abe . . . a still plainer one this evening. The result is that I have reluctantly consented to take command here and try to save the Capital . . . I don't know whether I can do it or not, for things are far gone. I hope I shall succeed . . . if when the whole army returns here (if it ever does) I am not placed in command of all, I will either insist upon a leave of absence or resign.[24]

That afternoon a more formal order was issued from the War Department. "Major-General McClellan will have command of the capital."[25] (See Appendix E, Documents 2 and 3.) This was the first official order given McClellan in regards to his position with the Federal Army since removal of over-all command in March of that year. One must interpret it quite loosely, as did McClellan, in order to understand the events that followed.

As of September 1, McClellan had, in effect, been detached from the Army of the Potomac. Technically, he was still in command. Halleck's order of August 30 had not relieved him; rather it had merely reduced his command to his own staff for the purpose of integrating his army with the Army of Virginia. Now on September 2, he was being formally reinstated. He could have his men back now that Pope no longer needed them. But he was being restricted, or so it seemed. The next morning when McClellan moved three corps of the army (The Second, Twelfth, and Ninth) out into Maryland to cope with "any attack upon the city from that side," Halleck cautioned him to remember that his command "included only the defenses of Washington, and did not extend to any active column that might be moved out beyond the line of works; [and] that no decision had . . . been made as to the commander of the active army." According to McClellan, Halleck repeated this warning several times.[26]

When Lincoln asked McClellan to resume his duties as commander of the Army of the Potomac and to defend Washington, he meant exactly what he said and nothing more. Not only did he mistrust the general militarily, but he was highly perturbed at his attitude and the attitude of his officers towards Pope and the Army of Virginia. McClellan had demonstrated on the Peninsula that he was incapable of conducting an offensive campaign, which was what the President desired so much. In addition, Lincoln would talk personally with Pope and would read his official reports, both confirming the accusations against Fitz-John Porter and others of McClellan's command which had filtered into the War Department. The President stated specifically, on several occasions during this period, that McClellan's assignment was not permanent, that it was a temporary stop-gap, and that he intended to use the general for only one purpose—that of bringing reorganization out of chaos.

The President knew perfectly well that he had no other who could command the loyalty of the army as did McClellan, nor one who could whip them back into shape in the all too-brief breathing spell they would be granted. It was abundantly clear that if the general had not possessed this one fortunate quality, his military career would have ended abruptly on September 2 rather than gained a renewed insurance as it did. Secretary of the Navy Gideon Welles recorded in his diary that the President was "more offended with [the general] than he ever was before," but, and he quoted Lincoln, " 'I must have [him] to reorganize the army and bring it out of chaos, but there has been a design—a purpose in breaking down Pope, without regard of consequences to the country. It is shocking to see and know this; but there is no remedy at present, McClellan has the army with him.' "[27]

There are no official documents or letters which would reveal the President's real thoughts during these trying days. Occasionally his correspondence can be interpreted to such results, but by and large, history has been forced to rely on "second hand accounts" from his close associates. Even these must be interpreted in light of the association itself. In addition to Welles's prolific writings, which have been judged fair and honest, there are the diaries of Lincoln's two secretaries, John Hay and John Nicolay. The President was quite frank in his conversations with both men. To Hay he confessed:

I am of the opinion that this public feeling against him [McClellan] will make it expedient to take important command from him. He has acted badly in this matter, but we must use the tools we have. There is no man in the Army who can man these fortifications and lick these troops of ours into shape half as well as he. If he can't fight himself, he excels in making others ready to fight.[28]

The President stood firm at the cabinet meeting on the afternoon of the 2nd. It was a trying moment in his political career. Every member of the cabinet, with the exception of Postmaster General Montgomery Blair, disliked McClellan personally and each had, in one form or another, urged Lincoln to remove the general from the army.

On August 30, Stanton had drafted a vicious and vehement attack on McClellan with intentions of passing it on to Lincoln. The Secretary looked on it with pride for indeed it was a unique document. Probably no other paper in government circles ever reeked with such hatred and villification of one man. It was addressed to the President and read:

The undersigned feel compelled by a profound sense of duty to the government and the people of the United States, and to yourself as your constitutional advisers, respectfully to recommend the immediate removal of George B. McClellan from any command in the armies of the United States. We are constrained to urge this by the conviction that after a sad and humiliating trial of twelve months and by the frightful and useless sacrifice of the lives of many thousand brave men and the waste of many millions of national means, he has proved to be incompetent for any important military command, and also because by recent disobedience of superior orders and inactivity, he has twice imperiled the fate of the army commanded by General Pope and while he continues in command will daily hazard the fate of our armies, exhibiting no sign of a disposition or capacity to restore by courage and diligence the national honor that has been so deeply tarnished in the eyes of the world by his military failures. We are unwilling to be accessory to the destruction of our armies, the protraction of the war, the waste of our national resources, and the overthrow of the government, which we believe must be the inevitable consequence of George B. McClellan being continued in command, and seek, therefore, by his prompt removal to afford an opportunity to capable officers under God's providence to preserve our national existance.[29]

In short, it was an ultimatum. "We are unwilling to be accessory . . ." Either McClellan must be drummed out of the military, posthaste, or the President would have to look for a new cabinet.

Stanton was at his best. Regardless of the authenticity of his accusations, he could not have leveled a more devastating blow at McClellan. Not everyone in the cabinet agreed with him. Secretary of State William H. Seward, not wishing to be caught in the middle, conveniently left town for a few days. Postmaster General Blair obviously could not be approached for a signature. Gideon Welles, although agreeing with the substance of the document, could not approve of Stanton's methods. He felt that to secure cabinet sanction without first consulting the President was wrong and therefore refused to sign. "Why not take the matter up in face to face conversation with Mr. Lincoln instead of putting the matter so uncompromisingly in writing," Welles asked Secretary of the Treasury Salmon P. Chase. Chase replied that this had been tried but to no avail. "A more decisive expression must be made and that in writing," said Chase. Welles still declined. "I do not choose to denounce McC[lellan] for incapacity," Mr. Welles said, "or to pronounce him as a traitor, as declared in this paper, but I will say, and perhaps it is my duty to say, that I believed his removal from command was demanded by public sentiment and the best interests of the country." To Welles, the entire intrigue was disrespectful to the President and indicated an internal cabinet revolution to gain control. He would have no part of it.[30]

Two others, besides Stanton and Chase, signed the paper—Attorney General Edward Bates and Secretary of the Interior Caleb Smith. But without Welles, it would be ineffective. Stanton had a majority but neither Bates nor Smith held any prominent position in either public opinion or with Lincoln.

On September 1, a second paper, similar to the first, was submitted to Welles. It was toned down somewhat but still insisted that "it is not safe to entrust to Major General McClellan the command of any army of the United States." Again the four—Stanton, Chase, Bates and Smith—signed. This time they left a blank space for the Navy Secretary, but Welles stood firm. Later he wrote, "My refusal, and perhaps my remarks prevented the matter from proceeding further. The President never knew of this paper."[31]

Stanton still had paper number two in his pocket when Lincoln arrived at the afternoon session of September 2. Word had reached the Secretary of McClellan's reappointment and he was seething with rage, fairly "trembling with excitement," as Welles recorded.[32] During his discussion with the other members, the President walked in, calm and controlled, but with a troubled brow. Stanton immediately took the initiative and jumped at Lincoln with demands to know if the rumors were true. Quietly the President assured him that just that morning he had asked General McClellan to assume the command of the city's defenses.

"No orders to that effect have been issued from the War Department," replied the Secretary. "The order is mine," said Lincoln, "and I will be responsible for it to the country." He admitted that McClellan had many faults but that he was the only one qualified to pick up the pieces of a broken army and bring it back to fighting condition. He made it firm that the appointment was only temporary and that no field command was being given McClellan. This, however, was no appeasement to the vehement Chase and Stanton. It would be a "national calamity," predicted the Secretary of the Treasury. "I cannot but feel that giving the command to McClellan is equivalent to giving Washington to the rebels."[33]

Lincoln then said that he would gladly shelve his plan if the cabinet could provide a better solution to the problem. Generals Hooker, Burnside, and Sumner were all suggested in a desperate attempt to replace McClellan on the spot. Burnside had already been offered the command and had declined. Lincoln could not agree that Hooker or Sumner could do the job any better, so the meeting ended with the President depressed and his cabinet frustrated. Welles considered this meeting one of the greatest moments in Lincoln's life. Several days later he noted: "From what I have seen and heard within the last few days, the more highly do I appreciate the President's judgement and sagacity in the stand he made, and the course he took."[34] Stanton, determined to have the last jab at McClellan, saw to it that the formal order issued that afternoon placing him in command of the Washington defenses went out over Halleck's name and not his.

While McClellan interpreted the case for his reinstatement in his own fashion, Lincoln received much criticism for his decisions; but two of his severest critics, in a moment of unusual understanding, pronounced fair judgement. Secretary Chase, after a visit to the War Department, wrote that Secretary Stanton commented with severity on Lincoln's humiliating submissiveness to McClellan:

It is, indeed, humiliating [wrote Chase] but prompted, I believe, by a sincere desire to serve the country, and a fear that, should he supersede McClellan by any other commander, no advantage would be gained in leadership, but much harm in the disaffection of officers and troops. The truth is, I think, that the President with the most honest intentions in the world, and a naturally clear judgement and a true, unselfish patriotism, has yielded so much to Border State and negrophobic counsels that he now finds it difficult to arrest his own descent towards the most fatal concessions.[35]

There was still the question of who would command the army in the field. Since McClellan, technically, was still commander of the Army of the Potomac, would he be removed again? So much trouble had already occurred over this problem, how could it possibly be resolved without Lincoln giving in to Stanton and his associates? And would the army be pulled from its assignment at Washington or would a new field army be formed? Each question would have to be resolved fast, for there seemed to be no question in Lincoln's or Stanton's mind that Lee would make an offensive move soon.

Again the President called on Burnside; again the general turned down the appointment. In Lincoln's opinion, Burnside was the only one with independent command experience whom he could trust. But each time he was summoned, the general would decline in favor of McClellan. There seemed to be little choice for Lincoln. If Lee struck, as he undoubtedly would, McClellan would have to take the army to meet him whenever and wherever it might be.

Herein lies one of several mysteries surrounding the Maryland Campaign. Although McClellan denied many times ever receiving any specific instructions to take to the field, there is some evidence to the contrary. Halleck's remarks in testimony to a Congressional investigation some years after the war indicated that the President had paid McClellan another or perhaps several more visits September 2-5, during which he asked the general to "take command of the forces in the field," and that he, Halleck, was present. Halleck added: "The question was discussed by the President for two or three days as to who should take command of the troops that were to go to the field. The decision was made by himself and announced to General McClellan in my presence." The order was: "You must find and hurt this enemy now."[36]

McClellan, in testimony before this same Congressional committee, could not recall such a meeting with the President; but a letter to his wife on September 5 rings of the brave soldier, donned in military finery, off to war. "Again I have been called upon to save the country. The case is desperate, but . . . I will try unselfishly to do my best, and . . . accomplish the salvation of the nation. My men are true and will stand by me till the last. It is probable that our communications will be cut off in a day or two . . ."[37] Lincoln's only comment on the situation was to Welles in which he said: "I wish you to understand it [the assignment] was not made by me. I put McClellan in command here . . . for he has great powers of organization, and discipline; . . . and there his usefulness ends. He can't go ahead— he can't strike a blow."[38]

On September 3, something occurred which tends to confirm that McClellan did have complete control of the army. The following order in Lincoln's handwriting was forwarded from the White House to the War Department:

Ordered, that the General-in-Chief, Major-General Halleck, immediately commence, and proceed with all possible dispatch, to organize an army for active operations, from all the material within and coming within his control, independent of the forces he may deem necessary for the defense of Washington, when such active army shall take the field.

It was delivered in departmental form over Stanton's signature to Halleck at 10:00 P.M."[39]

By this time the situation was thoroughly confused. Halleck, who had earlier shown marks of severe strain, was left holding the proverbial bag. If Burnside had turned down the appointment and Lincoln had found no other, whom could Halleck assign to the job? There was only one answer. Within the hour, on the same day, the following order was sent to General McClellan:

There is every probability that the enemy, baffled in his intended capture of Washington, will cross the Potomac, and make a raid into Maryland or Pennsylvania. A movable army must be immediately organized to meet him again in the field. You will, therefore, report the approximate force of each corps of the three armies now in the vicinity of Washington, which can be prepared in the next two days to take the field, and have them supplied and ready for that service.[40]

It was decided then, after days of wrangling, that McClellan would lead the army after all. Regardless of his denials, McClellan did receive orders to this effect. T. Harry Williams states that "either [he] forgot the conference at his house with Lincoln, or he was lying."[41] McClellan later wrote:

As the time had now arrived for the army to advance, and I had received no orders to take command of it, but had been expressly told that the assignment of a commander had not been decided, I determined to solve the question for myself, and when I moved out from Washington with my staff and personal escort, I left my card, with P.P.C. written upon it [pour prendre conge; French; military formality for officer informing superior of departure], at the White House, War Office, and Secretary Seward's house, and went on my way.

I was afterwards accused of assuming command without authority [there is no record of any such accusation], for nefarious purposes, and, in fact, fought the battle of South Mountain and Antietam with a halter around my neck; for if the Army of the Potomac had been defeated and I had survived I would, no doubt, have been tried for assuming authority without orders, and . . . I would probably have been condemned to death.

On May 30, 1885, McClellan's only visit to Sharpsburg after the battle, the general repeated these thoughts to Henry Kyd Douglas, late of Stonewall Jackson's staff in the Confederate army and then officiating in Antietam's memorial services. McClellan "stated that he firmly believed that if he had been defeated in the battle he would have been tried, cashiered, and perhaps shot."[42]

In the pressure of endless hours of crisis, men do forget or unconsciously rationalize. It is conceivable that McClellan actually did doubt his status as field commander. Though he carried the "halter around his neck" through the next weeks, he failed to explain, as have his biographers, why he labeled his orders from September 6 on "Headquarters, Army of the Potomac."[43] He also failed to clarify a statement he made in his report of October 15, 1862. "Being honored with the charge of this campaign, I entered at once upon the additional duties imposed upon me with cheerfulness and trust, yet not without feeling the weight of the responsibilities thus assumed and being deeply impressed with the magnitude of the issues involved."[44] If his conjectures were correct, it was rather presumptuous of him to assume a command title to which he was not entitled. And why he should think the death penalty justified when no such precedent existed is beyond comprehension.

One significant fact remains. On November 5, the following order was issued from the White House over Lincoln's signature: "By direction of the President, it is ordered that Major-General McClellan be relieved from the command of the *Army of the Potomac, . . .*"[45] With this one statement, all doubt should have been expelled from his mind.

As if nothing at all had happened at the White House and the War Department, "as if," wrote Secretary of the Treasury Chase, "the disastrous expenditure of near eight months had been only the absence of a few days,"[46] McClellan set about his new duties with the same vigor and determination that exemplified his first weeks of duty in 1861. "My conscience is clear,"[47] he wrote. The President had given him a job to do. Although both Nicolay and Hay disputed McClellan's statements on Lincoln's fears that the city was lost, the general believed it could be saved and was just as sure that he was the man to do it. Scant hours after Lincoln's visit, he had dispatched staff officers and orderlies on various assignments. By afternoon he was in the saddle and on the road to meet the army returning from Manassas.

Before he had ridden far, he met General Pope and his staff—the man he was relieving and officers who would soon be absorbed into his command. It was a strained but polite meeting. McClellan bowed and saluted. Pope did the same, but certainly with some emotion.

General Pope would soon be stripped of all command, but he still had the army under his control. According to Halleck, McClellan's orders did not become effective until the army reached the city. He informed Pope of this. With dignified military formality, Pope requested permission to continue to Washington. McClellan nodded and suggested where the general should place his men as they arrived. The two saluted and rode on, never to meet again on the battlefield.

McClellan's return to the army had the psychological impact of a decisive victory for the beaten men. It was exactly as Lincoln knew it would be. "Little Mac" was the medicine the sick army needed. General John Hatch, whose division led the retreat to Washington, was near Pope and McClellan when he overheard their conversation. Hatch had a personal dislike for Pope; and in an effort to avenge what he considered unjust treatment from the general, he shouted in a voice loud enough for Pope to hear, "Boys, McClellan is in command of the army again! Three cheers!"[48] Pandemonium broke loose. A tumultuous roar spread through the ranks.

Such a hurrah as the Army of the Potomac had never heard before [wrote an eyewitness]. Shout upon shout went out . . . and as it was taken up along the road and repeated by regiment, brigade, division and corps, we could hear the roar dying away in the distance. The effect of this man's presence . . . was electrical, and too wonderful to make it worthwhile attempting to give a reason for it.[49]

From the depths of despair and depression, the exhausted veterans of the ill-fated Second Manassas Campaign were raised to heights of excitement and hope. It was almost unbelievable, more easily imagined than could be described, as one eye witness reported:

Suddenly . . . a mounted officer, dashing past our bivouac, reined up enough to shout " 'Little Mac' is back here on the road, boys!" From extreme sadness we passed in a twinkling to a delirium of delight. A Deliverer had come. A real "rainbow of promise" had appeared suddenly in the dark political sky. The feeling in our division upon the return of General McClellan had its counterpart in all the others, for the Army of the Potomac loved him as it never loved any other leader. General McClellan may have had opponents elsewhere; he had few, if any, among the soldiers whom he commanded.[50]

The magic of McClellan's attraction to his men is an American military phenomenon. No other general up to that time, with the possible exception of old Zach Taylor during the Mexican War, commanded the undivided and lasting devotion and loyalty shown to George B. McClellan. At a moment of utter defeat and disaster, "Little Mac" performed a miracle of transformation. Veterans on the verge of desertion, tired, hungry, and dusty from the long march to Washington were suddenly, within a matter of a few hours, changed into a wildly cheering throng, their sore aching feet, growling stomachs, and wounds forgotten. They threw their caps in the air and danced and chanted the happy news—McClellan was back.

Throughout all Civil War literature, particularly among individual eyewitness accounts, no real explanation has been found for this god-like adulation. At this point, McClellan had been with the army for nearly fourteen months, from training to the field, and from the very beginning he had held the admiration of his troops. The cold, precise manner with which he trained and disciplined won him laurels rather than rebuff. Officers requested to serve with him. Enlisted men swelled with pride at the mention of his name. He had taken away their liquor, their self-styled freedom and liberties; he had punished their shenanigans and mutinies with imprisonment and threats of the firing squad; he whipped them into military formalities, clothed them, fed them, and drilled them as real soldiers; and he brought to them, for the first time, a sense of self respect and pride. He nursed them through "infancy" and praised them when they became men.

Whenever he appeared, even at the most formal military reviews, the soldiers cheered with delight. And when he smiled and turned in the saddle to acknowledge their cheers they could not restrain themselves from letting go again. "He had a taking way of returning such salutations," recorded one officer.

He went beyond the formal military salute, and gave his cap a little twirl, which with his bow and smile seemed to carry a little of personal good fellowship even to the humblest private soldier. If the cheer was repeated he would . . . repeat the salute. It was very plain that these little attentions to the troops took well, and had no doubt some influence in establishing a sort of comradeship between him and them.[51]

This was the one phase of McClellan's career he was justified in bragging about. "You have no idea," he wrote his wife, "how the men brighten up now when I go among them. I can see every eye glisten. Yesterday they nearly pulled me to pieces in one regiment. You never heard such yelling.[52] I hear them calling out to me as I ride among them, 'George, don't leave us again!' 'They sha'n't take you away from us again,' etc., etc."[53]

Soldiers are often the first to find fault with their leaders, but not so with the Army of the Potomac. "Little Mac" could do no wrong. He kept them in camp through the fall and winter of 1861, but that was all right; they did not see the enemy. He led them to a ridiculously unfruitful victory at Manassas; this, too, was all right; he lost not one man. The spring campaign on the Peninsula was long and weary but there were no mass slaughters, as there would be with Grant at Richmond, and the men were well fed. A maze of blind hero worship cloaked the fighting McClellan and hid his military incapacities.

The men of the Army of the Potomac were not stupid. On the contrary: their keen minds had sniffed out the fallacies of the Second Manassas campaign before Pope relinquished his command. One combatant wrote of how much they were disheartened by recent reverses.

The men [had] scattered about in groups, discussing the events of their ill-starred campaign, and indulging in comments that were decidedly uncomplimentary to those who had been responsible for the mismanagement. We did not know, of course, the exact significance of all that had happened, as we afterward learned it, but being mainly thinking men, we were able to form pretty shrewd guesses as to where the real difficulty lay.[54]

Col. Francis C. Barlow wrote to his mother: "The affairs of the country look melancholy enough. It is not worthwhile to make any predictions, but I think there is no prospect or hopes of success in this war. The Govt. is too rascally and corrupt besides being imbecile. I am in a state of chronic disgust."[55]

If the men could see through the military blunders at Manassas, why had they not ferreted out the "real difficulties" on the Peninsula? Why had they not made "shrewd guesses" about the mismanagement of the Seven Days Battle? They knew McClellan had enemies in

Washington as well as they knew he had friends in the military, but he was their guardian and they could see no reason to question the whys and wherefores of the general they loved. They were secure in his arms.

In the Maryland Campaign, McClellan demonstrated once again that peculiar but noble trait which would prevent him from being classified as a fighting general. In his last message to his wife before leaving Washington, he wrote:

> It makes my heart bleed to see the poor, shattered remnants of my noble Army of the Potomac, poor fellows! . . . I can hardly restrain myself when I see how fearfully they are reduced in numbers, and realize how many of them lie unburied on the field of battle, where their lives were uselessly sacrificed. It is the most terrible trial I ever experienced.[56]

McClellan was one of the most prolific letter writers of all Civil War generals. His daily, almost hourly, communications to his wife and close associates are most revealing, and have aided the historian in unmasking what would have otherwise been the greatest mystery of the war. On one such occasion he summed up his entire military career in a most strikingly prophetic statement and in so doing, wrote his own epitaph.

> No prospect of a brilliant victory [he wrote] shall induce me to depart from my intention of gaining success by maneuvering rather than fighting. I will not throw these raw men of mine into the teeth of artillery and entrenchments if it is possible to avoid it. I am trying to follow a lesson learned long ago—i.e., not to move until I know that everything is ready, and then to move with the utmost rapidity and energy.[57]

General George Gordon Meade wrote: "McClellan's star is again in the ascendant."[58] And seemingly it was. Lincoln was giving him another chance, and although in his opinion another chance was superfluous, McClellan set out immediately to prove himself. By nightfall of the 2nd, the bedraggled, defeated Federal army was back within the defenses of Washington under the guardian wings of their old commander. With a great sense of security, the men set about their duties, knowing full well that there would not be much time. Within two days, they would be on the march again. But again

"Little Mac" wrought miracles. He worked like "a beaver," Lincoln commented.[59] Complete reorganization was necessary. Broken ranks were refilled. New uniforms and weapons were issued. Supplies for battle were prepared. Wounds were mended and stomachs were filled. The old master was plying his art again.

Within two days, McClellan had Halleck's "movable army" ready for battle. It was far from the army which he took to Virginia in the spring for here he had the remnants of the Manassas disaster. Much reorganization would have to be done on the road. As it stood, the army consisted of six corps and a cavalry division; about 84,000 men on paper, or between 67,000 and 74,000 effectives. Administrative red tape would cover a period of a week or more, i.e., the First Corps would not be officially transferred back from the Army of Virginia until camp had been established at Frederick, Maryland,[60] but for purposes of expediting combat-ready troops, McClellan had his army.

This was by no means all of the Army of the Potomac. Washington, vulnerable as it was, must be defended. Although McClellan did well in a few days of reorganizing, he could not do all. His plan was to finish the job following whatever action he would be required to take in the field:

The purpose of advancing from Washington [the general wrote] was simply to meet the necessities of the moment by frustrating Lee's invasion of the Northern States, and, when that was accomplished, to push with the utmost rapidity the work of reorganization and supply, so that a new campaign might be promptly inaugurated with the army in condition to persecute it to a successful termination without intermission.[61]

As it was, stragglers and deserters would wander the streets of the city for weeks, and the nerve center of the government would be on pins and needles throughout the campaign. To complete the job and to man the defenses, McClellan left three corps, the Third Corps under Brig. Gen. S. P. Heintzelman, the Fifth Corps under Maj. Gen. Fitz-John Porter, and the Eleventh Corps under Maj. Gen. Franz Sigel, plus other provisional and "home guard" units—about 73,000 men in all. The commanding officer was Maj. Gen. Nathaniel P. Banks. In effect, McClellan had divided his army in half, taking one half to battle and leaving the remainder for defense and "to prevent the tail of the army from being cut off."[62]

The last remaining Federal force of any size south of the Potomac was garrisoned at Harpers Ferry, where the Shenandoah River joined the Potomac. Col. Dixon S. Miles commanded approximately 12,000 troops of what was known as the Railroad Brigade of the Middle Department, Eighth Army Corps.[63] They were not under McClellan's command, but they were uppermost in his consideration. Harpers Ferry sat in the bottom of a bowl surrounded on all sides by mountainous heights, thus making it extremely vulnerable and impracticable to defend. The garrison had no value at all unless Lee's crossing would be in its vicinity. Even then the troops could not be permitted to sit still. It was plain to see that Lee would risk no crossing that near, so McClellan proposed to Halleck that Miles be ordered to evacuate and join the active army. An additional 12,000 men would mean a great deal to him. If they remained at Harpers Ferry, they would be lost.

"Halleck received my statement with ill-concealed contempt; said that everything was all right as it was," wrote McClellan. "[He said] that my views were entirely erroneous . . . leaving matters at Harpers Ferry precisely as they were."[64] Still, according to McClellan, Halleck had not specifically spelled out who was to command this "movable army" he had organized. Time was running out. Lee was crossing the Potomac into Maryland. The Harpers Ferry matter would have to wait. "I was fully aware of the risk I ran [in moving the army out]," wrote McClellan, "but the path of duty was clear and I tried to follow it. It was absolutely necessary that Lee's army should be met, and in the state of affairs . . . there could be no hesitation on my part as to doing it promptly."[65]

And so the Maryland Campaign began. In the early pre-dawn hours of September 4, 1862, Lee's Army of Northern Virginia began crossing the Potomac, a move that would culminate in one of the most decisive battles of the Civil War. It would make, and subsequently break, the military career of George Brinton McClellan; it would change the entire political, economic, and ideological aspects of the war; on it would hinge the fate of the Confederacy and the continued existence of the United States of America.

That afternoon a farmer on horseback raced through the main streets of Washington announcing the dreaded news that the Confederate army was entering Maryland.[66] The invasion had come.

3

"The Flower of Lee's Army"

Lee invaded Maryland first because he had to, and secondly because he wanted to. In his considered judgment, he had an excellent chance of bringing the war to a quick conclusion. Each of the several reasons for invasion tend to prove the confidence with which he faced the future. Despite overwhelming odds, which were decidedly not in his favor, Lee found the move an absolute necessity. The northern counties of Virginia had been stripped of forage for both men and animals. Supplies for future operations would have to be "trained" from over 100 miles away. The army would have to go where the "grass was greener." If Lee went south, his army would not only become a greater burden on his own people, but he would also lose the initiative. On the other hand, Lincoln had called for 300,000 additional men for the Federal army in July. Lee had it on good authority that at least 60,000 recruits had just arrived in Washington. The most men he counted on taking into Maryland was 70,000, and this number would probably be depleted even more by the time he crossed the Potomac. McClellan should have half again as many.

Lee clearly recognized his limitations: "The army is not properly equipped for an invasion of an enemy's territory," he wrote Jefferson Davis. "It lacks much of the material of war, is feeble in transportation, the animals being much reduced, and the men are poorly provided with clothes and in thousands of instances, are destitute of shoes." He made a desperate appeal to the President:

What occasions me most concern is the fear of getting out of ammunition. I beg you will instruct the Ordnance Department to spare no pains in manufacturing a sufficient amount of the best kind, and to be particular, in preparing that for the artillery, to provide three times as much for the long-range guns. The points to which I desire the ammunition to be forwarded will be made known to the Department in time. If the Quartermaster's Department can furnish any shoes, it would be the greatest relief. We have entered upon September, and the nights are becoming cool.[1]

Quite obviously, Lee suffered apprehension. Aside from those expressed in letters to Jefferson Davis, however, there is only one record of open discussion concerning the success of the invasion: "General Lee, on account of our short supplies, hesitated a little," wrote General James Longstreet, " but I reminded him of my experience in Mexico, where sometimes we were obliged to live two or three days on green corn. I told him that we could not starve at that season of the year so long as the fields were loaded with 'roasting ears.' "[2] Stonewall Jackson, too, supported the invasion: "I am . . . in favor of carrying the war north of the Potomac," he wrote to a friend.[3]

Not only was the Richmond *Dispatch* in favor of carrying the war north of the Potomac, but it was telling its subscribers, on September 8, that this was the hour of Confederate triumph; this was the appointed time. "We confess to a slight touch of superstition," the editor wrote. "We almost believe in lucky days, and have a very strong propensity to put faith in coincidence." September was an auspicious month in American history, indeed in world history, he pointed out. There were the battles of Brandywine, Lake Erie, Lake Champlain, and the bombardment of Fort McHenry—all in September. The victory in Mexico had come on September 14. Titus had entered Jerusalem and Napoleon had entered Moscow, both on this date.

But should our army push its successes so far as to enter Washington on the 14th [the editor said], it will have accomplished a feat of far more memorable significance than any other of the events enumerated save only the capture of Jerusalem. We have rarely ever seen a season as well adapted to military operations as the present. The weather is splendid, the air is bracing, and the sun brilliant. It is neither too hot nor too cold, but exactly tempered to the convenience of man and beast. That our leaders will take advantage of it to complete our late victories, we do not doubt.[4]

After he had weighed all the factors of invasion, General Lee moved with typical speed and purpose. On the morning of September 4, before the first Confederate had crossed the Potomac, he wired Davis: "I shall proceed to make the movement at once, unless you should signify your disapprobation."[5] Before he could receive a reply, indeed before his message could reach Richmond, he ordered his troops forward. "I am aware that the movement is attended with much risk," he had written.[6] But it was a calculated risk. Three important factors were in his favor—leadership, spirit, and time. He would make the most of all three.

Lee's first Maryland objective was Frederick ("Frederick City" on some reports). It was one of the largest towns in the western part of the state, on a direct route into Pennsylvania, and far enough from Washington to give him a head start on McClellan should the Army of the Potomac choose to leave the city. Jackson urged Lee to cross the river at a point near Harpers Ferry, to sweep through Winchester and Martinsburg at the northern end of the Shenandoah Valley, and to capture troops and badly needed supplies along the way.[7] Inasmuch as Lee's objective was to pull the Federal army out of Virginia, the commanding general, feeling that a Valley route might cause just the reverse, opposed Jackson's plan. Instead, the Army of Northern Virginia crossed the Potomac at White's Ford, where the river depth was only two to three feet, about 23 miles to the south of Frederick and 32 miles north of Washington. To the Marylander's eye, the Rebels little resembled an invading army. Lee, himself, in no way appeared the conquering hero. It seems almost symbolic that the "big three" of the Confederacy—Lee, Longstreet, and Jackson—rode into Maryland in a fashion that would soon be used by hundreds of Confederates when they left; by means of ambulance.

It had rained on the last day of August. Lee was wearing a rather cumbrous pair of rubber overalls and a poncho. He was just preparing to mount his horse when someone shouted "Yankee Cavalry!" As Lee reached for the reins to control his frightened horse, he tripped in his heavy clothing and fell forward, bracing his fall with his hands. As a result, he broke a small bone in one hand and badly sprained the other. Under doctor's orders, both hands were splinted. Unable to handle his mount, the commander of the Army of Northern Virginia rode into enemy territory in an ambulance wagon.[8]

Lee was not the only officer incapacitated. The day after Stonewall Jackson crossed the river, he too had an accident that put him flat on his back. A reception committee of Southern sympathizers met him on the Maryland shores and presented him with a young mare as a gift. When the general mounted for the first time, the animal refused to move. Jackson dug his spurs into its side. When he did, the horse reared, losing its balance, and toppled backward. Jackson was thrown to the ground with a severe jolt. Fearing a serious injury, doctors ordered him to an ambulance.[9] And General Longstreet, Lee's "Old War Horse," had rubbed a raw blister on one heel. He wore a carpet slipper into Maryland and throughout the campaign;[10] a rather undignified uniform for a general.

In addition to these mishaps, two of them serious, the Army of Northern Virginia was further denied the glory of a truly triumphal entry into the North by serious internal conflicts. Brig. Gen. John Bell Hood was under arrest for insubordination. He had been ordered to the rear of his division to await trial on charges of refusing to relinquish some captured wagons. Following Manassas, Hood's men had spied several new Federal wagons outfitted with stretchers and medical supplies, which they easily raided and captured. Before long a squabble arose as to who should be authorized to keep them. In the ensuing argument, Hood and Brig. Gen. N. G. "Shanks" Evans, who had "titular authority" over Hood's Division, fell to bitter words. Evans insisted that the ambulances be turned over to his brigade. Hood refused, saying that he would "cheerly have obeyed directions to deliver them to General Lee's Quartermaster for the use of the army, [but] I did not consider it just that I should be required to yield them to another Brigade of the Division, which was in no manner entitled to them." Evans asked Longstreet to arrest Hood on insubordination and he made the charge stick. Lee interceded because the whole thing had blossomed into a ridiculous state of affairs and because Hood was much too valuable to lose in view of impending battle. Hood was returned to the ranks but without command. Resentment ran high among the men, so intense that before the campaign was over, Lee would return Hood to his division.[11]

The Army of Northern Virginia was staffed with the best the South had to offer and Lee could ill-afford petty differences among his generals at this time. Yet two of his most valued men had entered into another serious quarrel enroute to the Potomac, a quarrel that lasted throughout the Maryland Campaign. Ambrose Powell Hill and Thomas Jonathan Jackson, West Point classmates, had been thrown together under Lee's command and their personalities clashed. Hill led a division of Jackson's Corps. Late on the evening of September 3, Jackson issued orders for the advance the following morning, spelling out specific times for specific units. As was his custom, he was on the scene the next morning to see that his instructions were obeyed. Hill's Division was delayed and Jackson was mildly perturbed. Hill was nowhere in sight.

Already antagonized, the determined Jackson rode in full surveillance of the column when it moved. As it progressed, now with Hill at its head, the rear ranks began breaking as stragglers moved off to the sides of the road. Jackson noted that Hill rode on with his staff, apparently unconcerned. Jackson's temper, which had erupted on lesser occasions, began to boil. Soon it was time for an ordered rest-halt. Hill's Division continued to march. Jackson, holding off his fury, raced to the front and commanded the first brigade to stop as he had directed. Hill, every bit as tempestuous as Jackson, rode back and demanded to know who had ordered the halt. Col. Edward Thomas, who had received Jackson's directive, nodded to the stalwart general, who was silently watching the scene from his horse nearby, and said, "I halted because General Jackson ordered me to do so."

Filled with rage and contempt, Hill drew his sword and handed it to Jackson. With no attempt to conceal his anger, Hill snarled, "If you take command of my troops in my presence, take my sword also." "Put up your sword and consider yourself under arrest," replied Jackson. With this, Hill rode to the rear of his column. On September 7, he requested a copy of the formal charges being made against him. Jackson informed him through an aide that when the proper time arrived, military procedure would be followed. In the meantime, he was to ride with his division as before. From that day until the surrender of Harpers Ferry, Hill rode to the rear of his troops. Before the war ended, both men fell mortally wounded, their differences unresolved.[12]

As a whole, the Confederate army was not much better off, figuratively speaking, than its generals. It did not make a very good impression on the crowds that watched the crossing. One young man wrote:

They were the dirtiest, lousiest, filthiest, piratical-looking cut-throat men I ever saw. A most ragged, lean, and hungry set of wolves. Yet there was a dash about them that the Northern men lacked. They rode like circus riders. Many of them were from the far South and spoke a dialect I could scarcely understand. They were profane beyond belief and talked incessantly.[13]

Although the Southern soldier took great pride in his army, he was never too proud to admit its shortcomings. The army was in bad shape, and if no one else knew it, the men did. One of the rank and file put it this way:

All the roads of northern Virginia were livid with soldiers, comprehensively denominated "stragglers;" but the great majority of these men had fallen out from the advancing column from physical inability to keep up with it; thousands were not with General Lee because they had no shoes, and their bleeding feet could carry them no further, or the heavy march without rations had broken them down.[14]

A young officer in Jackson's Corps wrote:

We had been faring badly since we left Manassas Junction, having had only one meal that included bread and coffee. Our diet had been green corn, with beef without salt, roasted on the end of ramrods. We heard with delight of the "plenty" to be had in Maryland; judge of our disappointment when, about 2 o'clock at night, we were marched into a dank clover-field and the order came down the line, "Men, go into that corn-field and get your rations—and be ready to march at 5 in the morning."[15]

For nearly three weeks the men lived off of green corn and little else but potatoes. Twenty years later one man wrote that he would always remember the Maryland invasion as "the green corn campaign."[16] It was marked heavily with broken health and widespread desertions. Diarrhea and dysentery took a devastating toll. One young private documented the march with some interesting observations, giving a picturesque, yet pathetic, look at the Army of Northern Virginia:

Still no signs of our commissary wagons, and not a mouthful of food did we have all day. The 4th found our column halted, and green corn served out. . . . for six days not a morsel of bread or meat has gone into our

stomachs—and our *menu* consisted of apples and corn. We toasted, we
burned, we stewed, we boiled, we roasted these two together, and singly,
until there was not a man whose form had not caved in, and who had not
a bad attack of diarrhea. Our under-clothes were foul and hanging in strips,
our socks were worn out, and half the men were bare-footed, many were
lame, and were sent to the rear; others, of sterner stuff, hobbled along and
managed to keep up, while gangs from every company went off into the
surrounding country looking for food, and did not rejoin their commands
until weeks after. [Jed Hotchkiss, Lee's famous cartographer, said that as
many as 5,000 came up the night after the battle at Sharpsburg.] Many
became ill from exposure and starvation, and were left on the road. The
ambulances were full, and the whole route was marked with a sick, lame,
limping lot, that straggled to farm-houses that lined the way, and who, in
all cases, succored and cared for them.[17]

Sgt. Berry Benson of the 1st South Carolina Volunteers, whose
diary is a constant source of Confederate revelations, wrote: "I became more and more weak [as we continued the march, moving toward Leesburg], marching out of rank nearly all the time. Early in the
morning, before the line could get started, I would go ahead in order
not to be left too far behind at night."[18] Lee, himself, was well aware
of the straggling; "I fear from a third to one-half of the original
numbers," he wrote.[19]

Shoeless feet and ill health from exhaustive marches and continued
battle for three months were responsible for the most serious depletions
in Lee's ranks. Because of the incomplete and often inaccurate records
of the Confederate army, it will never be known exactly how many
men Lee lost due to these conditions. John Esten Cooke, soldier and
later a leading Southern writer, estimated that the ranks were depleted
by between 20,000 and 30,000 men who remained in Virginia. "This
great crowd toiled on painfully in the wake of the army," wrote Cooke,
"dragging themselves five or six miles a day; and when they came to
the Potomac, near Leesburg, it was only to find that General Lee had
swept on, that General McClellan's column was between him and
them, and that they could not rejoin their command."[20]

One of Lee's objectives in Maryland would be the purchase of new
shoes. On September 3, he had informed President Davis that "the
men are poorly provided with clothes, and in thousands of instances
are destitute of shoes."[21] There was no such thing as two pair per man

and even if such abundance existed, it is doubtful that the men would have bothered bringing them along. A newspaper correspondent with an unusual eye for logistics estimated that before Lee's army could progress further in the war, it would need at least 40,000 pairs of shoes.[22] Bell I. Wiley, in his *The Life of Johnny Reb,* states: "It may easily have been true that the difference between a victory and a draw for Lee at Antietam was his want of a few thousand pairs of shoes."[23] Southern shoes were not made to stand the punishment they were receiving. Unpaved, dirt roads of the South were no comparison to the hard-surfaced highways of Maryland. One officer commented that the average Southerner had ridden so much and walked so seldom in his life, that proper care was nearly ignored.[24] Douglas Southall Freeman commented: "After another six months of hardening, most of the troops were to find themselves possessed of feet so tough that shoes in summer were a nuisance. It was far from being so in September, 1862."[25] When questioned about his absence from duty at Antietam, one Georgia soldier replied, "I had no shoes. I tried it barefoot, but somehow my feet wouldn't callous. They just kept bleeding. I found it so hard to keep up that though I had the heart of a patriot, I began to feel I didn't have patriotic feet. Of course, I could have crawled on my hands and knees, but then my hands would have got so sore I couldn't have fired my rifle."[26] Lee's quartermaster was ultimately able to purchase some 1,700 pairs of shoes between Frederick and Hagerstown, but not nearly enough to help.

An editorial in the Richmond *Dispatch* of October 9, 1862, contained a devastating epitaph to the Maryland Campaign:

Posterity will scarcely believe that the wonderful campaign which has just ended with its terrible marches and desperate battles, was made by men, one-fourth of whom were entirely barefooted, and one-half of whom were as ragged as scarecrows. . . We cease to wonder at the number of stragglers, when we hear how many among them were shoeless, with stone bruises on their feet.[27]

Not only were shoes and uniforms sadly lacking, but the army had discarded much of their kits, reducing traveling gear down to the "simplest elements and smallest dimensions."[28] Tents were left behind and so were trunks and carpetbags. This army was traveling bare, figuratively and literally.

Many stragglers were truly sick, but deliberate absenteeism was not uncommon at this point in the war. Soldiers were tired of fighting; some, too, were tired of what they were fighting for. The Army of Northern Virginia, known throughout history for its devotion and bravery, was not so unique as to preclude a significant wave of political mutiny. Some counties in North Carolina, for example, had been pro-Union before the war began. A regimental historian wrote that their men "had volunteered to resist invasion and not to invade; some did not believe it right to invade Northern Territory."[29] The same feeling was also quite evident among South Carolina troops. At the battle of South Mountain, a mortally wounded Lt. Col. James from the 15th South Carolina told Capt. Charles Walcott of the 21st Massachusetts, who comforted him in his last moments, that the colonel of his regiment refused to cross the river, "saying that the regiment had enlisted to defend the South and not to invade the North." James had taken command and led the volunteers on, all to their death, he feared.[30] "There were two opinions in the army as to the propriety of the move," wrote a soldier to his daughter. "A minority believed that as a matter of *prudence* at least we should not leave our own soil; that it looked a little like *invasion*. The consequence was a large number hung back and would not cross the river—while others were willing to retire from the fight sooner than they would have done on our own soil."[31]

It was difficult to segregate those who feigned illness from those whose excuses were justified. Some were severely punished, but even drastic disciplinary measures failed to curb one of Lee's most serious problems. Straggling is our "one great embarrassment," he wrote Jefferson Davis.[32] The public was requested to help. Newspapers in Richmond pleaded with its citizens not to aid and comfort those who returned without leave. Police officials and railway agents examined passes, but still the ranks suffered incalcuable damage. Lee, with much dismay, informed President Davis that straggling was becoming intolerable and respectfully requested that something be done on a higher level. "Nothing can surpass the gallantry and intelligence of the main body," he told Davis, "but there are individuals who, from their backwardness in duty, tardiness of movement, and neglect of orders, do it no credit. One of the greatest evils, from which many minor ones proceed, is the habit of straggling from the ranks. It has become a habit difficult to correct." Lee recognized that many were ill and that the dropping from the ranks in these cases were accepted, but the greater number came "from design." "I know of no better way of correcting this . . . than by the appointment of a military commission of men known to the country, and having its confidence and support, to accompany the army constantly, with a provost-marshal and guard to execute promptly its decisions."[33] (See Appendix E, Document 6.) It was a bold measure, but one which Lee saw a necessity. In the meantime, his General Order No. 2 would have to suffice. (See Appendix E, Document 4.)

It was with great pain that Lee issued this order, but behind that familiar mask of gentleness was a stern military mind. He was a West Point man and had served in the military all his life. He knew it could be no other way. The Confederacy was undergoing its most severe test. "This army is about to engage in most important operations," the general wrote. "A provost guard . . . will follow in rear of the army, arrest stragglers, and punish summarily all depredators, and keep the men with their commands." If this failed to illustrate the urgency of the moment, Lee further explained:

Stragglers are usually those who desert their comrades in peril. Such characters are better absent from the army on such momentous occasions as those about to be entered upon. They will, as bringing discredit upon our cause, as useless members of the service and as especially deserving odium, come under the special attention of the provost-marshal, and be considered as unworthy members of an army which has immortalized itself in the recent glorious and successful engagements against the enemy . . .[34]

A Federal soldier passing over the Confederate route towards South Mountain observed pointed examples of Lee's discipline. He wrote:

During this short march we saw a terrible example of the discipline then enforced in the rebel army; two corpses in ragged gray uniforms were hanging on a tree beside the road, and we were told by citizens that they were two of Jackson's men whom he had ordered to be hung for stealing. Although the rebel army (ragged and half-fed) had just passed over the road by which we were moving, the ripe apples were left hanging untouched on the trees that lined the road; . . .

In a note of comparison between the two armies, this man added, "the straggling, plunderers from our well provided delivering army, left few apples, chickens, or young pigs behind them on the march."[35]

Despite the appearance and difficulties of the Confederate army, spirits were high. Longstreet said that Lee would have had to do little more than dismiss the troops in Virginia, give them a half-hour for a dip in the Potomac to wash off the dust and dirt for the Maryland damsels, and then reform in Frederick, so great was their faith in the friendship and generosity of the Marylanders.[36] Every attempt was made to prepare the army for impending action. Broken equipment which was repairable was quickly put into shape. Horses not fit for travel were put to pasture while as many healthy animals as could be obtained were assigned to the various units. All superfluous or unreliable modes of transportation were left behind. Major Heros Von Borcke, Jeb Stuart's Chief of Staff, described the excitement of the preparation:

On the morning of the 5th September there was again presented throughout the Confederate camps a scene of bustling activity. Every regiment was preparing for the march, officers were riding to and fro, and the long artillery-trains were moving off along the turnpike, their rumbling noise combining with the rattle of the drums and the roll of the bugles to wake the echoes for miles around. Our direction was northward, and as we rode onward towards the little town of Leesburg, inspirited by this fact, our horses exhibiting new life from yesterday's report, many a youthful hero looked forward to his triumphant entry into the Federal capital, or to a joyous reception at the hands of the fair women of Baltimore, whose irrepressible sympathies had been always with the South.[37]

As the men reached the Potomac, the 10th Virginia was in front with flags flying and bands blaring the exciting strains of "Maryland, My Maryland," long before adopted as a Southern song. Cheers and shouts spread from one regiment to another. Shoes were off and pants were rolled up. "It was a noble spectacle," wrote Jed Hotchkiss in his diary. "The broad river, fringed by lofty trees in full foliage; the exuberant wealth of the autumnal wild flower down to the very margin of the stream and a bright green island stretched away to the right."[38] Von Borcke added:

It was, indeed, a magnificent sight as the long column of many thousand horsemen stretched across this beautiful Potomac. The evening sun slanted upon its clear placid waters, and burnished them with gold, while arms of the soldiers, glittered and blazed in its radiance. There were few moments, perhaps, from the beginning to the close of the war, of excitement more intense, of exhilaration more delightful, than when we ascended the opposite bank to the familiar but now strangely thrilling music "Maryland, My Maryland." As I gained the dry ground, I little thought that in a short time I should recross the river into Virginia, under circumstances far different and far less inspiring.[39]

The excitement of the occasion seemed to spread in a rather peculiar manner to one of Jackson's staff — a man who became the real hero of the crossing. As might be expected in an operation of this sort, the old army mule could be counted on to snarl traffic, and it did. At a critical point, midstream, the jumble of wagons threatened to bring havoc to what had otherwise been a smooth movement of the army. Jackson, who by this time was hardly in any mood to tolerate any more insubordination, whether it be human or animal, ordered his chief quartermaster, Maj. John A. Harman, to clear the river. Harman was a profane man with considerable experience at handling mules. His "crisis" created one of the lighter moments of the campaign:

Harman dashed in among the wagoners, and, in the voice of a stentor, poured out a volume of oaths that would excite the admiration of the most scientific mule-driver. The effect was electrical. The drivers were frightened and swore as best they could, but far below the major's standards. The mules caught the inspiration from a chorus of familiar words, and all at once made a break for the Maryland shore, and in five minutes the ford was cleared. Jackson witnessed and heard it all. Harman rode back to join him, expecting a lecture, and, touching his hat said: "The ford is clear, general! There's only one language that will make mules understand on a hot day that they must get out of the water." The general smiled and said: "Thank you, major," and dashed into the water at the head of his staff, and rode across.[40]

It was a beautiful day. It was an exciting day. Behind this army lay a war-torn, desolated country. Before it lay a peaceful land, bountiful with the luxuries the men had dreamed about for weeks. By a stroke of luck, there was a boat loaded with melons waiting in one of the Chesapeake and Ohio Canal locks for transport to Washington. With little hesitation, the men proceded to "buy" the treasure for mess that evening. Jackson was on the lookout for early signs of subsistence and once across saw to it that a field of corn was purchased. The men were given orders to have "one day's ration" cooked that night and in their haversacks by dawn.[41] "Thus far we have met with a cordial hospitality," wrote a correspondent for a Charleston, South Carolina newspaper. "Along the road the farmers . . . opened their houses, and spread their boards with the fat of the land. One Marylander whom I met has fed in twenty-four hours six hundred men free of charge."[42] It was indeed going to be a bountiful land.

The army had confidence—confidence in its cause, confidence in Lee. On September 6, Lee gave the men cause for lifted spirits. Maj. Gen. Kirby Smith had had a victory in the west at the same time as the Manassas victory. Smith had captured a Federal general (William Nelson), his staff, and 3,000 prisoners complete with wagons, artillery, and small-arms in the battle for Richmond, Kentucky. "Soldiers, press onward," Lee told his men in General Orders No. 103.

Let each man feel the responsibility now resting on him to pursue vigorously the success vouchsafed to us by Heaven. Let the armies of the East and the West vie with each other in discipline, bravery, and activity, and our brethren of our sister States will soon be released from tyranny, and our independence be established upon a sure and abiding basis.[43]

Nearly every community in Maryland through which both Confederate and Federal troops marched was divided in sentiment. Opposition always showed, but, generally speaking, the townfolks would turn out in full force with the flag of the day. One such incident took place in Keedysville (Centreville on some Confederate military reports), and is to this day told with great relish and amusement. During the march to Sharpsburg by the two armies, both were greeted with equal enthusiasm. The Confederate flag was displayed for Lee. When McClellan rode through later, he found the Union flag flying from every window. Neither party knew of the little trick and Keedysville maintained its neutrality, serving the wounded of both armies during the battle.[44]

William M. Owen, an officer in the Washington Artrillery, wrote: "Every one we meet says he is a 'rebel' and we are most hospitably received wherever we go."[45] On the first night in Maryland, Jackson told the farmer, on whose ground he was camped, that he "would be obliged to take some [fence] rails for cooking rations." "Burn away," said the farmer, "that's what rails are for when there's no other wood about."[46]

Owen wrote that the "young ladies" were wild to see General Lee. They would come out to the camp in caravans of family carriages and surround Lee, kissing him and hugging him, much to his embarrassment and to the chagrin of his men. "We young ones look on, and only wish that they would distribute those favors a little more 'permiscus', so to speak;" wrote Owen, "but the fair ones, though coy, are very agreeable, and we each forth with select one whose colors we shall wear until we reach the next town."[47]

Von Borcke described the cavalry's reception:

The inhabitants of Maryland whom we met along the road, with some exceptions, did not greet us quite so cordially as we had expected, this portion of the state being less devoted than others to the Confederate cause. It was different, however, at Poolesville. We remained in Poolesville about an hour, and in this brief space the enthusiasm of the citizens rose to fever heat. A number of young men became so much excited that they immediately mounted their horses and insisted on joining our ranks. Two young merchants of the village, suddenly resolving to enlist in the Cavalry, announced the peremptory sale of their extensive stock of groceries upon the spot for Confederate money. Our soldiers cleared out both establishments during the hour, to last pin. Soldiers, on such occasions, are like children. They buy everything, and embarrass themselves with numberless articles which they soon afterwards are thrown away as useless. I, myself, could not resist the temptation of purchasing a box of cigars, a parcel of white crushed sugar, some lemons, and a pocket-knife, in the possession of which treasures I felt as happy as a king.[48]

On the morning of September 6, the main headquarters tent was pitched at Monocacy Junction on the Baltimore and Ohio Railroad. Lee had reached the first of his objectives. From here a plan would evolve to disrupt two main arteries to the west; the B & O and the Chesapeake and Ohio Canal. As it would turn out, interruption of rail traffic would be one of the few objectives he would achieve in Maryland.

Here at a spot known as Best's Grove, camped Lee, Jackson, Longstreet, and for a brief spell, Jeb Stuart. Here was the backbone of the Confederate army—and citizens loved it. Seldom had such an array of talent assembled on the field. With the exception of one dinner invitation to a private home which he accepted, Lee seldom left his tent. His injured hands pained him much. Jackson did not stray far either. Once when he did, two young girls from Baltimore, obviously admirers, ran to him, threw their arms around him and "talked with the wildest enthusiasm, both at the same time, until he seemed miserable." When they finally departed, the general "stood paralyzed, and . . . did not venture out again . . ."[49] Such was not the case with Longstreet and Stuart. Longstreet's "carpet slipper" was an oddity and Stuart's reputation with the fairer sex had preceeded him by many miles. The dashing cavalry general was "ready to see and talk to every good-looking woman," commented Henry Kyd Douglas.[50]

Douglas, the youngest member of Jackson's staff, was born in Shepherdstown, Virginia (West Virginia), but his home was now on the Maryland side of the river, just three miles from Sharpsburg. He was a Marylander returned home as an invader. On Saturday, the 6th, his mother drove to Monocacy Junction to pay him a visit. With great ceremony, he presented her to the four generals. Each received her with typical charm and dignity. It was a proud day for the 22-year-old lieutenant. Little did he realize that in less than two weeks his mother would be a prisoner in her own home, the farm gutted by war's scavenging fingers.[51]

Capt. W. T. Faithful of the 1st Maryland Regiment of the Potomac Home Brigade commanded all that was left of Federal troops in Frederick—some 600 sick and wounded in hospitals. While the Confederates were establishing their camp, Faithful conjured up enough transportation to get his men out and sent them quietly off to Harpers Ferry. What supplies he could get on wagons, he sent to Pennsylvania. The rest he burned.[52]

The next day was Sunday. There had been battles on Sunday. The first battle at Manassas had been fought on the Sabbath, but, generally speaking, the men of both armies respected the day. Religion was a strong force in both camps. Sunday, September 7, 1862, was not a particularly special day. The men were in Maryland. Lee had plans. McClellan had plans too; he was searching for Lee. But this would not interfere with activities in Frederick. Jackson found no excuse to keep him from going to church. Little, if anything, including battle, ever interrupted his worship in one form or another. On Sunday evening, Jackson asked his young brother-in-law and aide-de-camp, Lt. J. G. Morrison, and Kyd Douglas to attend services with him in Frederick. The young officers rode their mounts, the general in an ambulance. A short way out from camp, Jackson decided that he should have a pass to go through the lines. Reminded that it was his army, Jackson said that Lee had given orders and he intended to obey them. Douglas went back to camp and returned with the pass. It read:

Guards and Pickets
 Pass Maj. Genl. T. J. Jackson and two staff officers and attendants to Frederick to church, to return tonight.

By command of
Major Genl. Jackson
E. F. Paxton
A. A. Genl.

Jackson was a Presbyterian but that evening he attended services at the Reformed Church, and "as usual . . . went to sleep at the beginning of the sermon, and a very sound slumber it was," wrote Douglas. "His cap, which he held in his hand on his lap, dropped to the floor, and his head upon his breast, the prayer of the congregation did not awaken him, and only the voice of the choir and deep tones of the organ broke his sleep." Dr. Zacharias, the minister, was congratulated after the service for having pulled one over on the general. He had offered prayer for the President of the United States and Jackson had missed it. Douglas observed later: "The General didn't hear it, but if he had, I've no doubt he would have joined in it heartily."[53] Jackson admitted sleeping, but defended himself by stating that he was sitting so far to the rear of the church that he could not hear the sermon.[54]

This was Jackson's only visit away from camp and he was pleased with what he saw. The next day he wrote his wife:

The town appears to be a charming place, neat and beautiful. The ladies and gentlemen were sitting in front of the doors, and all looked so comfortable, and I may say elegant, according to my ideas, and their enjoyment looked so genuine, that my heart was in sympathy with the surroundings. If such scenes could only surround me in Lexington, how my heart would, under a smiling Providence, rejoice![55]

On Saturday, September 6, Lee informed Davis that "two divisions of the army have crossed the Potomac. I hope all will cross today. Navigation of the Chesapeake and Ohio has been interrupted and efforts will be made to break up the use of the Baltimore and Ohio Railroad."[56] The following morning he wrote: "Mr. President: I have the honor to inform you that all the divisions of the army have crossed the Potomac . . ."[57] In addition to the men that Lee had brought with him from Manassas, fresh troops from the Richmond defenses joined the march into Maryland. Bringing up the rear of the column, but crossing three miles farther up the river, were three divisions under Lafayette McLaws, Daniel Harvey Hill (another of Jackson's brothers-in-law), and John G. Walker. All three would play an important role in the action to follow. A brigade of cavalry, under Wade Hampton, and reserve artillery brought the total additions to about 20,000 men. But even this would not offset completely the overwhelming losses incurred before the crossing. At best, Lee could count only 50,000, a disappointing figure for what he had in mind.

Lee had an important job to do. He was now in Maryland and he must make the most of his time. On Saturday morning, September 6, the first Confederate troops moved into Frederick. Col. Bradley T. Johnson, a native of that city, was immediately appointed provost marshal. Johnson wasted no time in informing the people of Maryland why the Confederates were there. "Remember the cells of Fort Mc-Henry," he stated. Remember "the insults to your wives and daughters! the arrests! the midnight searches of your house! . . . rise at once in arms and strike for liberty and right."[58]

While these may have been Lee's sentiments, he preferred to put the matter more persuasively and diplomatically. Certainly Johnson's manner did little to arouse any interest. Lee waited for some specific reaction from Frederick or state officials on the invasion. One official in particular which he hoped to hear from was ex-governor Enoch Lowe, a known Confederate sympathizer. When Lowe made no effort to respond, and the state government passively accepted the Confederate army on its soil, Lee issued his formal proclamation to the people of Maryland. It came two days after Johnson's speech and was aimed primarily at the Federal government's military control of the state and the suspension of the writ of habeas corpus. Lee explained that he represented not an enemy but a friendly government, and that he was sent into Maryland to aid its citizens in repelling the "foreign yoke" of militant oppression. (See Appendix E, Document 9.) The Confederate army was there to assist them with "the power of its arms in regaining the rights of which you have been despoiled." There would be no constraint upon their free will. The decision to secede, if, indeed, they would go this far, would be in their hands. "This army will respect your choice whatever it may be," Lee told them.[59]

The words were impressive but it seems obvious that Lee really expected little. On the previous day he had written Davis: "Notwithstanding individual expressions of kindness that have been given, and the general sympathy in the success of the Confederate States, situated as Maryland is, I do not anticipate any general rising of the people in our behalf. Some additions to our ranks will no doubt be received, and I hope to procure subsistence for our troops."[60] Nonetheless, Davis had sent his personal political ambassador, E. Loring Lowe, along with Lee's army to negotiate any terms with Maryland should a victory in that state call for Confederate civil representation.[61] There are no accurate reports on how many Maryland recruits Lee persuaded. Longstreet claimed he expected 25,000,[62] though Lee's letter to Davis would dispute this. Recruiting estimates range from "comparatively few" in a Confederate account,[63] to 15,000 in a Richmond newspaper.[64] Some Marylanders came, of this we know. But when they saw the bare feet and ragged uniforms, many left, disillusioned. At best, Lee gained only a few hundred. Whatever he gained, however, he lost by straggling between Frederick and Sharpsburg.

Lee had been warned that the section of Maryland he would be entering was pro-Union. Bradley Johnson spent three hours with Lee and Jackson on the evening of the 4th giving them many valuable tips on Maryland. He told Lee that though there were many Southern sympathizers in Maryland, they could offer little help to the army without some assurance of a prolonged occupation. Confederate loyalties were frowned upon by both local citizens and the military. It had become risky business to speak out and Johnson warned Lee not to expect too much.[65]

Eyewitness accounts of Lee's reception in Frederick differ with the individual point of view. Yet it is safe to generalize that no pronounced hostility was displayed toward the uninvited guests. There was more curiosity than alarm. Some looked at the victors of Manassas with disappointment. Stonewall Jackson and Robert E. Lee had been magical names. They had heard of Jackson's peculiar habits and many came just to gaze at him, hoping to catch him sucking a lemon or praying while on horseback. When Jackson ordered the crowds away from his tent, one man was heard to say, "Oh, he's no great shakes after all!"[66]

A Union physician who observed the Confederate arrival noted: "Their reception in Frederick was decidedly cool; all the stores shut, no flags flying, and everything partook of a churchyard appearance."[67] Although the young people felt great excitement in the invasion, a number of the citizens of the county fled to Pennsylvania, taking their cattle with them.

The physician continued: "Every man seemed to have plenty of money, which they stated had been furnished to them freely to purchase whatever they wanted when they got to Philadelphia! The stores were entered, and the proprietors were either compelled to give their goods away or else take Confederate scrip."[68] Frederick citizens were not overly enthusiastic about accepting Rebel currency. Nothing short of military victory or total state secession would have made it worth anything more than paper. A young soldier wrote: "We found a grocer, a good, sensible fellow, with 'rebel sympathies,' and we invested a few hundred dollars, 'Confederate scrip,' in coffee, sugar, whisky, Scotch ale, champagne, and a few other 'necessaries of life,' much to the disgust of his partner, who did not take a bit of stock in 'Jeff Davis,' and who felt remarkable sore when the last of his stock of groceries, was exchanged for Confederate notes."[69]

The demand for supplies was great. Lee told Davis of the problem, but there was really little the government could do at this point. "Many of the farmers have not yet gotten out their wheat," wrote Lee, "and there is a reluctance on the part of the millers and others to commit themselves in our favor. Some cattle, but not in any great numbers, are obtained in this country."[70] Nearly every store that opened its doors was sold out. Coffee jumped to one dollar a pound and other prices soared to unprecedented heights. But there was no looting. Discipline was firm:

Their behavior towards every one was very carefully managed—no bad treatment of any one was permitted [wrote a local citizen]. No straggling was allowed, and although no discipline measures was observed, implicit obedience was maintained; for if a man declined or moved tardily, a blow sabre or butt of a pistol enforced the order. It was stated by the men that four of the army had been shot for straggling since leaving Leesburgh. All the doctors slept at the hospital, as the streets were filled with soldiers who had been drinking freely, though, to their credit, when they commenced drinking they speedily became dead drunk and were then harmless. Did any one of them attempt to create a disturbance, a guard would slip up to him and say something to him, and the songster would immediately cease his brawling and go quietly to the guard-house.[71]

George W. Shreve, a member of the Stuart Horse Artillery, wrote: "Genl. Lee [had] issued stringent orders against taking any property by the soldiers. Some of the men came into camp one morning with a pig, and declared that the pig attacked them, and they were obliged to kill it in self defense. It was keenly enjoyed for breakfast and no questions [were] asked."[72]

Von Borcke's description of the Frederick reception was somewhat different in viewpoint from that of the physician:

Entering the good old city of Frederick, I found it in a tremendous state of excitement. The Unionists living there had their houses closely shut up and barred; but the far greater number of the citizens, being favourably disposed to the Confederate cause, had thrown wide open their doors and windows, and welcomed our troops with the liveliest enthusiasm. Flags were floating from the houses, and garlands of flowers were hung across the streets. Everywhere a dense multitude was moving up and down, singing and shouting in a paroxysm of joy and patriotic emotion, in many cases partly superinduced by an abundant flow of strong liquors.[73]

The only trouble which occurred during the brief occupation was caused by several men who entered the offices of the Frederick *Examiner,* a Republican newspaper, and proceeded to disrupt business. Damages were quickly repaired and the offenders arrested by Provost Marshal Johnson.[74] Johnson was so vehement in his determination to present the best side of the Confederate face to the North that when he spotted a soldier in the street cheering for "Jeff Davis," he rode up, smashed him on the head with a revolver, and said, "There, you damned ————, see if you disobey orders again."[75]

While behavior was good, appearance left much to be desired. Frederick citizens remembered for a long time the ragged look of their invaders. "They were the filthiest set of men and officers I ever saw; with clothing that . . . had not been changed for weeks. They could be smelt all over the entire inclosure."[76] One man described them as "the dirtiest, lousiest, filthiest, piratical-looking cut-throats white man ever saw."[77] Another wrote:

Every evening, hundreds could be seen, sitting on the roads or fields, half denuded with clothes in laps, busily cracking, between two thumb-nails, these creeping nuisances [graybacks or body lice] . . . the men would boil their clothes for hours—next day these confounded things would be at work as lively as ever . . . many used to place their under-raiment, during the night, in the bottom of some stream and put a large stone to keep them down; in the morning they would hastily dry them and get a temporary relief . . .[78]

One Frederick woman's account has become a classic description of the Confederate soldier during the autumn of 1862. She wrote to a relative:

I wish, my dear Minnie, you could have witnessed the transit of the Rebel army through our streets. . . Their coming was unheralded by any pomp and pageant whatever. No burst of martial music greeted your ear, no thundering sound of cannon, no brilliant staff, no glittering cortege dashed through the streets; instead came three long, dirty columns that kept on in an unceasing flow. I could scarcely believe my eyes; was this body of men moving so smoothly along, with no order, their guns carried in every fashion, no two dressed alike, their officers hardly distinguishable from the privates, were these, I asked myself in amazement, were these dirty, lank, ugly specimens of humanity, with shocks of hair sticking through holes in their hats, and dust thick on their dirty faces, the men that had coped and encountered successfully, and driven back again and again, our splendid legions with their fine discipline, their martial show and color, their solid battalions keeping such perfect time to the inspiring bands of music? I must confess, Minnie, that I felt humiliated at the thought that this horde of ragamuffins could set our grand army of the Union at defiance.

Why it seemed as if a single regiment of our gallant boys in blue could drive that dirty crew into the river without any trouble. And then, too, I wish you could see how they behaved—a crowd of boys on a holiday don't seem happier. They are on the broad grin all the time. O, they are so dirty! I don't think the Potomac River could wash them clean; and ragged! There is not a scarecrow in our cornfields that would not scorn to exchange clothes with them; and so tattered! There isn't a decently dressed soldier in the whole army.

I saw some strikingly handsome faces though, or rather they would have been so if they could have had a good scrubbing. They were very polite, I must confess, and always asked for a drink of water, or anything else, and never think of coming inside of a door without an invitation. Many of them were barefooted. Indeed, I felt sorry for the poor, misguided wretches, for some of them limped along so painfully, trying to keep up with their comrades.[79]

"There was no one there who would not have been 'run in' by the police had he appeared on the streets of any populous city," wrote a Confederate soldier. "Yet those grimy, sweaty, lean, ragged men were the flower of Lee's army."[80]

The comparison between the two armies staggered the imagination in this frank but honest account by an admitted Union sympathizer:

In manners, in the conduct of soldiers and the discipline, these bundles of rags, these cough-racked, diseased and starved men excel our well-fed, well clothed, our best soldiers. No one can point to a single act of vandalism perpetrated by the Rebel soldiery during their occupation of Frederick, while even now a countless host of [Federal] stragglers are crawling after our own army devouring, destroying or wasting all that falls in their devious line of march. God knows I have no need to praise Confederate forebearance, but the fact that we are confronted by an army perfectly under the control and discipline of tried and experienced officers is incontrovertible. It accounts for the excellence of their fighting, and the almost powerlessness of our own army.[81]

Artist Alfred R. Waud, to whom we now look as the master of Civil War editorial illustrators, was trapped behind Confederate lines during the Frederick encampment days. Not one to be idle, Waud made good use of his time. An opportunity came to sketch the 1st Virginia Cavalry, one of the "crack regiments" of the Confederate army. With the drawing, which was later engraved and published in the September 27, 1862, edition of *Harper's,* the artist left an equally vivid word picture, one of the best descriptions of the Southern soldier:

They seemed to be of considerable social standing, that is, most of them—F. F. V.'s [First Family of Virginia], so to speak, and not irreverently; for they were not only as a body handsome, athletic men, but generally polite and agreeable in manner. With the exception of the officers, there was little else but homespun among them, light drab-gray or butternut color, the drab predominating; although there were so many varieties of dress, half-citizen, half military, that they could scarcely be said to have a uniform. Light jacket and trousers with black facings, and slouched hats, appeared to be (in those cases where the wearer could obtain it) the court costume of the regiment. Their horses were good; in many cases, they told me, they provided their own. Their arms were the United States cavalry sabre, Sharp's carbine, and pistols. Some few of them had old swords of the Revolution, curved, and in broad, heavy scabbards. Their carbines, they said, were mostly captured from our own cavalry, for whom they expressed utter contempt—a feeling unfortunately shared by our own army. Finally, they bragged of having their own horses, and, in many cases, of having no pay from the Government, not needing the paltry remuneration of a private.[82]

As far as receptions in Maryland went, Stuart's Cavalry was faring much better in surrounding communities than the army was in Frederick. On the evening of September 8, at Urbana, the socially-minded Jeb Stuart hosted a dance for the local belles, an affair that probably did more for Confederate public relations than Lee's eloquent proclamation. All families were invited regardless of their sympathies, and the girls flocked in from far and wide.

The halls of the old Academy on the hill were "aired and swept and festooned with roses, and decorated with battle-flags borrowed from the different regiments." Music was provided by the 18th Mississippi regimental band and everyone had a gay time dancing fancy polkas and reels for an hour or so. And then, suddenly, the guns at the outposts blazed away. Within a matter of seconds, the men had made their gentlemenly bows to their pretty partners, strapped on their sabres and cleared the hall. As they rode away, they assured the girls that they would be back before long.

By 1:00 A.M. they were back, fresh with victory, spirits high, and ready to have another go at the dance. The band had stayed and so had some of the girls. Those who had gone home, came flying back and the festivities continued until dawn, when the wounded from the skirmish were brought in. Activities took on a more somber note as the hall was converted to an emergency hospital, and the girls, in their gowns, to nurses. The wounds were slight so the whole affair was declared a success—the only romantic touch to an otherwise unglamorous campaign.[83]

In general, then, Lee's army, though it lacked the appearance of the dashing cavaliers, presented a kaleidoscope of the Southern society from which it came; well mannered, faithful to its cause, and full of the legendary spirit of fighting rebels. Its reception in Maryland was cool; reaction to the proclamation, indifference. The governor made no attempt to see General Lee or his representatives. As far as the army was concerned, the state seemed void of any responsible officials. Though Lee had been apprehensive in his correspondence with Davis, he was disappointed in the results of his primary objective. He had been in Maryland for four days; time enough for a show of support. He was not being pressed by McClellan nor by his own government, but he could ill afford to waste any more time. The army was satisfied that it had been treated fair in Frederick. With this as his only consolation, General Lee sat down to map his next move.

Meanwhile, the people of Richmond waited for news of the invasion. Word began to trickle in on the afternoon of September 8. On the morning of the 9th, newspapers were reporting that latest intelligence (this meant the latest rumor to leak out of the War Department) gave cause to believe that Lee's men were in Maryland. By the 10th they were certain the invasion had started, and for the next few days, while autumn drifted interminably by, newspapers editorially assured the people that what Lee was doing was morally right and fully warranted. "Now is the time to strike the telling and decisive blows of the war . . . our soldiers burn with impatience to retaliate," wrote the *Dispatch*. "The movement which Gen. Lee has now made is bold, but it is sagacious, and justified by the highest military authorities."[84]

Let not a blade of grass, or a stalk of corn, or a barrel of flour, or a bushel of meal, or a stack of salt, or a horse, or a cow, or a hog, or a sheep, be left wherever they move along [wrote the *Dispatch*]. Let vengenance be taken for all that has been done. . . Let retaliation be complete, that the Yankees may learn that two can play at the game they have themselves commenced.[85]

4

"All the Plans of the Rebels"

No general of any American army had ever conceived of such a bold and daring campaign as did Lee in September, 1862. His subordinates were awed at the calmness with which he described in detail his proposals on September 8. Pointing to Harrisburg, Pennsylvania, on his map, Lee explained his plan:

That is the objective point of the campaign. You remember, no doubt, the long bridge of the Pennsylvania railroad over the Susquehanna, a few miles west of Harrisburg. Well, I wish effectually to destroy that bridge, which will disable the Pennsylvania railroad for a long time. After that I can turn my attention to Philadelphia, Baltimore, or Washington, as may seem best for our interests.[1]

Turning to Maj. Gen. John G. Walker, whose eyes betrayed his skepticism, Lee said, "You doubtless regard it hazardous to leave McClellan practically on my line of communication, and to march into the heart of the enemy's country?" Walker nodded and Lee asked him if he was acquainted with General McClellan. "He is an able general, but a very cautious one," he said. "His enemies among his own people think him too much so. His army is in a very demoralized and chaotic condition, and will not be prepared for offensive operations—or he will not think it so—for three or four weeks. Before that time I hope to be on the Susquehanna."[2]

Here was truly a calculated risk—following this campaign Lee would be called the master of the calculated risk. His judgement of McClellan was correct but, unknowingly, his judgement of the Federal army was in error. As will be seen later, Lee's mistake concerning the condition of McClellan's army would be a costly one .

To reach his objective, Lee planned to travel by way of Hagerstown. Here he could re-establish his lines of communication with Richmond, which he had moved to the Shenandoah Valley. His present contact was "from Rapidan Station to Manassas, thence to Frederick." "It is too near the Potomac," Lee said, "and is liable to be cut any day by the enemy's cavalry. I have therefore given orders to move the line back into the Valley of Virginia, by way of Staunton, Harrisonburg, and Winchester, entering Maryland at Shepherdstown."[3]

Speaking to Walker, Lee outlined a proposal:

I wish you to return to the mouth of the Monocacy and effectually destroy the aqueduct of the Chesapeake and Ohio Canal. By the time that is accomplished, you will receive orders to cooperate in the capture of Harper's Ferry, and you will not return here, but, after the capture of Harper's Ferry, will rejoin us at Hagerstown, where the army will be concentrated. My information is that there are between 10,000 and 12,000 men at Harper's Ferry, and 3,000 at Martinsburg. The latter may escape toward Cumberland, but I think the chances are that they will take refuge at Harper's Ferry and be captured.[4]

Harpers Ferry had been a Federal garrison since June 14 of the previous year when Confederate troops under Jackson had abandoned it, burning everything as they left. McClellan, fearful of Lee's strength, wanted those men to join him as quickly as they could. Halleck, by this time nearly frantic with fear, had ordered Col. Dixon S. Miles, commander at Harpers Ferry, to hold the gap at all costs, keeping a watchful eye on Lee at Frederick. McClellan disagreed with Halleck, and sensing that Miles could be caught in a vise, wired Halleck: "Colonel Miles . . . can do nothing where he is, but could be of great service if ordered to join me by the most practicable route."[5] Halleck flatly refused. Not until three days later, after Lee had placed himself between Miles and McClellan, did Halleck offer the troops to McClellan's commmand. Then it was too late.

And so, on the morning of September 9, the stage was set for Lee's dramatic and famous Special Orders No. 191. McClellan was approaching Frederick, the road to Harpers Ferry was open and the Federal garrison was literally Lee's for the taking, and Pennsylvania was offering little or no opposition. Lee called in his adjutant and dictated instructions for the continuation of the campaign.

Simply interpreted, Special Orders No. 191 divided Lee's army into four distinct parts; Jackson, McLaws, and Walker on separate routes to Harpers Ferry, and Longstreet and D. H. Hill to Boonsboro for screening. Stuart's Cavalry was itself split four ways. (See Appendix A.) Few generals would have attempted what Lee had in mind. To split an army in such a manner and further divide it with two rivers and several troublesome mountain formations, could be suicidal. But Lee was counting on McClellan to be himself. The risk would not be excessive if McClellan moved in his accustomed manner, and if the Federal army was still in a state of confusion, Harpers Ferry could be taken and Confederate forces regrouped and into Pennsylvania before discovery. Lee's goal would have been accomplished. He would be on the Susquehanna, Britain and France would recognize the Confederacy, and the war would be over.

Lee's plans did not meet with the approval of his generals. Longstreet had already expressed his opinion a few days earlier when, as he and Lee rode together toward Frederick, the subject of Harpers Ferry was discussed. According to Longstreet, Lee suggested a siege of the Federal garrison and proposed that he, Longstreet, organize the forces. "I thought it a venture not worth the game . . ." wrote Longstreet. Unlike Lee, Longstreet felt that though the Federal army was beaten, it was not disorganized and that with McClellan's ability to whip life into the army, any risky exposure would certainly bring rapid repercussions. The men were in no condition to accomplish such a long march. Any alarming move from McClellan could force them into a regrouping action that might well be impossible.[6]

Lee dropped the subject, and Longstreet forgot about it until the morning of September 9 when he interrupted a conference between Lee and Jackson. They were discussing the Harpers Ferry proposal. Longstreet again voiced objection, commenting that the "entire army" should be used in the campaign rather than dividing it as Lee proposed at the time.[7] Before the order was written, Lee intended to split the army even further by sending Longstreet on to Hagerstown, while leaving D. H. Hill at Boonsboro. The purpose in going to Hagerstown at this time was to prevent stores and supplies from being shipped into Pennsylvania, thereby preventing capture by the Confederates. Lee bowed to Longstreet on this one point—Longstreet would remain at Boonsboro with Hill.[8]

"They had gone so far that it seemed useless for me to offer any further opposition," wrote Longstreet.[9] With this statement, history has concluded that Jackson was in complete accord with Lee on the Harpers Ferry expedition. Longstreet was the only one of the three generals who recorded the conference so that his statements have been accepted as fact. Some historians have theorized that Jackson was delighted with the assignment. This theory is logical for Jackson had proven his agility at such diversive actions and Harpers Ferry he knew well for he had commanded there the year before. The theory would go unchallenged were it not for the fact that the papers of Daniel Harvey Hill have revealed a conversation between Jackson and his brother-in-law which took place following the Fredericksburg Campaign in December, 1862. As the year drew to a close, Jackson talked about the military advances made by the Confederacy and, as if adding an epitaph to the Maryland Campaign, he said, "At the council held at Frederick, I opposed the separation of our forces in order to capture Harper's Ferry. I urged that we should all be kept together."[10] But in Harpers Ferry, Lee saw a definite threat to his plans. He ignored the suggestions of his generals. Whether or not Jackson agreed, it seems obvious that his knowledge of Harpers Ferry, its strength and its weaknesses, influenced Lee in making the decision.

Immediately following the "council," nine copies of Special Orders No. 191 were written—one for Jackson, who would command the Harpers Ferry expedition; one for Major Taylor of Lee's staff, who would arrange for the sick and wounded to be sent to Winchester; one for General Stuart, who would cover the rear of the army's movements; one for Longstreet, who, although assigned no major role until later, was entitled to Lee's confidence; one for Lee's "confidential," or order book; and one for Maj. Gen. Daniel Harvey Hill, who would hold the rear guard at Boonsboro. Each copy was signed by Robert H. Chilton, Lee's Assistant Adjutant-General. The orders were immediately sent out by courier and receipts of delivery returned and filed. (The "nine" copies mentioned above is purely conjecture. It is based on Chilton's statement to D. H. Hill some years later that the order was sent to all commanders affected by the order. It is assumed then that each officer mentioned received a copy. See Appendix A for a complete appraisal of the "lost order" incident.)

Longstreet, conscious of the risk Lee was taking, and aware of the results if the enemy should discover the instructions, committed them to memory, then tore the paper into small pieces and chewed them like a plug of tobacco into insignificant pulp.[11] Walker, too, knew the importance of what Lee was doing. "On receiving my copy of the order I was so impressed with the disastrous consequence which might result from its loss that I pinned it securely in an inside pocket."[12] It can only be assumed that Taylor, Stuart and McLaws took proper precautions with their copies for no reference is made by any one of them. Anderson informed Hill following the war that he did not receive a copy. When Jackson received his copy he carefully put it away in his coat, but before doing this he committed a breach of his own security principles.

When Jackson entered Maryland, D. H. Hill was under his command. Lee intended that the order in question would remove Hill from Jackson, placing him under his own personal command. Jackson did not interpret it in this manner. Not knowing that Lee had designated a copy for Hill, and having read that Hill would play an important role in the strategy, he made a copy in his own handwriting and dispatched it to Hill.[13]

Hill received the copy of Special Orders No. 191 prepared by Jackson that same evening and carefully placed it away for safe keeping. He was unaware that Lee was sending a copy also—a copy that never arrived. At that moment, Lee knew nothing of the lost and duplicated orders, the significance of which would not be apparent for several days. It was time to move on.

On the morning of September 10, the Army of Northern Virginia broke camp and moved northwestward on the old National Road. It was a bright, clear day, and the men seemed to be in a gay mood. Frederick citizens crowded the streets in the early dawn and throughout the morning as the troops filed by. Some were demonstrative and waved, others looked coolly on. Two little girls waving a Union flag, shouted, 'Hurrah for the Stars and Stripes! Down with the Stars and Bars!" This was a source of great amusement for the boys.[14]

Jackson, up at 3:00 A.M., was the first to leave. His faithful Negro servant, Jim, had been up for several hours packing for the trip. Jim once told Kyd Douglas that he could always tell the "condition of the military atmosphere by the General's devotions." He accepted the daily prayers as merely routine, but when Jackson got up in the night to pray, "then I begin to cook rations and pack up for there will be hell to pay in the morning."[15] Jim was busy that night.

While his infantry moved through the main streets, Jackson and his staff rode by the Presbyterian parsonage. He had known the Rev. Dr. John B. Ross in Lexington and wanted to pay his respects. The household was not yet awake—it was 5:15 A.M.—so he left a message and continued on his way, by Mill Street, to the head of his column. "Regret not being permitted to see Dr. and Mrs. Ross," wrote Jackson," but could not expect to have that pleasure at so unseasonable an hour."[16]

To the west of town on the main highway, as it crossed Town Creek Bridge, there lived an elderly woman whose rise to sudden and lasting fame was attributed to Jackson and his men. John Greenleaf Whittier's stirring words of Barbara Fritchie and her encounter with Stonewall Jackson rank high among Civil War poetry and to this day are accepted as fact by many. The truth of the matter is that the poem has no historical credence. Had Jackson not detoured to stop at the home of Dr. Ross, he might well have passed directly by the Fritchie home. General Bradley Johnson, who was a native of Frederick, traced Jackson's route years later for a lecture series, and proved without a doubt that the general joined his troops west of town, well past the Fritchie residence. Henry Kyd Douglas wrote:

We . . . went by the most direct route through Mill Street to the head of the column. As for Barbara Fritchie, we did not pass her house. There was such an old woman in Frederick, in her ninety-sixth year and bedridden. She never saw Stonewall Jackson and he never saw her. I was with him every minute while he was in town, and nothing like the patriotic incident so graphically described by Mr. Whittier in his poem ever occurred. The venerable poet held on to the fiction with such tenacity for years after, that he seemed to resent the truth about it. If he had known that the real sentiments of the old lady had the flavor of disloyalty and that had she waved a flag on that occasion, it would not have been the Stars and Stripes, his fervid desire to make her immortal would have cooled off more quickly and he would not have been so anxious for that poem to live.[17]

Jackson and Longstreet moved on towards Middletown; McLaws headed for Maryland Heights by way of Jefferson and Burkittsville; Walker had left camp the evening before on Lee's verbal instructions to destroy the C & O Canal aqueduct. The pattern of Lee's plan was beginning to take shape.

Jeb Stuart, the "eyes" of Lee's Army, had almost hourly reports on McClellan's advance delivered to Lee. The Army of the Potomac had been moving at the rate of about six miles a day, exactly what Lee had anticipated. At the same time, however, Stuart's counterpart in the Federal army, Brig. Gen. Alfred Pleasonton, was making the same kind of reports to McClellan. The little "feeler" skirmishes in which the two engaged slowly moved towards Frederick until at last McClellan was told that Lee had evacuated. The pursuit was stepped up. Lee began his move on September 10. The Federal Army moved in from the east on September 12, encountering the tail end of Stuart's Cavalry. Frederick heard the first spattering of rifle fire as hoofs clattered rapidly to the west.

While Lee was drafting plans for his next move, McClellan was probing to the west. Washington knew that Lee had crossed the Potomac. Army officials also knew that he had headed toward Frederick. The big puzzle was what would Lee do next. General Halleck was obsessed with fear for the defenses of Washington. Lincoln, too, was worried. Other government officials were near hysteria. If Lee turned toward the capital before McClellan could regroup Pope's forces from Second Manassas, the city would surely fall. Oddly enough, the only man who remained calm and collected was McClellan.

Washington as a wartime capital was as out-of-place as Halleck was as chief of the armies or as McClellan was in the field. The District of Columbia was surrounded on the south by Virginia, on the east and southeast by the only section of Maryland that had openly opposed the Union, and on the north and west by Maryland territory that always had the administration in doubt. The capital was vulnerable, and the situation called for most extensive fortifications. When the eye was not on the land, it was on the Potomac. Officials were constantly in fear of a naval attack. From the executive office windows, on the second floor of the White House, Lincoln could see the Potomac. "Both he [Lincoln] and Stanton," wrote Gideon Welles, "went repeatedly to the window and looked down the Potomac— the view being uninterrupted for miles—to see if the Merrimac was not coming to Washington."[18] The worse was expected. Howitzers were placed in the Treasury building. Each door of the capital building was barricaded with sandbags piled ten feet high. The 6th Massachusetts camped in the Senate chamber and Pennsylvania troops occupied the House of Representatives.[19]

To have moved the center of government would have been loss of face—an admission of open fear, and would be analyzed in the Southern press as an acceptance of defeat. McClellan could not have cared less. The troops needed to protect Washington were much more important to him in the field. "Even if Washington should be taken," he wrote, "this would not, in my judgement, bear comparison with the ruin and disaster which would follow a signal defeat of this army."[20] The fact that the better part of these same "defense" troops remained in Washington after Antietam while Lee escaped back into Virginia has not been overlooked in the final judgement of the fateful month of September, 1862. Be that as it may, Lincoln and Halleck refused to let Washington stand alone, no matter where Lee was or in what direction he was headed. Thus, for the third time since the war began, the Union would be on the defensive.

Northern newspapers tried to soft-peddle the invasion. It was just a raid for food, they reported. "The whole invasion is only for foraging purposes . . ."[21] wrote the Baltimore *American*. But the War Department would not be lulled into apathy. Knowing that Lee had headed for Frederick, McClellan moved his army in that direction on the old National Road on September 5, dividing it into three wings; the right under Maj. Gen. Ambrose E. Burnside with the First and Ninth Corps, the center wing under Brig. Gen. Edwin V. Sumner with the Second and Twelfth Corps, and the left wing under Maj. Gen. William B. Franklin with the Sixth and Maj. Gen. Darius Couch's division of the Fourth Corps (the remainder of which was still on the Peninsula) and Brig. Gen. George Sykes' division of the Fifth Corps.

The remainder of the Fifth Corps (13,000), under Porter, was held in reserve. In addition to this, there were the 70,000 men left behind to protect Washington. In total, McClellan had 158,000 on the march and in reserve, more than three times as many as Lee. (See Appendix C.)

On September 4, the day Lee crossed the river, the Army of the Potomac was still in scattered positions, some yet in Virginia, others in Washington, but by the 7th, a reorganization pattern could be seen. The "movable army" began to take shape. Though at least ten days would pass before full scale battle was launched, the army was logistically shaky, particularly among newly recruited units. McClellan would claim as late as weeks following Sharpsburg that the army was still not fully reorganized, while others in the general's defense would excuse his actions during the campaign because of his reorganization problems. It is true that his time was limited and there is evidence of ill-trained regiments breaking under the pressure of battle, but in the general, over-all picture, this defense is weak. Only a small percentage of the effective strength of the army was inexperienced and those cases of units completely exhausting their ammunition in battle can be blamed, in great part, on poor planning.[22]

Nevertheless, some units had legitimate gripes about the way their commissary was managed. The 16th Maine, in the service only about one month prior to the battle, expressed great "dissatisfaction" at having to leave their tents, knapsacks and overcoats behind at camp when they left Washington. "In our greenness," wrote their regimental historian, "we expected they would follow us in a few days, as a matter of course. The officer's tents followed the regiment, but the men sheltered themselves, as best they could, with fence rails and cornstalks." Though the 16th Maine did not enter the action at Antietam, they were still without shelter of any kind in November.[23]

Lagging supplies presented not the only problem with some regiments. Many went into battle and quickly crumbled under the strain. When it became apparent that the 16th Maine would face the enemy in Maryland, Col. Asa W. Wildes lodged a vigorous protest with General Hooker. Not only did his regiment lack proper equipment, but they were extremely deficient in instructions and training. The protest was disregarded and Wildes resigned stating his unwillingness to command under the circumstances. He was later restored to his position when it was discovered that the regiment was never intended for active duty and that the whole thing was a big mistake.[24] If this was what McClellan meant when he later cried "reorganization" problems, then perhaps there was some justification.

As the days would go by, the army would fan out on several parallel roads, thereby giving it the effect of a broad three-pronged forward movement. The right wing moved on the Brookeville-New Market road: the center took the National highway; the left, under Franklin, followed the route towards Seneca along the river.

The object of these movements [wrote McClellan in his official report] was to feel the enemy—to compel him to develop his intentions—at the same time that the troops were in position readily to cover Baltimore or Washington, to attack him should he hold the line of the Monocacy, or to follow him into Pennsylvania if necessary . . . and if I had marched the entire army in one column along the bank of the river, instead of upon five different parallel roads, the column, with its trains, would have extended about 50 miles, and the enemy might have defeated the advance before the rear could have reached the scene of action. Moreover, such a movement would have uncovered the communications with Baltimore and Washington on our right and exposed our right and rear.[25]

McClellan had received a number of reports that Lee was heading for both Baltimore and Washington. His slow and cautious movements can be credited somewhat to the deliberate rumors Stuart's cavalry was spreading. Lee had instructed Stuart to "divide his cavalry and threaten both Baltimore and Washington on both flanks of McClellan, giving out on each flank that he [Lee] was behind with his whole force."[26]

On the afternoon of September 7, McClellan moved his own headquarters out of Washington for the first time to Rockville, about 12 miles to the northwest. Once established, he spent the evening looking over his reports. The accumulative dispatches showed him that the enemy had started their crossing of the Potomac sometime on September 4 at a point near Leesburg, and that they had arrived in Frederick early that morning, the 7th. With the additional information which had been given him, almost on an hourly basis, McClellan could have drawn the enemy's route on the headquarters map, so positive was his identification of their movements. The fact that the Confederates had deliberately started rumors of proposed attacks on Philadelphia, Baltimore, and Washington seemed to be secondary in his thoughts. Though he had scouts on the lookout on both flanks, he was fairly certain that, as bold as Lee was, he would not try to outflank the Army of the Potomac. The big questions in his mind were the condition and number of the converging forces.

Of the two, he was best informed on the condition of the army. McClellan knew that the Army of Northern Virginia had been marching and fighting since June 25. There are limits to the endurance of all armies. When the first reports arrived, they could only confirm the logic:

"The men [looked] worn out and hungry . . ."[27]

"A man from Leesburg states that the rebel soldiers are running over the country, hunting something to eat, and are a hard-looking set, with a large number of stragglers."[28]

"[The] rebel soldiers [are] badly cared for . . ."[29]

"Many barefoot and clothes much worn out. This information is correct."[30]

After the Confederates arrived in Frederick, this report: "[The soldiers] were shoeless, unclad, taking possession of all stores having shoes, army goods, or other supplies . . ."[31]

The Richmond *Dispatch* poked a finger in the ribs of the Northern press when they wrote that "Yankee correspondents make a lugubrious attempt to be funny over the ragged and barefoot condition of the Confederate soldiery. This is a poor consolation for the whippings they have received from 'ragged and barefooted' men." But "Yankee correspondents" were not trying to be funny.[32] The next day McClellan would read newspaper "glimpses behind the rebel lines," accounts taken from prisoners following Second Manassas. They were most revealing and remarkably accurate, all things considered. Both condition and numbers were given openly. "This is the plain unvarnished truth," the New York *Tribune* stated, "we have been whipped by an inferior force of inferior men, better handled than our own."[33] After his bout with correspondents following the "occupation" of Manassas in the spring, it is doubtful that McClellan paid much attention to such articles. The facts were there, nevertheless. He was about to face that same army and those same generals.

Though McClellan's relationship with the press had been an on-again-off-again proposition—when it was to his advantage he used it effectively; when it criticized him he rebuked it—by South Mountain it had resolved to little more than indifference. He had received his share of criticism and praise from the press. Correspondents knew him from as far back as the western Virginia campaign when McClellan's appointment to Major General had been questioned by the Cincinnati *Daily Gazette*.[34] When he came to Washington, however, he had forgotten this and determined to start his new career off on the right foot. He granted interviews and gave receptions, delivered impressive talks on the important role of the correspondent in the war and, in diplomatic terms, told the boys just how far they should go in reporting what should be classified information, never once denying privileges to any: they were impressed. Then came the long delay and Manassas and finally the last straw. The December 4, 1861, edition of the New York *Times* published a map showing the defense lines of Washington and listed the forces.[35]

Correspondents endured the wrath of Secretary of War Stanton and lately of Gen. Halleck; both of whom had issued edicts banning correspondents from the front. They were particularly careful, therefore, to avoid McClellan's headquarters on the march to Frederick. With luck the general would forgive and forget.

By the time McClellan had set up his headquarters, a dozen or more estimates of Confederate strength were before him, all confirming the *Tribune* headline, "The strength of the rebel army exaggerated."[36] Not one report exceeded 60,000. Most of these figures came from eyewitnesses—"respectable Union citizens," "a spy in whom I have confidence," "a rebel deserter," and railroad laborers whose observations were wired direct to President Garrett of the B & O and later to army headquarters. There were no Pinkerton figures available at this moment and it would not be until the next day that the "scare" figures of 100,000 and more would appear. So, with a true picture of the enemy's physical condition and numerical statistics of 30,000 to 60,000, it can be established that on McClellan's first day in Maryland, he knew as much about Lee's army as there was to know. He could pinpoint their route and location and could estimate their strength within a few thousand. His greatest fear was what the Confederates intended to do, and it was this fear that dictated his course of action for the next several days, a slow and deliberately cautious movement of about six miles a day in the direction of Frederick.

At 7:30 P.M. on September 9, McClellan, still in Rockville, sent the following wire to Halleck: "From such information as can be obtained, Jackson and Longstreet have about 110,000 men of all arms near Frederick . . ."[37] From this point on, no official report put the Confederates at less than 100,000. Obviously the Pinkerton boys were back on the job and McClellan accepted their estimates with the same relish he did on the Peninsula. Twenty years later, Allan Pinkerton wrote a book covering his war experiences with McClellan. In his chapter on the Maryland Campaign, he gives Lee credit for having 40,000 men at Antietam.[38] Though the detective altered his figures over the years, McClellan did not, as will be seen. Without delay he began his series of telegrams to Washington requesting additional troops. General Jacob Cox, whose postwar writings were most outspoken and openly critical of McClellan, wrote: "The fiction as to the strength of Lee's forces is the most remarkable in the history of modern wars. Whether McClellan was the victim or an accomplice of the inventions of his 'secret service,' we cannot tell. It is almost incredible that he should be deceived, except willingly."[39] Though Maj. Gen. Dan Butterfield, in testimony to the Committee on the Conduct of the War, spoke of the army of 1863, his comments essentially covered the Army of the Potomac throughout 1862. "We were almost as ignorant of the enemy in our immediate front as if they had been in China."[40] McClellan had written, as far back as the western Virginia campaign, that the "information obtained [there] . . . is exceedingly vague and unreliable. I hope to inaugurate a better system."[41] His better system was Allan Pinkerton. It should be pointed out, however, that Pinkerton was not the only source of exaggerated figures. Not all newspaper reports were as accurate as that of the Tribune. On September 9, the New York Herald estimated Lee's forces at no less than "150,000 strong."[42]

In McClellan's official report, dated August 4, 1863, the second of two he did for the War Department, he offers a set of figures tabulating all Confederate forces under Lee. These were drawn up for him by Col. John S. Clark, an aide to Maj. Gen. Nathaniel P. Banks who commanded the defenses of Washington, from "information obtained by the examination of some 250 prisoners" taken "previous to the battle of Antietam." For no apparent reason, McClellan gives the impression that the following information was in his hands before he met the enemy:

General T. J. Jackson's corps	24,778
General James Longstreet's corps	23,342
General D. H. Hill's two divisions	15,525
General J. E. B. Stuart cavalry	6,400
General Ransom's and Jenkins' brigade	3,000
Forty-six regiments not included in above	18,400
Artillery, estimated at 400 guns	6,000
Total	97,445[43]

In Washington, Banks evidently conducted an extensive interrogation of prisoners taken at Second Manassas. This was standard procedure and an intelligence practice used today. "It consists in examining each prisoner apart," wrote Banks to McClellan, "and comparing the statements of each with that of others. The result, if the prisoners are numerous, must be very nearly approximate to the truth." The old law of averages was working for Banks, or so he thought. The fallacy behind this assumption is that the common soldier may know his regiment's disposition on the field, the fighting condition of his comrades, and maybe even the number of artillery or officers his unit might have, but seldom does he have the faintest idea of the strength of his unit. Johnny Reb, in particular, was prone to exaggerate or boast a little of his army. This seems obvious from the average Banks's investigation netted. Some of these men were also deserters, an extremely unreliable source of information. Yet Banks told McClellan that the "method adopted . . . will be found, upon full consideration, to be a very reliable one. I am persuaded that a careful and thorough examination of prisoners, East and West, in this manner, would give a reasonably accurate view of the rebellion."[44]

Despite Banks's miscalculations, which served only to confirm McClellan's suspicions that Lee had nearly 100,000, the report was not submitted to McClellan until October 20. The fact that his report of a year later contained this, indicates quite clearly his readiness to accept, and to retain through the years, Lee's overwhelming odds.

On September 11, McClellan sent a rather amazing message to General Halleck. It was almost an apology for what might happen during the "coming battle," and clearly illustrated McClellan's uncertainty. He began by explaining why he had left a "sufficient force" to defend the city, how he had figured that the Confederate move could have been a feint to draw troops away from Washington, and of how he now knew that this condition no longer existed:

All the evidence that has been accumulated from various sources since we left Washington goes to prove most conclusively that almost the entire rebel army in Virginia, amounting to not less than 120,000 men, is in the vicinity of Frederick City. These troops, for the most part, consist of their oldest regiments, and are commanded by their best generals. Everything seems to indicate that they intend to hazard all upon the issue of the coming battle. They are probably aware that their forces are numerically superior to ours by at least 25 percent. This, with the prestige of their recent successes, will, without doubt, inspire them with a confidence which will cause them to fight well. The momentous consequences involved in the struggle of the next few days impels me, at the risk of being considered slow and over cautious, to most earnestly recommend that every available man be at once added to this army.[45]

Though McClellan had, only a few days earlier, an exact picture of the Confederate army, he was now ready to admit that it was a better army in all respects than the Army of the Potomac.

He "believed" that his army would fight well, but "the result of a general battle with such odds as the enemy now appears to have against us, might, to say the least, be doubtful; and if we should be defeated, the consequences to the country would be disastrous in the extreme." It is one thing to be realistic, but it is another to accept defeat so easily. It is almost unbelievable that the commanding officer of such a fine army could have so little confidence in its abilities. In the same paragraph, he asked for three corps from Washington and all 12,000 men from Harpers Ferry, an additional 25,000.[46] During the Peninsula Campaign, Stanton had remarked of McClellan: "If he had a million men, he would swear the enemy had two millions, and then he would sit down in the mud and yell for three."[47]

McClellan concluded his message to Halleck with an urgent appeal that must have brought the general-in-chief to sudden panic:

From the moment the rebels commenced the policy of concentrating their forces, and with their large masses of troops operating against our scattered forces, they have been successful. They are undoubtedly pursuing the same now, and are prepared to take advantage of any division of our troops in future. I, therefore, most respectfully, but strenuously, urge upon you the absolute necessity, at this critical juncture, of uniting all our disposable forces. Every other consideration should yield to this, and if we defeat the army now arrayed before us, the rebellion is crushed, for I do not believe they can organize another army. But if we should be so unfortunate as to meet with defeat, our country is at their mercy.[48]

A few days earlier McClellan had assured the President that he could save Washington. Now, before he had hardly sighted the enemy, he was admitting possible defeat. It was becoming increasingly apparent to Washington that this McClellan was the same McClellan that commanded the army on the Peninsula. He had not changed. The Maryland Campaign would be fought with the same hesitation, the same lack of drive and spirit which had, only weeks previous, brought Lincoln to desperation.

Dispatches during the next two days once more brought McClellan vital information on Confederate plans. Once the exaggerations were sifted out, a clear picture of Lee's intentions was presented. At 8:00 P.M. on September 11, McClellan received the following message from Governor Curtin of Pennsylvania: "We have advices that the enemy broke up whole encampment at Frederick yesterday morning, 3 o'clock, and marched in direction of Hagerstown . . . Man who gives information said rebel army marching 5 A.M. to 9 P.M. yesterday out of their camps at Frederick."[49] The governor again wired the next afternoon: "I have advices that Jackson is crossing the Potomac at Williamsport . . ."[50] (McClellan had once made the statement that he did not like Jackson's movements. "He will suddenly appear when least expected."[51])

This rather remarkable piece of information was forwarded by the governor late on the evening of September 12:

A reliable gentleman came from Hanover to give me the following information: "I left the rebel encampment at Liberty, Md., last night at 12 o'clock. I spent twenty-four hours among their men and officers, from whom I learned the following general programme, after satisfying them that

I was a citizen of Maryland and favorable to their cause: They intend to cross about 70,000 men, forming their reserve at Williamsport, and occupy the Virginia Shore as a general depot for all supplies they can gather. Part of this reserve to attack and capture Martinsburg and Harper's Ferry. The main rebel army to occupy Maryland between Williamsport and Hagerstown, from which they will move on Cumberland Valley and other points in Pennsylvania. Their force in Maryland was about 190,000 men. That they have in Virginia about 250,000 men, all of whom are being concentrated to menace Washington and keep the Union armies employed there, while their forces in Maryland devastate and destroy Pennsylvania."

The gentleman who gives me this information is vouched for as reliable and truthful by the best citizens of the place where he lives. I give it to you for consideration.[52]

By the time McClellan himself arrived in Frederick, then, he knew, or should have known, providing his intelligence officers were carefully analyzing these bits of information, the basic outline of the Confederate plans of operation. Although many of the reports blew Confederate strength way out of proportion, some were fairly accurate. Had an average been taken of all "eyewitnesses," a much more realistic figure would have developed. McClellan knew the exact departure time from Frederick, the route which the main body of the army took, and the length of time it took to pass a given point. He further knew that Jackson had recrossed the Potomac, and that Harpers Ferry, as well as certain points in Pennsylvania, were marked for occupation.

Had the Pinkerton Agency or a military intelligence department been fully efficient, the event which happened on the 13th would have been secondary and served only as a means of confirmation. D. H. Hill said that "McClellan would have been the most inefficient of generals, could he not have gained that information in a friendly country from his own scouts and spies."[53] Instead, to McClellan, the discovery of Lee's lost dispatch became an event of prime military importance. His reaction, and its effect on the campaign, would forever remain the mystery of Antietam.

With the exception of cavalry skirmishes, the Federal move to Frederick was uneventful. The fall climate was good; the marching was slow and easy; the army grew in strength and confidence. Varying degrees of hospitality were experienced along the route. Some communities were openly hostile, while others greeted the army with red-carpet treatment. Ridgeville, Maryland, leaned somewhat to the Confederates. The small population had opened its doors en masse to the boys in gray, feasting them "with the fatted calf." But when the 16th Maine arrived a few days later, doors were locked and gardens were "guarded with fidelity." Though a few loyalists visited the Federal camp with baskets of food, the new recruits could not get a canteen of fresh water for less than six cents.[54] Such problems seldom dismayed the resourceful, however. At Rockville, Thomas Livermore of the 18th New Hampshire was told by his colonel, "Mr. Livermore, don't you on any account let two of your men go out and get one of those sheep for supper." Within moments, "two stout and willing privates" had bagged two sheep while the owner was chasing off another regiment. A bushel of potatoes neatly confiscated on another diversionary action made a "most delicious stew" for dinner that evening.[55]

Some menus were not quite as appetizing. Those regiments whose commissary wagons lagged far behind fared less well at meal time. Green apples and an occasional cider or whisky keg was all that kept the men going, and that only for a day or so at a time. Cooked wheat was not uncommon. "Nature abhors a vacuum," wrote a member of the 124th Pennsylvania, "especially when it is under the cartridge belt."[56]

"Fine marching weather; a land flowing with milk and honey; a general tone of Union sentiment among the people, who, being little cursed by slavery, had not lost their loyalty; scenery, not grand but picturesque, all contributed to make the march delightful." This is how Maryland appeared to an officer in the Army of the Potomac; "like the Israelites of old, we looked upon the land and it was good."[57] "Of all the memories of the war, none are more pleasant than those of our sojourn in the goodly city of Frederick," wrote another. "Hundreds of Union banners floated from the roofs and windows, and in many a threshold stood the ladies and children of the family, offering food and water to the passing troops, or with tiny flags waving a welcome to their deliverers."[58]

McClellan wrote his wife:

I can't describe to you for want of time the enthusiastic reception we met with . . . at Frederick. I was nearly overwhelmed and pulled to pieces. I enclose with this a little flag that some enthusiastic lady thrust into or upon Dan's bridle. [McClellan's horse was named "Dan Webster."] As to flowers they came in crowds! In truth, I was seldom more affected than by the scenes I saw . . . and the reception I met with . . .[59]

The trip to Frederick was not without its problems. The Army of the Potomac was plagued with stragglers and marauders, so much so that McClellan was forced to issue an order, similar in some respects to that issued by Lee before the Confederate army crossed the river. It read, in part:

Each division should have a strong rear guard, behind which no straggler . . . should be permitted to remain. . . The bayonet must be used to insure obedience to these orders. Marauders will be at once brought to trial . . . the sentence of death will be executed, if awarded by the court, with promptness and as publicly as possible.[60]

Open defiance of orders was not uncommon. The Civil War would be several years old before any real close relationship between officers and men was established in the Federal army, and even then, in many cases, only in battle. Though insubordination was exemplified mostly in the language of the ranks, direct disobedience was frequent. Sgt. William Potts of the 124th Pennsylvania saw his chance to "fall out" on the way to Antietam, and did so taking fully half of the regiment with him. "When we arrived at camp we had more men than the Colonel went into camp with the night before," he wrote.[61] In retaliation, General Crawford, brigade commander, force-marched the men "so fast that our wagon train could not keep up with us, and the men went into camp very hungry." The boys figured that this was part of McClellan's strategy—to keep them tired and hungry for the fight, too tired and hungry to run away. But such speculation did not alter their attitude toward Crawford. Some of the boys threatened to "square with him" if the opportunity ever presented itself. "I told them that was very wrong," wrote Potts, "but if I was aiming at a

Reb and the General got in the way, I would not stop firing on his account."[62]

If straggling and insubordination were not problems enough, camp followers threatened to disrupt army life completely. Prostitutes followed the army from Washington in droves. They had done it before and they would do it again, but this campaign in particular was one in which the girls felt an interest. Their life blood was being taken away. With 450 houses of ill-repute, and at least 7,500 prostitutes reported in Washington in the fall of 1862, and 70,000 men leaving the city, there was little choice but to take to the road. Tents of iniquity were established in Frederick and did a thriving business. Some soldier's letters indicate that even the battle at South Mountain failed to slow things down. There is evidence that enterprising harlots made their way as close to Antietam as Boonsboro. Frederick was known as "a great place for liquor," "a grog-shop every few doors on various streets, where sentries seem almost useless."[63]

As the various Federal regiments arrived in Frederick, they pitched their tents in the same fields as the Confederates, used the same water supplies, and, in many cases, made friends with the same farmers. At about noon on September 13, the 27th Indiana arrived. The arms were stacked, regimental flags furled, and the brisk business of establishing normal camp operations were set into motion. Those without specific duties wandered off to rest from the morning's pace.

Private Barton W. Mitchell and Sergeant John M. Bloss tossed their gear aside and lay down on the cool grass. They lapsed into the idle talk of soldiers, discussing McClellan's return as their leader, or perhaps a recent letter from home. Mitchell had just rolled over and was about to pull his cap over his eyes, when he spotted a piece of paper wrapped around what appeared to be several sticks. Upon investigation, he found it to be three cigars of some expense. This type of luxury was not easy to come by for the common soldier. While they leaned back like men of leisure and prepared to light up, they opened the paper and made a quick survey. Suddenly the cigars became insignificant. The paper they held in their hands was of obvious vital military importance. Bloss read the names of Jackson, Longstreet, and Lee, names which he knew well. At once the two men rushed to their commander, Col. Silas Colgrove. Colgrove immediately saw that he held in his hands the key to the Confederate plans. It read: "Head-quarters, Army of Northern Virginia, Special Orders No. 191" and it was addressed to D. H. Hill. The paper was signed: "By command of General R. E. Lee: R. H. Chilton, Assistant Adjutant-General."[64] (See Appendix A.)

In a matter of minutes Colgrove had placed it in the hands of Col. S. E. Pittman, division adjutant (1st Division, Twelfth Corps) and a good friend of Chilton's, who quickly identified the handwriting.[65] Pittman hastened to General McClellan's tent and requested an immediate audience. McClellan was in conference at the time, but summoned Pittman in and took a look at the paper. The general's cautious nature put him on the defensive right away. Was it an elaborate hoax? Pittman doubted it since he was quite familiar with Chilton's signature. There could be no doubt in his mind about its authenticity. McClellan was overjoyed. The game was over. He now knew Lee's secret. A quick move would crush the Army of Northern Virginia. A few moments later, while talking to his close friend, Gen. John Gibbon, McClellan exclaimed, "Here is a paper with which, if I cannot whip Bobbie Lee, I will be willing to go home. I will not show you the document now," he told Gibbon, "but here is the signature, and it gives the movement of every division of Lee's army." As if all his plans were made in those few moments; as if he was ready right then to bag the entire Confederate army, McClellan told Gibbon that *tomorrow* "we will pitch into his center, and if you people will only do two good, hard days' marching I will put Lee in a position he will find it hard to get out of."[66]

A wire was sent to the President displaying McClellan's regained confidence. "I have all the plans of the rebels," he wrote Lincoln, "and will catch them in their own trap . . ." But he added his usual cautious note; ". . . if my men are equal to the emergency."[67]

In a more detailed telegram to General Halleck, McClellan said, "An order from General R. E. Lee, addressed to D. H. Hill, which has accidentally come into my hands this evening—the authenticity of which is unquestionable—discloses some of the plans of the enemy . . ."[68]

On September 8, from his camp near Rockville, McClellan had told Halleck, "As soon as I find out where to strike, I will be after them without an hour's delay."[69] There was no doubt now that he knew *where* to strike. The plans spelled it out specifically. Years later McClellan wrote: "I was satisfied in regard to the genuineness of the order and made no further inquiries."[70] But there was one thing Lee's orders did not state—the strength of the Confederate army. No matter how delighted McClellan was to see the dispatch, it only nurtured the seeds of doubt that had been sown through the weeks before. In the message to Halleck on the 13th, McClellan had concluded: "I feel confident that there is now no rebel force immediately threatening Washington or Baltimore, but that I have the mass of their troops to contend with, and they outnumber me when united."[71] It was obvious that he had no intentions of attacking Lee's united army, but he failed to tell Halleck why he would not force the Confederate hand now that he knew the army was divided.

Despite his eagerness to move rapidly and overtake Lee's separated army, McClellan could not. Longstreet and Hill were directly in front at Boonsboro with an undetermined number of troops. In between was South Mountain, a natural barrier which Lee would use to delay McClellan until Jackson, who had gone to Harpers Ferry, could rejoin the army. McClellan's one chance was to force the mountain passes; Turner's Gap on the old National Road leading to Boonsboro, and Crampton's Gap, six miles to the south. This could conceivably accomplish three things—crush Lee's rear guard just west of the mountain, capture McLaws' Division, the Maryland phase of the Harpers Ferry operation, and release the 12,000 Federal troops bottled up at the garrison.

By 6:00 P.M. on the evening of September 13, the day he received Lee's orders, McClellan had made up his mind. There was no need to wait for replies from Lincoln and Halleck. There would be none coming. Apparently neither of McClellan's superiors were sufficiently impressed with the discovery; or were they, too, skeptical of Confederate trickery?

5

Harpers Ferry

Special Orders No. 191 had been written on September 9. It was now the 13th. Three days had passed since the Army of Northern Virginia had left Frederick and Lee was having troubles. He had anticipated that Jackson would have Harpers Ferry in his hands by the 12th ("Friday night," as the orders stated). Unfortunately, it was not until the morning of the 13th that Maryland, Loudoun, and Bolivar Heights were first sighted by the Confederates. It would be another full day before positions could be taken for the assault. As it was, McClellan had a three day advantage over Lee. Now he would have two more.

Exactly where was Lee's army now? Jackson had led the withdrawal from Frederick with three divisions of about 11,500 men under his direct personal command—A. P. Hill's, Ewell's Division under Brig. Gen. A. P. Lawton, and Jackson's own division under Brig. Gen. John R. Jones. His assignment called for him to occupy Bolivar Heights, overlooking both the Shenandoah and Potomac Rivers, the only direct land approach to the town of Harpers Ferry. He was to march by way of Boonsboro, cross the Potomac at "the most convenient point" near Sharpsburg and either capture the Federal outpost at Martinsburg or drive the troops into the trap at Harpers Ferry.

Brig. Gen. Lafayette McLaws, with his own division of four brigades and that of R. H. Anderson with six brigades, or a total of some 8,000 men, would follow Longstreet to Middletown, move southwest across South Mountain into Pleasant Valley and then on to Maryland Heights where he would cover the Federal garrison from the north. Walker, with his own division, would travel south from

Frederick, cross the river at Cheek's Ford, and take position on Loudoun Heights, the Virginia or south side of Harpers Ferry. Upon completion of their mission, the three wings were to rejoin Hill and Longstreet at Boonsboro and continue on to Lee's objective, Pennsylvania. Lee fully expected the army to move as one body by September 14 at the latest. (See Appendix A.)

Jackson was noted for his secrecy. He never divulged his plans until the last possible moment. More than once his men and even staff officers marched completely blind. To thoroughly confuse the enemy, he would often deliberately camp at a crossroads. Federal informers and spies never knew until he climbed into the saddle into which of the four directions he would actually move his army. The army was literally on a crossroads the morning of September 10 when Jackson left Frederick. As the general rode through the city that morning, he pulled one of his master strokes of genius. He stopped by a group of curious citizens who had gathered to see the army depart, and asked for a map of Chambersburg, Pennsylvania, and directions to various other northern and western points.[1] It was his way of assuring the enemy's confusion. It was not until they neared Middletown, across the Catoctin mountain range from Frederick, that Jackson reversed his character and called Kyd Douglas to his side and revealed his plans. He had good reason in doing so for Douglas had been raised only a few miles from Sharpsburg. He would know the roads and river, knowledge no map could offer. From that moment on, Douglas rode close to his beloved commander.[2]

At Middletown, Jackson met with opposition. More amused than angered, he was confronted by two young girls with red, white, and blue hair-ribbons and small Union flags which they waved "defiantly" in the general's face. Jackson lifted his cap and bowed courteously, and then with a smile, quietly remarked to an aide, "We evidently have no friends in this town."[3]

By nightfall on the 10th, they had crossed South Mountain through Turner's Gap and had camped on the western slopes leading to Boonsboro, about 14 miles from Frederick. Jackson's headquarters tent was staked in a field opposite the John Murdock house. A squad of the Black Horse Cavalry, Jackson's escort, had preceded him and rode on towards Hagerstown on a scouting mission. Col. S. B. French, one of Jackson's aides, rode alone following them. Douglas also wanted to go on ahead, at least as far as Boonsboro, where he had friends. He was certain to pick up some helpful information. Much against Jackson's wishes, Douglas, along with a courier, rode at a leisurely gait into town. Just as they reached the United States Hotel in the center of Boonsboro, they were met by shots from a company of Federal cavalry coming in the opposite direction. The two men wheeled around and raced for their own camp, the Federals in hot pursuit. Douglas fired a few random shots from his "trusty revolvers" and in answer had his new hat shot from his head. "I wanted to stop and get it," he wrote, "but thought better of it."[4]

As they started up the mountain, they saw Jackson taking one of his frequent solitary strolls along the roadside, leading his horse with one hand and swinging his hat in the other. When Jackson realized what was happening, he quickly mounted and rode to the rear. The Federals began to slow their pace. Douglas, who was fast learning Jackson's quick thinking habits, whirled about and with a cry to nonexistent reinforcements, charged back down the mountain. Not being able to see what size force might be following, the Federal cavalry fled into the night.

The squad of Confederate cavalry, which had gone on to Hagerstown, turned when they heard the shots and, racing down the pike, met the Federals head on. One bluecoat was killed and several were captured. From the prisoners it was learned that they were based at Kearneysville, near Shepherdstown, a force Jackson might have to reckon with on his way to Harpers Ferry.[5]

Riding back into town, Douglas discovered that Colonel French had stopped at the hotel and was having dinner when the action started. A colored servant had taken him to a coal cellar for hiding. His face and uniform were hardly in shape for inspection, but he was safe and somewhat chagrined over the whole thing. His "colored brother" earned himself a ten dollar Confederate bill for the deed.[6]

Douglas recovered his hat and, much to his surprise, Jackson's gloves, which the general had dropped in flight. "When I reached Headquarters," wrote Douglas, "the General, with an I-told-you-so air, congratulated me on my escape and my fast horse; but when I, in response, produced the gloves he had [lost], he saw the 'retort courteous' and with a smile retired to his tent."[7]

The march was resumed the next morning, and by early afternoon

Jackson had crossed the Potomac at Williamsport to the tune of "Carry Me Back to Ole Virginny" from the regimental bands. Jackson had taken the long route rather than the "most convenient," but he may well have considered the back way the most likely to support the element of surprise on the garrison at Martinsburg. At any rate, by that evening, the 11th, the three Confederate divisions were camped within four miles of Martinsburg. Brig. Gen. Julius White, who was commanding some 2500 Federal troops there, made no hesitation about pulling out in the face of the Confederates. He had left the night before for the haven of Harpers Ferry, a move Jackson fully expected.

Early the next morning, Jackson entered Martinsburg and for the next several hours was rendered helpless by the friendly, almost hysterical, reception given him by the townspeople. It was afternoon before he found escape. That evening his men camped on the banks of the Opequon Creek. And that evening A. P. Hill was restored to command.

Hill had been under arrest for more than a week, marching to the rear of his division, while Brig. Gen. L. O'B. Branch commanded. He could sense battle coming and wanted desperately to be on the front line with his men. To say the least, for an officer of the fiery nature of Hill it must have been humiliating to be on display to his men in such a position. He walked with his own rear guard, "an old white hat slouched down over his eyes, his coat off and wearing an old flannel shirt, looking as mad as a bull."[8] Sending for Kyd Douglas, Hill requested that Jackson be informed of his desires, that "he did not wish any one else to command his division in an engagement, [and] that he asked to be restored to it until the battle or battles were over . . ." Douglas gladly delivered the message for he liked Hill, and he undoubtedly embellished the request with a few supporting comments of his own for Jackson immediately consented. The next morning Hill was at the head of the column, "looking like a young eagle in search of his prey," much to the satisfaction and delight of his men.[9]

Late on the morning of the 13th, Jackson deployed his troops at Halltown, within sight of Bolivar Heights, and "immediately shut up his side of the pen," as Douglas put it.[10] Already Jackson was behind schedule. He had been on the road for three days covering what amounted to roughly 57 miles. His men had encountered no enemy until they reached Halltown, and the fording of the river had presented no problems. Jackson had been known to march his men much faster than this, but now he was leading bone-weary soldiers, many still without shoes, and armies tend to reach a limit on the strain they can bear. No matter how much they were pushed, they could go only so fast. The delay was costly, and it substantiated Longstreet's warnings that the Army of Northern Virginia was in no condition to undertake such a complex operation.

McLaws, whose assignment was to occupy Maryland Heights, left Frederick about the same time as Jackson on the morning of September 10. His march was to be about twenty miles by way of Middletown and Burkittsville, but it took him three days to get into position to take the heights, thus placing his two divisions also behind schedule. This particular phase of the operation was by far the most important and the most difficult, and only a proper understanding of the geography makes it clear.

Harpers Ferry nestles at the convergence of the Potomac and Shenandoah Rivers, the Shenandoah flowing from the southwest, the Potomac from the northwest and on to the east. With the exception of the three water passages, the small community is surrounded by large mountainous bluffs; on its own land mass to the west by Bolivar Heights, Jackson's position; to the southeast by Loudoun Heights, Walker's position; and by McLaws' position, Maryland Heights, to the northeast, the southern extremity of Elk Ridge, a short mountain running south from Keedysville. With all three heights in Confederate hands, the Federal garrison would be vulnerable to attack and ultimate surrender. There could be no way out. It was, in the words of men who served there, "a complete slaughter pen," "a pot hole or death trap," "no more defensible than a well bottom."[11] Both Jackson and A. P. Hill freely admitted "that they had rather take it forty times than to undertake to defend it once."[12]

Col. Dixon S. Miles, the Federal commmander, had stationed some 7,000 men across Bolivar Heights in a line stretching from river to river. Walker would have no trouble at Loudoun Heights for it was void of any defenders, but there were 2,000 men on Maryland Heights. The Maryland bluff was much higher than Bolivar by some 700 feet, and Loudoun by about 100 feet.[13] From this point properly placed guns with distance capacity could command both the town and Bolivar. "So long as Maryland Heights was occupied by the enemy," wrote McLaws, "Harper's Ferry could never be occupied by us. If we gained possession of the heights, the town was no longer tenable to them."[14] McLaws, therefore, held the key to the operation. He also held the most critical position. Not only did he face the enemy in the front, but he was constantly in danger from the enemy in his rear, the only one of the three wings so jeopardized. Throughout his dispatches, Lee clearly indicated much more concern for the safety of McLaws than either of the other two segments of his army surrounding Harpers Ferry.

McLaws crossed the South Mountain range at Brownsville Gap and moved into Pleasant Valley between South Mountain and Elk Ridge. At this point the two Confederate divisions were four miles from the Potomac. They were also in a position to see the back of their objective. It is formidable and somewhat awe-inspiring even today. The thought of dragging artillery up the sheer face of the mountain must have staggered McLaws. But soon he had the information he needed and began making the necessary dispositions. It was now September 12 and time was pressing.

To McLaws' right was a "slight depression" in Elk Ridge, a pass known as Solomon's Gap. From this point south to the heights ran a narrow road, rugged in some spots, nearly impassable in others, but nevertheless a road giving access to the Federal fortifications. Generals Kershaw's and Barksdale's brigades were directed "to proceed along that road and carry the heights, using infantry alone, as the character of the country forbade the use of any other arm."[15] Wright's Brigade of Anderson's Division was sent back up the mountain and along the ridge to the southernmost point where it could command the B & O Railroad, the canal, and the road running to the east along the river. Semmes's and Mahone's Brigades were left on the valley road opposite Brownsville Gap to guard the South Mountain passes against the enemy. Cobb's Brigade was sent across the valley to the foot of Elk Ridge where he would follow Kershaw's movements and render any assistance if needed. McLaws' men were spread thin but he had a job to do. With the rest of the two divisions, he moved on south through the valley, keeping pace and in constant signal commmunications with Kershaw.

On top of Elk Ridge, the going was not easy. Almost immediately upon ascent, Kershaw ran into Federal pickets, a good five miles from the heights. Splitting into two columns, skirmishers scattered to the left and right of the road and in the first encounter threw back "three companies of cavalry." The terrain did not lend itself to any spirited action other than infantry. At the most, the road was little more than a trail cut through the trees, just wide enough for single lane buggy traffic. So hazardous were the precipitous sides that movement was slow and tedious. At 6:00 P.M., after marching less than four miles, Kershaw and Barksdale were stopped by an "abatis" or log fortification constructed across the ridge from rock to rock, forbidding any passage. "A sharp skirmish ensued," wrote Kershaw, "which satisfied me that the enemy occupied the position in force."[16] Deploying his men in two defensive lines, he settled down for the night.

By sunup the next morning, the Confederates were pushing the attack on past the abatis, which was abandoned under heavy fire, and on to another and much stronger fortification of earthworks and logs some 400 yards ahead. The night before, Barksdale had been directed to move to the left down the east side of the mountain and approach the enemy from the flank and the rear. It was no easy job and was only accomplished after severe strain and great labor, but as the morning attack continued, Barksdale made his way to an advantageous point "in the rear of the enemy." Kershaw was encountering heavy losses against "a most obstinate resistance" when Barksdale asked him to hold his fire. If the enemy was to be flanked, Confederates would be firing at Confederates.

I sent to direct our fire to cease [wrote Kershaw], hoping that we might capture the whole force if General Barksdale could get up. Before this order was extended, the right company of Colonel Fisher's regiment, Barksdale Brigade, fired into a body of the enemy's sharpshooters lodged in the rocks above them, and their whole line broke into a perfect rout, escaping down the mountain sides to their rear. This took place at 10:30 o'clock A.M.[17]

Although it has never been positively identified because of variations in Federal and Confederate reports, this break was in all probability caused by the 126th New York, a "perfectly new" regiment that had arrived in Harpers Ferry only the night before and had not as yet had a rifle in their hands.[18]

There was little left to do but clean out the few remaining pickets and lay claim to the stores which the Federals had left behind. Three heavy guns were spiked and were of no use to Kershaw, but food, ammunition, and tents, what could be carried, was unexpected bounty and loaded on the men's shoulders.[19] By 4:30 that afternoon, the last retreating Federal had crossed the pontoon bridge over the Potomac and entered Harpers Ferry.[20] Maryland Heights was in Confederate hands. The key to the Federal garrison was lost. General White declared later, in an investigation of the surrender, that he firmly believed the evacuation of Maryland Heights was the surrender of Harpers Ferry. That evening Brig. Gen. Howell Cobb's Brigade was moved up the valley to the river road sealing it off as any possible escape route. Harpers Ferry was now commanded from the east and the north.

The next day was Sunday, September 14. McLaws was a full day behind schedule. He had not as yet heard anything from Walker and Jackson. The morning was spent in cutting a road from the base of the mountain to the fortifications for the transport of artillery. This was not a case where the enemy guns could be turned on them. Confederate ingenuity was given a severe test, for it was not an easy operation. Racing against time, McLaws' men performed a herculean feat. In seven hours—by 2:00 P.M.—the road was finished and four rifled Parrott guns were in position and firing. The use of animals was impossible (neither the road-space or terrain permitted it), so as many as 200 men were employed to carry each piece by hand.[21] In the process several carriages were damaged, one beyond repair.[22]

While his guns were shelling the town, McLaws' attention was called to the rear. Off in the distance he could hear the muffled roar of cannon at Crampton's Gap:

But I felt no particular concern about it [wrote McLaws], as there were three brigades of infantry in the vicinity, besides the cavalry of Colonel Munford, and General Stuart, who was with me on the heights and had just come in from above, told me he did not believe there was more than a brigade of the enemy. I, however, sent my adjutant-general to General Cobb . . . with directions to hold the gap if he lost his last man in doing it, and shortly afterward went down the mountain and started toward the gap.[23]

While McLaws forced his way along the crest of Elk Ridge and through the valley toward Maryland Heights, Walker, too, was having his problems, not with the enemy, but with nature. His first assignment was to destroy the aqueduct of the C & O Canal at the mouth of the Monocacy River. This direction was issued by Lee on September 9, the day before the army broke camp at Frederick, putting Walker on the road when Special Orders No. 191 was issued. By 11 P.M. that night, his division of some 3,400 men was at the aqueduct where he was met by the courier with further instructions to proceed to Loudoun Heights and cooperate with Jackson and Mc-Laws. After several hours of fruitless labor on the masonry at the aqueduct, it was decided to move on. Not a crack could be found in the "solid mass of granite in which to apply a crow-bar and dull drills made blasting with powder impossible."[24] The work we had undertaken was one of days instead of hours, wrote Walker. Any delay would have placed the division alone in the face of the enemy "while it would be engaged in destroying the aqueduct, in a most exposed and dangerous position." Tools were packed and movement resumed during the early morning hours with Federal infantry coming up quickly on Walker's heels to occupy the canal.[25]

Late on the night of the 10th, Walker's division reached Point-of-Rocks, their fording point on the Potomac. They ditched plans to cross at Cheek's Ford because of "superior" enemy forces there. But even here the prospects did not look good. The canal bridge had been destroyed and the river banks were steep. Lieutenant Waddill of the 46th North Carolina wrote:

This ford will be remembered as one of the many impossibilities triumphed over by Lee's foot cavalry. The chill of the water, the multitude of boulders which literally covered the bottom of the river, coupled with the depth of the stream (which came to the shoulders of the shorter men) all served to impress this bit of experience indelibly upon the memories of those who took that early morning dip.[26]

Once across the river, Walker made camp. "My men being much worn down by two days' and nights' marching, almost without sleep or rest, we remained in camp during the 11th, and proceeded the next day toward Harper's Ferry, encamping at Hillsborough."[27] While here, Walker had a brief encounter with what he assumed was an enemy agent. A woman sent him a message requesting a meeting at the local hotel, saying she had an important message from "our friends" in Washington to be delivered to General Lee in person. "I saw at once that I had to do with a Federal spy . . ." wrote Walker. Professing ignorance of Lee's whereabouts, he detained her through the night on the pretense of trying to find the general. The next morning before leaving camp, he had her arrested and taken to Leesburg.[28]

A day of rest and intrigue now put Walker behind schedule. He did not reach the base of Loudoun Heights until Saturday morning, the 13th, and only then did he send two brigades to the top (27th North Carolina and 30th Virginia). Loudoun Heights was totally unfortified by the Federals, an example of the gross negligence of Miles's administration. Despite repeated warnings from his subordinates that once Loudoun was occupied by Confederate forces, they would have direct command of Harpers Ferry and possibly Bolivar, Miles refused to believe that it would come to pass. The enemy would come the front way, through Bolivar, and not the back way, thought Miles.[29] While McLaws was cutting his road to the crest of Maryland Heights Sunday morning, Walker was personally leading three Parrott guns and two rifled pieces to Loudoun. The climb was as arduous as that of his comrade, but by 1:00 P.M. he, too, was in firing readiness. "I informed . . . Jackson of this, by signal, and awaited his instructions." Before a reply came, his batteries attracted the attention of the Federal artillery on Bolivar, and the duel was on.[30]

McClellan had first raised the Harpers Ferry question with Halleck before the Army of the Potomac left Washington. He wanted Miles and his 12,000 men to join the main army. "I regarded the arrangements there as exceedingly dangerous," wrote McClellan. In a conversation with Secretary Seward, who expressed some uneasiness about Miles's position, the general stated:

In my opinion the proper course was to abandon the position and unite the garrison . . . to the main army of operations, for the reason that its presence at Harper's Ferry would not hinder the enemy from crossing the Potomac; that if we were unsuccessful in the approaching battle, Harper's Ferry would be of no use to us, and its garrison necessarily lost; that if we were successful, we would immediately recover the post without any difficulty, while the addition of 10,000 men to the active army would be an important factor in insuring success. I added that if it were determined to hold the position, the existing arrangements were all wrong, as it would be easy for the enemy to surround and capture the garrison, and that the garrison ought, at least, to be withdrawn to the Maryland Heights, where they could resist attack until relieved.[31]

Impressed, Seward asked McClellan to join him in a trip to see Halleck where these thoughts should be repeated. But Halleck regarded the generals remarks with "ill-concealed contempt," and the matter was dropped.

The men in the Harpers Ferry garrison felt the growing tension. Some openly opposed the senile Colonel Miles and his passive attitude on defenses. Waiting for the enemy like so many sitting ducks was not to their liking. The 12th New York Militia wanted out. Col. W. G. Ward sent an urgent wire to Maj. Gen. John E. Wool, departmental commander, on behalf of his men. Wool, with an unusual tolerance for Ward's insubordination in going over Miles's head, replied:

I thank you for your telegram. Surely your regiment will not desire to leave at the present, when their general asks them to remain a few days. They would not be well received at New York if they should return at this moment. They would be branded as cowards. I am not willing that they should lose their good name, when but a few days' delay will entitle them to carry the proud name of brave soldiers. You and your officers, who consent to remain, merit the thanks of myself and of the whole country.[32]

These were nice words but they did little for Ward. A second plea was sent to Wool. "A few days is too indefinite," wrote Ward. "I must most respectfully but earnestly urge that my command be sent home on Saturday next at very latest. Please answer, naming the day when they will be sent home."[33] There was no reply. If the message impassioned Wool at all, it did little more than strengthen his instructions to Miles: ". . . remain at Harper's Ferry until further orders."[34]

By the time Lee had started his Potomac crossing, Halleck had second thoughts on McClellan's suggestions of evacuation. On the 5th he wrote Wool in Baltimore: "I find it impossible to get this army into the field again in large force for a day or two. In the meantime Harper's Ferry may be attacked and overwhelmed." There was merit to moving the troops to Maryland Heights, Halleck thought, but, not knowing the ground himself, he left the decision to Wool.[35]

On the 7th, two days after McClellan left Washington, Lincoln stepped into the act. He wired Wool: "What about Harper's Ferry? Do you know anything about it?"[36] Wool replied: "I think Harper's Ferry will be defended."[37] And so Miles sat. There were no orders to tell him to do anything different, and apparently no initiative to compel him to take matters into his own hands. The telegraph wires were cut that day and communications ceased, but Miles had been ordered to stay, and stay he would. "I am ordered by General Wool to hold this place," he told his officers. "God damn my soul to hell if I don't hold it against the enemy."[38]

Three days passed. Then on the 10th, McClellan wrote to Halleck: "Col. Miles is at or near Harper's Ferry, as I understand . . . He can do nothing where he is, but could be of great service if ordered to join me."[39] This was the second time McClellan had asked for Miles's release, and for the second time, Halleck turned him down. "There is no way for Col. Miles to join you at present; his only chance is to defend his works till you can open communication with him." Halleck was right this time, but McClellan was not seeking to reinforce his army so much as he was trying to spring Miles from an inevitable trap. He thought Miles could march out of his position easily and quickly while there was still time, cross the river at Williamsport, and make for Pennsylvania, thereby escaping capture and ultimately supporting the main army on the flank. Since Halleck still did not accept McClellan's suggestions, there was little to do but try to relieve Miles.[40]

Though Halleck did not realize it (and he could not even have known had he been on the field), by refusing to release Miles he had turned the trap around and was inadvertently using the hapless troops at Harpers Ferry as bait for Lee. Halleck was rattled by the downright confusing reports he was receiving from dozens of sources. To Wool, he seemed receptive to any open suggestions for saving Miles, yet in the next breath to McClellan, he shut that same door. But now McClellan had a copy of Lee's Harpers Ferry plans. The shoe was on the other foot. The Army of the Potomac was in a position to both relieve Miles and crush Lee. The orders had reached McClellan late but he felt certain that with the present disposition of Lee's Army, he could "cut the enemy in two and beat him in detail."

The incompetence of Dixon Miles as commander at Harpers Ferry gave rise to a military investigation some months after the surrender.[41] His conduct was certainly to be questioned. Gross neglect of proper defenses, complete disregard of orders from the department commander, and an unstable relationship with his officers and men all contributed to what was later described as a military "disgrace," "unjustified," and "inexcusable."[42] Unfortunately, Miles was not around to defend himself. He did little, however, at the time to insure acquital.

Colonel Ward of the 12th New York was not the only one who wanted out. Much of the dissatisfaction was not revealed until the investigation, but one man had an idea for a mass cavalry escape, openly opposed Miles on it, and was successful. There were some 1,300 to 1,500 cavalry at Harpers Ferry; the 1st Maryland, 1st Rhode Island, 12th Illinois, a detachment from the Maryland Potomac Home Brigade, and the 8th New York.[43] They were all under the command of Col. Arno Voss of the 12th Illinois,[44] but it was Col. Benjamin F. (Grimes) Davis who instigated the idea and who did most of the talking. Davis was a Mississippian, one of two Southern officers who had remained with the regular army. He held the rank of Captain in the 1st Cavalry (regular army), but had been breveted to Colonel of the 8th New York Volunteers. Davis held an impressive record. Graduating from West Point in the class of 1854 along with Jeb Stuart, John Pegram, and Custis Lee, he had received his early training in the west against the Apache.[45] Now he was well seasoned in the saddle, well liked by his men, and on the night of the 14th, ready to demonstrate his daring. Davis knew as well as Voss and the others that it would be a grossly unjustified sacrifice to surrender the horses and men to Jackson. Since there was no possible way the cavalry could help defend the garrison, why not make a break for it? Capture on the road or pinned in at the Ferry; it made little difference. As long as there was the slightest chance of cutting their way out, there was absolutely nothing to lose. Davis felt that the cavalry had done all they could and they had. The skirmishes against Kershaw on Elk Ridge and the reconnaisance reports were all handsomely performed, but that was the extent of it. Futhermore, there was no forage for the horses. Should the garrison hold out for another two or three days, which Davis and others considered highly unlikely, a surrender of such a large, hungry, cavalry force would be humiliating.

Davis's own particular unit was restless. They had been issued their horses only a few weeks before and had not yet seen action. Their first action had been on foot against Jackson at Winchester in May and they had performed rather badly.[46] Now the prospects of prison camp or even parole before "dipping their swords in blood" was unthinkable. William M. Luff of the 12th Illinois spoke for nearly all the garrison when he wrote:

> The situation was extremely depressing. Surrounded on all sides by the enemy, with no hope of succor or opportunity to make an adequate defense, and with the prospect of early capture or surrender, the minds of officers and men naturally turned toward escape. They had not been there long enough to become attached to the place, and the surroundings were far from pleasant.[47]

Davis went to General White, who, although he was senior officer, had not assumed any command, and presented his proposal. He "desired the privilege of cutting his way out."[48] It was as simple as that. What other logic could anyone offer for keeping the cavalry there? White agreed and so did Lt. Col. Hasbrouck Davis of the 12th Illinois.[49] Together they went to Miles. As was expected, Miles opposed the move. He had disagreed with nearly every other plan for saving his men; why should he make an exception for this? It was impracticable and involved too much risk, Miles said. The whole idea was "wild, impractical and sure to invariably result in serious loss to the government."[50] Miles was an old army man, meaning that if it didn't go by regulations it was dangerous. But Davis was undaunted. He was representing all the cavalry, he told Miles, not just his own regiment. They saw no excuse for staying. Colonel Miles could not be so unreasonable as not to see this. Had the colonel forgotten that just the night before he had suggested to Captain Charles Russell of the 1st Maryland a mass escape for the cavalry? Davis had been there and heard him.[51] But what about the infantry and artillery, Miles wanted to know. They too would want to go. That was Miles's problem. He would have to deal with those boys. Davis had his own men to think of. He was going to go, with or without Miles's consent, and he let it be known in no uncertain terms.[52] After some deliberation and more heated words, Miles consented, providing a suitable route was chosen. The unit commanders could meet in his office at 7:00 P.M.[53]

Davis was on time with his fellow officers and several plans. The first was to cross the Shenandoah River into Loudoun County, skirt the enemy on the heights, and set out for Washington. It was immediately pronounced "impracticable." Among the lesser evils, the river was full of deep holes at that point, making it unsafe.[54] Then Davis suggested the south side of the Potomac to Kearneysville and Shepherdstown, thence to Hagerstown and on into Pennsylvania. This, too, was rejected as too risky.[55] Finally an agreement was reached. The men would take the pontoon bridge across the Potomac to the Sandy Hook-Sharpsburg road, running along the base of Maryland Heights, the same road John Brown had used several years before, and from there proceed north.[56] This was perhaps the most risky plan of all. Confederate infantry was in Sandy Hook and McLaws was on top of the mountain with an undetermined number of troops in undetermined positions. Undoubtedly, this road would be covered. It was almost unbelievable that it would not be. But once Miles had set his mind, there was no changing it. Besides, McClellan was assumed to be in the vicinity of Sharpsburg and South Mountain. The plan was immediately put down in black and white: "The cavalry forces at this post, except detached orderlies, will make immediate preparation to leave here at eight o'clock to-night . . ." There would be no baggage-wagons, ambulances or extra horses. "No other instructions can be given to the commander than to force his way through the enemy's lines and join our own army."[57] And there was a word of caution from Miles. There were to be no bugle calls. Everything must be quiet lest the infantry be forewarned. "He was afraid . . . [of] a stampede among them."[58]

There was some consternation caused by Miles's decision to let the cavalry go. Much of the sting had gone from the insult to the infantrymen by the time of the investigation, but some attempt was made to use the Davis escape as a direct slap in the face to the foot soldier. In the questioning, two schools of thought were developed.

General White to Captain William H. Grafflin of the 1st Maryland Cavalry:

Question: Do you or not believe that the force at Harper's Ferry could have escaped over the route you took?

Answer: I think they might. To be sure, they could not have escaped without an engagement. It is very likely we might have had considerable of a fight before we got out; but I think the best portion of them might have got out; that is, if they had been stripped of everything but their ammunition and arms. They could not have carried anything with them.

Question: Do you think infantry could have been marched with sufficient rapidity to have gone through as you did?

Answer: I think the best portion of them could; some, no doubt, would have given out.

Question: What do you think about taking artillery along?

Answer: Well, sir, with an addition of horses we might have taken artillery.

Question: How long that night would it have taken to have got over the bridge all the troops there, cavalry, artillery and infantry? Would it have taken all night?

Answer: If they had commenced at dark, they might have got their artillery and infantry over before I got over. It was about 10:30 o'clock before I moved out of the street.

Question: You think we might have moved 10,000 or 12,000 men in that time with the artillery we had?

Answer: I think so.

Question: Could not a portion of them have crossed the ford?

Answer: They could all have crossed the ford, all the cavalry.

Question: Would it not have expedited the movement very much if some of them had crossed the ford?

Answer: I do not think it would; but I know one thing, that it took that cavalry longer to cross than it would have taken four times that amount of infantry.

Question: Could or not both cavalry and infantry have been crossing at the bridge and at the ford at the same time?

Answer: Yes, sir; the river was very shoal then.[59]

One cavalry officer said he was positive Stonewall Jackson could have escaped with his infantry,[60] but not everyone agreed with Grafflin that Federal infantry would have been as successful. One witness claimed: "The route was not practicable for artillery and infantry at the rate we marched . . . It was not a very good road at any time . . . it would have been utterly impossible for the artillery and infantry to have accompanied us, even if the road had been good."[61] And another:

The road was very narrow and difficult; infantry could not have kept up with us. The road was too rough for artillery, passing, as it did, frequently over ravines, fields, and fences. If we had taken a different route, over which infantry . . . could have passed, we should have alarmed the enemy at Hagerstown, Funkstown, and Williamsport, and from either of these points they could have brought artillery and successfully resisted us.[62]

Some of the infantry and artillery officers did catch on to what was going on and protested. If the cavalry was going, they wanted to go too. They said they did not see the necessity of staying there and being butchered by artillery without the opportunity of using their men and arms in any way. Capt. John C. Phillips of the 2nd Illinois Light Artillery arrived at Miles's headquarters armed with a request for permission to attempt escape just as the cavalry was preparing to leave. "I told Colonel Davis if he would wait until such time as I could get back from Colonel [Frederick] D'Utassy [commanding 39th New York], there might be some arrangements to go with them."[63] But Davis did not wait, and Miles, reiterating his firmness to hold the town "to the last extremity," refused to concede. The infantrymen were ordered back to their places.[64]

Davis had little time to prepare for the escape. There was no packing. The men were ordered into the saddle just as they were, "leaving everything, but our overcoats."[65] This included their tents and the regimental band. "We missed the tents afterward, but managed to get along without the band," one man wrote.[66] What forage they had was evenly divided among the horses, and then they mounted. They would need a guide and a scout for the expedition. Tom Noakes, a civilian who knew this country like the back of his hand, had been employed regularly as a government guide, and he was a good one. He had just come in from a scouting part and knew the enemy's location. Davis immediately assigned him to the lead position.[67] With Noakes he put Lt. Hanson Green of the 1st Maryland, a man who was a native of the region.[68] After a briefing to the men on the hazards of the mission and a stop to invite General White to join them, an invitation White refused because he felt he was needed there, the cavalry was on its way.[69] By morning they would be in "Pennsylvania, on the way to Richmond, or in Hell!"[70] This statement by a member of the Rhode Island regiment indicated not only their determination but the fact that they knew absolutely nothing of what the trip held in store for them. They were going out blind, and they hoped the Confederates would be also.

The night was moonless and "intensely dark," perfect for a mass escape. The big question was, would McLaws' pickets see them? Oddly enough, the one road which the Confederates had failed to cover was the old Sharpsburg road running along the base of the mountain, the road the Federals had selected. Jackson had expressed some concern to McLaws that afternoon about an attempted break-out from the Federal garrison. Walker, on Loudoun Heights, was watching the Shenandoah River. The 12th Virginia Cavalry was on Jackson's left to prevent any sneak-through along the Potomac. "Fearing lest the enemy should attempt to escape across the Potomac," wrote Jackson, "by means of signals I called the attention of Major-General McLaws, commanding on Maryland Heights, to the propriety of guarding against such an attempt."[71] Stuart had gone with McLaws to the edge of the heights that afternoon and, because of his familiarity with the roads in that area (he had served in the United States Cavalry during the John Brown episode), "repeatedly urged the importance of his [McLaws] holding with an infantry picket the road leading from the Ferry by the Kennedy [John Brown] farm toward Sharpsburg."[72] But luck was with Davis from the start. McLaws was too busy to see him. Perhaps luck would ride with them. They already had their sign. Just as they mounted, the commissary boys came up with some "little tinfoil packages of tobacco," sort of a "bon voyage" gift which the surprised boys cherished as their "good-luck piece."[73]

Quietly and slowly, the party began crossing the bridge in single file, turning left on the road leading northwestward. The 12th Illinois was in front, the New York, Maryland, and Rhode Island regiments following.[74] Once on the Maryland side, the pace quickened. Two columns were formed in order to expedite the movement. It would take nearly two hours, so long in fact that the head of the column was ten miles into Washington County before the last man crossed.[75] Soon they were galloping in columns of fours, each group seeking desperately to keep up, watching for sparks from the horses hoofs on the stones or listening for the rattle of sabres, so intense was the darkness.[76] One company had a close call and nearly gave the whole secret away. Instead of turning left toward Sharpsburg, Company D.,

12th Illinois, turned right toward Sandy Hook and directly into the arms of Confederate pickets. It was a nasty moment or two, but since there was no Confederate cavalry to follow, the men made it back to the bridge in time to join the column.[77] Twice on the road to Sharpsburg, similar incidents happened. Davis came upon Confederate pickets a few miles out but scattered them quickly.[78] Several miles further on, they encountered a road block of overturned wagons set up by rebels evidently alerted by the first group. Here is where Noakes and Green came in handy. The entire line skirted the obstruction by taking winding paths through the fields—fields that only the guides knew.[79]

"It was a killing pace and very hard work to keep up," wrote William Luff of the 12th Illinois.[80] Men and horses were exhausted. Some slept in the saddle only to find when they awoke that they had strayed from the line of march. Quickly they would race back, some to drop their heads again. If a horse gave out, and some did, a comrade would make room for a rider.[81] No one was to be left for capture. Some strayed, unable to keep up. At least thirteen returned over the bridge that night, including one wounded and one killed from the skirmish.[82] The others ploughed on into the unknown. At this rapid pace, the first troopers reached Sharpsburg by 10:00 P.M.[83] At the edge of town, a shot and a cry was heard.

"Who goes there?" came the challenge.
"Friend to the Union," replied Davis.

"This reply was evidently unsatisfactory, for the pickets immediately fired upon us," wrote Luff in a rather amusing understatement of what could have been a serious situation.[84] Noakes was pressed into service again, and with the aid of a friendly citizen, who told them they were headed right for the Confederate army, they were off. To the left of the town and through forests, fields, and across streams, Noakes and Green led them, with artillery shells pounding at their heels.[85] Through the night they rode, by-passing houses, villages, and main highways until they reached the Hagerstown-Williamsport Pike about two miles north of Williamsport. The advance scouts reported noises from the highway—the rumblings of wagons off in the distance. Davis halted the column. Dawn was breaking but it was still dark enough to hide in the shadows along the roadside. The men were lined up quickly, the 8th New York on one side, and the 12th Illinois on the other, the rest in reserve. It was a spine tingling moment. After all these miles at breakneck speed and so close to the Pennsylvania border, it was a horrible thought to have to face up to the enemy here. Whatever was on the road, Davis was ready for it. He had 1,300 cavalrymen and every one of them was alert now.

Davis was not the first to escape Harpers Ferry under orders. On Saturday evening, the 13th, after Maryland Heights had been evacuated, Miles sent for Capt. Charles Russell of the 1st Maryland. Did Captain Russell think he could lead the cavalry force out of the post? "I'm willing to try," Russell told him.[86] Well then, would the captain be willing to take a few men out past the enemy lines and deliver a message to General McClellan? He was thought to be some place near Frederick, but since communications had been cut, no one knew for certain where the Army of the Potomac was located. Russell readily agreed to do the job. He knew the territory, and without hindrance he could be in Frederick by morning.

[Miles] asked me if I could . . . try to reach somebody that had ever heard of the United States Army, or any general of the United States Army, or anybody who knew anything about the United States Army, and report the condition of Harper's Ferry. He told me that if I could get to any general of the United States Army, or to any telegraph station, or, if possible, get to General McClellan . . . to report, that he thought he could hold out forty-eight hours; that he had subsistence for forty-eight hours, but if he was not relieved in that time, he would have to surrender the place.[87]

Miles was worried. His language, as Russell reported it, was an indication of the anxiety which Miles himself had helped create at the garrison. Without any delay, Russell was on his way with nine hand-picked men. It was an important mission so they chose to stay on the south side of the Potomac until they reached Blackfords' Ford below Shepherdstown. Outrunning Conderate pickets several times, including seventy-one of them at South Mountain, Russell and his party made it to Middletown where they met the first Federal lines. Refreshed after a few moments rest, and with new horses, they were on their way to McClellan's headquarters in Frederick.[88] Around 9:00

A.M. on the morning of the 14th, Russell was escorted to the general's tent where, in a fair exchange for a hearty breakfast, he gave McClellan the verbal message from Miles;[89] "the first authentic intelligence I had received as to the conditions of things at Harper's Ferry," wrote McClellan.[90]

Russell felt that it would be impossible for his men to return to the post so McClellan sent them off to join Franklin's Sixth Corps and dispatched another courier off to Miles via a different route. "You may count on our making every effort to relieve you," he wrote. "You may rely upon my speedily accomplishing that object. Hold out to the last extremity." Then as he moved ahead, McClellan had the artillery fire at frequent intervals to let Miles know "relief was at hand." It was a rather slow, suspenseful, dramatic touch, but Miles was getting the message.[91]

By the morning of the 14th, Jackson had a signal station established on a hill back of Halltown and was in touch with Walker's brigades. Capt. J. L. Bartlett, Jackson's signal officer, had been unable to raise McLaws so a message was rushed off to him by courier at 7:20 A.M. "I am gratified to learn that you have the main heights," he told him. "I desire you to move forward until you get complete possession . . . I hope you will establish batteries wherever you can to advantage, for the purpose of firing upon the enemy's camps, and at such other points as you may be able to damage him." He told McLaws to let him know as soon as he was in position. Walker was moving his guns up Loudoun Heights and once all were ready, he wanted a concerted firing. "The position in front of me is a strong one, and I desire to remain quiet, and let you and Walker draw attention . . . so that I may have an opportunity of getting possession of the hill without much loss." Jackson closed on a note of unusual determination so as to let McLaws finish his task. "Should we have to attack, let the work be done thoroughly . . . Demolish the place if it is occupied by the enemy, and does not surrender."[92]

At 10:00 A.M., Captain Bartlett reported that Walker had signaled that his six guns were in position. "Shall we wait for McLaws," Walker wanted to know? "Wait," answered Jackson.[93] Then the general sat down to detail his orders.

In 1886, Walker was invited to write an article for *Century Magazine,* which ultimately appeared in *Battles and Leaders.*[94] In that article he claimed that on the morning of the 14th he received "substantially the following dispatch" from Jackson: "Harper's Ferry is now completely invested. I shall summon its commander to surrender. Should he refuse, I shall give him twenty-four hours to remove the non-combatants, and then carry the place by assault. *Do not fire unless forced to.*"[95]

Walker was wrong. Jackson was behind schedule by two days. There is absolutely no evidence to show that he would wait another "twenty-four hours." He had told McLaws that morning in his message by courier that he planned to send in a "flag of truce" for the purpose of getting out all noncombatants, but in the same message, he also said, ". . . fire on the houses when necessary. The citizens can keep out of harm's way from your artillery."[96] These are not the thoughts of a man who would delay any longer reinforcing Lee's beleaguered remnants of the army. If, in fact, Jackson did send the message Walker claimed, it is extremely doubtful that he would have varied it so greatly between his two key men and their positions. In almost all cases, he sent duplicate messages to both McLaws and Walker; "Similar instructions will be sent to General Walker," he would tell McLaws. "I do not desire any of the batteries to open until all are ready on both sides of the river, except you should find it necessary, of which you must judge for yourself."[97] In Walker's own words this was "Do not fire unless forced to."

Obviously, Walker suffered from one of two things; a guilt complex for opening fire prematurely, or a hero complex from forcing Jackson to ditch his twenty-four hour delay plan, thus assuring early surrender at Harpers Ferry and saving the battle for Lee. One thing seems certain: Walker was nervous up on Loudoun Heights. He had heard the same distant cannon booming that McLaws heard and was fairly certain that McClellan was making some effort to seek out McLaws. If he felt keen concern for the safety of the remainder of the army, one cannot take that away from him. "It was certain that General Lee would be in fearful peril should the capture of Harper's Ferry be much longer delayed," wrote Walker. "I thereupon asked permission to open fire, but receiving no reply, I determined to be 'forced.' "[98]

To "force the issue," Walker advanced two brigades into the open in full view of Federal artillery on Bolivar Heights. "As I expected, they at once opened a heavy, but harmless, fire upon my regiments, which afforded me the wished-for pretext."[99] Within a matter of minutes, all six guns replied and the siege was on. McLaws and Jackson followed suit immediately.

For this action, Walker had no need for guilt. It was only a matter of time before artillery fire would have been ordered. Though Jackson had said in a combined message to both McLaws and Walker, "I will let you know when to open all the batteries," he had left the door wide-open for each commander to make his own judgement.[100] Certainly, Jackson made no censorious moves against Walker. "Thus it would appear," wrote Bradley T. Johnson in reply to Walker's *Century* article, "that General Walker forced the attack on Harper's Ferry, and prevented the delay of twenty-four hours which General Jackson proposed to give; and that to this prompt attack was due the capture of Harper's Ferry, and the salvation of that part of the Army of Northern Virginia which . . . was waiting at Sharpsburg . . ."[101]

Though Walker could lay no more claim to being a hero than McLaws, and perhaps not as much, his artillery was doing the intended job at the Federal garrison, or so he claimed: a "plunging fire" doing "great execution," while McLaws' guns were "ineffective, the shells bursting in mid-air without reaching the enemy."[102] Whose guns they were made little difference; they did considerable damage to artillery emplacements in the town, and, what was probably worse, irreparable damage to the already deteriorating morale of the Federal garrison. Jackson wasted little time in taking advantage of the opportunity. A. P. Hill was ordered to move to his right, along the left bank of the Shenandoah with the thought to turning the enemy's left in the morning. He did so with five brigades; three under Brockenbrough, Archer, and Pender, who gained a hill overlooking the extreme left of the enemy line, and two under Branch and Gregg, who skirted the edge of the town by the river and, under cover of darkness, slipped in behind the Federal lines. Jackson's own division under J. R. Jones moved into position on the left. The old Stonewall Brigade, along with the batteries of Poague and Carpenter, found a hill, took it after a brief skirmish, and that part of the line was secure.

Ewell's Division was advanced by three columns to the center. The encirclement was nearly complete. That night batteries under Pegram, McIntosh, Davidson, Braxton, and Crenshaw were moved to support Hill's right, and Colonel Crutchfield, Jackson's artillery chief, crossed ten guns over the Shenandoah so as to concentrate on the enemy's left flank. The trap was set and, as A. P. Hill put it, "the fate of Harper's Ferry was sealed."[103] Jackson had never had a chance to use his big guns. If things went well that night, the morning would bring on a new chapter in his military career.

After dark, as soon as things had settled down, Kyd Douglas took leave on a personal mission. He had seen his mother last while in camp in Frederick and not his father and sister for some months. Shepherdstown was within an hour's ride, about eleven miles, and home was just across the river. On the finest horse he could find, he rode through the night for a delightful three hour visit.[104]

While Douglas was away, Jackson was drafting one of the most important messages of the entire campaign, one that would influence Lee's third great decision. The dispatch was dated "Near Halltown, September 14, 1862, 8:15 P.M." and was addressed to Col. R. H. Chilton:

Colonel: Through God's blessing, the advance, which commenced this evening, has been successful thus far, and I look to him for success to-morrow. The advance has been directed to be resumed at dawn to-morrow morning.[105]

6

South Mountain

There was one thing Special Orders No. 191 did not tell McClellan. After Lee started his move to Boonsboro, he received word that Federal militia based in Pennsylvania was moving to Hagerstown to cut him off. Douglas S. Freeman calls it a "vague rumor,"[1] presumably passed on by a sympathetic citizen. The rumor was later proven to be groundless. There were Federal pickets in the Greencastle-Chambersburg area, but the force was not sufficient to cause the Confederates any injury. To ward off any potential trap, however, Lee further divided his army into a fifth wing, sending Longstreet's Corps on to Hagerstown as he had originally intended. Hagerstown, with its rail connections to the North, was to be the springboard for the drive on Harrisburg, and it must be protected at all costs. Lee did not yet know that McClellan had a copy of his order so that the disposition of Longstreet, conceived at first as mere insurance, would ultimately aggravate the awkward dispersion of his forces. Lee himself accompanied Longstreet's men on the 13 mile march from Boonsboro, leaving D. H. Hill at the western base of South Mountain on the main highway to watch the east for Federal movements, and to guard against any escape attempts from Harpers Ferry which might come through Pleasant Valley.

Once in Hagerstown, Lee gave Davis a summary of his accomplishments. It was not overly impressive. Of those things he hoped to accomplish, drawing the Federal forces north of the Potomac and west of Washington was all he could claim. He fared better procuring supplies in Hagerstown than he did in Frederick, and this encouraging

159

news he told Davis. "The army has been received in this region with sympathy and kindness," he wrote. "We have found in this city about 1,500 barrels of flour, and I am led to hope that a supply can be gathered from the mills in the country . . ." They had collected some shoes, but, he said, "they will not be sufficient to cover the bare feet of the army." Then he told the President that he would wait in Hagerstown for news from Jackson at Harpers Ferry.[2]

The question now arises, what would McClellan have done had he known that Lee had sent Longstreet on to Hagerstown? Presumably, at the time the "lost dispatch" was brought to him, there was no knowledge of the further split in the Army of Northern Virginia. The orders specifically stated that Longstreet's command would "halt at Boonsboro" and that D. H. Hill would form the "rear guard," meaning that both commands were just over the mountain. The defense for McClellan could rest with ease at this point were it not for the fact that at sometime on the same day as the Confederate plans were revealed, Governor Curtin sent the following wire to Federal headquarters, addressed to Gen. McClellan: "Longstreet's division is said to have reached Hagerstown last night."[3]

Governor Curtin was, in many ways, like Halleck. He was frantic over the safety of Pennsylvania. His telegrams to McClellan, Halleck, and Lincoln were numerous and frequent and often bordered on hysteria. Many times his information was in error, but, on the other hand, he was quite frequently accurate as far as basic troop movements were concerned. On September 8, McClellan had informed Curtin that he was "endeavoring to get all the information about the movements of the rebel army possible," and respectfully requested the governor to "obtain all possible information of the enemy's movements and communicate them to me should he advance toward your state."[4] The governor complied with McClellan's request to the best of his ability. There is no evidence that any serious reconnaissance was made to determine the actual strength of the forces covering Turner's Gap on the main highway, nor was there any attempt to check out the governor's message. He was not even given the courtesy of a reply to his all-important piece of information.

The question of whether McClellan would have taken advantage of the situation becomes lost in the complexity of the man himself.

There can be no question, however, that his headquarters knew long before they broke camp in Frederick that Lee's army was greatly weakened now, and that at the most, only one division stood between them and a quick decisive victory. For some unknown reason, McClellan refused to accept basic information. Lee, in enemy territory, and with full knowledge that the Army of the Potomac was at his rear, refused to pass off a "vague rumor" as insignificant. Clearly, Lee had as much at stake by chasing down the Hagerstown story as did McClellan in reading Curtin's telegram.

There can be found no plausible reason for McClellan's delay in moving on South Mountain immediately upon receipt of the "dispatch." His most fervent supporters can offer no excuse for such negligence. The situation on this most fateful day could not have been spelled out more specifically than if Lee had paid a visit to Federal headquarters and described the plans in detail. Such opportunities rarely present themselves in battle. McClellan was plainly not the man to accept them. Kenneth P. Williams, one of McClellan's severest critics wrote: "It is to be hoped that some capable smokers derived more good out of the three cigars than McClellan was to get out of the order in which they were wrapped."[5]

Lee had no intentions of defending the mountain gaps as evidenced by his troops stationed there. His report stated:

General Stuart, with the cavalry, remained east of the mountains, to observe the enemy and retard his advance. The advance of the Federal Army was so slow at the time we left Fredericktown as to justify the belief that the reduction of Harper's Ferry would be accomplished and our troops concentrated before they would be called upon to meet it. In that event, it had not been intended to oppose its passabe through the South Mountains, as it was desired to engage it as far as possible from its base.[6]

With one mighty thrust, the Federal army could have dealt the fatal blow, destroying Hill, McLaws, and, in all probability, taking Longstreet and the prize catch, Lee, with it. Only Jackson and Walker, if fortunate enough to escape to the Valley, would have remained of the Army of Northern Virginia; a staggering thought.

In his official report, McClellan stated that upon finding the "lost dispatch," he "immediately gave orders for a rapid and vigorous forward movement."[7] The orders were not given immediately, but at

6:20 that evening, and the movement was neither rapid nor vigorous. Gen. Alfred Pleasonton's cavalry was already on the old National Road pursuing Stuart, who was screening the rear of the Confederate army. At 3:35 P.M., the Kanawha Division of the Ninth Corps was ordered to proceed as far as Middletown to support Pleasonton.[8] Neither of these two movements, however, can be directly connected to the finding of the "dispatch" since one was in action at the time and the other specified as a support.

Years after the war, McClellan still clung to his story that immediate orders were given to his army. Why, no one can be certain. His very first communique that afternoon was at 3:00 P.M. to his cavalry chief, in which he enclosed a copy of the dispatch for verification. Pleasonton, who now held the extreme western advance position, was requested to ascertain whether the order of march had "thus far been followed by the enemy."[9] If McClellan was uncertain as to what Lee's order meant, this was a meager attempt at finding out. He would wait another three hours before doing anything about it. When all the official orders had been compiled, it was evident that he had delayed for about six hours before making initial contact with any of his commanders. When he did, it was with Franklin's Sixth Corps at Buckeystown, several miles directly south of Frederick.

The message was dated "September 13, 1862—6:20 P.M." and explained the basic Confederate plans. Franklin was instructed to cut off or destroy McLaws' command on Maryland Heights by driving through Crampton's Gap, about 12 miles from Franklin's position, the southernmost route through the South Mountain range. ". . . you will move *at daybreak* in the morning, by Jefferson and Burkittsville, upon the road to Rohrersville."[10] "At daybreak," meant a delay of at least ten or eleven more hours. One military critic has stated: "Jackson would have got his men on the move within one hour."[11] Another, in writing of the campaign, commented:

Franklin's troops, like all troops of a force marching to meet and fight an invading army, were, or should have been, in condition to move at a moment's notice. The weather on the 13th was extremely fine, and roads in good condition. There was no reason why Franklin's Corps should not have moved that night, instead of at daybreak the next morning.[12]

"I ask of you, at this important moment," wrote McClellan to Franklin, "all your intellect and the utmost activity that a general can exercise."[13] This was a strange request, indeed, coming from a general whose intellect and activity failed him at "this important moment." Without a doubt, McClellan knew that a rapid forward movement would be disastrous to the Confederate army. His continued insistance that such a movement was accomplished, substantiates this fact.

An immediate march by Franklin would have taken him to Burkittsville or the base of the mountain range by midnight, giving him at least five hours of rest before striking the pass at daybreak. This must have been quite apparent to both McClellan and Franklin. What was not known, but what could have been an educated guess, should anyone have cared to make one, was that a daybreak drive through Crampton's Gap would have closed the campaign.

It is interesting to note at this point that McClellan sent either a postscript to his message to Franklin, or a second message. Appearing in a supplement volume to the *Official Records*, it, too, is dated "September 13, 1862, 6:20 P.M." Bearing tremendous significance in the McClellan controversy, it has been generally overlooked in historical analyzations. To some minor extent, it relieves McClellan of some of the blame for the retarded movement of the Sixth Corps. He wrote: "Knowing my views and intentions [already transmitted in the first message], you are fully authorized to change any of the details of this order as circumstances may change, provided the purpose is carried out; that purpose being to attack the enemy in detail and beat him." Further on in the same message, he suggested that "if . . . you consider it preferable to crush the enemy at Petersville before undertaking the movement I have directed, you are at liberty to do so . . ."[14]

In two separate statements, McClellan gave Franklin the opportunity to alter the orders as he saw fit. In other words, had Franklin chosen to move his corps that night in preparation for an early morning attack on the pass, he was free to do so. The message, therefore, sheds light on Franklin for the first time as a "McClellan disciple." As will be indicated later in his actions following the battle for Crampton's Gap, Franklin played the McClellan "waiting game" with some vigor.

McClellan also knew, as evidenced by his first message to Franklin, that he had nothing to gain by delay. Col. Francis W. Palfrey wrote:

He was playing for a great stake, and fortune had given him a wonderfully good chance of winning, and he should have used every card to the very utmost, and left nothing to chance that he could compass by skill and energy. But there are some soldiers who are much more ingenious in finding reasons for not doing the very best thing in the very best way, than they are vigorous and irresistible in clearing away the obstacles to doing the very best thing in the very best way.[15]

McClellan had long before proven to Lincoln that he fitted Palfrey's description. He was doing nothing now to vindicate himself. Years later, in writing of the Maryland Campaign, General Ezra A. Carman was reminded of Napoleon and one of his generals who claimed he could not ascertain the position and strength of the enemy's army. "Attack him and you will find out," replied Napoleon. "The general who is ignorant of his enemy's strength and dispositions," wrote Carman, "is ignorant of his trade."[16]

Gen. Jacob D. Cox, who commanded the Kanawha Division under Burnside, commented on the approach to Frederick in his memoirs:

We moved forward by very short marches of six or eight miles, feeling our way so cautiously that Lee's reports speak of it as an unexpectedly slow approach. I see no good reason why it might not have advanced at once to the left bank of the Monocacy, covering thus both Washington and Baltimore, and hastening by some days Lee's movements across the Blue Ridge. We should have at least known where the enemy was by being in contact with him, instead of being the sport of all sorts of vague rumors and wild reports.

And on the finding of the "lost orders" Cox wrote:

If his [McClellan's] men had been ordered to be at the top of South Mountain before dark, they could have been there; but less than one full corps passed Catoctin Mountain that day or night, and when the leisurely movement of the 14th began, he, himself instead of being with the advance, was in Frederick till after 2 P.M. The failure to be "equal to the emergency" was not in his men. Twenty-four hours, as it turned out, was the whole difference between saving and losing Harper's Ferry . . .[17]

While Federal troops rested on the night of September 13, there was considerable activity on the Confederate side of South Mountain.

That morning, when McClellan opened D. H. Hill's copy of Special Orders No. 191, he was in conference with several businessmen of Frederick, possibly discussing arrangements for supplies. One of his guests was a Southern sympathizer. It was difficult for this man to conceal his shock when McClellan threw his arms in the air and exclaimed that he now knew Lee's secret. As soon as the conference was completed, the man made immediate arrangements to pass through the lines. Near dusk, he approached Confederate pickets at the base of South Mountain. He had a message for General Lee, he told the men. They took him to Jeb Stuart who, with his cavalry, had been screening the move through Turner's Gap. Stuart questioned the stranger extensively.

The story the man told was utterly fantastic, but certainly one that could not be ignored. Lee's plan had been risky and to have them fall into the hands of the enemy at this point would be sheer disaster. Lee must be notified, but he was in Hagerstown. It would mean sending a courier, a two-hour ride at least. Stuart wasted no time. The courier was dispatched and by 10:00 P.M. Lee received the message. He now knew that McClellan had a copy of the plans.[18]

What could he do? Jackson was at Harpers Ferry; McLaws was on Maryland Heights; Walker was on Loudoun Heights; Hill was at Boonsboro, and Longstreet was in Hagerstown. Not only had he split his army into four parts, but now it was split five ways, with only two parts in Virginia that could get away. Now that the Hagerstown report had proved false and they were in no danger of a Pennsylvania ambush, he must focus his attention to the east. McClellan was sure to come, and he was sure to at least make an attempt to dislodge McLaws. But McLaws would have to take care of himself. At 10:00 P.M. Lee sent a message to McLaws to beware of a Federal attempt to take the heights and to watch for an escape from Harpers Ferry.[19] He then ordered Longstreet to march to Boonsboro the next morning to help Hill defend Turner's Gap.

Just as the "lost order" was a great opportunity for McClellan, so it was a great crisis for Lee, and as McClellan had failed to rise to the occasion, so Lee failed to take advantage of the few precious hours he had been given by the warning of the "friend" from Frederick. In not doing so, he illustrated two fallacies of the Confederate command system—his overconfidence in some generals and his inability to enforce his authority on others. As a result, six to eight extremely vital hours slipped by him, as will be seen by the development of the action at South Mountain.

Lee and Longstreet were at odds. They had been at odds before and they would be again, but the strained relationship at Hagerstown would be detrimental to the army. Longstreet was somewhat bitter over the whole strategy. He had already lost out in his objections to the Harpers Ferry diversion. Now he was asking for Hill's immediate withdrawal from Boonsboro to meet him at Sharpsburg for a stand which he felt would be a better defensive position than South Mountain. "Lee listened patiently" but overruled him and again that night ordered him to Hill's aid. During the middle of the night, Longstreet, unable to sleep, got up and wrote a note of protest to Lee, arguing that he could not race to Boonsboro and effectively fight with exhausted troops (it would be impossible to do anything) and appealed to Lee to reconsider his Sharpsburg suggestion. To this, Lee never replied.[20] His order was firm. No general could be more sympathetic to the needs of his men than Lee but this was no time for such concern, especially since the troops had been in Hagerstown for more than twenty-four hours. Longstreet's men had done little in Hagerstown but rest. They had received a much better reception than in Frederick and the merchants had opened their doors to sell them dress patterns, oilcloth and beaver-skin hats.[21] Despite their commanders' concern for their physical condition, there seemed to be little to warrant any further delay in the resumption of the movement of the corps. Still, Longstreet waited until daybreak. E. P. Alexander theorized that Longstreet would have been much better off at Crampton's Gap, stating that if Longstreet had not gone to Hagerstown, the battle of Sharpsburg might "otherwise have probably been fought upon the mountain."[22] The Federal push through the mountain passes may have been delayed, but it is extremely doubtful that McClellan would have been stopped. Had Longstreet gone to Crampton's Gap, Hill's subsequent position on the National road would not have held. Though Alexander's theory is weak in nature, it does emphasize the significance of Longstreet's delay in moving.

Why didn't Lee order an immediate advance that night rather than waiting until morning? Perhaps he was in agreement with Longstreet that his men needed rest, but had they spent the night marching rather than the hot morning and afternoon as they did, they would have fared no worse and would have been on the field when battle commenced. No one has attempted to defend this delay, indeed, no one has questioned it. The whole thing seems to have been overshadowed by Hill's inadequacies in the defense of Turner's Gap at South Mountain.

Four roads cross South Mountain from the Middletown Valley: the main highway, or the old National road at Turner's Gap (called Frog Pass in one Confederate report);[23] the old Sharpsburg road at Fox's Gap about a mile to the south; the Burkittsville road at Crampton's Gap; and the old Hagerstown road which ran to the north of, and parallel to, the main highway. All four points would see action, but until the afternoon of the 13th, none seemed particularly important to the Confederates. Even then, the main pass was not of enough concern for D. H. Hill, in whose hands it had been placed, to visit himself. This was Stuart's job. Was not the underlying tactic to pull McClellan as far from home as possible? It was obvious that the Federal army would cross the mountain range. No special effort had been planned to stop him. By the time McClellan would get there, according to Lee's schedule, the Confederate army would be well on its way to Pennsylvania. Hill's orders were to watch for any escape from Harpers Ferry. Guarding the passes was secondary.

Hill had five brigades at Boonsboro, less than 5000 men.[24] When Stuart notified him at noon on the 13th that two Federal brigades (Pleasonton's cavalry) had pushed him out of the Catoctin range and were pressing on through the valley, Hill sent Col. A. H. Colquitt's brigade to Turner's Gap and placed Brig. Gen. Samuel Garland's brigade on the alert. The three remaining brigades were to continue their surveillance at Boonsboro. Hill himself stayed at his headquarters. Was he negligent? He did not think so. Covering the pass was not his job. He had much more important duties at Boonsboro.

When Colquitt arrived at the pass, he witnessed Stuart's withdrawal and the advance of the Federal infantry. His men "were thrown rapidly into position at the most available points, and the infantry disposed upon the right and left of the road [somewhat downhill and east of the crest]. The enemy made no further efforts to advance, and at dark withdrew from my immediate front."[25] The threat having subsided, Colquitt and Stuart discussed their position. Stuart seemed as unconcerned as Hill. Neither believed that there was any great danger. Stuart told Colquitt that his position and strength was sufficient to hold the Federal brigades, and that he, Stuart, must move on toward Harpers Ferry. In his official report, Stuart put his excuse in a little different light: "This was obviously no place for cavalry operations, a single horseman passing from point to point on the mountain with difficulty."[26] Col. Thomas L. Rosser, whom Stuart had positioned at Fox's Gap, later gave his own thoughts on Stuart's behavior: "Stuart did not expect the enemy would advance on Boonsboro, and was careless in guarding the roads leading that way."[27]

Colquitt did not share Stuart's views on the adequacy of the defense. As he later indicated, he believed that Stuart was wrong in his estimate of Federal strength. He informed General Hill, who ordered Garland's Brigade up for support. Colquitt wasted no time in deploying his men for whatever might come:

To the right and left of the turnpike, a mile distant on either side were practicable roads leading over the mountain, and connecting by a crossroad along the ridge with the turnpike. Upon each of these roads I threw out strong infantry pickets, the cavalry being withdrawn, and my main body was retired to the rear of the cross-road, leaving a line of skirmishers in front.[28]

During the early morning hours, Garland arrived and by daybreak his brigade was ready to take position. The line when formed, stretched from the Hagerstown road to Fox's Gap, with Garland on the extreme right, guarding the right flank and the connecting road between Turner's and Fox's Gaps. They had with them two batteries of artillery, a total of eight guns. Two Georgia regiments from Colquitt's Brigade were positioned behind stone walls on the eastern face of the mountain, flanking the turnpike. Leaving only a skeleton cavalry force to support Colquitt and Garland, Stuart proceeded to Crampton's Gap which he believed "was as much threatened as any other."[29] He felt confident that Turner's Gap was in capable hands, confident that he had done all he could to prepare for the approaching enemy, which he considered small in number and insignificant in intent. He wrote that "it was believed the enemy's [main] effort would be against McLaws, probably by the route of Crampton's Gap."[30]

By midnight, the 13th, Lee had had an opportunity to survey the situation at South Mountain from the dispatches he had received. Harpers Ferry had not fallen as he had hoped. This meant that McLaws on Maryland Heights was extremely vulnerable. For the first time since the division of the army, Lee began to feel uneasy. The mountain passes, which to this point carried little importance, now suddenly caused deep concern. A message was sent to Hill with orders for him to personally survey Turner's Gap come daybreak, and with the information that Longstreet was coming to his support. Lee also wrote Stuart that Longstreet was moving and that he expected the gap "to be held at all hazards until the operations at Harper's Ferry are finished."[31] Lee knew nothing of Stuart's side trip to Crampton's Gap, nor did Hill. Both thought he would be at Turner's Gap when they arrived. Stuart and Hill were not on the very best of terms, which may account for the failure of communications between the two. Stuart had rather free license with his maneuvering, so he offered no excuse for his failure to contact Lee on his actions.

When Hill arrived at the Mountain House "between daylight and sunrise,"[32] he found, much to his amazement, that during the night Colquitt had moved his brigade down the eastern side of the mountain and had stationed them at the base, apparently under the belief that, since no action had come, the Federals had withdrawn. Hill immediately ordered them back to their original defensive positions behind the stone walls just below the crest. This prompt action probably averted serious repercussions, for at that very moment Federal infantry and artillery were moving along the old Sharpsburg road towards the summit. Alarmed at the position his men held, and with the sudden realization that Stuart would not be there to help him, Hill made some fast decisions which obviously should have been done before. "An examination of the pass . . . satisfied me that it could only be held by a large force, and was wholly indefensible by a small one. I accordingly ordered up G .B. Anderson's Brigade. A regiment of Ripley's brigade was sent to hold another pass, Hamburg Pass, some 3 miles distant, on our left."[33] This was the 4th Georgia under Col. George Doles.[34] The remainder of Ripley's Brigade and a full brigade under Rodes were left at Boonsboro to guard the army's supply train and artillery which had been left behind. Hill was also putting some credence in Stuart's theory that the big push would come through Crampton's Gap. If this proved true, no chances could be taken by leaving Boonsboro uncovered.

Once Hill was satisfied that Colquitt was in position, he and his aide, Maj. Ratchford, rode towards Fox's Gap to observe. Before they had gone far, they heard the voices of the enemy and rumblings of their wagons. This meant that the Federals had a head start on them and might have occupied Fox's Gap. Garland was pressed into action with his five regiments of about 1000 men, nearly all of them untried soldiers, and a battery of artillery. At about nine o'clock, first contact was made and the battle of South Mountain was underway.

Hill had seen the Federal Army spread out in the valley east of the mountain:

The marching columns extended back far as eye could see in the distance; but many of the troops had already arrived and were in double lines of battle, and those advancing were taking up positions as fast as they arrived. It was a grand and glorious spectacle, and it was impossible to look at it without admiration. I had never seen so tremendous an army before, and I did not see one like it afterward. For though we confronted greater forces at Yorktown, Sharpsburg, Fredericksburg, and about Richmond under Grant, these were only partly seen, at most a corps at a time. But here four corps were in full view, one of which was on the mountain and almost within rifle-range. The sight inspired more satisfaction than discomfort; for though I knew that my little force could be brushed away as readily as the strong man can brush to one side the wasp or the hornet, I felt that General McClellan had made a mistake, and I hoped to be able to delay him until General Longstreet could come up and our trains could be extricated from their perilous position.[35]

If Hill had not realized his perilous position before, he knew it now. Longstreet was still many miles off and Stuart was some five or six miles away to the south. At full strength, he had five brigades with which to face the Army of the Potomac. "I do not remember ever to have experienced a feeling of greater *loneliness*. It seemed as though we were deserted by 'all the world and the rest of mankind.' "[36] Despite the odds against him, Hill had two advantages: McClellan's delay in moving gave him the opportunity to place at least two of his brigades into position, and although the enemy could not see him, he could see the enemy. Unless McClellan would take Governor

Curtin's message as serious intelligence, the Federal army still thought that Longstreet was with Hill. McClellan would move cautiously for he did not yet know that he outnumbered the Confederates on the mountain by four to one. In actuality, McClellan expected battle at Boonsboro and nothing more than a skirmish at Turner's pass. He would soon know how stubborn the Confederates could be.

As Franklin's men slept at Buckeystown, so did the remainder of the army. Resting in the Middletown Valley that night was the Kanawha Division of the Ninth Corps under Brig. Gen. Jacob D. Cox. Cox had moved his division across the Catoctin mountain on the National road the afternoon of the 13th as support for Pleasonton's cavalry which had been detailed for reconnaissance. Pleasonton had left early on the morning of the 13th. Cox received his orders at noon of the same day. McClellan would lead one to believe that this was the big push he was making as a result of finding the "lost dispatch," but Pleasonton departed much too early and Cox makes no mention of his movement being instigated by McClellan's find. It is clear, therefore, that those Federal troops in the Middletown Valley on the 13th were merely a part of normal operations and not the "vigorous move" McClellan claimed he made. Cox failed to explain why he stopped at Middletown or why he permitted his campfires to reveal his strength. Again, in this case as with Franklin, an educated guess would have told Cox and Pleasonton that a continued night march would have netted favorable results. With little or no effort, the Kanawha Division alone could have altered the course of the campaign as well as the war. It was not until six o'clock the following morning, September 14, that the first brigade of infantry moved toward the mountain.

In McClellan's message to Franklin on the 13th, he had spelled out his plan of action, which in essence was a good one: "My general idea is to cut the enemy in two and beat him in detail."[37] It was basically quite simple. Special Orders No. 191 told McClellan that Lee's army was divided. In order to cut it "in two" he would have to drive a wedge between the command at Boonsboro and the command at Harpers Ferry. If he moved fast enough, Colonel Miles could help him turn on McLaws, Walker, and Jackson. The main body of the army could then turn on Hill and Longstreet. McClellan had the grandest opportunity of his military career. How he squandered away precious time is a matter of military history and one of the saddest moments of the war for the Union.

Pleasonton's cavalry had left Frederick at daybreak on the morning of September 13, headed in the direction of Hagerstown on the National road. About three or four miles west of town, the Federals had their first encounter with Stuart's rear guard located near the crest of Braddock Heights. Both cavalries were dismounted and both used artillery and carbine. Pleasonton described the action as "severe" and "warm."[38] Inasmuch as Stuart regarded his job as primarily screening, his efforts were more defensive than aggressive. It was his job to judge the position and strength of the enemy. "Every means was taken to ascertain what the nature of the enemy's movement was; whether a reconnaissance feeling for our whereabouts, or an aggressive movement of the army," wrote Stuart in his report.[39] The skirmish was indeed warm for it was not until two o'clock that Stuart abandoned his position and pulled back to the east side of Middletown, there to stand another duel with Pleasonton. Again the action was spirited, but Stuart held his ground long enough to insure that Turner's Gap was protected. Before leaving Middletown, Stuart's men destroyed the small bridge over Catoctin Creek and set fire to a barn nearby as a final effort to retard the Federal advance. Pleasonton easily forded the stream and by dusk reached the base of South Mountain, "which was found to be too strong a position [Colquitt's Brigade] to be carried by my force . . . satisfied that the enemy would defend his position at Turner's Gap with a large force . . ."[40]

Behind Pleasonton came three divisions of the Ninth Corps. Camp for the night was established in fields just west of Middletown, in full view of Confederate lookouts on the mountain. While they rested, McClellan, back in Frederick, sat down to draft orders for the following day. Between 6:20 of the 13th when Franklin's orders were issued, and 1:00 A.M. of the 14th, the Army of the Potomac received their instructions. Marching orders ranged from "daylight" to 7:00 A.M. (McClellan's own report listed this schedule, thereby further denying his claim to a "rapid and vigorous forward movement.")[41] With the exception of Franklin and Cox, nearly all the army spent the night within a two-mile radius of Frederick.

At six o'clock Sunday morning, September 14, Pleasonton and one brigade (about 1500 strong) from the Ninth Corps, under the command of Col. E. P. Scammon, moved out from camp. At the village of Bolivar, a hamlet situated at the eastern base of the mountain on the main highway, the old Sharpsburg road branched to the left, taking a winding course to the crest (Fox's Gap). Scammon was ordered up with instructions to reach the right flank of the Confederates and to turn them toward Turner's Gap. Cox rode with them until he met Col. Augustus Moor of the 28th Ohio, who had been taken prisoner the day before in the action on the Catoctin range. Moor had been paroled and was returning to his regiment when Cox found him walking along the main highway. When Cox explained the plan of action to Moor, all Moor could say was "My God! Be careful."[42] With this warning, Cox alerted Col. George Crook, who had taken over the 2d Brigade following Moor's capture, and told Scammon that Crook would follow him, promising the whole division if it was needed. As Scammon started up the mountain, Cox placed his artillery into position on a knoll near Bolivar. A duel with Colquitt's guns started about 7:30 A.M.

The mountain was steep and the men moved slowly, but Cox was right along with them urging them to press forward. At about 9:00 A.M., just short of the crest, they ran head on into heavy fire from Rosser's cavalry. Dismounted, the cavalrymen were well hidden behind the thick trees and stone walls at the edge of an open field with both rifles and artillery. Scammon's men scattered and soon were returning the fire. Crook's brigade came up and closed in behind them. About this time, Garland's Brigade of North Carolinians came puffing in from Turner's Gap, the main highway, to support Rosser.

There was a road to the left, which rose to a summit overlooking open fields, and then circled to run across the crest and on to Turner's Gap. Scammon ordered the 11th Ohio and then the 23d Ohio, under Lt. Col. Rutherford B. Hayes, to move out on this road in an effort to attack the enemy both from the flank and the rear. Amidst the snarling undergrowth and dense forests, the battle raged. Bayonets were fixed, and the Ohioians and North Carolinians went at it hand to hand until finally the Confederate right gave way. Garland was mortally wounded. Immediately his command collapsed and his rookies raced to the rear and to the protection of the western slope of the mountain.

The fighting was fierce for more than an hour. "Our men fell fast, but they kept their pace," wrote Cox.[43] The Federals had the advantage now. Cox had attacked uphill, due west, had turned the Confederate line at Fox's Gap, and was now attacking due north along the crest toward the Mountain House. Hill turned with the right flank of Colquitt's Brigade, his center, using "dismounted staff officers, couriers, teamsters, and cooks," and two guns which poured a devastating fire in Cox's direction.[44] This stubborn resistance discouraged Cox from pressing any further. He held Fox's Gap, his lines running diagonally across the crest of the mountain. He chose to rest his men there in position until the remainder of the Ninth Corps arrived. It was now about eleven o'clock and for the second time since McClellan had come into possession of the "lost dispatch," a clear-cut advantage rested in the hands of the Federals and with no one to exploit it. Cox had fought hard and well for Fox's Gap and in so doing had wrecked one of Hill's brigades. From some 200 prisoners captured, he had learned that Hill had only five brigades and that three were still on their way. He learned too that Longstreet was coming in support. Hill later thought that the prisoners might have given the impression that Longstreet was just over the crest, and he attributed the lull in the battle to this bit of intelligence.[45] This meant, then, that at about 11:00 A.M., Cox was facing only one brigade, Colquitt's, and that one was on the National road and could not be spared. The Ohio boys were exhausted. The march up the mountain had drained much of their fighting spirit. They had been on the road for nearly three hours and had been in battle for at least two. Cox could do nothing without aid, and aid would not be coming for at least another three hours.

Hill could hear artillery far off in the distance and at one time wondered what action might be taking place at Crampton's Gap. But it was a fleeting thought. He was cumbered with grave responsibilities with his own command. His orders from Lee had instructed him to guard the wagon train at Boonsboro and to watch Pleasant Valley for any Federal escape from Harpers Ferry. Checking the Federal advance through Turner's Gap, in Hill's mind, had been secondary. Now the situation had reversed. He would have to pull his remaining brigades from Boonsboro and use them on the mountain. He was facing the better part of the Army of the Potomac.

Had he been so inclined, Hill should have counted his blessings.

McClellan had given him an undeserved break. Two of the remaining three divisions of the Ninth Corps had camped east of Middletown and did not move from camp until about noon on the 14th. Maj. Gen. Jesse L. Reno, who would soon meet his death, was in command. Brig. Gen. Orlando B. Willcox, commanding the 1st Division did not state in his report exactly what time he received his orders, but Brig. Gen. Samuel D. Sturgis, commanding the 2d Division, stated that "about 1 o'clock P.M. . . . my division moved . . . to the support of General Willcox . . ."[46] Reno, whose report would be sorely missed by historians, failed to explain to anyone why he delayed so long in supporting Cox's Division. General Cox had sent a courier to Reno at about 7:30 that morning with a detail of his plans. Before Cox reached the field of battle, Reno had replied that he was sending the rest of the corps.[47]

Hill could not know that Willcox and Sturgis were still so distant, but turning to his rear, he could see by the dust in the air that his three remaining brigades were on their way. Anderson was up first and immediately took position to the right. Rodes and Ripley followed. Rodes's Alabamians were pressed to the extreme left, which to this time had not been protected with any strength. This was high ground overlooking the main highway at the gap. Hill was positive that an effort would be made there. Every indication from troop movements in the valley below pointed to this. Ripley, and what could be re-formed of Garland's Brigade under Col. D. K. McRae, was sent to the right to support Anderson.

As sporadic picket firing kept the air lively during the noon hours, Willcox rode onto the field with Sturgis close behind. They reported to Cox who, as senior officer, was commanding the field. It was now about two o'clock in the afternoon. Willcox had come close to causing a serious blunder not too long before. When he reached Bolivar on the main highway at the mountain base, instead of turning left to go up the Sharpsburg road towards Fox's Gap, he turned right and was well up the rugged slopes on the old Hagerstown road when he was called back.[48] This delay was just enough time for the first of Longstreet's men to arrive from Hagerstown. The Federal army had given Hill another break.

Longstreet left Hagerstown at the crack of dawn. With him was Lee, his hands still bandaged, the right in a sling, still riding in an ambulance.[49] Behind in Hagerstown, they had left Brig. Gen. Robert Toombs's Brigade in command and the 11th Georgia of G. T. Anderson's Brigade, under Maj. F. H. Little, in charge of Longstreet's wagon train of ammunition and subsistance.[50] A small, insignificant detachment of cavalry was assigned escort duties. There had been about 125 wagons in the train to Hagerstown, but now Gen. E. P. Alexander was bringing eighty, loaded with ordnance for ready use, back to Boonsboro.[51] The corps was marched fast and hard. It was nearly 13 miles, and the most hardy soldiers would find nine hours of this kind of pace quite exhausting. It was hot and dry and the dust choked the resistance from literally hundreds. Regiments and brigades were reduced to mere fractions.[52] There was no time to deal delicately with their worn condition. Hill was waiting on the road to funnel them into position immediately. For the Confederates to adequately defend their present position, Longstreet's men must be prepared for momentary battle.

Lee had paused at Boonsboro and was watching the men pass on towards the mountain when Hood's Division came up. When the men saw Lee, they shouted, "Give us Hood." General Hood was riding at the rear of his command, still in a state of arrest following his clash with General Evans. The demonstration impressed Lee and with a tip of the hat, he said, "You shall have him, gentlemen." A few minutes later, when he encountered Hood, Lee offered to release him from arrest and return him to command if the general would express an apology for the incident. Hood, determined man that he was, flatly refused. "Well," replied Lee, "I will suspend your arrest till the impending battle is decided." With this, Hood rejoined his men amid their wild shouts and cheers.[53]

D. R. Jones's Division was the first of Longstreet's Corps to arrive at the crest. Brig. Gen. Thomas F. Drayton's Brigade, followed by Col. George T. Anderson's, was sent to the right to join Ripley. Hill personally ordered the officers to cooperate with G. B. Anderson, giving command of the three brigades to the senior officer, General Ripley. Almost at once Ripley bungled the situation by ordering an ill-timed advance before the men were properly positioned. In the process, his own brigade marched off in the wrong direction, down the mountain to the west, and failed to return until some hours after the battle was over. His brigade was of absolutely no use to Hill that day. Naturally,

Hill was perturbed. Ten years later he wrote: "I received a note from Ripley saying that he was progressing finely; so he was, to the rear of the mountain on the west side. Before he returned, the fighting was over, and his brigade did not fire a shot that day."[54]

Cox pressed the 1st Division of Gen. Wilcox into action almost immediately upon arrival. They clashed head-on with Drayton and the two Andersons, but the confusion was so great that little or nothing was accomplished. Ripley had left a hole that could not be plugged before the Federal advance penetrated. The two flanks fought vigorously, and, indeed, threatened to turn the Federal left.

The contest for the next hour and a half raged between stone wall and forest, each army keeping check on the other; Cox holding on to his precious positions on the left and center high ground, his right pressing for the last elevation between themselves and Turner's Gap. At about four o'clock, Sturgis' and Rodman's brigades arrived to support Cox; simultaneously, Hood's two brigades under Col. W. T. Wofford and Col. McIver Law came up the west side of the mountain to fall in beside Drayton. Hood went in about halfway between Turner's and Fox's Gap. By this time, General Reno had arrived and was in personal command of the east field. Furious battle raged back and forth in a seesaw manner with neither side giving or gaining any substantial ground. The Confederates had made good use of the up-and-down terrain, and between knoll-placed artillery, stone walls, and dense forests, had held off all Federal advances.

During one lull in the fighting, Reno, apparently thinking that the Confederates had retreated, rode out into the open to personally reconnoiter. Confident that the position was clear, he ordered the 51st Pennsylvania to prepare to march forward. He formed his men into position and then gave them permission to rest and have coffee. As he turned to speak to the next regiment in line, the forest came alive with devastating fire. The Pennsylvanians were scattered and Reno was instantly killed.[55] Hood's men had moved into the sector the Federals planned to take "when their coffee was finished." The confusion which followed was frightening. As the Pennsylvanians tried to pick themselves up, the 35th Massachusetts, directly behind, opened up a returning volley. Caught in the cross-fire, the astonished Pennsylvanians fumbled their way back to the lines until at last the officers had them under control and pressing forward. (These men would later redeem what they considered serious damage to their reputation by carrying the Burnside Bridge.) Overpowering lines of blue pushed through the field and to the woods, cracking the Confederate position and driving their right deeper to the Mountain House. Fighting continued through the evening and night with the Conefderate right trying in vain to turn the Federal left, and Willcox and Sturgis, essentially in the center on the National road and just to the south, struggling desperately to gain the last stronghold, Turner's Gap. By ten o'clock, the battle on this side of the mountain had spent itself. Little had been accomplished on either side since morning. The thin Confederate line held on. Fox's Gap was in Federal hands but the center was safe, at least from the south. Hill's left was another story in itself.

All morning and afternoon, the long columns of blue had filed across Catoctin Mountain and into the Middletown Valley. With them had come their commander, McClellan, who, perched atop a knoll near Bolivar, watched the men wind their way to the top of South Mountain.

Maj. Gen. Joseph Hooker, who would command this same army at Chancellorsville the following year, was now in command of the First Corps. It took all day for him to move these three giant divisions from Frederick. They had broken camp on the Monocacy River, to the south of Frederick, at daybreak, making their arrival at Middletown about one o'clock in the afternoon. It was several more hours before the 3d Division under George G. Meade, who too would command the army later, was ready for any assault on the mountain. The 1st Division under James B. Ricketts was ordered to deploy immediately to the right for support.

Under McClellan's directions, Hooker sent his corps off to the right on the old Hagerstown road to turn the Confederate left. As the battle had raged mainly on his left, McClellan now sought to squeeze Lee off the mountain by throwing a corps at him from each side. His delay in moving from Frederick and his bare knowledge of the terrain would give him little advantage, however. The Federal army was totally unfamiliar with this part of the country, least of all the back mountain roads. The slopes to the north of the main highway were rugged and steep, pierced with gorges and ravines that made marching in battle formation nearly impossible. It was particularly difficult for infantry, Hooker wrote, "even in absence of a foe in front."[56] There were no mountain climbers in the Army of the Potomac. They had not been trained for such warfare nor had the veterans scaled any mountains in the Virginia campaigns. What few veterans remained from the war with Mexico, where there was much rugged terrain, were of little help. This was one problem the boys would have to tackle by themselves.

The ascent was slow and arduous. As rough as was the terrain facing Cox, it was even then not as precipitous as that on the Federal right. The First Corps managed to form battle lines about four o'clock, but by the time they reached the main Confederate positions, the sun was setting. The whole day had been used in marching and climbing and they were exhausted. To add to their problems, the Confederates were well entrenched behind stone walls and in dense timber growth. They advanced with great determination, however, and with vast numbers were soon routing the Confederates.

Mead's division moved on the right with Hatch on the left. It was an impressive sight to Hill, who watched from above: "the sight was grand and sublime, but the elements of the pretty and the picturesque did not enter into it. Doubtless the Hebrew poet whose idea of the awe-inspiring is expressed by the phrase, 'terrible as an army with banners,' had his view of the enemy from the top of a mountain."[57] Hill could see the bluecoats for some distance as they made their advance through open fields to the base of the mountain. It was "grand and imposing . . . Hatch's division in three lines, a brigade in each . . . colors flying."[58] Doubtless, Hill reflected on what this imposing sight would soon mean to his own men, for later he wrote: "Meade was one of our most dreaded foes; he was always in deadly earnest, and he eschewed all trifling. He had under him brigade commanders, officers, and soldiers worthy of his leadership."[59]

General Hill had reason to ponder. The Army of the Potomac was spread out before him, 20,000 strong. He had been fighting all morning and afternoon against four of its best divisions. Casualties were high and hundreds had been lost as prisoners. Now approaching on his left was the entire First Corps of three divisions. And behind them, pressing for room to come into line, was the Twelfth Corps and the Fifth Corps called up from the defenses of Washington. When all his available troops were accounted for, he had fourteen brigades at the most, five of his own and nine of Longstreet's.

Rodes's Brigade of Alabamians, upon arrival at the Mountain House at about 2:00 P.M., had been sent to the left and north of the main highway to protect that flank. He had 1,200 men in five regiments which he was forced to divide to some extent because of a ravine and a high knoll to his extreme left, the key to his defense. The knoll had to be held at all costs for it commanded access, not only to his rear, but to Turner's Gap. The men were well dug in behind trees and stone walls, however, and had several hours of inactivity in which to brace themselves before the attack came.

Just as Hatch and Meade made first contact with Rodes, Longstreet came up to Hill with the remainder of Jones's Division and parts of Hood's Division. The brigades of Kemper, Garnett, Jenkins, and Evans were immediately sent to support Rodes. These men were sufferering from extreme fatigue. Someone at Boonsboro had gotten their orders and directions mixed and sent Garnett, Kemper, and Jenkins to the south of the turnpike. By the time they had found out where they were supposed to report, they had traversed over miles of back lanes and plowed fields and it was dusk, much too late to be of any substantial use. Garnett reported many stragglers, men who had managed the march from Hagerstown, but who, because of sheer exhaustion, could not make it up the mountain.[60]

Rodes's Brigade faced the greatest hazard on South Mountain that day. He held one of the key Confederate positions against two full Corps. The odds were overwhelming, but few units of the war fought with such bravery and determination. The Federal advance was slow and steady, outflanking Rodes "on either side by at least half a mile."[61] In setting up his defensive position, Rodes had deployed and dispersed over the eastern face of the mountain. The first skirmish lines had gone as far as the base.

Brig. Gen. Truman Seymour, commanding the 1st Brigade of Meade's 3d Division, reported to his commander that he thought he could take the knoll to his right. If so, he could swing into the left and sweep the Confederates off the crest. Meade consented, and Seymour moved off on a narrow road which ran about one quarter-mile to the north (the old Hagerstown road) and then swung to the west and up. Rodes was waiting for him with Col. John B. Gordon's 6th Alabama, a regiment which received highest praise from Rodes as one "handled in a manner I have never heard or seen equaled during this war."[62] It would display its splendid spirit again at Antietam in the Sunken Road.

While Gordon gallantly held off Seymour, Hatch's division, supported by Ricketts moved on Rodes's right. It was Hatch's job to move up both sides of the ravine that divided the mountain and that had separated Rodes's Brigade. It was a sticky problem for the 1st Division. It was some time before any definitive battle formation could be arranged, but once confusing orders were translated and a lost brigade pulled into line, the division moved steadily forward. While placing his men into position, Brig. Gen. M. R. Patrick, commander of the 3d Brigade, rode out in front to reconnoiter. Rodes's men saw him and opened fire, thus revealing their positions. With this, the Federals moved forward.

The blue lines moved steadily "under a most galling fire from the enemy above us, posted behind the trees and among the rocks," wrote Patrick.[63] About thirty paces from the top of the mountain, there was a cornfield fence, which the 80th New York spied about the time the Alabamians made a dash for it. The firing was at extremely close range and as deadly as any that day. General Hatch was out in front, directing his brigades, when a Confederate shot sent him to the rear, wounded. Brig. Gen. Abner Doubleday took over. The fence was theirs, but Rodes continued his relentless firing from the trees at the crest. Doubleday writes: "At last I ordered the troops to cease firing, lie down behind the fence, allowed the enemy to charge to within about 15 paces, apparently under the impression that we had given way. Then, at a word, my men sprang to their feet and poured in a deadly volley, from which the enemy fled in disorder, leaving their dead within 30 feet of our line."[64]

Realizing that his right was finished, Rodes concentrated all his available forces on his left with a last ditch stand to prevent Seymour from taking the heights. The Confederates fought fiercely under heavy pressure from their left and center but valiantly held the hill until it was too dark to distinguish anything at close range. As darkness fell, both sides ceased their firing. The crest of the mountain belonged to the Federals. They had taken their left, Fox's Gap, and they had the right, the old Hagerstown road, but they did not have Turner's Gap, the main thoroughfare across the mountain.

Not all of the action at South Mountain took place around Turner's Gap. Six miles to the south was another important passageway, perhaps the most important in terms of McClellan's objective which was to arrest the collapse of Harpers Ferry. Crampton's Gap led to Pleasant Valley, which lay between Elk Ridge and the South Mountain range. (Elk Ridge was the northern end of Maryland Heights.) Once access had been gained to the valley, it was McClellan's hope that Franklin with his Sixth Corps, and a division under Maj. Gen. Darius N. Couch, would "cut off the retreat of, or destroy, McLaws's command," which was employed on Maryland Heights in the joint effort of Jackson to take Harpers Ferry.

When McLaws had crossed the South Mountain range, he left two brigades under Brig. Gen. Paul Semmes and Brig. Gen. William Mahone at Brownsville Gap to defend the rear of his Maryland Heights operation. One battery from Semmes's artillery, and three regiments from Mahone's Brigade, were sent north to Crampton's Gap. Stuart had already posted cavalry under Col. Thomas T. Munford to defend the gap, and upon reporting the accessibility of the pass to McLaws, Howell Cobb's Brigade was sent back as additional reinforcements.

Munford utilized his small force to good advantage. Advance infantry was placed at the base of the mountain behind a stone wall while troops lined both sides of the only road leading to the top. Two batteries of artillery were positioned about halfway down the steep mountain side. The Confederates were well entrenched with the advantage of being able to see the enemy long before they arrived. As would soon be obvious, only larger numbers could dislodge them. One Confederate soldier pondered over the odds:

We had only three companies of infantry, one brigade of cavalry, and six pieces of artillery to defend the pass against at least two, perhaps three, divisions of Yankee infantry, with accompanying artillery and a big bunch of cavalry. The whole country seemed to be full of bluecoats. They were so numerous that it looked as if they were creeping up out of the ground— and what would or could our little force of some three or four hundred available men standing half-way up a bushy, stony mountainside do with such a mighty host?[65]

Franklin came upon the Confederate wall at about noon. The Sixth Corps had been marching since daybreak with one delay—when General Couch brought his men into co-ordinated marching position. Once the army reached Burkittsville, about one and one-half miles to the southeast of the pass, the Confederate artillery opened fire. Slocum's division was ordered into position with three brigades—Torbert on the left, Newton in the center, and Bartlett on the right. Why there was a delay of nearly three hours before the Federal line began to move forward is not explained by Franklin but, according to reports, it was 3:00 P.M. before the initial attack was made.[66] With artillery support from batteries located east of Burkittsville, the Federals advanced slowly and steadily. First the stone wall, and then the skirmish lines on each side of the road fell under overwhelming fire. The Confederates had little opportunity to make a stand under the odds, but they held the Federals back three hours before being forced to break and retreat. There was considerable confusion as the remnants of Mahone's Brigade fled to Brownsville (in the valley) and Munford's cavalry to Rohrersville. They left behind nearly 400 prisoners and several hundred pieces of valuable equipment.

McLaws had been warned by Stuart, as had Hill, that the Federals were approaching their respective positions. Hill had only two brigades at Turner's Gap at the outset. McLaws had even less to protect his rear at Crampton's Gap. Crampton's Gap was now penetrated. Franklin had accomplished the first phase of his orders, but, like McClellan, he too, was overly cautious. Although he was keeping schedule and obeying orders, once he reached this point, he came to a complete standstill. How Franklin had accomplished the breakthrough is rather amusingly described by a Confederate who witnessed the Crampton's Gap action:

To observe the caution with which the Yankees, with their vastly superior numbers, approached the mountain put one very much in mind of a lion, king of the forest, making exceedingly careful preparations to spring on a plucky little mouse. For we had only about three hundred men actually engaged, and they were mostly cavalry, which is of very little use in defending a mountain pass.

As usual, correspondents of Northern newspapers will say that a little band of heroic Union patriots gallantly cleaned out Crampton's Gap, defended by an overwhelming force of Rebels strongly posted and standing so thick that they had to crawl over each other to get away.[67]

The retreating Confederates had formed a defensive line of battle a little further down the valley. Franklin sent out feelers and came to the conclusion that the Confederate position was strong and that he was "outnumbered two to one."[68] His 18,000 against only a few brigades left McLaws' back door wide open. Whether or not Franklin really believed he was outnumbered is immaterial. The point of the matter is that he missed the last possible opportunity to save Harpers Ferry by not following through with his attack. Instead, he remained where he had stopped on the night of the 14th, until the 17th when he joined McClellan at Sharpsburg.

By late in the evening on September 14, the battle for South Mountain and its three passes was over. A gallant band of some 18,000 Confederates, less than half of Lee's Army of Northern Virginia, had suffered heavy losses against overwhelming odds. McClellan would boast of a great and glorious victory. True, the Confederates retreated and the battle left Lee in a perilous position, making him cancel all his plans for advancing into Pennsylvania and, ultimately, to Washington. But McClellan had thrown away the greatest opportunity of his lifetime. The physical disadvantages of one army counterbalanced the command inadequacies of the other. McClellan had known the complete Confederate plans. By moving too late and too slowly, he had afforded Lee an unrequested, but badly needed compensation for the "lost dispatch." Lee had gained an additional twenty-four hours— twenty-four more hours for Jackson to complete his Harpers Ferry operations and join the main army. Without this advantage, Lee would undoubtedly have been forced to immediately withdraw into Virginia, and the battle at Sharpsburg would never have been fought. McClellan had failed to see the weak link in Lee's defenses—Crampton's Gap. By sending the bulk of his army against Hill at Turner's Gap instead of against the one brigade of infantry and some scattered cavalry at Crampton's, he had virtually tossed away the campaign.

That morning, services were held in the little German Brethern Church at Sharpsburg, Maryland. It was a peaceful Sunday, and this was a peaceful congregation—their religion forbid them to take up arms. Following the sermon, the men, women, and children, dressed in the simple garb that was indicative of their faith, journeyed to the Samuel Mumma farm, a short distance away, for dinner. From there they could see the black smoke of battle and hear the roar of cannons rising above South Mountain. By Wednesday evening of that week, their church would be wrecked by war and filled with the bodies of gallant soldiers—both blue and gray. By Wednesday evening, Mr. Mumma's beautiful farm would be a heap of ashes.

7

"Harper's Ferry Is To Be Surrendered"

A heavy mist hung over the crest of South Mountain on that Sunday night in September as Robert E. Lee, James Longstreet, Daniel Harvey Hill, and John B. Hood met near Boonsboro to consider the next day's plans. Since Lee could not ride to the Mountain House, his generals came to him. Their mood was one of concern. All hope for a successful campaign seemed to be quickly vanishing. Although they had protected their supply wagons at Boonsboro and had delayed the Army of the Potomac another day, they had paid dearly for it. There was little doubt in their minds that they could hold out another twenty-four hours. No one recorded the conversation that night, but it seems certain that Lee ordered the withdrawal from South Mountain with combined relief and disappointment. He still had no word from Jackson at Harpers Ferry and McLaws' safety was somewhat in doubt. Aside from the one brigade Longstreet had left in Hagerstown, there were no available reinforcements to hold off McClellan. To expect Hill to repeat his performance was out of the question and to reconcentrate his army overnight was impossible. The men must be retired from the field. Lee calmly told his aides to relay the withdrawal orders. It must be done immediately. There would be no time to bury the dead.

Quickly and quietly the individual regiments gathered their equipment and made their way down the western slope of the mountain. The general movement began about 11 o'clock and continued throughout the night. From the viewpoint of the tactician, it was a masterpiece of quiet, skillful, undetected, disengagement. It was not without its prob-

186

lems, however. Though much credit is given Longstreet and Hill for an orderly withdrawal, and the rumors of a demoralized rout were later denied, there is some evidence that the march that night left much to be desired. It is not surprising to find that many companies and regiments were broken and scattered. Actually there was great straggling after South Mountain and it took "sharp play with the flats of our swords on the backs of these fellows" to keep them in line, wrote Moxley Sorrel of Longstreet's staff. "We had a bad night on the mountain extracting D. H. Hill."[1]

The western side of the mountain was littered with Confederate stragglers as late as the Federal pursual the next day, some openly admitting their desire to be captured. One officer pounded on the door of a farm house seeking information that might lead him to his company. "We have been badly whipped," he said, "and I don't know where a single man can be found."[2]

On the other side of the mountain it was a different story. David L. Thompson of the 9th New York walked over the quiet battlefield that night and recorded a grim epitaph to the Confederate defenders:

All around lay the . . . dead—undersized men mostly . . . with sallow, hatchet faces, and clad in "butternut"—a color running all the way from a deep, coffee brown up to the whitish brown of ordinary dust. As I looked down on the poor, pinched faces, worn with marching and scant fare, all enmity died out. There was no "secession" in those rigid forms, nor in those fixed eyes staring blankly at the sky. Clearly it was not "their war." Some of our men primed their muskets afresh with the finer powder from the cartridge-boxes of the dead. With this exception, each remained untouched as he had fallen. Darkness came on rapidly, and it grew very chilly. As little could be done at that hour in the way of burial, we unrolled the blankets of the dead, spread them over the bodies, and then sat down in line, munching a little on our cooked rations in lieu of supper, and listening to the firing, which was kept up on the right, persistently.[3]

"The command rested on their arms during the night," wrote General Meade. "The ammunition train was brought up and the men's cartridge-boxes were filled, and every preparation made to renew the contest at daylight the next morning should the enemy be in force."[4] "Drawing our blankets over us," Thompson wrote, "we went to sleep, lying upon our arms in line as we had stood, living Yankee and dead Confederate side by side, and undistinguishable."[5]

The scene the next morning was a horrible one. Trees were "shrivered," broken and twisted into grotesque shapes as if the battle had left a ghastly monument to the dead. Ragged, dirty bodies were strewn over the ground, some in groups indicating a fierce stand for one vantage point. One New Hampshire lad was astounded to find eighteen bodies piled on top of each other like a cord of wood. Another saw forty corpses lined behind about five rods of stone wall, their faces blackened in death, their feet bare, brown as the earth and calloused as hard. "I have seen all of war I ever wish to," wrote a recruit of about four weeks. "The thing is indescribable."[6]

Confederate stragglers roamed the fields around South Mountain throughout the night and morning; some searching for their companies, some searching for the enemy to give themselves up, others looking for the quickest and easiest way back to the Potomac and safety in Virginia. A search party from the 21st Massachusetts was quite surprised to find a half-dozen Rebel survivors who had "21st Mass." painted on their knapsacks. They had been picked up at Manassas only a few weeks before where the Northern boys had left them in a hurried withdrawal.[7]

In the ensuing friendly conversation between victor and captive, the Confederates were asked how their food was. "We have plenty of rations," replied one of the prisoners. Upon investigation it was found that their knapsacks yielded "less than a dozen dirty little balls of corn meal, covered with the ashes in which they had been baked. The rebels hung their heads at the exposure of their scanty fare."[8]

Burial of the dead presented a problem in several ways. Many of the dead had fallen into deep crevices between boulders.[9] It was a difficult job, besides being an unsavory one. When there was not room or time, the details balked. One group of Ohio troops was assigned a rather large "portion of rebel dead." Seeing a deep well on the Wise farm at Fox's Gap, they began tossing the bodies in. The ground was too hard to dig anyway; this was the easy way out, but Mr. Wise caught them in the act. Stuck with the uncompleted work, Wise made a deal with General Burnside to bury the remainder for one dollar a piece. As long as the well was already spoiled, he might as well finish the job. Fifty-eight more bodies were dumped in, filling the hole to capacity. Wise, however, did not do such a good job either, for a few weeks later the Sanitary Commission spotted "a man's hand projecting through the sunken earth, with which it had been covered."[10]

While burial crews made their way over the field, checking both blue and gray, McClellan's headquarters was busier than it had been for days. The men on the front lines reported no answer to their scattered fire. Advance pickets sent out raced back with the news that the Rebels had retreated during the night. The only sign of gray uniforms was the hundreds of dead and dying that covered the mountain top. McClellan was ecstatic. The victory was his. At sunup, Pleasonton's cavalry was ordered out in pursuit. His job was to overtake Lee's rear and harass until Federal infantry could be deployed.

After the necessary instructions were issued, McClellan sat down to transcribe the good news for Washington. His dispatches were many and each was filled with typical enthusiasm and exaggeration. To Halleck he wrote that the Confederate army was in "perfect panic" and "demoralized." "General Lee is reported wounded and . . . gives his loss as 15,000. . . . Lee last night stated publicly that he must admit they had been shockingly whipped."[11] (Northern newspapers, in an effort to minimize the damage to the Federal army, reported that Hill and Longstreet were both dead.)[12] McClellan even took time to send a message to the old man who had given him his job over a year before, retired General Winfield Scott:

We attacked a large force of the enemy yesterday, occupying a strong mountain pass . . . Our troops, old and new regiments, behaved most valiantly and gained a signal victory. R. E. Lee in command. The rebels routed, and retreating in disorder this morning. We are pursuing closely and taking many prisoners.[13]

Scott replied: "Bravo, my dear general! Twice more and it's done."[14]

Lincoln, who had been keeping in close contact with the War Department, was prompt in his congratulatory wire. Filled with hope for the future and compassion for his army, Lincoln wrote: "God bless you, and all with you. Destroy the rebel army, if possible."[15] Within 15 minutes the President had telegraphed the jubilant news to his friend, J. K. Dubois in Springfield, Illinois: "I now consider it safe to say that Gen. McClellan has gained a great victory over the great rebel army in Maryland between Fredericktown and Hagerstown. He is now pursuing the flying foe."[16]

Lincoln had appraised the messages from McClellan and felt justified in calling it a great victory. Had not the general stated that the Confederate army was in a "demoralized condition" and that Lee had openly admitted defeat? The President had taken McClellan at his word, accepted his reports as valid, and rejoiced with him. No one knows if Lincoln suppressed inward fears of what McClellan might or might not do next, or, indeed, of what interpretations should be given to the reports just received. Only one clue bears his anxiety— "Destroy the rebel army, *if possible*." The next day he would write Governor Curtin: "What do you hear from Gen. McClellan's army? We have nothing from him today."[17]

Gideon Welles, Lincoln's close friend, was not so quick to accept McClellan's "victory." His quite frank statements recorded in his diary under September 15 might well have reflected Lincoln's innermost thoughts:

Some rumors yesterday and more direct information to-day are cheering to the Union cause. McClellan telegraphs a victory, defeat of the enemy with loss of 15,000 men, and that "General Lee admits they are badly whipped." To whom Lee made this admission so that it should be brought straight to McC. and telegraphed here does not appear. A tale like this from Pope would have been classed as one of his fictions. It may be all true, coming from McClellan, but I do not credit Lee's confession or admission. That we have had a fight and beaten the Rebels, I can believe. It could scarcely have been otherwise. I am afraid it is not as decisive as it should be, and as is the current belief, but shall rejoice if McC. has actually overtaken the Rebels, which is not yet altogether clear.[18]

While McClellan mapped his next strategy, Lee and his army made their way through the streets of Boonsboro and Keedysville toward Sharpsburg. As early as the evening of the 13th, the night before South Mountain, Lee had selected Sharpsburg as a rendezvous point for the separated segments of the army. He had ordered McLaws to move to Sharpsburg immediately upon the completion of his mission at Harpers Ferry. Again the next morning, after urging McLaws to push his operations to a rapid conclusion, Lee directed him to Sharpsburg.[19] At these early hours, Lee's chief concern was to see that McLaws' command of two divisions should extricate itself from Maryland Heights and move north on a road that would prevent interception by any direct Federal push into Pleasant Valley.

As the hours went by, however, Sharpsburg took on a new significance to Lee. The village, established in the early 1760's and probably the oldest in Washington County, was about one mile from the nearest river fording point, Blackford's or Boteler's Ford. Aside from protecting McLaws' withdrawal route and assembling his divided army on the Maryland side of the river, Lee had chosen the Sharpsburg area as a potential or practical escape route back to Virginia. At this particular moment, Lee was quite seriously considering crossing the river without giving battle to McClellan. At 8:00 P.M. on the night of the 14th, as the battle at South Mountain was reaching its climax, Lee ordered McLaws to retire immediately and make his way to the nearest ford, stating that "the day has gone against us . . . this army [referring to Hill and Longstreet] will go by Sharpsburg and cross the river."[20] To further clarify his intentions, Lee directed McLaws to use any ford but the one at Shepherdstown, which at that time, was assumed to be suitable for crossing. This was being reserved for the South Mountain army. Lee also instructed Jackson to "take position at Shepherdstown to cover [the] crossing into Virginia."[21] He had not told anyone but McLaws and Jackson, aside from a few of his own staff, what he actually proposed to do, so the decision was never developed into a major issue. His report to President Davis carefully avoided mention of a considered withdrawal. But while Lee was writing the messages to his Harpers Ferry army, Jackson was preparing a message of his own.[22] It would give Lee cause to give second thoughts on immediate withdrawal.

The long Confederate line made its way down the mountain through the darkness. There was no moon. Hill's Division was first; Longstreet followed. When they reached Boonsboro, they turned to the left on the road to Sharpsburg. At this intersection Fitzhugh Lee, General Lee's nephew, met them with his brigade of cavalry. He had been ordered by Stuart to cover the withdrawal and he would do it well.

In the haste and excitement of the withdrawal, Ripley and Hill both forgot the regiment they had sent to Hamburg Pass. The 4th Georgia had been sent three miles north of Turner's Gap that morning and had remained at that "obscure pass" all day "without molestation." The

Federals did not know they were there and if it had not been for thoughtful Colonel William DeRosset of the 3d North Carolina, they might well have been cut off from the rest of the army. DeRosset discovered their absence in the nick of time and sent a courier off to notify them. It was not a moment too soon. Another ten minutes and they would have been lost. Just as they reached Boonsboro on a side road, the enemy was coming in on another.[23]

While the battlefield at South Mountain was being evacuated, one of the most daring and exciting events of the entire campaign was taking place some twenty miles away. Gen. Robert Toombs, left in Hagerstown that morning when Longstreet moved his corps towards Boonsboro, had been in travel-readiness since the night before. There was little to do that day but put out the usual watches and stand on the alert should an order come from Longstreet or the enemy make itself known. At 10:00 P.M. on Sunday evening, orders came to join the main army at Sharpsburg. Assuming that Toombs was correct in reporting the time, this would tend to pinpoint, within reason, a time for the command decision to quit the mountain. Toombs left immediately with his four regiments, the 2d, 15th, 17th and 20th Georgia.[24] Major Little's 11th Georgia, which had been detached from G. T. Anderson's Brigade to escort the reserve supply wagons, moved to Funkstown where it was due to pick up Hill's wagons coming up from Boonsboro.[25] Lee had directed that these wagon trains be sent to Williamsport, "with a view to its safety, and, if necessary, to its crossing the river."[26] At about the same time he was directing General Alexander to take his train of eighty ammunition wagons to Williamsport, cross the river at that point and then double back to Shepherdstown where he was to park them.[27] The significance of this abandonment of Hagerstown as a launching terminal for an invasion of Pennsylvania and the escorting of his wagons to the Virginia side of the Potomac will be seen later in the light of other similar movements.

The 11th Georgia split up among the wagons, a right wing under a Captain Mitchell towards the front, the left under Little to the rear.[28] The 1st Virginia Cavalry rode to the rear, "that being the only direction from which an attack was apprehended."[29] This rear echelon has been called only a "guard" in Confederate reports. Since Toombs received his orders at 10:00 P.M. and marched "immediately," in all probability the wagons were on their way by midnight. The 11th

Georgia historian states that the rear guard was in motion before day-light.[30] There was no moon that night, only starlight, so the trip to Williamsport would be painfully slow and tiresome.

As the procession approached Williamsport in the gray of the dawn, the men nodding occasionally, the rattling of wheels signaling their advance, a cavalry officer appeared from the dark. The man spoke in a thick southern accent, ordering the lead wagon to halt. The teamster stopped, assuming that there was a roadblock of some kind ahead. Successively, each wagon behind brought their horses and mules to a standstill. It was a chance for a few minutes of dozing. No one expressed any apprehensions except the officer in charge of the cavalry detail. He rode ahead to see what was wrong.[31]

Col. Benjamin F. Davis was giving orders to Capt. William Frisbie of the 8th New York Cavalry to take the wagons on to the Greencastle road when the Confederate officer rode up. Sensing something amiss, he asked the lead teamster why he had stopped. "The woods are full of Yanks," he replied. "By what authority have you stopped this train?" the Confederate asked Frisbie. "By the authority of an officer of the United States Army," said Frisbie with his hand on his revolver. Realizing he was surrounded, the officer surrendered quietly and the wagons rolled into line on the Greencastle Pike. Each wagon followed with no questions asked. So quiet and smooth was the operation that the cavalry did not know what had happened until their turn to pass through the check-point. Davis's southern accent and the advantage of the morning grayness completely fooled the Confederates into think-ing their route was detoured to a more convenient river crossing. "A change of governments was probably never more quietly or speedily effected," wrote William Luff of the 12th Illinois.[32] But not all the wagons were taken. Apparently Davis was interested only in the am-munition supplies.

Frisbie was to lead the train across the Pennsylvania border into Greencastle some 12 miles away. He was told to proceed at the rate of eight miles an hour, considerably faster than normal. The average rate of wagon travel was four miles at the most. The young New York captain had a tough assignment, and to make matters worse, he had not the faintest idea where Greencastle was or how to get there. "Find it and be off, without delay," Davis told him. Fortunately Frisbie found a Marylander who knew the way and the train was off.[33]

Many of the teamsters rode along in total ignorance of their capture until it was light enough to see the uniforms of the cavalry that was now escorting. When they asked the Federals what units they were from, they soon learned that they were not in good hands. One teamster turned to Henry Norton of the 8th New York in the early light of the dawn and said, "To what regiment do you belong?" "The Eighth New York," replied Norton. "The hell, you say!" said the Confederate.[34] Several drivers deliberately ditched their wagons though they had been given orders to keep in line or be shot. As a result, at least five wagons were burned to prevent their falling back into Confederate hands.[35] The men were mad and made other attempts to stop the train. Davis assigned guards with cocked revolvers to each wagon.[36] And he had other problems to contend with. As the wagons moved towards the Pennsylvania border, the Confederate cavalry, which had gotten away after their first alarm, returned with reinforcements, including some artillery. The 12th Illinois was kept busy holding them off until the last wagon was over the line.[37]

When Captain Mitchell, who had the right wing of the 11th Georgia, learned what was happening, he consulted with his officers and decided the best thing to do would be to break off the train as quietly as possible. He did and linked up with Major Little later on in the morning. According to the regimental historian, "the Federals meditated nothing more than a passing notice."[38]

Davis did not know that he had barely missed Alexander's eighty wagons loaded with ammunition which probably crossed his path within an hour or so of the big capture, nor did he know that he came close to encountering Lee's reserve artillery also headed for the Williamsport crossing. At sunrise that morning, Brig. Gen. William N. Pendleton, commanding Lee's reserve artillery, reached the intersection of the Hagerstown-Sharpsburg Pike and the Boonsboro-Williamsport road. Here he received "reliable intelligence" that a large Federal cavalry force was just ahead. Positioning his guns out to the front and all the flanks, he sent a patrol forward to investigate. The road was clear for two miles, they reported. Pendleton sent for some of Toombs's men to come back to support him and then, proceeding cautiously, he moved on to Williamsport and then to Shepherdstown with Alexander's ammunition train. "We thus narrowly missed a rather strange encounter," wrote Pendleton.[39] Toombs sent his 15th and 17th Georgia back towards Williamsport where they joined with the 11th regiment to see the remainder of the wagons safely across the Potomac.[40]

Meanwhile, Davis was pushing on to Greencastle. Sometime between nine and ten o'clock on the morning of the 15th, the cumbersome wagon train with its weary cavalry escort pulled into town. Immediately the telegraph operator at the railroad station got a message off to Governor Curtin. It was a short message, but full of the kind of information Curtin liked to fire off to Washington. Davis had arrived with 1,300 cavalry, forty wagons from "Longstreet's ordnance train," and forty prisoners. The cavalry commander was passing along some reliable intelligence that Washington might be interested in. "Colonel Davis says he thinks Colonel Miles will surrender this morning."[41] Colonel Voss, who was over-all commander of the cavalry at Harpers Ferry, also had a few words to say. He sent a telegram to General Wool in Baltimore stating that they had captured "over 60 wagons" and "675 prisoners."[42] Herein lies one of the mysteries of this spectacular operation.

Davis reported forty prisoners, a figure which corresponds with the number of wagons captured. Presumably, these would be the teamsters or drivers. On the other hand, Colonel Voss names 675 prisoners. Both reports were dated at the same time and from the same place. Other than the Confederate cavalry, which had gotten away, the only escort the wagon train had was the 11th Georgia. Neither the 11th Georgia, or any other Confederate unit, reports a loss of that many men during the campaign other than battlefield casualities. To make the situation even more complex, Major Little, who commanded the 11th, reports no loss of prisoners at all. As a matter of fact, he does not even discuss the wagon train incident with the exception to say that the "left wing" of his regiment, under the command of a "Capt. John W. Stokes," had been detailed to guard "D. H. Hill's commissary train" at Martinsburg.[43] From the rather sketchy reports available, it must be assumed that Hill's wagons got through the Williamsport crossing without incident and that Little's men were detailed for guard duty at that point. On the night of September 16, Little was on the south side of the river at Shepherdstown with his "right wing," only 140 men out of his regiment, the left being detained in Martinsburg by the provost marshal.[44]

Lee and Longstreet barely mention the capture of the wagon train in their reports. Longstreet fails to acknowledge it as being a part of his corps. Even Federal reports, strangely enough, seem to play the incident down. With the exception of a message from McClellan to General Halleck, dated September 23, recommending Capt. B. F. Davis for promotion to " brevet major" for "conspicuous conduct in the management of the withdrawal of the cavalry from Harper's Ferry,"[45] little credit is given for one of the more spectacular cavalry deeds of the war. But Davis had a right to be proud of his men and their achievement. They had traveled over fifty miles in a little more than 12 hours and had come through some narrow scrapes with the enemy. The loss of the Confederate wagons had little consequence on the battle but they did not need to know that. Davis now had possession of forty wagons loaded with everything from chains to horseshoes.[46] To him it was just that much less scrap iron to be shot at their comrades. He had escaped from the Harpers Ferry death trap against the advice and better judgement of the commander and in the process had lost only 178 men, many of whom eventually caught up in time for the battle on the 17th.[47] If nothing more, they had earned comment from Confederate General Longstreet ("The command seems to have exercised more than usual discretion and courage.")[48] and the title "Harper's Ferry Skedaddlers," which they carried through the war.[49]

When Lee decided on September 9 to divide his army in order to take the Federal garrison at Harpers Ferry, he made the second of three fateful decisions in the Maryland campaign. His third came on the 15th when the decision to fight at Sharpsburg was made. Longstreet had been opposed to the plan. He had objected to the Harpers Ferry diversion and now that Jackson was running late and South Mountain had resulted in defeat, he supported an early and complete withdrawal from Maryland. Jackson, on the other hand, delighted with the way things had gone at Harpers Ferry, was in favor of taking the stand. After the battle he would tell Lee "it was better to have fought the battle than to have left . . . without a struggle."[50]

The decision was a bold one. "So bold and so hazardous," wrote John C. Ropes, one of the leading military writers in the 1890's, "that one is bewildered that he should even have thought seriously of making it."[51] The odds were very much against Lee. He had, just the day before, withdrawn from a battlefield the loser. D. H. Hill and Longstreet had been outnumbered and the main artery or mountain pass which they had held was now in the hands of the enemy. A second pass also had fallen to McClellan. The Federal commander, victorious and refreshed by the accomplishments of his men, would have every reason to move on with new speed and vigor. Delaying the Federal army one more day was a possibility, but battle was sure to come by Tuesday, the 16th. At that time Lee saw no chance of McLaws, Walker, and Jackson returning to Sharpsburg soon enough to support him.

Though the defensive nature of the fields of Antietam had merits, the remnants of the Army of Northern Virginia literally had its back to the wall. Should the impending battle bring defeat, there was only one retreat route; one river ford that was usable. The speculation of a rout — the prisoners, the loss of lives — was a grim thought. It would surely be catastrophic. Why then did Lee risk the future of the Confederacy; the future of his beloved Virginia? The fervent hopes of foreign intervention were, most assuredly, on his mind. But such thoughts were remote in view of more immediate probabilities. Lee was in Maryland. He had committed himself to this campaign by merely crossing the Potomac River. The division of his army and the subsequent discovery by McClellan further committed Lee to battle. The victory would, of necessity, have to be a decisive one. Failure to offer battle to McClellan would be open admission that the entire campaign was based on faulty strategy. This Lee could not afford to do.

Though the invasion of Maryland carried with it certain obligations, there is no reason to believe that the honor and prestige of protecting the Confederacy's name before the people of this state motivated Lee's decision to stand at Sharpsburg. The situation had gone far beyond a matter of losing face. Lee would fight at Sharpsburg for a good, sound "Lee" reason. He honestly believed that he could beat McClellan.

Lee continued to entertain thoughts that the Army of the Potomac was in a "demoralized" condition. His underestimation of its "recovery power" was his greatest mistake. Neither the Seven Days Battle nor Second Manassas offered any substantial proof that the Federal army was incapable of fighting. Ropes states that Lee was "unable to discriminate between successes obtained against poor troops, and successes obtained against good troops — poorly led."[52] It would seem too that Lee was unable to discriminate between the human limit of his own army and the spirit with which his men fought. This combined miscalculation would spell the end to the Maryland Campaign.

Lee's effective strength on the morning of September 15 was 14 of 39 brigades, the remaining 25 still at Harpers Ferry, or a total of about 9,262 infantry, plus cavalry and artillery. On the morning of the 17th, his effective strength would be about 35,255.[53] McClellan had a total of 87,164[54] on both dates, odds of better than two to one, meaning that should he choose to attack on either the 15th or 16th, Lee would be overpowered by sheer force.

The condition of both men and equipment in the two armies was by no means a matter of small consequence. Lee's men were ragged and battle weary. Their diet had been low in quantity and quality and their arms were inferior, all of which compounded the problems facing the general. On the other hand, the Army of the Potomac had gained a new spirit with McClellan at the helm. There were fresh troops and plenty of reserves, and their equipment was superior. Each of these important considerations were on Lee's mind when he made his decision to stand at Sharpsburg, but it is not likely that any one can be called a deciding factor. London, England, was far away and whatever action might come from Palmerston and Russell certainly would not arrive the day after the battle. The condition of the Federal army was really immaterial at this point. Lee had fought it before when he was outnumbered. Certainly Lee would not have fought for prestige alone. Too much risk would be involved for such an empty prize. He would not fight for any of these reasons individually, but would fight for them collectively. The day before at South Mountain, he had lost the initiative. He would try once more to gain it back. With so much at stake, he must take this chance.

Of those factors that influenced Lee's decision to stay in Maryland and fight, the terrain surrounding the small village of Sharpsburg was of prime consideration. In every respect, it afforded Lee the defensive elements he wanted and needed — the Antietam Creek, which would provide a natural barrier between the two armies; a long ridge of land running north and south, paralleling the Antietam; the Potomac River and Virginia to his rear. A road leading to Sharpsburg ran directly from the base of Maryland Heights. Blackford's Ford connected conveniently with a road from Harpers Ferry.

The Potomac River, after running an eastward course from the western Maryland counties to Williamsport, turns and goes through a series of erratic loops and curves to the south until it reaches Harpers Ferry, where its course again turns east. Antietam Creek, stemming from the Pennsylvania border, flows to the south and empties into the Potomac about three miles south of Shepherdstown. In the southern apex of this peculiar triangle of land lying between creek and river is Sharpsburg. Striking a base line east from the Potomac near Mercerville, Maryland to the Antietam, a distance of three and one-half miles, gives the approximate area of land on which Lee would fight. From the middle of the base to the town runs the Sharpsburg ridge carrying the Hagerstown Pike.

The countryside around Sharpsburg, Maryland was peaceful, inhabited by prosperous farmers, good, religious people, who knew nothing of war, but who would rise to the occasion and bind the wounds of both Confederate and Federal. These were the fields that Lee had chosen. They would soon be drenched in blood.

Then, Lee received Jackson's message. "Success to-morrow," it said. He could count on Jackson to change the whole outlook of things at the last moment. Apprehensions began to subside; not altogether, but enough to cause reconsideration of his withdrawal plans.

At daybreak when it was discovered that the Confederates had evacuated Turner's Gap, the Federal pursuit was organized. Pleasonton's cavalry led the columns of infantry, the corps of Sumner, Hooker, and Mansfield. South Mountain inhabitants had informed McClellan's headquarters that Lee's army was "disordered" and "retreating in the greatest haste." "There was such a concurrence of testimony on this point," wrote McClellan, "that there seemed no doubt as to the fact."[55] So McClellan readily believed the story and finally made the rapid movement he had written so much about.

Fitzhugh Lee had set up his artillery at the east end of Boonsboro and then had ridden his cavalry on to the base of the mountain. As the blue infantry slowly approached in the morning light, Lee edged back toward the town, engaging the enemy with small fire as he did, until his big guns were uncovered. When the columns were within range, his artillery opened fire. The Federal lines halted. Again they moved and again Lee fired. It was a holding action. The Confederates were in no position nor did they have the strength to fight a full-scale skirmish. This soon became apparent as the Federal lines spread to the left and right and threatened to outflank them. Quickly Lee gathered his guns and withdrew toward the town. As he did, the center of the Federal line broke to let through a dashing cavalry charge. Lee called up his 3rd Regiment which took Pleasonton on and beat him back to his lines. The Federals increased their attacks, however, and Lee was forced to deploy the 9th Regiment under Col. W. H. F. ("Rooney") Lee, General Lee's second eldest son, in a series of rotating positions in order to insure the safe passage of his men through the town. It was soon discovered that the streets were little safer than the fields to the east. The streets were so narrow and Union sentiment so hot, that passage without being hit by random shots from windows was extremely difficult. In the mad scramble of the cavalry clashes, "Rooney" Lee was thrown to the ground, stunned, but not seriously hurt. After hours of close contact with the enemy, he finally made his way to the west and late that night met his men again near Sharpsburg.[56] Fitzhugh Lee, in the meantime, successfully slowed the Federal advance through Boonsboro and later engaged the enemy in a delaying action at Keedysville. The mission was accomplished. The Army of Northern Virginia crossed the Antietam and began taking up position in the fields surrounding Sharpsburg.

D. H. Hill's Division was the first to cross the creek about daylight. His weary brigades made their way to the high ground between the main Sharpsburg ridge and the west bank of the Antietam. D. R. Jones's Division of Longstreet's Corps was next, taking position to Hill's right and commanding the Boonsboro Pike and the middle bridge. The rear guard, Hood's Division, and several brigades of Jones's Division formed on Hill's left, overlooking the Hagerstown-Sharpsburg Pike and extending from the Dunkard Church into the West Wood. As Hood moved into position, Jones extended his right on to cover the high ground overlooking the lower bridge, the third of three stone bridges crossing the Antietam in this immediate area. The first or upper bridge would not be protected by Confederate forces. It would later be used for Federal troops crossing to the northern part of the field. Evans's Independent Brigade moved in to the center position and blocked the Boonsboro Pike. Stuart's Cavalry, including his short range guns, occupied a small hill, Nicodemus Heights, to the extreme Confederate left. Munford's cavalry detachment covered the extreme right, guarding the creek and the Harpers Ferry road below Jones's position. The line was long, about five miles, and winding over the terrain covered an area of about three miles from the West Wood to the lower bridge.

At sunrise that morning, Harpers Ferry was sealed in. A heavy mist covered the basin and its perimeter. Jackson's guns were poised. The climax was at hand. The general had been up since 3:00 A.M. sending his couriers from one battery to another. It had been four days since his "expedition" had left Frederick. Time passed all too rapidly, but now it was just a matter of touching that spark, executing the final blow — if in blood, so be it. The gunners had their targets; they had their sights aimed since the day before; the mist would pose no problem. Orders came and they commenced firing, one battery taking its signal from the other.

"It was perfectly terrific," said Col. William H. Trimble, who was stationed at the garrison with the 60th Ohio Infantry. Trimble had been in three other artillery bombardments, but they were "so perfectly insignificant in comparison with this that there was just no comparison at all." Every foot of ground was commanded by the Confederates, "not a place where you could lay the palm of your hand and say it was safe."[57] There was a terrible cross-fire. "Nothing could stand before such a raking cannonade," wrote Lt. Henry Binney, aide-de-camp to Colonel Miles, the commanding officer. In his daily journal, under September 15, he recorded, "We are surrounded by enemy batteries."[58]

Within an hour, Federal guns had ceased their opposition. By prearranged signal — the silence of Hill's artillery — Pender's Brigade started forward to storm the works. Immediately the enemy guns opened again. All Confederate batteries were moved forward to pour "a rapid fire" onto the post.[59] General Julius White, who was on rather shaky ground when it came to command decisions (he was senior officer, but diplomatically had requested Colonel Miles to continue), cautiously suggested to Miles that a consultation of officers was in order. Miles agreed and the call went out. The decision was made and the white flag went up. For some unknown reason, the Confederate artillery fired again just as Miles and Lt. Binney started for Jackson's lines. Miles had just said, "Well, Mr. Binney, we have done our duty, but where can McClellan be?" At that moment he was hit by a fragment of an exploding shell. Binney immediately administered what emergency measures he could until some men were found to carry the colonel to an ambulance.[60] The wound was mortal, however, and Miles, the old man who said that he would defend Harpers Ferry to the very last, died. "He had done his duty; he was an old soldier and willing to die," wrote Binney, quoting the colonel's last words.[61] Immediately General White assumed command and made preparations for negotiations with the Confederates. The firing ceased and the men stripped their regimental colors from the staffs.[62]

Henry Kyd Douglas and A. P. Hill went out to meet the approaching Federal officers. One was White, the other, Miles's assistant adjutant-general. White was resplendent in full dress uniform with "untarnished" sabre, white gloves, and polished boots, mounted on a handsome black horse. He asked to be taken to Jackson. "He must have been somewhat astonished to find in General Jackson the worst-dressed, worst-mounted, most faded and dingy-looking general he had ever seen anyone surrender to, with a staff, not much for looks or equipment," wrote Douglas.[63] But this was war and Jackson had been marching and fighting. White had not.

The meeting was formal and over in a few minutes. The terms of surrender were to be unconditional. General Hill would stay and handle the arrangements, and, according to Jackson's instructions, they were to be liberal.[64] Then Jackson rode down into Harpers Ferry to inspect the garrison. Federal soldiers lined the streets. "He's not much for looks," one of them said, "but if we'd had him we wouldn't have been caught in this trap!"[65] Jackson's men stocked up on supplies, prepared rations for two days, and then, "in obedience to orders from the commanding general," struck out on the seventeen mile, overnight trek to Sharpsburg.[66] Messages were sent to Walker and McLaws to join the movement immediately. By the time Jackson left, Walker fell in behind. McLaws, having to elude Franklin in Pleasant Valley, departed much later.

Hill was most liberal with his terms. All 11,000 men in the garrison were paroled. This meant that officers could retain sidearms and personal belongings; the men, their equipment for personal comfort. To Hill, as with men in both armies, a parole was freedom granted in return for an oath not to take up arms again until a legitimate exchange of prisoners could be arranged. The soldier was honor bound and in most cases, the parole was observed. Hill was somewhat perturbed, however, when it took two months for the return of wagons loaned to the officers for the transportation of their baggage. According to the rules of war, this was legal Confederate property. Hill regretted that his "magnanimity was not appreciated by the enemy."[67]

Besides the impressive catch of 11,000 Federal troops, the Harpers Ferry "booty" netted the victors some 12,000 rifles and 70 pieces of artillery. There were uniforms, large stores of food and ammunition, and a few horses. All too few horses, lamented W. W. Blackford. He had heard about the great escape of the night before. " To think of all the fine horses they carried off, and carbines of the best kind, and the spurs, all of which would have fallen to our share, and the very things we so much needed, was enough to vex a saint."[68] Jackson said, "I would rather have had them [Davis's cavalry] than everything else in the place."[69]

That morning Jackson had taken time from his busy affairs to write General Lee; " Through God's blessing, Harper's Ferry and its garrison are to be surrendered."[70] The courier who rode off to Sharpsburg stopped off on the Maryland shore of the river to hand a message to the Douglas family. "Dear Father," it read. "Harper's Ferry has surrendered. Nobody hurt on our side. H. K. D."[71] Then the courier raced on to join Lee who was taking up position on the western fields of the Antietam.

Over in Pleasant Valley they could hear Jackson's guns. The continuous roar echoed through the hills telling the men that the seige was on. To Franklin's Sixth Corps it meant that it was too late to rescue the garrison; to McLaws' beleaguered forces, it meant that unless Jackson was successful, their only route back through to Virginia would be cut off. Franklin was pressing to the river. Time was running out. "Their skirmishers were within two hundred yards of our lines when . . . Jackson's guns suddenly ceased," wrote Lt. Col. W. W. Blackford. It was an ominous silence. The enemy noticed it too and halted. Then in relay fashion, from Maryland Heights down through the valley came the news. Harpers Ferry had surrendered. Cheers went up and the thin Confederate line came alive with wild excitement. "What the hell are you fellows cheering for?" shouted a Federal skirmisher who jumped up on a stone wall. "Because Harpers Ferry is gone up, G—— d——— you," shouted back one of Stuart's men. "I thought that was it," grimly replied the Federal and then he jumped down.[72]

Jackson's courier arrived in Sharpsburg as the various regiments of Lee's army were selecting their positions. "This is indeed good news," said General Lee as he read Jackson's dispatch, "let it be announced to the troops . . ."[73] A mighty roar thundered through the air. Harpers Ferry had fallen. This was a good omen.

As the First, Second, and Twelfth Corps advanced to Boonsboro on the old National highway, Burnside was ordered to send the Ninth Corps over the Sharpsburg road through Fox's Gap, meet the main body of the army at the foot of the mountain, or, if possible, establish some contact with Franklin who would be coming from Pleasant Valley under orders. The combined operation would have as its objective Keedysville, where it could cut off the retreat of the Confederates.

McClellan stated in his official report that "it had been hoped to engage the enemy during the 15th."[74] His orders were to that effect and gave every indication that a sincere effort was being made at headquarters to co-ordinate the movements of his seperate wings. Here, however, the inadequacies of his command system began to show. Burnside did not begin his advance until shortly after noon, thus delaying the general pursuit and stalling plans which would not gain force enough again during the day to accomplish the objective. Early that morning, Burnside had requested permission to leave headquarters so that he could personally catch up to his men who, he had indicated, were already in motion. McClellan consented, but when he later rode over the field, he found the Ninth Corps still in bivouac. Although Burnside could not be found, he later gave extreme fatigue and hunger as his excuse.[75]

It soon became apparent that Burnside and Franklin would both be problem children to McClellan, for orders from this point on the 15th became more and more confused. McClellan had some second thoughts about Franklin joining with Burnside at the head of the valley. In one order McClellan instructed Franklin to pursue the enemy at his front, but not so until he had determined his strength.[76] To the Sixth Corps commander, this, in so many words, relieved him from making any movements to connect with the main body of the army, and, in the end, Franklin would accept this interpretation.

When, on moving out of Washington, McClellan had formed the three wings of the Army of the Potomac, he had as much as given the three commanders independent command. That is to say that each of the three generals should have accepted command responsibilities. It would normally be expected that in seperate operations, each would act at their own discretion when any suitable occasion arose. Such was the case when McClellan gave Franklin the opportunity on the night of the 13th to interpret his orders according to the prevailing circumstances. This delegating of wing command functions, which certainly applied under actual battle conditions, was applicable also in noncombat. Franklin, however, was reluctant to move on his own and indicated throughout the campaign that he had no intentions of going one step further than specifically instructed. As a result of the inactivity of Franklin and the delay of Burnside, McClellan's initial drive after South Mountain lost momentum. The "rapid pursuit" failed to catch and check Lee, and thus became another of the deciding factors in the campaign. This same lack of co-ordination would show once the Antietam was reached.

Richardson's division of the Second Corps was the first to reach the high ground east of the creek. When the head of the column came into view, the Confederate batteries opened fire. Federal light artillery was immediately brought up and retaliated, but little damage was done on either side. When McClellan arrived and had acknowledged the cheers of his men, he examined the situation and quickly concluded that it was merely a "feeler" action and that since it was too late in the day to initiate any kind of an attack, he would deploy the troops on hand, await the arrival of others, and settle down for the night.

Only a token attempt was made to determine the Confederate defenses. Several artillery shots were fired; no cavalry reconnaissance was made; no pickets sent out for spying. If McClellan knew what he was going to do, he gave no indications. He rested that night with an army that outnumbered the Confederates four to one. While Lee waited for Jackson, McLaws, and Walker, McClellan obligingly waited for them also. As he did, the odds dropped to two to one — that is, the actual odds. Despite the 18,000 McClellan thought Lee had lost at South Mountain, he still believed the Army of Northern Virginia outnumbered him two to one.

By this time, Lee knew McClellan better than most. He still could have quietly slipped across the Potomac that night, met Jackson, and pulled back into Virginia. It seems evident now that McClellan would never have pursued him for it was the Federal commander's intentions to get Lee out of Maryland and not much else. Instead, Lee counted on McClellan's continued delay and settled down for a night's rest. It was almost as if Lee was pulling the strings of a Federal puppet. This was the way the night of the 15th was spent — Lee ready for battle (as ready as he could be at that moment) and McClellan in an undefined position with no battle plans whatever — the two armies less than two miles apart.

The composure of these two gentlemen that night clearly indicates certain qualities the forthcoming battle would bear out. Both slept well. Lee, facing great odds, had been strengthened by the news of Jackson's victory at Harpers Ferry. He was confident that Stonewall would be up by daybreak. He was glad now that he had not taken Longstreet's advice to withdraw to Virginia. Also, he felt he had McClellan marked. If the Federal commander started out in the morning, it would be a slow start, one that the Confederate army could detect early and meet with all their force.

McClellan, too, slept well. He had just completed a "glorious victory" at South Mountain. Reinforcements were on their way. Although he was "outnumbered," the Confederates had not yet made an offensive attack in Maryland and after the "beating" it took on the 14th, it was not likely to do so that night. Lincoln had wired him after South Mountain: "God bless you and all with you. Destroy the rebel army if possible."[77] He would try, but not that night. The next day perhaps. McClellan knew Lee. What he did not know was that Lee knew McClellan.

The morning of the 16th came quietly. The only sounds were distant bugles and the rumblings of wagons. A heavy mist hung over the valley, hiding Confederate positions from view. McClellan was inclined to believe that Lee had withdrawn and telegraphed his wife that he believed he had already delivered Pennsylvania and Maryland from the enemy's hands.[78] At 7:00 A.M., he sent a message to Halleck: "This morning a heavy fog has thus far prevented us doing more than to ascertain that some of the enemy are still there. Do not know in what force. Will attack as soon as situation of enemy is developed."[79] Later when the mist had burned away and Federal and Confederate batteries traded shots, it became obvious to McClellan that Lee intended to stand and fight. For a few brief moments volley after volley thundered through the air. Then all would be quiet until another exploratory shell found its way into the lines. McClellan, in viewing Confederate positions, exposed himself on several occasions. Rebel batteries tried, unsuccessfully, to drop a shell in his path. Each time McClellan withdrew below the hills only to pop up again at some other point. He later would state that he had personally and purposely exposed the Confederate artillery positions,[80] a factor that meant very little to the outcome of the battle. Nevertheless, Lee rode the lines too, ordering his men not to waste their ammunition. He was in no position to offer McClellan reason to start an artillery duel.

About noon, a cloud formation cast a heavy shadow over the field and a slight breeze began to stir. It was a sigh of relief for Lee, for with it came Jackson and Walker from Harpers Ferry. Lee's headquarters were located in a grove of trees just west of Sharpsburg on the Shepherdstown road. All morning he had watched anxiously for his "right arm," as he would come to call Jackson. Jackson had reported that he planned to leave for Sharpsburg as soon as his men had made all the necessary arrangements for A. P. Hill to guard the prisoners and after they had had their evening meal.

Walker's observations on his arrival at Lee's headquarters are indicative of the character of the Confederate commander history has immortalized. "Anxious enough, no doubt, he was," wrote Gen. Walker, "but there was nothing in his look or manner to indicate it, on the contrary, he was calm, dignified, and even cheerful. If he had had a well-equipped army of a hundred thousand veterans at his back, he could not have appeared more composed and confident."[81]

As soon as the divisions were up, Lee placed them into position; Jackson to the far left behind Hood, and Walker, whose men were farther behind and needed rest after the long march from Loudoun Heights, to the right to strengthen the defense of the lower bridge. It was not until the morning of the 17th that all of Walker's men would be in position.

McClellan's ride along the lines revealed many things, or so he would have historians believe. Aside from "exposing Confederate artillery," he made an extensive study of the area around the lower bridge. This was obviously the key to the southern approach to Sharpsburg from Harpers Ferry, a route which he knew would be used by one or more of the Confederate divisions in that action. According to his own testimony, he ordered Burnside to move up at noon, control the bridge, and be ready, supposedly at a moment's notice, to block the Harpers Ferry road.[82] Burnside moved, but not until that night.

That afternoon as the various Confederate units met on the field, a dramatic and touching reunion was held. Harpers Ferry veterans embraced South Mountain veterans as nearly every regimental band struck up "Dixie." Thousands of voices joined in the "inspiring, soul-stirring music. It seemed to put new life into both men and animals and . . . we felt ready for anything our beloved general might undertake," wrote William T. Poague.[83]

By 2:00 P.M. McClellan had made up his mind on the plans of battle. He would first attack the Confederate left and right as diversions for a main attack at the center. Orders went out. Hooker's First Corps, at Keedysville, crossed the creek and late in the afternoon reached the Hagerstown Pike, north of Hood's position. McClellan himself had led the way, somewhat disturbed over repeated delays in getting the columns moving. At about 6:00 P.M. they made their first contact with Confederate pickets.[84]

Lee, Jackson, and Longstreet were in conference at the time. One can only surmise their reaction at the sound of infantry fire and its supporting artillery from across the creek. Lee had been waiting battle for nearly two days. This must be it, but why so late in the day, he could not understand.

Hood was ordered forth to meet the attack and Jackson moved in on his left. By this time, Hooker was the one doing the exposing. Although darkness fell before it developed into open battle, Lee knew that this was where the first attack would fall the next morning. Both sides settled down for the night and as they did, Lee sent urgent messages to McLaws and A. P. Hill to come as rapidly as they could. And McClellan sent a message to Franklin to quit Pleasant Valley and move into battle position. Hooker grumbled, "If they had let us start earlier, we might have finished tonight."[85] It was too late, however, to be thinking about this now.

It was only a matter of time. Daylight would bring what Lee had been waiting for. Once again McClellan was obliging him. He was giving time for Hill and McLaws to rejoin Lee. McClellan, and he alone, was bringing the odds down, and down, and down.

About 9:00 P.M. it started to rain.

8

The Gleam of Bayonets

It was not a peaceful night. The atmosphere was tense, the air bristling with activity. Pickets, almost close enough to touch, fired at one another throughout the dark hours. One green Union regiment nearly caused a major clash in the early morning when a recruit tripped over the regimental dog in the dark and tumbled a stack of rifles. The clatter sent men scurrying for cover all along the lines.[1] Throughout the night, couriers raced from brigade to brigade relaying orders. Although there was little talk among the men, each knew instinctively that the morning would bring a mighty and fierce clash of arms. Unlike Wellington's troops at Waterloo, who took rain the night before battle as a sign of good fortune, the men at Antietam saw their rain as an evil omen.

Strange and almost ghostly things happened during the night for which no explanation could be offered. Behind the Confederate lines, the cavalry was bedded down for a few hours rest when the horses belonging to the Jeff Davis Legion mysteriously stampeded. They broke the picket ropes and scattered in all directions "in the greatest panic and excitement and wild confusion." Fortunately they headed away from the front lines, otherwise the battle might well have had an earlier start. The rest of the night and a good deal of the next day was spent in recovering them. What started the whole thing was never known but it certainly did little to ease the tension.[2]

The thoughts of men on the night before battle vary. Some are frightened; others accept their fate calmly. Young Thomas Livermore of the 5th New Hampshire recorded his emotions and revealed how a soldier resigns himself to the will of God, and the enemy:

209

Whether we were to attack or to repel, whether the fight was to be in the woods on our right in the ravine, or in the hills in our front, or on the crest amid the hostile batteries, I knew not, and then, when was the fight to begin? How long would it last? Who would win? Was I to be killed, to be torn with a shell, or pierced with a bullet? What was death? How quickly should I be in the other world if I were killed? I am not aware that I once wished we should not fight. I know that to stay out or shrink from the battle in any way never entered my head; yet I can venture to say that while we waited in the twilight, time flew with slow wings, and the quicker I was in it and through it, alive or dead, the better I thought I would be. This contemplating for a long time the black-muzzled cannon, and conjuring up the hosts who are to blaze at you with death-dealing musketry, is not pleasant.[3]

For some strange reason, McClellan took extra measures of security that night. The Confederates had watched the Federal army take position for two days and Hooker had already given away his plans, but still McClellan ordered no fires and complete silence.[4] The men grumbled at their commander's lack of consideration. These restrictions would mean no light for the customary card games, all the more important on a night like this, and munching on dry coffee grounds in a steady drizzle was hardly a soldier's idea of spending what might be his last night alive.

Hood's Division had had little more than coffee for the past three days, actually only a half ration of beef, and they were near collapse. Hood approached Lee's headquarters and respectfully requested permission to pull his men back for a hot meal. It was imperative that they have some food in their stomachs if they were going to fight the next day. Lee consented, but reluctantly, for he had no replacements along that part of the line. He suggested that Hood see Jackson about stretching the defenses a little thinner to take up the slack. If Jackson agreed, then permission was granted.

Jackson was as reluctant as Lee but he nodded his approval providing that Hood would drop everything the moment he was called to the front. It was not like Hood to reject such conditions, for his men were always ready for a fight. Their incredible insulation from fear and their undaunted bravery would make Jackson proud of them on the morrow. So at 10:00 P.M. Hood's Division of two brigades, some 2,400 indispensable men took their rifles in hand and silently made their way to the grounds around the Dunkard Church.[5]

At about the same time, General Mansfield was receiving his orders for the Federal Twelfth Corps to pack their belongings and file into marching order; they were moving to the front. Mansfield followed Hooker's path until he reached a field northeast of where the First Corps had camped. Here his men gained a few extra hours of rest before dawn.

Daylight was slow in coming. The rain had stopped but it had left a heavy overcast, a foggy mist that covered the fields. Incidental firing, which had started at about 3:00 A.M., began to pick up. As dawn broke and the gray shroud slowly lifted, the soldiers became more alert. They began to make out the shadowy images of pickets each had heard during the night. The least movement amongst the trees stirred a hornet's nest of firing. Then the big guns roared. Four batteries of Federal artillery lining the eastern bank of the Antietam shattered the morning air with their barrage, raking the Confederate line. The ground beneath fairly trembled as the dense air first held, then echoed, the thunder from the mountains to the river. William Thomas Poague, "gunner with Stonewall," made a pointed observation on artillery conditions that morning: "A fire of any sort from the rear [of the enemy's lines] is very disturbing and makes one feel, whenever made conscious of it by roving missiles, that the enemy are not fighting fair, but he soon gets over his irritation as he remembers that he is playing a game in which all things are fair."[6] Fair or not, the game was on.

Hooker was up early—"The old man would have liked to be with the pickets," one of his staff said[7]—and so were McClellan and Lee. Lee had been up since before 4:00 A.M. At 4:30 A.M. he had notified Pendleton to guard well the fords with his reserve artillery and to send all others up to the front.[8] He knew now, beyond the shadow of a doubt, that McClellan would strike. McClellan was waiting for Franklin. Without the Sixth Corps, he had about 70,000 men on the books. Lee was waiting for McLaws' and Anderson's ten brigades from Maryland Heights and A. P. Hill's four brigades from Harpers Ferry. Without their combined 9,000, he had about 26,000 to face the Federal army.[9] Neither man was satisfied with these figures. But time was running out. Before 6:00 A.M., the First Corps began to move. The actual time is not known but it is estimated between 5:30 and 6 o'clock. Though it was an overcast morning, most accounts give the time of initial movements at first "faint streaks of daylight;"[10] "at the peep of day 'ere the sun had cast a ray over the towering Blue Ridge."[11] Official recorded sunrise that morning was 5:43 A.M.[12] The temperature at daybreak was 65 degrees. It would rise to about 75 degrees by afternoon and the relative humidity would measure 71 per cent. The winds would run at two miles per hour from the west and the clouds would be scattered.[13] All in all, it would be a typical September day. The humidity would be a little higher than normal, keeping powder smoke at a low level and accounting for the choking sensation expressed by so many of the soldiers, otherwise it was little more than the Mummas, the Poffenbergers and the Millers would expect for this time of the year. The difference lay in the uninvited guests which now camped in their fields.

Hooker stood at the northern apex of a triangle—the North Wood, a large patch of trees that served as his launching point. To his left, at the eastern base, was the East Wood, and to the right was the West Wood and the little white Church of the Brethren. In between lay the D. R. Miller farm and its cornfield of some 30 acres. The high ground at the church would be his objective, but he did not know yet how heavily the farm had been fortified. His intelligence failed to tell him anymore than the enemy was there in force. This much he discovered the evening before.

Hooker had ten brigades in the divisions of Doubleday, Ricketts and Meade, numbering between 7,000 and 9,000 men. They faced seven Confederate brigades from Jones's (Jackson's) and Lawton's(Ewell's) divisions, numbering about 5,500 men; the old Stonewall Brigade with some 300.[14] This was not the first time that some of these men had come face to face. Many of the Federal regiments had opposed Jackson's men at Cedar Mountain and at Second Manassas and were keenly aware of the determination with which these Confederates fought. Early reports from the front lines told them it would not be an easy fight.

The main attack was aimed at the church which sat on the Hagerstown Pike about 1,000 yards to the south. In formation, the First Corps was bent like a bow, the right astride the pike facing south towards the church, and the left with its left flank brushing the East Wood, facing southwest. Each flank overlapped the Confederate positions. Doubleday's division was on the right with the brigades of Gibbon in front and Phelps directly behind. Patrick's brigade followed Phelps, being detained by Hooker for about twenty minutes. Seymour's brigade of Meade's division formed on Doubleday's left at the edge of the East Wood supported in the rear by Duryea of Rickett's division. Christian and Hartsuff of Rickett's division formed behind Duryea to add force to the four brigade attack on the left and the three brigade attack on the right. One brigade from Doubleday's (Hofman's) and two from Meade's (Magilton's and Robert Anderson's) divisions were held back as reserves.

Hooker described the opening scenes of the battle:

We had not proceeded far before I discovered that a heavy force of the enemy had taken possession of a cornfield in my immediate front and from the sun's rays falling on their bayonets projecting above the corn could see that the field was filled with the enemy, with arms in their hands, standing apparently at "support arms."[15]

A member of the Stonewall Brigade saw Hooker's men coming. "In apparent double battle lines, the Federals were moving toward us at charge bayonets, common time, and the sunbeams falling on their well polished guns and bayonets gave a glamor and a show at once fearful and entrancing."[16]

A little to the right of where Hooker formed his line there was a slight rise on the Nicodemus farm; "Nicodemus Heights" it was called. This was the key to the morning phase of the battle. The army which occupied this knoll, commanded the Hagerstown Pike. Fortunately for Lee, who was on the field first, Jeb Stuart's artillery was there in force. Had he not been, commented one contemporary, "the low timbered ground around the Dunkard Church . . . could not have been held fifteen minutes."[17] As it was, Stuart had a clear shot on the attackers as they came out of the North Wood. He watched Gibbon's brigade move down the road and as they reached the open, his guns charged the air with fire. As though Stuart's guns had given an unannounced signal, the entire Miller farm came alive with the Rebel yell. The tall corn shimmered as a vast sea of Confederate infantry, Lawton's Division, opened up on the Federals who were maneuvering in the encircling movement. The oncoming lines were an impressive sight. Jackson's brigades crouching behind fences, waited. Jackson had two divisions on the field. His own division was commanded by J. R. Jones with two brigades (Jones's own and Winder's) and was deployed across the Hagerstown Pike from the West Wood to the cornfield. Lawton's Division formed on Jones's right with his own and Trimble's brigades to the extreme right astride the Smoketown Road facing in a northeasterly direction. Early's Brigade was to the far left supporting Stuart. When the first wave of Federals were within close firing distance, Rebel shouts echoed the first shocking volley. The musket fire was heavy and fierce, the air "alive with shells," a "terrific storm of shell, canister, and musketry,"[18] and enough to halt the blue line momentarily. Patrick wrote that up to this point the fire had been brisk, "not heavy," but at this moment "a most galling fire" poured in from the enemy.[19] The advance was impetuous, and the Confederate resistance was stubborn.

Before Hooker could move his men again, he ordered some thirty-six guns from the rear to be placed in a ravine between the North Wood and the Miller farm and aimed at the cornfield.[20] Their fire was deadly accurate and the carnage was terrible. Bits of bodies, rifles and fence rails flew in the air as the corn was ripped to shreds. At the same time, twenty-four 20-pounder rifled Parrott guns from across the Antietam opened up on the same target. They fired continuously. Eye witnesses claimed to have heard one gun every second.[21] The Confederates took an unmerciful pounding. There was little chance for escape. Most of the men simply dug in where they were—many dying without having moved an inch. The line of battle now extended over one-half mile through the corn and trees, offering a grim testament to the adage that "war was hell." Jackson had called for support from D. H. Hill on his right. As no direct attack had yet been made on the center, Hill felt he could spare three of his brigades and sent up Colquitt, Ripley, and Garland's Brigade under McRae. Immediately they were drawn into the line of fire.

Patrick's brigade had now moved to Gibbon's right and was invading the West Wood from the north. Hartsuff and Christian were in the East Wood relieving Seymour. Had G. F. R. Henderson's comment on Hooker's advance been made at the time of the battle, it would have been most significant and would have set the theme for the day. He wrote years later that "the battle opened with a resolution which, if it had infected McClellan, would have carried the Sharpsburg ridge ere set of sun."[22]

Shortly the fire died down and the blue columns pressed forward. George Smalley, New York *Tribune* correspondent, who had wormed his way onto Hooker's staff, was on the front line in advance of the general's personal aides. Once Hooker spied him:

"Who are you?"

"Special correspondent of the New York Tribune, sir," replied Smalley.

"Will you take an order for me? Tell the colonel of that regiment to take his men to the front and keep them there," said the general pointing to a line being hard pressed.

Though Smalley had managed to get himself in uniform, he had no rank or insignia. It was with some doubt that the colonel looked him over.

"Who are you?"

"The order is General Hooker's," said Smalley.

"It must come to me from a staff officer or from my brigade commander."

"Very good," replied Smalley. "I shall report to General Hooker that you refuse to obey."

"Oh, for God's sake, don't do that!" and with that the colonel proceeded to carry out the orders.

"Don't let the next man talk so much," Hooker told Smalley when he returned with the story, and then sent him off on another errand.[23]

Smalley continued to distinguish himself throughout the morning, taking chances that brought the admiration of all who saw him. "In all the experiences I have had of the war," General Hooker is reported to have said, "I never saw the most experienced and veteran soldier exhibit more tranquil fortitude and unshaken valor than was exhibited by that young man."[24] Twice Smalley's horse was shot from under him and several times he narrowly escaped death-dealing blows of enemy artillery, but on he went serving one of his favorite generals and gathering, at the same time, some of the most exciting news copy of the war.

The lines wavered back and forth, neither one being able to see exactly what was happening. Dense black smoke from exploding shells and hot muskets hung heavy over the field. The Mumma farm buildings at the southeast edge of the cornfield had been set afire by the Confederates to prevent their use by the Federals as a base.[25] From a distance, no one could see. Only the murderous clatter of close range rifle fire and screaming voices told observers what was happening. Hand to hand combat—charge and countercharge—it was a fight to the finish such as neither army had ever experienced. There was an

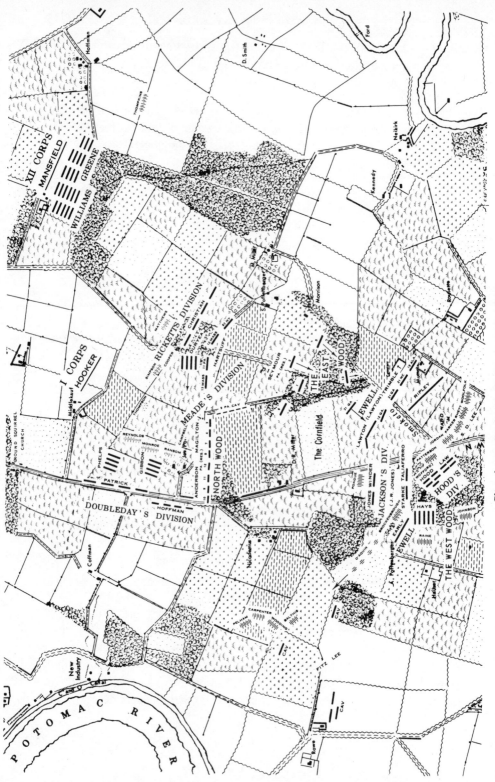

Situation at daybreak, September 17, 1862.

intense, almost hysterical excitement among the men; an eagerness, a recklessness, a complete disregard of everything and everybody, of nothing but victory. The two lines nearly tore each other to shreds. Men wrote later that there was never anything like this—that the bullets were like hail stones dropping on an "enormous tin roof"[26] in a fierce storm. "Men and officers of New York and Wisconsin are fused into a common mass in the frantic struggle to shoot fast," wrote a member of the 14th New York. "Everybody tears cartridges, loads, passes guns or shoots. Men are falling in their places or running back into the corn. The soldier who is shooting is furious in his energy and eagerness to win victory. Many of the recruits who are killed or wounded only left home ten days ago."[27]

As seconds and minutes flew by, regiments were whittled away to nothing. Divisions took ghastly losses, some as high as 60 per cent. The 12th Massachusetts under Hartsuff sent in 334 new recruits; 114 survived. Rickett's division was reduced by one-third, 153 killed and 898 wounded, having taken the brunt of Confederate force at the edge of the West Wood. Gibbon's brigade lost 380 men while Phelps's brigade lost 40 per cent.[28] In the confusion and chaos, Pennsylvanians were mixed with New Yorkers; charges and retreats overlapped; strange voices gave commands, strange colors led the way. One Federal enlisted man wrote:

Some of our own men mistaking us in the smoke and fog for the enemy fired into us, and we were forced to move to the rear, having got separated from the regiment. [When] I joined the regiment which I found had been badly cut up, some companies had not more than a half dozen men left. Our company has about 20 men fit for fighting now out of 104 which it had 14 months ago.[29]

Confederate mounted officers, unable to maneuver in the mass confusion, took to foot, turning their horses loose to gallop to the rear. Just as one North Carolina colonel was being pulled from his horse by an attentive aide, a minie ball, whistling over the empty saddle, struck his hand which was still holding on to the pommel.[30]

One of the thrilling narratives of the cornfield came from Rufus R. Dawes of the 6th Wisconsin:

After a few rods of advance, the line stopped and, by common impulse fell back to the edge of the corn and lay down on the ground behind the low rail fence. Another line of our men came up through the corn. We all joined together, jumped over the fence, and again pushed out into the open field. There is a rattling fusillade and loud cheers. "Forward" is the word. The men are loading and firing with demoniacal fury and shouting and laughing hysterically, and the whole field before us is covered with rebels fleeing for life, into the woods. Great numbers of them are shot while climbing over the high post and rail fences along the turnpike. We push on over the open fields half way to the little church. The powder is bad, and the guns have become very dirty. It takes hard pounding to get the bullets down, and our firing is becoming slow. A long and steady line of rebel gray, unbroken by the fugitives who fly before us, comes sweeping down through the woods around the church. They raise the yell and fire. It is like a scythe running through our line. "Now, save, who can." It is a race for life that each man runs for the cornfield. A sharp cut, as of a switch, stings the calf of my leg as I run. Back to the corn, and back through the corn, and headlong flight continues. At the bottom of the hill, I took the blue color of the state of Wisconsin, and waving it, called a rally of Wisconsin men. Two hundred men gathered around the flag of the Badger state. Across the turnpike just in front of the haystacks, two guns of Battery "B," 4th U. S. Artillery were in action. The pursuing rebels were upon them. General John Gibbon, our brigade commander, who in regular service was captain of this battery, grimed and black with powder smoke is himself sighting these guns of his old battery, comes running to me, "Here, major, move your men over, we must save these guns." I commanded "Right face, forward march," and started ahead with the colors in my hand into the open field, the men following. As I entered the field, a report as of a thunderclap in my ear fairly stunned me. This was Gibbon's last shot at the advancing rebels. The cannon was double charged with canister. The rails of the fence flew high in the air. A line of Union blue charged swiftly forward from our right across the field in front of the battery, and into the corn-field. They drove back the rebels who were firing upon us. It was our own gallant 19th Indiana, and here fell dead their leader, Lieutenant Colonel A. F. Bachman; but the youngest captain in their line, William W. Dudley, stepped forward and led on the charge. I gathered my men on the turnpike, reorganized them, and reported to General Doubleday, who was himself there. He ordered me to move back to the next woods in the rear, to remain and await instructions. Bullets, shot and shell, fired by the enemy in the corn-field, were still flying thickly around us, striking the trees in this woods, and cutting off the limbs. I placed my men under the best shelter I could find, and here we figured up, as nearly as we could, our dreadful losses in the battle. Three hundred and fourteen officers and men had marched with us into battle. There had been killed and wounded, one hundred and fifty-two. Company "C" under Captain Hooe, thirty-five men, was not in the fight in front of the corn-field. That company was on skirmish duty farther to our right. In this service they lost two men. Of two hundred and eighty men who were at the corn-field and turnpike, one hundred and fifty were killed or wounded. This was the most dreadful slaughter to which our regiment was subjected in the war. We were joined in the woods by Captain Ely, who reported to me, as the senior officer present, with the colors and eighteen men of the second Wisconsin. They represented what remained for duty of that gallant regiment.[31]

The Confederates were drastically reduced in numbers. One brigade of 1,150 lost 554, another 323 out of 550. Regimental commanders and their staffs were wiped out. One-third of Lawton's, Hay's and Trimble's brigades were killed or wounded. Aside from Early, who had not yet been drawn into the main fight, there was only one general officer of brigade level on the field. Jackson's Division was reduced to 600 men and was being commanded by a colonel; Winder's Brigade by a major; Jones's Brigade by three successive captains.[32] The overwhelming tide of blue forced them to withdraw to the West Wood where they turned to pepper the Federals as they broke into the open, south of the cornfield. Lee's left was in a perilous position, on the verge of complete extinction. Were it not for the able maneuvering of Stuart's master artillerymen, the Confederate left would not only have been in trouble, it would have tipped its desperate hand to the Federals. Through the shifting of guns from one spot to another, the Federals were deluded into thinking that they had run into a stubborn wall. Brilliant move that it was, it was only enough to sustain Confederate strength until the wall could materialize.

It was now 7:00 o'clock. Jones and Lawton were both wounded and off the field. Ripley, from Hill's Division, was wounded and Col. Douglas, who was commanding Lawton's Brigade, was killed. Brig. Gen. W. E. Starke, who had assumed division command from Jones, was dead; Col. A. J. Grigsby had taken over. On the Federal side, Seymour and Duryea were out of action. It was now time for Hood to fulfill his promise. The men were still at breakfast when Hood called them out. This counterstroke was devastating to the Federals. Hood drove from the West Wood with a ferocity that has long been attributed to the angry mood of soldiers denied the comforts of "behind the

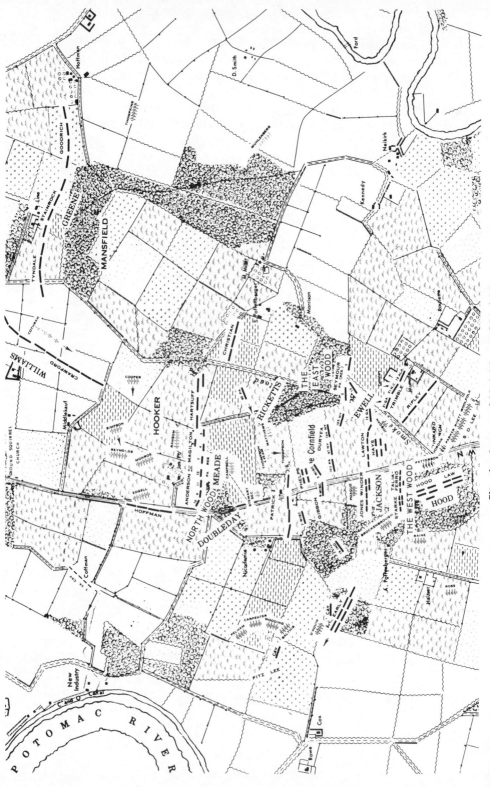

Situation between 6:00 A.M. and 6:20 A.M.

lines." Their first volley stopped the advancing blue line cold. Then with a burst of fury they pushed into the cornfield, or what was left of it, sending the Northern boys fleeing for cover. The cornfield, which had just been won by the Federals only a few minutes before, changed hands again.

Back on the ridge the Federals reformed their lines as best they could amongst the artillery and fired alternately from between and behind the guns. Hooker quickly put his reserve brigades (Anderson's and Magilton's) into action. Wofford's Brigade of Hood's Division was pressing hard against Gibbon and Phelps. Law, on Wofford's right, struck out for Christian and Hartsuff. Anderson fell in behind Gibbon but before Magilton could reach the East Wood, his brigade was hit on the flank. Before Hood's men could break through the Miller farm, Gibbon's battery of six guns checked the action at a range of about 50 feet. Shell after shell tore into the Texans halting their advance just short of a complete rout on the part of the Federals. Regrouped, the boys in blue headed for the cornfield again. And again the action seesawed back and forth until the Confederates finally faded to the south edge of the cornfield and the West Wood.

Few men were able to record with any degree of accuracy this phase of the battle so great was the confusion. Official records speak in generalities, unable to determine the hour, the direction of specific troop movements or the casualities incurred. Hood called it the "most terrific clash of arms, by far, that has occurred during the war."[33] The First Corps commander summed it up rather aptly when he later described the horrid results. "In the time I am writing every stalk of corn in the northern and greater part of the field was cut as closely as could have been done with a knife, and the slain lay in rows precisely as they had stood in their ranks a few moments before. It was never my fortune to witness a more bloody, dismal battle-field."[34]

Hooker did not exaggerate. He had been on the field with his men and had watched each wave of blue as it plowed through the holocaust. It is doubtful that history has ever recorded a more terrible clash in so small an area. Casualities were appalling. The First Corps had lost 2,500 out of 9,000 sent into action. The Confederates, who held the Miller farm against the initial attack, lost at least 50 per cent. Hood's Division and Hill's three brigades were beaten to a pulp—all of this in less than two hours. A New York *Tribune* corre-

spondent recorded his view of the Miller farm: "Pale and bloody faces are everywhere upturned. They are sad and terrible, but there is nothing that makes one's heart beat so quickly as the imploring look of sorely wounded men who beckon wearily for help you cannot stay to give."[35] But the fighting was not yet finished. One member of the 124th Pennsylvania remembered a general riding up to his regiment "telling us to hurry, as his men were getting cut to pieces. Feeling that we might experience the same, I had no desire to accept the invitation. About that time things began to get warm—our Captain thought it was hot and remarked, it was too hot for him, and if we wanted to go in we might, but he would be ——— if he would, and he retired to the rear . . ."[36] Mansfield's Twelfth Corps was coming on the field. McLaws and Anderson, who had spent the night marching from Maryland, were now being pressed into action by Lee; McLaws to support Jackson, and Anderson to fall in behind D. H. Hill on the center. There would be no pause in the battle.

The Twelfth Corps, which had moved up from the Antietam during the night, was camped about a mile to Hooker's left rear. Since Mansfield did not survive the morning, there is no report to give a time when Hooker summoned him forth. It is reasonable to assume that the Twelfth Corps started moving with the early firing for he was on the field by about 7:30 A.M. Maj. Gen. Joseph K. F. Mansfield was the oldest general then serving in the Army of the Potomac. He had served in the war with Mexico and had made a name for himself in planning the attack on Buena Vista. Now, at the age of 59, he was commanding the Twelfth Corps. He had only been with the men for two days, having joined them at Frederick, but in this short time he had become a favorite. The men all liked him. He had a certain air that defied his age and brought wild cheers from his men when he appeared.

Mansfield had the weight of the battle on his shoulders. With Hooker's attack spent, his task was to restore order on the field and check the Federal rout. The condition of the field came as a shock to the old general. He had thought that Hooker's advances were successful and that his job would be merely a mopping up operation, further tipping the scales and cleaning the Confederates from the field. He had two divisions, the 1st under Brig. Gen. Alpheus S. Williams with two brigades of new recruits under Crawford and Gordon, and the 2d Division under Brig. Gen. George S. Greene with three brigades, Tyndale's, Stainrook's and Goodrich's.

A rare photograph, previously unpublished and until recently unknown, of Confederate troops prior to the battle of Antietam. The picture was taken from a second-story window of a clothing store in Frederick, Maryland, and is dated sometime between September 6 and September 10, 1862. With the exception of one, or possibly two, men in the foreground, apparently no one knew the photograph was being taken, making it, therefore, one of the few candid, unposed pictures of the Civil War. This particular unit cannot be identified, but the photograph clearly illustrates and verifies all contemporary accounts of the type of uniform worn by the Southern soldier. Note the blanket rolls and the odd assortment of hats. (Courtesy Benjamin B. Rosenstock)

George Brinton McClellan. (Courtesy Kean Archives, Philadelphia)

Ambrose E. Burnside. (Courtesy National Archives)

Henry Wager Halleck. (Courtesy Kean Archives, Philadelphia)

Thomas Jonathan ("Stonewall") Jackson. (Courtesy National Archives)

James Longstreet. (Courtesy National Archives)

John Bell Hood. (Courtesy Kean Archives, Philadelphia)

Henry Kyd Douglas—a photograph taken in Richmond, 1863. (Courtesy University of North Carolina Press)

A candid photograph of Federal troops assembled on North Market Street in Frederick, Maryland. Neither the military unit nor the date of the photograph can be identified. The owner of the original negative seems reasonably certain that it is September 1862, prior to the Battle of Antietam, basing this on family memoirs. One historical fact will verify the time; it had rained just prior to the arrival of the Federal army in Frederick. Close observation will reveal what appears to be puddles of water on the streets. (Courtesy Benjamin B. Rosenstock)

Confederate troops crossing the Potomac River.

Harpers Ferry as it looked in 1865; view facing down the Potomac River with Maryland Heights to the left. Shenandoah River joins Potomac on right. (Courtesy Library of Congress)

General McClellan's arrival in Frederick, Maryland.

Confederate encampment at Hagerstown, Maryland.

Battle of South Mountain—Turner's Pass, Sunday, September 14, 1862; scene looking west from Bolivar on Hagerstown-Frederick road. From a contemporary sketch. (Courtesy Maryland Historical Society)

Special Orders No. 191 written by Stonewall Jackson (from a copy sent to him by R. H. Chilton) and delivered to D. H. Hill. According to Hill's testimony, this is the only copy he received. It remained in his personal possession until he died as his only tangible evidence in the mystery. Note the certification of authenticity in the left margin of second page. It reads: "I hereby certify that I am familiar with the hand writing of Gen. T. J. Jackson and know this order to be in his hand writing. J. G. Morrison, Capt. & A.D.C. to Gen. T. J. Jackson." (Courtesy North Carolina Department of Archives and History) enemy at Harpers Ferry & vicinity.

VI Genl. Walker with his division, after accomplishing the object in which he is now engaged will cross the Potomac at Cheeks Ford, ascend its right bank to Lovettsville take possession of Loudon heights if practicable by Friday morning Keys Ford on his left and the road between the end of the Mountain and the Potomac on his right. He will as far as practicable co-operate with Genl. McLaws & Genl Jackson in intercepting the retreat of the enemy

VII Genl. D. H. Hills division will form the rear guard of the army, pursuing the road taken by the main body. The reserve Art.y Ordnance & Supply, trains &c will precede Genl. Hill.

VIII Genl. Stuart will detach a squadron of cav.y to accompany the commands of Genls Longstreet, Jackson & McLaws & with the main body of the cav.y will cover the route of the army & bring up all stragglers that may have been left behind.

IX The commands of Genls Jackson McLaws & Walker after accomplishing the objects for which they have been detached will join the main body of the army at Boonsboro or Hagers town

X Each Reg.t on the march will habitually carry its axes in the Reg.t ordnance wagons for the use of the men at their encampments to procure wood &c

By command of Genl. R. E. Lee
R. H. Chilton
A. A. Genl.

Federal artillery in motion during battle on South Mountain, Sunday, September 14, 1862.

The Middle Bridge crossing the Antietam Creek on the Boonsboro-Keedysville-Sharpsburg Pike. Both Confederate and Federal troops used this southwesterly approach to Antietam. This photograph, taken following the battle, faces Sharpsburg and shows military supply wagons on their way to army bivouac areas. Maryland highway improvements have now replaced this old stone construction, the only one of the three "battle" bridges (Upper, Middle, and Lower) to be so destroyed. Note temporary telegraph wires along pike. (Courtesy National Archives)

Hooker's advance across the Antietam, September 16, 1862.

The German Church of the Brethren (Dunkard), identified as photographed before the battle. (Courtesy National Archives)

Confederate dead along Hagerstown turnpike. (Courtesy National Archives)

Burnside (Lower) Bridge as seen from the Federal side. Bluffs in background were held by Toombs's Georgia regiments. Note stone fences on crest of hill (upper right).

Bloody Lane following the battle. (Courtesy Library of Congress)

Edwin Forbes's famous illustration of the Federal charge across the Lower Bridge, which later became Burnside Bridge. (Courtesy National Archives)

Federal burial detail following the battle. Note man in process of actual digging. Many bodies were buried on the spot where they were found. Some were later removed to the National Cemetery at Sharpsburg. Through diaries, letters, and family reminiscences, members of the Hagerstown (Maryland) Civil War Round Table have recently plotted dozens of unmarked graves on the battlefield. (Courtesy National Archives)

Unidentified dead waiting burial following battle. (Courtesy National Archives)

Lincoln's visit to McClellan's headquarters, October 1862. The general's tents were pitched on the grounds of the Philip Pry house near Keedysville. (Courtesy U. S. Army)

The President and his general following Antietam. The features of the two men, remarkably clear in this photograph, show none of the strain of their earlier and later correspondence. (Courtesy U. S. Army)

With Mansfield, himself, in the lead, Williams moved on the Confederate positions, south and west from between the North and East Wood just at the time Gibbon's battery broke Hood's charge, at about 7:20 A.M. There was still confusion on the field. The men were so thickly scattered through the haze of smoke that it was difficult to see if they were firing at their own men or the enemy. Mansfield rode out into the open to survey the situation before advancing his men, having a dreadful fear of firing into the backs of Hooker's men. As he did, a bullet struck his horse and it threw him to the ground. While leading the wounded animal to cover, another bullet caught the general in the stomach. Four men quickly made a stretcher from muskets and a blanket and carried him back of the lines to the George Line house where he died before he could see any of his men in action.[37] The week before, Mansfield had called on Gideon Welles in Washington. They were from the same state and close friends. As they departed that day, Welles had said, "Farewell, success attend you." Mansfield replied, "We may never meet again."[38] By this time Hooker was wounded in the foot and retiring from the field. Meade took over the First Corps and withdrew to the bivouac area for reorganization.

Williams, senior division commander, immediately took command of the Twelfth Corps. He had a bear by the tail. Mass confusion resulted from the switch in command. Though Williams was never able to assemble the scattered pieces, his corps did as best they could. Two brigades approached the cornfield and marched through Hooker's shattered lines, Gordon pushing past the Miller buildings and Crawford hitting diagonally from the northeast. Once again there was fierce fighting as Hood made a last effort to hold. The odds were simply too much for him, and his men backed stubbornly down the pike rails until they were pulled out of line some distance below the church.

Further to the east of the cornfield, progress was being made by Greene's 2d Division. Here the Smoketown Road runs from the Upper Bridge and terminates at the Dunkard Church. Greene's 2,500 men moved through the East Wood and onto the road. Hill's three brigades, still on the cornfield, hit the advance broadside. Reinforcements from Jackson's or Grigsby's already depleted division were brought in for support, but superior Federal artillery once again cut through the Confederate defenses and Greene pushed on to the Mumma farm ridge just to the east of the church. The drive was spent. No reinforcements came up, and the fire was too heavy to advance further. McClellan's main thrust on the Confederate left had come close to breaking through. If Lee had any doubt whatsoever in his mind when he crossed the Potomac about the loyalty of his North Carolina boys, or for that matter, any of his troops, they were dispelled during those few morning hours. All his men had fought magnificently. What McClellan did not know was that had Hooker and Mansfield co-ordinated their efforts, there could have been no doubt that Lee's left would have been turned. Indeed, had McClellan co-ordinated the efforts of his three major corps movements that morning, the battle would have been over by noon. McClellan failed to take advantage of another opportunity Lee laid in his lap—this time not because of "lost orders," but because of necessity. The Federal left and center stood still while Lee shifted whole regiments to other parts of the field—right under McClellan's eyes, Federal reserves staying in line behind the front.

During these morning hours, the town of Sharpsburg received the brunt of McClellan's artillery. Shells zipped overhead, careening through the trees and crashing into houses, setting fires, and wrecking brick and stone constructions of long standing. Glass windows were shattered and bricks were scattered about. Those who remained behind the lines to administer to the wounded were kept busy extinguishing fires and dodging bullet-like debris. "I was never so tired of shelling in my life before," wrote Dr. J. R. Boulware, a surgeon with the 6th South Carolina, "I hate cannons."[39] Though the citizens of Sharpsburg had fled to the protective caves along the river edge, it was difficult to keep the inquisitive from Boonsboro and Keedysville in their homes. One reporter estimated that at one time as many as 5,000 spectators lined the hills behind the Antietam.[40]

McClellan, too, was behind the Antietam, venturing forth only occasionally. Some reporters would remember another time, another place where McClellan had remained behind the lines while his army fought Lee; McClellan was on the gunboat "Galeno" during the battle of Malvern Hill on the Peninsula, "the meanest picture that this bloody rebellion has painted."[41] At Antietam most of his time was spent with his close friend Fitz-John Porter, commander of the Fifth Corps. The two had established a "command post" along a rail fence near headquarters. McClellan's manner was "cool, and soldierly, his voice low-toned." He smoked, chatted frequently with his staff, always his glasses in his hand. He said to an aide, "By George, this is a magnificent field, and if we win this fight it will cover all our errors and misfortunes forever!"[42] Once when he rode toward the front, the distinguished Boston *Journal* correspondent, Charles Carleton Coffin, noticed a marked change in the reception the general was offered from his men. There were no cheers, no hurrahs, nothing but silent gazes.[43] It was almost as if they did not recognize him, almost as if they suspected what was happening on the field was their commander's fault. They seemed to sense that McClellan was putting his men in a paper bag and letting them fight their way out, blind and helpless. They were seeing him for the first time as the real McClellan, his glory stripped and fleeting with the tide of battle. If there seemed to be unrest in the eyes of the men, it was present among the officers also and would become more evident as the day progressed.

McClellan had a knack for not letting his men know what was happening on the field. Maj. Gen. Edwin V. Sumner, commanding the Second Corps, was in such a position that morning. At about 7:20 A.M., after spending the morning issuing preparatory instructions to his divisions, he was ordered to cross the Antietam with no foreknowledge of how Hooker was progressing.[44] Why McClellan detained Sumner at headquarters for so long and withheld information from him cannot be explained. As Mansfield, Sumner was under the assumption that the First Corps had the situation well in hand. He would come into battle totally unaware of the conditions of the field, unbriefed and depending solely on his own eyes. The severe inadequacies of the Federal command system would soon be abundantly clear.

Sumner had three divisions under Maj. Gen. John Sedgwick, Brig. Gen. William French, and Maj. Gen. Israel Richardson, nearly all composed of veterans. Sedgwick left camp at 7:20 A.M., French at 7:30 A.M., and Richardson at 8:30 A.M., after some delay in getting Morell's division of Porter's Fifth Corps as replacement.[45]

The Confederates, now in position at the extremities of the West Wood and beyond, watched Sedgwick's 2d Division march across the fields. It was a magnificent sight. Sedgwick's division was divided into columns of brigades about 70 yards apart as if in parade formation. Rifles and bayonets glittered in the bright sun which was now burning away the mist. Lee, whose hands were still bandaged from the earlier accident, was led on horseback by a courier to the hill east of Sharpsburg where he watched the approaching action intently.[46] "I saw

Situation at 7:30 A.M.

[him] standing erect and calm, with a field-glass to his eye," wrote General Walker, "his fine form sharply outlined against the sky, and I thought I had never seen a nobler figure. He seemed quite unconscious that the enemy's shells were exploding around and beyond him."[47]

Sedgwick's division entered the East Wood from the south and marched to the north. They were wasting no time now as it was becoming increasingly apparent that the Federal positions were in peril. Perhaps one reason for this was discovered by Col. Francis W. Palfrey. He wrote:

These were a grove of noble trees [the East Wood], almost entirely clear of underbrush. There were sorry sights to be seen in them, but the worse sight of all was the liberal supply of unwounded men helping wounded men to the rear. When good Samaritans so abound, it is a strong indication that the discipline of the troops in front is not good, and that the battle is not going so as to encourage the half-hearted.[48]

As the blue line reached the Mumma farm opposite the Dunkard Church, Sedgwick made a left flank movement bringing his men into attack position, parallel to the Hagerstown Pike and Jackson's front.

Jackson was not idly sitting by. Walker's troops had been called from the extreme Confederate right and were double timing through Sharpsburg toward the West Wood. McLaws' Division, resting near Lee's headquarters after their all night march from Maryland Heights, had been called and were on their way. Col. Stephen D. Lee, who was commanding five batteries of artillery under Hood, was sent to General Lee with an urgent appeal to send reinforcements as rapidly as possible "or the day was lost." He described McLaws' dramatic arrival on the field.

I met General Lee on horseback moving at a walk towards that part of the field, and about half-way between Sharpsburg and the Dunkard church. I reported the condition of affairs on the left and delivered General Hood's message. He quietly said, "Don't be excited about it, Colonel, go tell General Hood to hold his ground. Reinforcements are now rapidly approaching between Sharpsburg and the ford. Tell him that I am now coming to his support." I said, "General, your presence will do good, but nothing but infantry can save the day on the left." I started to return and had not gone over a hundred yards when he called me and pointed to McLaws' division, then in sight, approaching at a double quick.[49]

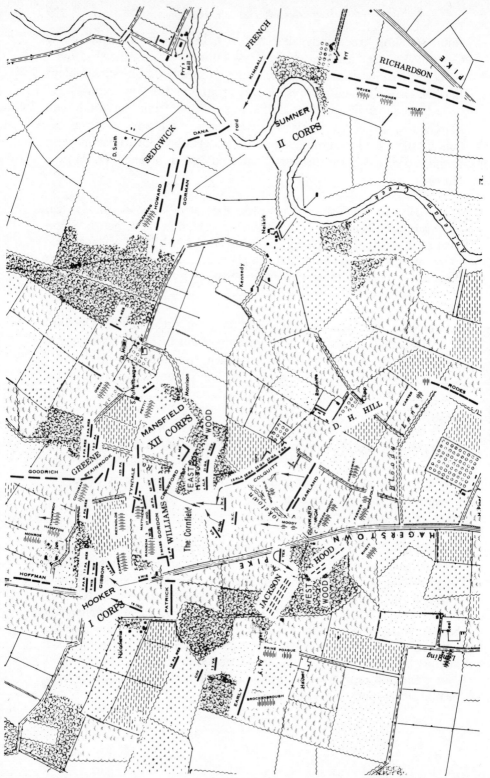

Situation at 8:00 A.M.

McLaws' men were tired but they eagerly helped Jackson work the pieces of his pattern as they pushed toward the West Wood.

Lee was not far from the front lines at any time. Freeman says that his movements are difficult to trace, but numerous little incidents crop up here and there showing that Lee was keeping a worried eye on his men. On two such occasions near the West Wood, he stumbled upon boys making rapidly for the rear. When one was asked where he was going, he replied, "Goin' to the rear."

"Leave your comrades and your flag at such a time?"

"Look'ee here, General, I've been stunted by a bung and I'm a leetle the durndest demoralized Reb you ever seen!"[50]

Lee let him go, but another did not strike his sympathy quite as much. A soldier dragging a stuck pig toward the rear caught Lee's eye and quickly aroused an indignant rage in the general. This was a flagrant violation of orders and with no hesitation, Lee ordered the man taken to Jackson with instructions to have him shot immediately. Jackson thought better of the situation, overruled his commander, and put the man on the front lines as his punishment. The man "redeemed his credit by his bravery, and came through the thick of the fight unscathed."[51]

The West Wood was now defended from the west and reinforcements were approaching from the south. The Confederates were in a position to encircle the Federal advance should it penetrate the wood. General Early, given command of Lawton's Division of about 600 men, was called in from the far left, and Stuart moved his artillery south to a more advantageous position. Jackson now had ten brigades either in position or on their way to face Sedgwick's three. The crisis facing Lee at the Dunkard church, the Federal salient threatening to crack his left center, his calculated gamble of pulling Walker off the lower Antietam ford, and the somewhat overlapping of brigades and regiments in the West Wood—many fighting under strange colors— all indicate that Jackson's position was not an ambush as it has sometimes been called. An ambush takes time and Jackson had no time. Troops would still be moving when the attack came. The almost spontaneous alignment of Confederate troops, however, could not have affected a better trap had it been worked out hours in advance. It was now shortly after 9:00 A.M.

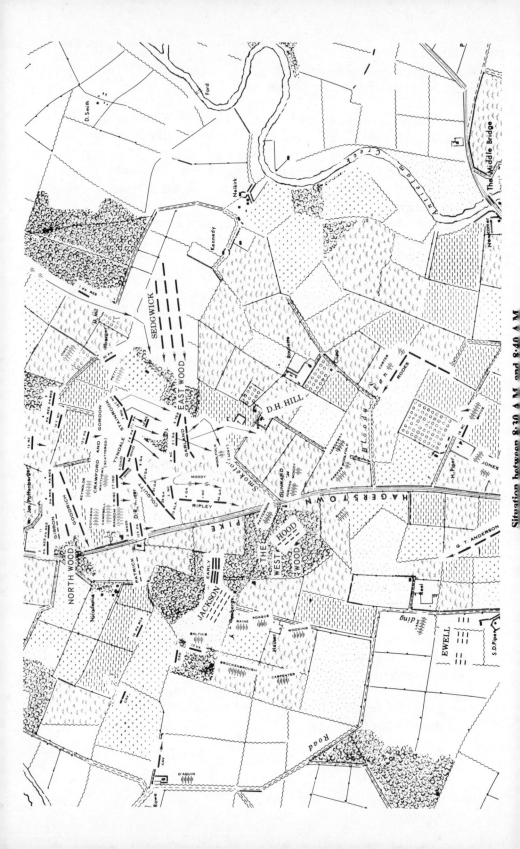

Situation between 8:30 A.M. and 8:40 A.M.

General Sumner, an old cavalry officer, was himself leading Sedgwick's Division. He made a fine picture, his hat off, white hair flying, as he rode with his men through the trees and the cornfield toward the Hagerstown Pike and the West Wood. He seemed to have the field to himself. All was quiet. The firing had stopped. The First Corps was virtually nonexistent and the Twelfth Corps was dissipated to the point of total inactivity. Sumner wrote:

I saw nothing of his corps [Hooker's] at all as I was advancing with my command on the field. There were some troops lying down on the left which I took to belong to Mansfield's command. . . . General Hooker's corps was dispersed; there is no question about that. I sent one of my own staff-officers to find where they were; and General Ricketts, the only officer we could find, said that he could not raise 300 men of the corps.[52]

Though it may have seemed so to Sumner, he did not have the entire field to himself. It was quiet to be sure, but only because both attack and counterattack had spent themselves. Off to his right was Doubleday's division of the First Corps. Though Gibbon, Phelps, and Patrick had been hit hard, they had reformed and were about a quarter mile to the north. And there was Hofman's brigade, still held in reserve. Their combined strength numbered about 1,000 men. The divisions of both Meade and Ricketts were somewhere to the rear, within a half mile, almost too far to be of any substantial help to Sedgwick.

The Twelfth Corps had fared little, if any, better than the First Corps. Mansfield's death early in the day very nearly shattered what strength it had. A great percentage of the corps was new and untried. Switching of commands to fill the vacancies merely piled confusion upon confusion. One regimental colonel did not find out until late in the day that he had been elevated that morning to brigade command.[53] It is doubtful therefore that General Williams, who replaced Mansfield, could have rallied sufficient force to be effective. With the exception of Gordon's brigade, now in front of the East Wood after successfully repulsing Hood, and the 125th Pennsylvania of Crawford's brigade, which had actually penetrated the West Wood and now just a few yards to the north of the Dunkard Church, Williams made little contribution to Sumner's attack. Williams' division, which fell to Crawford, operated independently from Greene's division of the same corps. They had failed to keep in touch with each other and so were

somewhat ignorant of one another's actions and intentions. Greene had his own problems and failed to let the command changes effect him. In all probability, he did not even know about them. The 3rd Brigade, under Goodrich, had been sent off to support Doubleday and so was in a position to render some assistance. Tyndale and Stainrook were with Greene on the extreme left of Sumner though they were out of sight.

Sumner, therefore, actually had support on the field to his right with Doubleday, support to strength of some 1,800 to his left with Greene, and another 1,200, and to his rear with Gordon's brigade of about 1,700. Had Sumner or Sedgwick been on the field earlier for reconnaissance, or had a proper intelligence system been in operation, he would have known that were at least 4,700 men at his command. As it was, he did not see them and so forged ahead on his own.

Sedgwick's men were now in order; Gorman's brigade in front, followed by Dana's and Howard's, nearly all of whom were veterans unlike the Twelfth Corps. They were passing through the cornfield, stepping lightly to avoid the bodies scattered by the earlier action. Stuart's artillery was taking its toll; the lines wavered but moved steadily on, the left and right dangerously exposed to a surprise flanking attack. There was a brief pause and then the order to "double-time." The charge picked up momentum. Gorman's brigade entered the West Wood, threading its way through the trees. Dana's brigade had halted, thinking it was to lie down when it saw and passed over Gordon's brigade which had taken a prone position. When orders were finally deciphered, there was a gap between the lines. Dana and Howard moved forward quickly until there was little more than 30 paces between the three lines.[54]

Gorman's brigade had been tramping over and around large limestone croppings. They were dangerous and afforded excellent hiding places for the enemy. Then there was a rail fence and a narrow road; just beyond this, the edge of the wood and the open fields. They came into the open and stopped. The West Wood action had already started when the 125th Pennsylvania had broken through the trees. The extreme left of Gorman's line, the 34th New York, had separated and come up on the right of the Pennsylvania regiment.[55] This left a hole in the line of about 400 yards, but to Gorman it was, at the moment, nothing serious. It looked as though it was just a matter of swinging to the left and sweeping into Sharpsburg. This was the farthest Federal penetration and this was Lee's weakened left. And then about that moment the air came alive with a fearful clash.

For the next twenty minutes, the most terrible holocaust of the day, some say of the war, engulfed Sedwick's division. Totally unexpected, primarily because no one had taken the time to survey what was thought to be a demoralized army, a whole new host of screaming Confederates came charging head on, bullets flying and unseen artillery shells ripping through the trees. The whole thing was so sudden that many of the men hardly had time to even raise their rifles into firing position. A New York reporter wrote:

The last of the charging lines had gone beyond, and was sweeping majestically into the jaws of death when the mass seemed to halt, while from the front line spouted forth a long angry sheet of flame from innumerable gun-barrels. Men were falling fast now, as unseen batteries were pelting the lines with an iron storm, and the Confederate bullets were finding the object of their flight. It was pitiful to see the men drop, at times in groups, knocked over by solid shot, or riddled with musket and rifle balls or bits of shell or case or canister.[56]

Fire came from three directions. The rear flanks were getting it just as much as the front lines. Confederate artillery, which had gotten the range of the open field behind, pinned down any hope of mass escape. McLaws' Division had lost none of its fighting power despite the long march from Maryland Heights. They had been in the vicinity of Sharpsburg for about an hour when Lee sent for them to join Jackson. Completely ignorant of the field or the disposition of the troops, McLaws relied on the guidance of several officers who sent him to the west of the town towards the West Wood. Cobb's Brigade led off, Kershaw, Barksdale, and Semmes falling in on his left. As they moved steadily forward toward the Federal left flank, Semmes reported seeing "an incessant current of wounded [flowing] to the rear, showing that the conflict had been severe and well contested."[57] McLaws hurried, directing his men to the left flank. Cobb's Brigade, under Lieutenant Colonel Sanders, failed to hear the command and marched straight ahead, missing the West Wood action completely and ending up along the Hagerstown Pike, falling in on the left Rodes's Brigade. It was just as well. At Crampton's Gap, Cobb had over 1,300 officers and men. He now had 357.[58]

While McLaws was moving into position, Walker's Division was rapidly approaching, not more than 15 minutes behind. At about 9:00 A.M., Walker had been summoned by Lee to reinforce Jackson. He had, just a few hours before, left Sharpsburg to take his assigned position in support of General Toombs opposite the lower bridge. Quickly he brought in his skirmishers and set out for the far left. It would take him about an hour. On his way he met General Ripley, who had been wounded, and was oriented on the progress of the battle. By this time it was evident that Jackson was in serious trouble. One of the general's aides was sent out to talk with Walker. Jackson considered the West Wood the "key to the battlefield" and urged that should Walker find the wood occupied, it was imperative that the enemy be driven out.[59] Walker was further informed that a gap of at least a third mile had developed between D. H. Hill's left and the West Wood and that it must be plugged. Immediately the 27th North Carolina and the 3rd Arkansas were dispatched under Col. John R. Cooke. The rest of the division moved on. Von Borcke said that it was "astonishing to see men without shoes, whose lacerated feet often stained their path with blood, limping to the front to conquer or fall with their comrades."[60]

Jubal Early, who supported Stuart through the attacks of the First and Twelfth Corps, had moved to the south and west behind the West Wood ridge and was out of sight re-forming his lines when the 125th Pennsylvania and 34th New York came up to the church. Seeing that these units posed a serious threat, Early advanced his column of about 900 men in that general direction. He had left the Stonewall Brigade (Grigsby) with some 200 men to hold Sedgwick until promised reinforcements arrived.[61] At about this same moment, McLaws came on the field.

Cobb's breaking off left Kershaw in command of the right wing of McLaws' advance. Kershaw ordered his men forward at double-quick time, several regiments actually forming in the process. The danger of two Confederate units colliding immediately became apparent. Early, aproaching from nearly due west, and Kershaw, from the southwest, were on a collision course that would be disastrous if they converged. The confusion was bad enough as it was. It was inevitable that someone would have to give. Kershaw veered off to his right, putting him on a due east course. Early turned slightly to the left, aiming at the left flank of Sedgwick's forces. In the face of these advancing troops, the 125th Pennsylvania and 34th New York withdrew back across the Hagerstown Pike, firing as they went. Sgt. Charles Burton, the regiment color bearer, was hit five times but held on long enough to hand the flag over to Cpl. G. S. Haskins with instructions not to let it fall. Colonel Higgins of the Pennsylvania unit later remarked: "Had I remained in position two minutes longer I would have lost my entire command."[62] The Confederates were coming on with wild enthusiasm. There seems to have been a noticeable surge of spirit among both Early's and McLaws' men despite the intensity of the fire they faced. "The troops needed little encouragement," wrote Semmes. Early tried to hold his men back but, once started, there seemed to be no stopping the pursuit.[63]

As the Pennsylvania and New York units backed off from the trees around the Dunkard Church, they fell into the arms of their own support — Greene's division behind the Mumma farm ridge and several batteries of artillery set up near the Mumma house and the East Wood. As Kershaw pursued these forces, he fell right into the path of this sweeping fire. Tompkins' Rhode Island Battery and Cothran's New York Battery opened up as the Confederates came through the wood and into the open. It was a devastating blow to Kershaw's South Carolinians. Tompkins noted that his guns were "pointed with care, and the accuracy of aim and length of fuse noticed."[64] But artillery does not distinguish between officers and men. As fast as the Confederates appeared, they were shot down. Kershaw described one of the most colorful scenes of the day:

> The Seventh [South Carolina], led by Colonel Aiken, trailed their progress to the cannon's mouth with the blood of their bravest, and, when borne back by resistless force, rallied the remnant left under command of Capt. John S. Hard, the senior surviving officer. Colonel Aiken was most dangerously wounded, and every officer and man in the color company either killed or wounded, and their total loss 140 out of 268 men carried in. The colors of this regiment, shot from the staff, formed the winding-sheet of the last man of the color company at the extreme point reached by our troops that day.[65]

Tompkins saw this dramatic event. He talked about the "sharp cannister fire" from his battery that caused the enemy to "retire in confusion, leaving the ground covered with their dead and wounded" and then he added, "and abandoning one of their battle-flags, which was secured by a regiment which came up on my right after the enemy had retreated."[66] The 28th Pennsylvania, Stainrook's brigade (Greene's division), was that regiment, and if it distinguished itself in no other way in this battle, it did so at this very moment. Cpl. Jacob G. Orth of Company D moved out and picked up the 7th South Carolina flag. He did not wrench it from the hand of the color bearer for this soldier was dead. The flag staff was broken and according to Kershaw's official report, the colors had fallen. Orth took the flag and brought it back to his commander as their trophy of war. For this he received the "medal of honor."[67]

Kershaw's Brigade was wrecked. There was no order and what was left was totally ineffective in the pursual of Sedgwick. Barksdale's Brigade, which was on Kershaw's left, had been stopped at the Hagerstown Pike by Tompkins' Battery and instead of driving through as Kershaw did, he joined on Early's right, made a left flank movement and hit the left of Sedgwick's men in the West Wood. Walker, meanwhile, was coming to Early's aid. It is not difficult to imagine the confusion of the mass of troops on the field at this particular moment for the fighting was at extreme close quarters. Walker had two brigades; Manning's and Ransom's. Two of Manning's regiments had been dropped off farther south to fill the gap in the Confederate line. His remaining three reported to Kershaw and inadvertently fell to the same fate as the brave South Carolinians. Ransom continued on and fell in with Early and Barksdale.

A solid wall of smoke stood between the two protagonists. Men in blue turned to fire and found themselves aiming at their own men. Dana's brigade, the second Federal line, fired through Gorman's brigade, the first, so close had the left of one come to the left of the other. Frantically, Lt. Col. J. W. Kimball of the 15th Massachusetts tried to stop the 69th New York from this "murderous fire." It was either bring them on through to the front or halt them altogether. General Sumner rode up about this time and in a vain effort tried to correct the "terrible mistake." But the men were in such close proximity to each other, it was next to impossible to maintain any semblance of order.[68]

Men scrambled for cover and there was none. In a matter of minutes, lines began to break. The third line, Howard's brigade, was the first to go. They were all Pennsylvanians and all from Philadelphia; thus the "Philadelphia Brigade." The fact that they came from the city of "brotherly love" had nothing to do with the unfortunate circumstance they found themselves in that morning. They had hardly a chance to raise their rifles when the shock wave hit them. Sumner, concerned for the rear and of the danger of complete encirclement by the Confederate troops now penetrating to the Hagerstown Pike, ordered Howard to turn about, indicating that he should face to the rear, but the brigade simply melted away across the field, the 72d Pennsylvania disappearing completely and not showing up until late in the day.[69] Fleeing regiments stumbled over bodies of their comrades, shells exploding in their faces as they ran. It was reported that the Confederate encirclement was so complete "a strong body . . . marched up northward through the open fields between the West Woods and the Hagerstown pike."[70] This was undoubtedly units from Early, Barksdale, or Ransom.

It was no easy fight for Sedgwick. His right was being bombarded by Stuart's artillery, his center was facing Grigsby and Semmes, and his left was being turned by Early, Barksdale and Ransom, and the remnants of Kershaw's and Manning's brigades. Slowly his command withered. So confused were battle orders and directions that few could be followed with any degree of accuracy. Men hardly knew which way to turn; it seemed better at times to merely race for cover.

The 15th Massachusetts pushed forward some ten yards until they were within fifteen yards from the Confederates, their right managing to chase Stuart's men from their guns on two occasions. Then the Confederates pushed out of the wood and across the pike. Once again they entered the cornfield, firing as they went at targets less than fifteen yards away. There was only one place for the Federals to go — back to the East and North Wood. Gibbons' batteries, which had been watching, but from a helpless position, now swung into action for the second time that morning. They opened up with full force, plastering the cornfield with canister. Tompkins and Cothran never ceased with their devastating fire. The Confederate line halted and then withdrew back to the protection of the rocks and trees.

The nearest support for Sedgwick was Greene's relatively fresh division which had rested throughout most of the West Wood action. Now at this late moment, he rose and pushed forward to the church. Contrary to most general studies of this campaign, this was the first time Greene had entered the West Wood. He remained for about two hours when he was pushed out by rallying troops under Ransom. As he was withdrawing to the East Wood, the first units from Franklin's Sixth Corps were arriving from Pleasant Valley. Irwin's brigade was immediately sent in to support Greene's retirement. Within moments Irwin's brigade was shattered and pulled back, thus retiring the big Federal push for the west side of the Hagerstown Pike. Sumner advised Franklin that it was fruitless to attempt any further action, that he was convinced the West Wood could not be taken.

Sedgwick's division was wrecked. Nearly half, or around 2,225, were casualties. Sedgwick himself was wounded three times and put out of action. Greene was re-forming in the East Wood. Meade had assumed command of the First Corps. Confederate losses were not light. They already had their share of casualties in the morning, but McLaws would suffer as high as 40 per cent. An educated estimate of the Confederate accumulative strength at this time would be about 3,500 under Jackson. The Federals, after considerable regrouping and command readjusting, had in the neighborhood of 11,000 troops.[71]

Four hours of steady fighting had left both sides exhausted. Hooker's first corps was broken; little was left of Mansfield's Twelfth Corps; now one-third of Sumner's Second Corps was on the run. And still Lee's left held. Dead and wounded in the cornfield numbered better than 12,000. Twelve thousand in four hours; three bitter Federal attacks; three equally bitter Confederate counter-attacks.

The fighting on Lee's left died out around 10:30 A.M. With the exception of occasional artillery exchanges, more annoying than anything else, there was no battle in this area the rest of the day. As the intense noise of battle faded, the horrible and pathetic sounds of human voices, crying in pain and death, drifted over the fields. Walter Clark of the 35th North Carolina heard a plea for help and crawled forward through the trees. The call had come from a Massachusetts colonel who reluctantly surrendered his sword and pistol in return for medical aid. Years later, Clark realized what a prize he had captured. The victim was Francis W. Palfrey, who distinguished himself in the famous *The Army in the Civil War* volumes published in 1897. Palfrey authored *The Antietam and Fredericksburg*.[72]

Situation at 10:30 A.M.

Jackson seriously considered at about this time a flanking movement that would carry his men around the Federal right and to their rear. To ascertain what opposition he would encounter, he sent a man by the name of Hood from the 35th North Carolina up a tall tree. When Jackson called to him for a count on the troops situated beyond the East Wood, Hood yelled down, "Who-e-e! there are oceans of them, General." "Count their flags," ordered Jackson, who wanted more specific information. When Hood reached thirty-nine, the general called him down.[73] That was enough to discourage the operation. The Confederate left, no longer on the Potomac, was grounded in the West Wood and here is where it would stay.

During the quiet period of the battle, a strange incident occurred which has all but escaped history. George Smalley was approached by a member of McClellan's staff. Would Mr. Smalley go to General Hooker and ask him to take command of the army? The battle was only half fought and only half won. There was still time to save the field and crush Lee if McClellan was ousted and the command given to Hooker. Would Mr. Smalley act as an intermediator? This was mutiny in its truest sense, subject to the most severe consequences. The officers knew this but still wanted Hooker. After some argument, Smalley agreed to visit Hooker on the pretense of a sickbed call. The reporter, who had already found favor with Hooker, questioned the general in his bedroom at the Pry house, where he had been taken, on his ability to resume his duties following the accident on the field earlier that morning. Hooker replied that he was helpless and could not return to the field. When Smalley pressed the question, Hooker suspected something and quizzed the reporter. Neither man gave an inch and the matter was dropped. Smalley's report ended the notions of mutiny. If the battle of Antietam itself did not forecast McClellan's military future, this incident surely did.[74]

9

Bloody Lane

To this hour all the action had taken place on Lee's left, the Federal right. McClellan had no troops directly facing Lee's center, which was entrenched to the east of the Hagerstown Pike between the East Wood and the Boonsboro Pike. McCellan's center, so to speak, was still on the eastern banks of the Antietam, being fed into battle one unit at a time as they were needed. The Ninth Corps, opposite the lower bridge, had not yet moved against Lee's right. It was a game of chess with McClellan moving only one piece at a time as if the same rules applied to war.

Lee proved to be the master chessman, however. As long as McClellan chose to move in this fashion, Lee would adjust his lines in like manner. That morning Lee had carefully moved Walker's Division from his already weakened right to the left, leaving only a token defense facing Burnside. D. H. Hill, commanding the center, had given Jackson three of his five brigades and now his line was stretched as thin as prudence would allow. Had Burnside chosen to attack as early in the morning as Hooker, Lee would most assuredly have been overwhelmingly defeated. But once more the Federal army was most obliging. McClellan would send no more troops against the Confederate left. He had probed with his pawns and lost three, each checked in their advance. The game would continue until little was left of the grey side but the king, a couple of battered titled pieces, and a pawn or two. There would be no checkmate — a stalemate, perhaps — but it was only 9:30 in the morning. There was more death and destruction to come.

Now that Lee's left was relatively quiet and it was apparent that fighting would not be resumed on that part of the field, it was time to shift the pieces. When Sumner came to the front he had had two divisions with him — Sedgwick's and French's. French had followed behind Sedgwick but instead of joining in with the attack, found himself facing south against D. H. Hill holding forth at the Piper farm. It was all quite by accident and little blame can be placed on French himself. He thought, as did Sumner, that his division would swing in on Sedgwick's right. Unfortunately for Sedgwick, French ran into Hill's advance pickets and quite unconciously turned the axis of the battle for the second time that day; back to a north-south direction.

Six hundred yards below the Dunkard Church on the Hagerstown Pike, a narrow lane turned to the east, ran for some 500 yards to a shallow and then another 500 yards to the crest of a ridge. At this point the road turned sharply south and then through a series of turns dipped through a deep ravine and back to the crest of the ridge to the Boonsboro Pike. For lack of a better name, the first 1,000 yards was called the Sunken Road which was apropos since the shallow dropped ten feet or more below the terrain level. On the south was the Piper farm, on the north the Roulette and Clipp farms.

It was in this section of the road that Hill had positioned his South Mountain veterans, the remnants of Garland's, Colquitt's Rodes's and Anderson's brigades, and in that order from left to right. The men of Ripley's, Garland's and Colquitt's brigades had been sent to Jackson's support earlier that morning. Part of Colquitt's brigade had returned and was now on the ridge above the shallow road looking north. Garland's Brigade, badly broken, slowly drew back and what was left of it formed with Colquitt. Ripley had gone off behind a ridge on the left of the Hagerstown Pike with Walker's Division, its commander badly wounded. The body of Hill's defense occupied the low section of the road, well entrenched behind a breastwork of fence rails. Originally these men had faced to the east, the Sunken Road bisecting their line. With the intense action on the far left, they had turned to face the north waiting for McClellan's next punch. Hill was full of fight and, despite depleted ranks, his men were equally determined. They had had a visit from General Lee with a word of encouragement and a warning of what it would mean to lose their ground. Col. John B. Gordon of the 6th Alabama replied to Lee in a loud voice so his men could hear: " These men are going to stay here, General, till the sun goes down or victory is won!" Years later when Gordon recorded these memories, he added, "Alas! Many of the brave fellows are there now."[1]

Major Alfred A. Woodhull, U.S.A., was standing near Weed's battery of artillery on the east bank of the Antietam when Capt. Weed spied a man on horseback with several companions on foot near the crest of the ridge at the Sunken Road. It was Hill, Longstreet, and Lee. Hill was on horseback begging forgiveness for his fatigue. The men had gone forward to view the Federal positions. Longstreet had asked Hill to ride apart so that the group would not be such a likely target. Capt. Weed thought they were just that as he sighted his gun for the horse and fired. Longstreet saw the puff of smoke. "There is a shot for General Hill," he said. And at that instant both front legs of Hill's horse were sheared off just below the knees. This was the third horse Hill had lost that day.[2]

As French moved south from the East Wood, he encountered the advanced Confederate pickets at the Roulette farm. Colquitt was out in front, but the best that could be expected was a delaying action. It was only a matter of minutes after initial contact that they were forced to withdraw. They made a stubborn stand but when Capt. T. P. Thomson of the 5th North Carolina (Garland's Brigade) yelled, "They are flanking us," the ranks broke and fled to the rear.[3] A number of Confederates headed for the old farm house, scrambling for the nearest and safest shelter they could find. The cellar door was open and they leaped in only to find the door slammed shut behind them by the enemy. For the 14th Connecticut, which had only been in uniform a few weeks, this kind of fighting was much more fun than battle.[4] Colquitt's Brigade had suffered the loss of ten field officers that morning; four killed and six wounded. This left Hill with only two brigades untouched thus far at Antietam; Rodes's which had so desperately held the Confederate left at South Mountain losing at least one-third of its strength, and G. B. Anderson's relatively fresh brigade. The few men that Colquitt could now muster were formed on Rodes's left. Off in the distance someplace was Cobb's Brigade and the two regiments of Manning's Brigade dropped off that morning, but Hill knew little about them. So he had two brigades facing a full division; the odds were hardly desirable. But Lee had told Hill that R. H. Anderson was

Situation at Lower Bridge, 10:30 A.M.

up from Maryland Heights and was on his way to support him. At least help was coming.

Longstreet described French's approach:

The signal of the approaching storm was the bursting of . . . French's division, through the field of corn, hardly ruffled by the affair at the Roulette House, spreading its grand march against our centre. They came in full appreciation of the work in hand, marched better than on drill, unfolded banners making gay their gallant step.[5]

During the advance of the 132nd Pennsylvania, a Confederate shell hit a colony of bee hives in the Roulette orchard. It was touch and go for awhile as the men ran for cover from an odd assortment of swarming bullets and bees. At this particular moment, the 132nd, a newly recruited regiment, could not have cared less whether it was more humiliating to break under the sting of lead or bees. The whole thing was a little too much for them. After considerable prodding by officers, the lines moved on to the high ground overlooking the Piper farm and the Sunken Road and out of danger, but these boys would never forget this incident. Long after time clouded their memories, long after battle lines and formations became sketchy images, they remembered their skirmish with the bees.[6]

There was an eerie quietness as the Federals formed on top. Hill held his fire until the line started to move down the slope. Confederate General Gordon and a Union soldier, T. F. Galway, both eyewitnesses, left dramatic accounts of what took place next.

GORDON: My troops held the most advanced position on this part of the field . . . the predicted assault came. The men in blue . . . formed in my front, an assaulting column four lines deep. The front line came to a "charge bayonets," the other lines to a "right shoulder shift." The brave Union commander, superbly mounted, placed himself in front, while his band in [the] rear cheered them with martial music. It was a thrilling spectacle. So far as I could see, every soldier wore white garters around his ankles. The banners above them had apparently never been discolored by the smoke and dust of battle. Their gleaming bayonets flashed like burnished silver in the sunlight. With the precision of step and perfect alignment of a holiday parade, this magnificent array moved to the charge, every step keeping time to the tap of the deep-sounding drum. As we stood looking upon that thrilling pageant, I thought, if I did not say, "What a pity to spoil with bullets such a scene of martial beauty!" But there was nothing else to do. Mars is not an aesthetic god; and he was directing every part of this game in which giants were the contestants. To oppose man against man was impossible, for there were four lines of blue to my one line of gray. The only plan was to hold my fire until the advancing Federals were almost upon my lines. No troops with empty guns could withstand the shock. My men were at once directed to lie down upon the grass. Not a shot would be fired until my voice should be heard commanding "Fire!"

The stillness was literally oppressive, as this column of Union infantry moved majestically toward us. Now the front rank was within a few rods of where I stood. With all my lung power I shouted "Fire!" Our rifles flamed and roared in the Federals' faces like a blinding blaze of lightning.

GALWAY: . . . the Confederates met us with a murderous fire.

GORDON: The effect was appalling. The entire front line, with few exceptions, went down in the consuming blast. Before the rear lines could recover, my exultant men were on their feet, devouring them with successive volleys. The first now became furious and deadly.[7]

It was the cornfield all over again. The first line halted, re-formed and moved again. And again they were stopped. Across the road, in the Piper fields, Rebel infantry fired over the heads of their comrades direct into the faces of the enemy. Confederate artillery, scattered to the left during the morning, was now being brought back and was, for a short time, holding the Federals back.

A Federal officer marveled at the stamina of Hill's men. He wrote:

It is beyond all wonder how such men as the rebel troops can fight on as they do; that, filthy, sick, hungry, and miserable, they should prove such heroes in fight, is past explanation—one regiment stood up before the fire of two or three of our long-range batteries and of two regiments of infantry, and though the air around them was vocal with the whistle of bullets and screams of shells, there they stood, and delivered their fire in perfect order; and there they continued to stand.[8]

Gordon came upon a gray-haired father and his son. The boy was dead, the father bending over him, mortally wounded himself, resolving to go back into battle with his name on his breath.[9]

R. H. Anderson arrived at Sharpsburg just as the action broke out on the center. Longstreet, who was commanding this section of the field, directed Anderson, with between 3,000 and 4,000 men, to fall in behind Hill. He moved rapidly across the fields from the Piper farm

Situation between 12:00 noon and 12:15 P.M.

to throw his weight into the battle. These were Hill's expected reinforcements.

Quickly, what little Confederate artillery was left, about twelve guns now, rolled up and pumped fresh fire into French's division. McClellan's big guns from across the Antietam got their range and amidst the air-shattering musket fire there gradually formed a fierce artillery duel that shook the very foundations of barns and houses for miles around. The black smoke rolled across the hills, blinding, choking, mingling with the sweat on the men's faces until they resembled charred ghost-like images from hell.

GALWAY: At one time a lull occurred in the Confederate fire from the lane, and then we saw perhaps a dozen white squares rise above the fence rails; whether they were white handkerchiefs or the white cotton haversacks used by the Confederates, we could not distinguish. It was quickly plain, however, that though there might be some in the lane who wished to surrender, these were in the minority, for we met a musketry fire so rapid and well aimed that we all unfixed bayonets and backed up step by step until we were on the old ground, where we dropped down again and resumed our fire as before.[10]

Galwey was not the only one who saw the white flag. Lt. Col. Vincent M. Wilcox, commander of the 132nd Pennsylvania, wrote: "At last he [the enemy] exhibited a white flag . . ." And Wilcox added: " . . . but in violation of that flag kept us an incessant fire of shell and musketry . . ."[11] Col. Joseph Snider of the 7th West Virginia was not happy at all with what he considered a downright trick. "The enemy endeavored to deceive us by hoisting a white flag, which for a moment caused our men to cease firing, during which time the enemy was discovered to be moving in large force with the view of flanking our left . . ."[12]

French's division was in trouble. Three regiments under Col. Dwight Morris were untrained and inexperienced. Their confusion simply complicated matters. Kimball's brigade was forced to march over and around Morris and finally formed itself on the lane leading from the Roulette farm to the Sunken Road and moved on to the crest. Kimball described what he saw:

Directly on my front, in a narrow road running parallel with my line, and, being washed by water, forming a natural rifle-pit between my line and a large corn-field, I found the enemy in great force, as also in the corn-field in rear of the ditch. My advance farther was checked and for three hours and thirty minutes the battle raged incessantly, without either party giving way.[13]

The Confederate position was so strong — much stronger than French had expected — that one Federal regiment after another fell in the path of Rebel resistance. Longstreet ordered an attack. "I endeavored to charge them with my brigade and that portion of Colquitt's which was on my immediate left," wrote Rodes. Rodes later claimed he failed because one regiment did not hear the command and another did not move up far enough.[14] But he underestimated the damage. Some men had broken through and had gotten as far as the Rouette barn, some 500 yards to the north of the Sunken Road, a considerable distance behind French's front lines. This, for a time, posed a definite threat to the Federal rear. It was stemmed only by the quick thinking of Brooke's brigade of Richardson's division then coming on the field.[15] All Federal regimental reports listed heavy casualities. The 14th Indiana had gone into battle with 60 rounds of ammunition. Just as the last was fired, "the enemy was discovered moving in heavy force" on their right flank. It was a mad scramble as the men struggled to get ammunition off the bodies of their dead comrades, but, as all reports say, "the line was held and the enemy repulsed."[16]

"Being foiled in this [Rodes's charge], he [the enemy] made a heavy charge on my center," wrote Kimball, "thinking to break my line, but was met by my command and repulsed with great slaughter."[17] This was Anderson's Brigade, but segregated advances would not work. "It became evident to me then that an attack by us must, to be successful, be made by the whole of Anderson's brigade, mine, Colquitt's and any troops that had arrived on Anderson's right," wrote Rodes. "My whole force at this moment did not amount to over 700 men — most probably not to that number."[18]

Countercharges were made. The 108th New York drove into the Confederate lines, taking 168 prisoners and the regimental colors from Anderson's 14th North Carolina. Young Henry Niles, Company K of the New York regiment, grabbed the North Carolina flag and raced to the rear with another trophy of battle. On his way to his colonel, he was stopped by an officer from another regiment. The officer said, "You'd better give me those colors, boy. You're liable to be shot by one of your own men." Not knowing any better, Niles handed over the flag.[19] Through the cleverness of one and the ignorance of another, the 108th New York was deprived of one of the highest regimental battlefield honors. Others lost similar honors when they pursued the enemy in flight. Kimball complained that "some parties outside the brigade" took several stands of colors while his men were busy rounding up some 300 prisoners.[20]

Just as Rodes initiated his attack, Maj. Gen. Israel B. Richardson with Sumner's 3d division, the one late in leaving camp, arrived on the field with his three brigades. On his right was Meagher's (pronounced "Mar") famous Irish Brigade, the 29th Massachusetts, the 88th, 63rd, and the celebrated fighting 69th New York. On the left was Brig. Gen. John C. Caldwell's Brigade, the 5th New Hampshire, 88th Pennsylvania, the 7th, 61st and 64th New York. Brooke's brigade supported the rear.

Richardson came on strong. He had personally led his division as the advance unit pursuing Lee after South Mountain, and here he was in personal command again. The division made an impressive sight, the band drumming the march, the Irish Brigade in front, green flag fluttering in the breeze. Proud names like Duffy, McGee, O'Neil, Murphy, Callahan, and Kelly were marching to battle, all God-fearing men with a set determination in their eyes that would have warned any enemy to step aside. It is said the flamboyant 69th took with them their own laundress and that, in the height of battle, she was standing with the regiment, swinging her bonnet, cheering the men on.[21]

While still in the depressions of land before the plateau confronting the Rebels, Richardson ordered a halt. Every man was ordered to remove all unnecessary equipment. Those who still carried blanket rolls tossed them aside. Canteens were removed until each man had only his rifle and cartridge box. "The men of the Irish Brigade instantly obeyed this order with a heartiness and enthusiasm which was rare to expect from men who had been wearied and worn by the unremitting labors of a nine months' campaign," wrote their commander.[22] It was going to be a hot battle. There would be no time to fool with extra equipment. They would go in light. Regiment after regiment received a last minute morale-boosting talk from their commanding officer. Colonel E. E. Cross of the 5th New Hampshire paced up and down in front of his men and said, "Men, you are about to engage in battle.

You have never disgraced your state; I hope you won't this time. If any man runs I want the file closers to shoot him; if they don't, I shall myself. That's all I have to say." The speech had a lasting effect on the men, but perhaps not so much on the officers. The man who so vividly remembered Col. Cross's words also remembered seeing "General ———— under the hill and behind the haystack out of harm's way, and I did not see him after that until we came out of the musketry fight."[23]

While Meagher's brigade moved into position from the northeast to face the right of Hill's line, Wright's Brigade from R. H. Anderson's Division formed on Hill's extreme right next to G. B. Anderson and extended the Confederate line out of the shallow road and onto the crest of the plateau. As Meagher approached, he came over the wide field of over 100 yards, giving him little cover from the fire of Confederates, now out of the road and approaching to meet him. "The enemy's column, with their battle-flag advanced and defiantly flying in front, was at this time within 300 paces of our line," wrote Meagher.[24]

The Irish Brigade was, in effect, stopgapping a break in French's line. Anderson's Brigade had their eye on it first and were determined to drive a wedge in and through. Fifty paces from the oncoming green flag, the Confederates formed their lines. Meagher described the reception:

On coming into this close and fatal contact with the enemy, the officers and men of the brigade waved their swords and hats and gave the heartiest cheers for their general, George B. McClellan, and the Army of the Potomac. Never were men in higher spirits. Never did men with such alacrity and generosity of heart press forward and encounter the perils of the battlefield. It was my design, under the general orders I received, to push the enemy on both their fronts as they displayed themselves to us, and, relying on the impetuosity and recklessness of Irish soldiers in a charge, felt confident that before such a charge, the rebel column would give away and be dispersed.[25].

But the enemy was not immediately dispersed despite the "persistant and effective" fire from the Irish. Meagher was forced to hold his ground within thirty paces of the Confederates. The general himself was injured when his horse was shot beneath him and he hit the ground rather heavily. He was carried off the field and put out of action until the next morning. Reports circulated later that he was drunk and had fallen from his horse. They were never proven true.[26]

Caldwell came onto the field on Meagher's left through a plowed field. Since the Irish Brigade was facing Hill's right, Caldwell found himself out in left field, so to speak, or much too far to do any good since he faced none of the enemy. At this particular point, the fate of Lee's center was in Caldwell's hands. Though he faced southeast, a turn to the right would have swept him down onto the Sunken Road, and, in all probability, would have carried him directly through Hill's line. Caldwell thought of this and was in the process of making the delicate move when Richardson ordered him to relieve Meagher's brigade. Caldwell gave a "right flank march" and his five regiments filed in behind Meagher, passing his line "in the most perfect order, under a severe fire of musketry." It was one of the smoothest exhibitions of troop movements in the entire battle. As Caldwell moved in, Meagher's brigade took a "left flank" and marched out and around to the rear. Now Caldwell faced the enemy's front, all of this in a matter of minutes and with hardly a falter in the face of the stout resistance.[27]

While Caldwell was shifting his regiments, two important things were happening. R. H. Anderson was swinging the main body of his division into position. While giving directions, he was shot and taken to the rear. Immediately the command system broke and little, if anything, was accomplished. With the exception of Wright's Brigade, which had formed on G. B. Anderson's right, this division contributed nothing substantial to ward off the Federal push.

Though Anderson's Division failed to aid Hill, Rodes's underestimated "attack" gave a few worries to the rear of the Federal lines. Brooke's brigade had been held in reserve by Richardson, and it was directly behind Meagher and Caldwell. When Rodes's unidentified troops (two brigades) reached the Roulette barn, Col. Paul Frank, commanding the 52nd New York, turned to his right to face them. It took about sixty rounds per man to dislodge the Confederates, but within thirty minutes the threat had withered away and Frank was able to devote his attention to the front.[28]

Chaplain H. S. Stevens of the 14th Connecticut had taken several wounded members of the regiment to the rear just as Rodes headed for the Roulette farm. Taking shelter in the basement of the house, Stevens kept an eye on the Confederate advance, knowing full well that only a stroke of luck would save them from capture. William Roulette himself was keeping an eye on developments for his family had been prisoners in their own home since early morning, unable to leave for the firing. Stevens stepped outside a few feet from the door to make the surrender obvious to the "Johnnies" before they took it on their own to destroy the house and all its hostages. "The foremost men in butternut came within about two rods of us," wrote the chaplain, "when the operations of a battery brought to bear upon the cornfield and of some infantry throwing a flanking fire into the field started those Johnnies on a retrograde movement of the most lively sort." In no time, Roulette was out in the fields shouting to his saviours, "Give it to 'em! Drive 'em! Take anything on my place, only drive 'em! Drive 'em!"[29]

By this time, the fighting at the Sunken Road had taken on a new violence. Shells from Confederate artillery tore large trenches in the plowed fields, speeding on with an irresistable force until their momentum was spent. Federal soldiers pushing forward hopped and skipped through the furrows, gingerly avoiding unexploded missiles, each, the boys were certain, marked for them. The noise was intense. "The thundering of artillery, the roaring of bursting shells, the rolling of musketry, and humming of deadly fragments and bullets, and sometimes the yells of the rebels and our own cheers all seemed to fill the whole horizon and drive peace away forever," wrote Thomas Livermore.[30] In 1960, a young boy searching for minie balls after a heavy rain unearthed a .69 calibre Confederate shell fused nose to nose with a .58 calibre Federal shell at the sunken road, vivid evidence of the fierce intensity of the fire.[31] An eyewitness to the battle claimed a count of seventeen bullet holes found in one Confederate body caught in the road.[32] Caldwell was moving in and the stubborn resistance was monstrous. "Fighting Dick" Richardson, as he was known, was on foot leading his men, bare sword in hand, his face blackened with powder, yelling and swearing at the top of his voice, barely heard above the terrible clash of weapons.[33] G. B. Anderson fell mortally wounded. Gordon took one bullet, then another and another, still on his feet encouraging his men on. Rodes was hit in the thigh, but neither man went down. Caldwell steadily gained ground and pushing forward broke the line from shallow to the crest of the road bed, sweeping Wright's and Anderson's Brigades back to the south side of the road and on into Piper's cornfield. Now only Rodes was left, still entrenched in the sunken part of the road. Barlow's 61st New York swung to its left facing Rodes's right. The Confederates were making a desperate attempt to hold, by now firing over their comrade's bodies. The fire was as intense as it was on any part of the field that day, but the Federals were now on the crest of the ridge and on the road, firing down. Now nothing could save the vulnerable Rebels.

Gordon by this time had received his fifth wound and was in critical condition:

A fifth ball . . . struck me squarely in the face . . . barely missing the jugular vein. I fell forward and lay unconscious with my face in my cap; and it would seem that I might have been smothered by the blood running into my cap from this last wound but for the act of some Yankee, who as if to save my life, had at a previous hour during the battle, shot a hole through the cap, which let the blood out.[34]

Lt. Col. J. N. Lightfoot had taken over the brigade and was making a desperate attempt to regroup his men. He reported to Rodes that his right was being turned. Rodes told him to go back and "throw his right back out of the old road." Lightfoot raced to the rear of his regiment and shouted, "Sixth Alabama, about face; forward march." Major Hobson of the 5th asked in astonishment if this meant the whole brigade. "Yes," cried Lightfoot. This confused order, accompanied by the roar of guns, broke what was left of Hill's line of defense. The men turned and ran for the rear.[35]

Rodes, though wounded, did his best to rally the men and, after some running about, managed to locate about 40 from the brigade near the Hagerstown Pike. Along with about 110 from other units, he formed a line 150 yards behind his original position. It was too late, however, to make any kind of a stand. Caldwell had taken over 300 prisoners and was now pushing the remnants of Wright's and Anderson's brigades across the road, through the cornfield and on into the Piper farm bottom. Federal troops were now within a few hundred yards of the hill commanding Sharpsburg.[36]

"Affairs looked very critical," wrote D. H. Hill. There were no reinforcements. Any resistance now would have to be organized from those broken regiments on the field. This Hill tried to do. "I got up about 200 men, who said they were willing to advance to attack if I would lead them." Grabbing a rifle and joining the ranks as if he was a private, Hill led his little band towards Caldwell's left.[37] It was a bold and magnificent show of courage and determination. The Confederates raced for a knoll, command of which would have enveloped the Federal left flank. Caldwell's 5th New Hampshire, under Colonel Cross, aimed for the small knoll. Cross was wounded in the head but was still on foot leading his men onward. Shouting out above the clash of weapons, he cried, "Men, put on the war paint!" Turning with astonishment, the men saw Cross, bare-headed, with a red handkerchief tied over his forehead, blood streaming down his cheeks, applying black powder to his perspiring face. Taking their cue, the boys tore the ends of their paper cartridges and streaked their faces with the powder. Then Cross yelled, "Give 'em the war whoop!" With a terrifying scream that rang out above the musket fire and with the fierce intensity of a thundering Indian charge, the rows of devilish-looking faces poured through the Confederate attack, scattering the line with close volley after volley. An officer of the New Hampshire regiment later wrote that he was certain that the alarm of painted faces and the "horrid whoop" helped repel the enemy. "At any rate," he wrote, "it reanimated us and let him know we were unterrified."[38]

Again the Confederates attempted a flanking movement, this time on Caldwell's right. Col. Francis Barlow of the 61st New York saw the movement. He ordered" 'Right shoulder shift arms,' and moved to the right, oblique to another hill . . . and commenced firing to the right upon the enemy. He fired about 20 rounds here, when the enemy's line broke in perfect disorder and ran in every direction."[39]

Several small but bold Confederate attempts were made to crack the oncoming Federal lines but to no avail. Brigades were practically extinct. Those which had not retreated completely off the field were rallied under individual commanders and pressed forward, some in groups as small as 40, others of 100. G. B. Anderson's Brigade had vanished. After the severe pounding they took and the loss of prisoners caught in Caldwell's sweep across the road, there was little left of Rodes's and Colquitt's men. Longstreet, who had kept a close eye on the events on the field, rode back and forth behind the lines searching for some kind of reinforcements to fill the gaps. Cooke's 27th North Carolina sent word to Longstreet that his ammunition was exhausted. The general ordered him to hold with the bayonet. Cooke's reply was that " 'he would hold till ice forms in regions where it was never known,' or words to that effect," wrote Longstreet.[40]

Sorrel, of Longstreet's staff, recorded the incident a little differently, but it still held the essence of fierce determination. Longstreet was always most generous with his compliments on good work, and he was forever passing along encouragement to the boys on the front lines. On this particular occasion he ordered Sorrel to pass his compliments on to the colonel of the 27th North Carolina. "Say he has fought splendidly and must keep it up," Sorrel quoted the general. "We are hard pressed and if he loses his position, there is nothing left behind him; his men have made noble sacrifices, but are to do still more." Sorrel continued:

Profanity is justly considered objectionable. I do not approve of it, but there are times when it may be overlooked, and never did such words sound so sweet as when I looked into Cooke's eyes and heard him: "Major, thank General Longstreet for his good words, but say, by ———— almighty, he needn't doubt me! We will stay here, by J. C., if we must all go to hell together! That ———— thick line of the enemy has been fighting all day, but my regiment is still ready to lick this whole ———— outfit. Start away, Major, quick, or you'll be getting hurt too, exposed as you are on that horse."[41]

Sorrel was hurt just then as a fragment of a shell struck him senseless from his horse, but he was able to report to Longstreet later and with a great deal of satisfaction.[42] When Hill found a battery of artillery near the Piper barn, he ordered it out and within range where it might to do some good. Immediately it drew fire from Federal guns which hit and exploded a caisson. Undaunted and without fear and with Longstreet himself shouting commands, they emptied what little ammunition they had left into the Federal lines, their guns jumping ten to twelve inches with their double charges.[43] They fired 70 rounds and lost 19 men and 15 horses.[44] "They seemed to forget that they had known fatigue;" wrote Longstreet. "The guns were played with life, and the brave spirits manning them claimed that they were there to hold or to go down with the guns."[45]

Another battery joined them and picked up the tempo of the firing. They took a terrible beating from the Federal artillery and soon the crews began to dwindle away to nothing. Longstreet was off his horse and with orders shouted above the roar of cannon had his own staff manning gunner's stations. It was an impressive sight and lived in the memory of the men for years—Longstreet, still with his bandaged heel encased in the uncomfortable carpet slipper, holding the reigns of his officer's horses while calmly passing on advice on the range of the enemy.[46]

Caldwell narrated the closing action:

The enemy made one more effort to break my line, and this time the attack was made in the center. Colonel Barlow hearing firing to his left, on our old front, immediately moved to the left and formed in line with the rest of the brigade. The whole brigade then moved forward in line, driving the enemy entirely out of the corn-field and through the orchard beyond, the enemy firing grape and canister from two brass pieces in the orchard to our front, and shell and spherical-case shot from a battery on our right. While leading his men forward under the fire, Colonel Barlow fell, dangerously wounded by a grape-shot in the groin. By command of General Richardson, I halted the brigade, and, drawing back the line reformed it near the edge of the corn-field. It was now 1 o'clock p.m. Here we lay exposed to a heavy artillery fire, by which General Richardson was severely wounded. The fall of General Richardson (General Meagher having been previously borne from the field) left me in command of the division, which I formed in line, awaiting the enemy's attack.[47]

But there would be no enemy attack and there would be no further Federal effort. The blue line had lost its power and the Confederates held tight. Lee, hearing the guns on his right and knowing that time would not permit another rapid shift of his line as he had done that morning, attempted to inaugurate a diversionary action on his left. Jackson was ordered to co-ordinate an attack with Stuart and Walker gathering as much force as possible. It would have been futile to "hazard the attempt," however, for Federal artillery had pushed so far forward and so near the Potomac as to make any Confederate effort certain suicide. Lee was forced to abandon the thought and turn his attention to his right. The tactics of the deployment were sound only in that Lee had good cause to believe McClellan's right demoralized. There had been little action there since early in the morning but with the army in the condition it was at the time, it was obvious to Jackson that little or nothing could be accomplished.[48]

Supporting artillery had been most effective for the Federal assaults throughout the morning, but, for some strange reason, at this point they ceased to be of any help. Their aim was now endangering their own men as much as the enemy. Word was sent back to headquarters to cease firing. Richardson determined to use what was available on the field, but much to his indignation, he received no cooperation. Finally, with only a battery of horse artillery—six-pounders—Richardson moved forward. Personally commanding his guns in an effort to silence the deadly Confederate batteries, the general received a mortal wound in the side from a shell fragment. He was borne from the field as rapidly as possible and taken to McClellan's headquarters, where, in Philip Pry's bedroom, after all efforts to save his life had failed, infection set in, and on November 3rd he died. "No one but a soldier," wrote one of his men, "could understand our sorrow at seeing him carried off the field."[49]

The battle for the little sunken road had lasted for three and a half hours. It was the bloodiest period of the day. Federal casualties numbered nearly 3,000. There was no way of determining Confederate losses. One Federal soldier wrote that the gray dead lay so thick in the road that a man could have walked its length without touching ground.[50]

Brig. Gen D. H. Strother of McClellan's staff described the horror of the scene:

I was astonished to observe our troops moving along the front and passing over what appeared to be a long, heavy column of the enemy without paying it any attention whatever. I borrowed a glass from an officer, and discovered this to be actually a column of the enemy's dead and wounded lying along the hollow road . . . Among the prostrate mass I could easily distinguish the movements of those endeavoring to crawl away from the ground; hands waving as if calling of assistance, and others struggling as if in the agonies of death.[51]

Legend has it that after the battle, when local citizens volunteered to aid the wounded and the burying of the dead, a little old lady rode over the fields to the Sunken Road. Surveying the sea of bodies twisted in death, some still moaning their last breath, she descended from her carriage, got down on her knees and with head bowed, asked the Master's blessings on the men who now lay in this "bloody lane." From that day to this, the Sunken Road has been called Bloody Lane, a lasting tribute to gallant soldiers, both North and South.[52]

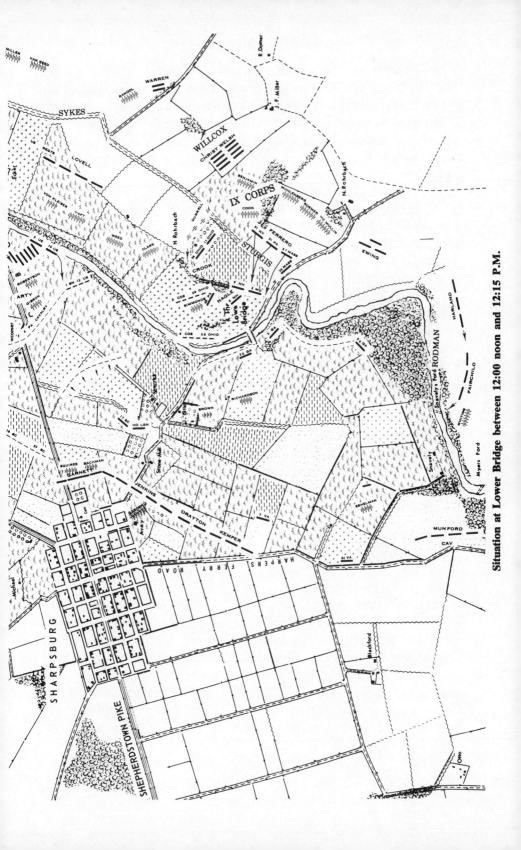

Situation at Lower Bridge between 12:00 noon and 12:15 P.M.

Lee's center had been shattered. Only a handful of Hill's division was left. Longstreet later stated that had ten thousand Federals been put in at that moment (1:00 p.m.) the Confederate army would have been swept from the field.[53] E. P. Alexander wrote: "Lee's army was ruined and the end of the Confederacy was in sight."[54] Never before had a battle come so close to ending, a war so close to a conclusion, and the victor not realized it.

The mysteries of Antietam number in the dozens, and this is one of the most puzzling. McClellan had the 10,000 Longstreet spoke of, and more. Franklin's Sixth Corps, after two peaceful days of rest in Pleasant Valley, came on the scene. He had crossed the creek behind Richardson and was poised ready for attack following the final phase of operations. Sumner had ridden the front, viewing the damages. He suggested that there was no use to further bloodshed. His suggestion did not settle too well with Franklin. They had a heated argument, but Sumner stuck to his guns. And what is more, McClellan supported him. "It would not be prudent to make the attack . . ." the general told Franklin.[55] Exactly why, he never explained. Fitz-John Porter's Fifth Corps was in reserve and ready, as was Pleasonton's cavalry and artillery.

General Peter Michie, commenting on the effective strength of Federal reserves, said, "Had McClellan put in his reserves across the Boonsborough [middle bridge] at the time when McLaws was pushing Sedgwick back, there is every reason to suppose that he would have achieved a great victory."[56] But McClellan did not have his victory on Lee's center. With the exception of periodical firing from pickets which occurred all along the lines, the action around the Sunken Road remained quiet the rest of the day. All attention was shifted to McClellan's left—Lee's weakened right—along the lower bridge.

When the final analyzation of the strategy and tactics of the battle of Antietam is made, the name of Maj. Gen. Israel B. Richardson may well gain new, and certainly deserved, prominence. From the viewpoint of troop direction and performance, Richardson's star rose high at the Sunken Road. It is difficult to imagine what might have taken place had he not been put out of action as the fight reached its climax. It is even more difficult to determine if his untimely, mortal wound actually affected that climax. The battle at this point seems to have almost come to a standstill when he fell. This is not to say that

Situation at 1:00 P.M.

Caldwell was unqualified for pursuit without Richardson, for Caldwell's brigade performed brilliantly that day, but there was still fight in Hill's line, as weak as it was. It is reasonable to state that given another hour or so, which could easily have been had not Sumner rebuffed the chances, Caldwell could have pushed D. H. Hill off the field and gained the all-important Sharpsburg hill.

Though little is known of Richardson's own views of McClellan's tactics that day, there is little doubt that his performance during the all-too-brief period he was on the field was indicative of a determined nature, and every reason to believe that, had fate granted him the opportunity, he would have pressed the fight through the Piper fields and on to Sharpsburg. Richardson was not a hero—there would be no Federal heroes on September 17—but he has remained in obscurity too long. In contrast to other division commanders, and even some corps commanders, Richardson emerges as a soldier's soldier, far too little appreciated by his superiors and by history.

Captain William M. Graham, commanding Battery K, First U. S. Artillery, who was talking with Richardson when the general was wounded, related one of the most touching events of the day, and, at the same time, created another of Antietam's mysteries:

In closing this report [Graham wrote in his official report to army headquarters] I feel called upon to mention the conduct of a citizen, a Mr. ———, who resides near the battle-field. This gentleman drove his carriage to my battery while under a severe artillery fire, and carried off my wounded, who were suffering very much for the want of proper surgical attendance, and distributed ham and biscuit among the men of the battery. He also returned a second time to the battery. One of his horses was wounded while performing this service.[57]

The good Samaritan of Antietam has never been identified.

10

Burnside's Bridge

The Federal Ninth Corps under Maj. Gen. Ambrose E. Burnside consisted of four divisions; 1st (Willcox), 2d (Sturgis), 3d (Rodman), and the Kanawha Division under Cox. This formidable array of military power had been a part of McClellan's right wing, had fought well at South Mountain, and was now assigned to the extreme Federal left at Antietam overlooking the lower bridge. At this point, Burnside was in a rather peculiar position. He had commanded the right wing of the army, which included both the First and Ninth Corps, since original orders were given in Washington, and it had been this wing that had battled D. H. Hill at Turner's Pass. McClellan, however, had removed Hooker's First Corps from Burnside on the 16th, sending it to the far right of the line. In order to handle wing command, Burnside had given temporary command of the Ninth Corps to Jacob D. Cox, and now without Hooker and with the Ninth Corps on the verge of battle, Burnside still considered this odd command arrangement in effect. Burnside was obviously miffed at Hooker's assignment and clearly let it be known that he blamed McClellan's decision on Hooker's desire for independent command.[1] Fitz-John Porter later said that Hooker was working for promotion to General-in-Chief and would "turn a somerset to get it."[2] As it would develop, Burnside's affection for McClellan diminished somewhat over this incident. At West Point they had always been "Mac" and "Burn" to each other,[3] but now the relationship took on an icy atmosphere.

It was felt by some of Burnside's staff that McClellan had placed their general in this peculiar position on purpose to try "to ruin him in battle by putting him where, with the force he had, he was sure to fail."[4] They attributed it to jealousy, McClellan being aware that Burnside had been offered command of the army several weeks before and that he was a great favorite with the men. One man later wrote that "the position of Porter's reserve and McClellan was shown me, and it seems an intended sacrifice of Burnside to see the course things took. I am sure I cannot look upon McC. as a *true* friend of the general."[5]

Burside, perhaps deliberately or from spite, passed on to Cox all orders sent from McClellan. He had also gone so far as to turn over his entire staff to Cox. Such strange actions would be costly and would develop into one of the several controversies involving the battle at Sharpsburg. McClellan had organized the three "wings" of his army for a specific reason. Each was in a position to accomplish one or more objectives. The right and left covered Washington and Baltimore from whatever diversive action Lee might take, and the center was aimed for attack should Lee develop a defensive line along the Monocacy River—these objectives being the expressed desires of McClellan. Once the army had arrived at Sharpsburg, there was no longer any need for this particular command system. It had been useful to a certain degree, but now with the choice of Hooker for the opening assault on the right, it was obvious that the "wing command" was ineffective. Even if an immediate pursuit of Lee after the battle had been put into action, a reorganization into the original three wings would have been totally impractical. When Cox urged Burnside to assume immediate command of the corps and let him lead his own division, Burnside "objected that as he had been announced as command of the right wing of the army composed of two corps, he was unwilling to waive his precedence or to assume that Hooker was detached for anything more than a temporary purpose."[6]

McClellan's actual plan of action at Antietam was vague. His plan for the Ninth Corps was confusing. In two separate reports, one written within a month after the battle and the other nearly a year later, he made three varying statements. On October 15, 1862 he wrote: "The design was to make the main attack upon the enemy's left—at least to create a diversion in favor of the main attack, with the hope of something more by assailing the enemy's right . . ."[7] It is difficult to ascertain here exactly what he had in mind; a simultaneous attack, or first an attack using Hooker and then later one using Burnside.

On August 4, 1863, McClellan wrote: "My plan for the impending general engagement was to attack the enemy's left with the corps of Hooker and Mansfield, supported by Sumner's and, if necessary, by Franklin's, and as soon as matters looked favorably there, to move the corps of Burnside against the enemy's extreme right . . ."[8] Here a separate movement is quite clear. But within eight pages of the same report, he changes the story. "The attack on the right was to have been supported by an attack on the left."[9] It is hardly possible to reconcile the three statements, therefore McClellan's plan of battle, the first source of research, immediately throws a cloak of fog on later developments. Only one thing is clear and that is the actual deployment of the troops, and even that carries with it a certain enigma remaining to this day.

The terrain around the lower bridge was unlike any on the field. The main road from Sharpsburg ran east until it met the Antietam, then gradually turned to follow it through a small ravine, crossing the creek about 200 yards downstream and moving on south. On the east, the ground rose to a gradual climb and then flattened out to farmland. On this rise and beyond were the four divisions of the Ninth Corps. To the west of the stone bridge was a high bluff, jutting sharply up from the road. Brig. Gen. Robert Toombs's brigade of Georgians held the bridge from rifle pits dug into the side of the bluff and with several batteries of artillery on top.

Little or no reconnaissance had been done by Burnside following his arrival two days earlier. McClellan's only orders had been to take up camp on the left of the line. Burnside, showing his disgruntled attitude, did only as he was told and no more. It could not have been more obvious that the bridge was a difficult target and to try to take it woud be costly, yet no attempt to check the stream for fording points was made. By the time Burnside received his first order to move, extremely little, if anything, was known of the target area; there was a stone bridge, the creek was high, or so they thought, and the enemy was on the other side. Henry Kyd Douglas, whose home was nearby and who undoubtedly had played or fished in the Antietam many times as a child, failed to understand why the creek itself was not checked out and used. "Go look at it and tell me if you don't think Burnside and his corps might have executed a hop, skip, and jump and landed on the other side," wrote Douglas. "One thing is certain, they might have waded it that day without getting their waist belts wet in any place."[10]

On the night of the 16th, McClellan visited Burnside's headquarters and informed him of his plans. He directed that the attack on the bridge would be initiated by his orders the next morning and that positions should be taken that night.[11] Subsequently, the Ninth Corps was moved up towards the ravine and there spent the night. The next morning at seven o'clock a stand-by message was delivered from McClellan's tent.[12] Already the left movements were an hour or more behind the right.

The next message, or actual attack order, was sent sometime between eight o'clock and ten o'clock. McClellan claimed in one report that it was sent at 8:00 A.M.;[13] later he claimed it was received at 10:00 A.M.[14] The order was actually dated at 9:10 A.M.[15] By now the double action timetable was off nearly five hours. The critical initiative over Lee at this point was lost. It would be further dwindled away throughout the morning hours. In a battle, two hours can make a difference. It seemed to mean little in the ultimate action at the lower bridge, but some speculation has been made on the two hour difference between the sending and receiving of orders. Again McClellan's reports merely confuse matters. It seems more and more obvious that the eight o'clock story, much like the "rapid movement" on the 13th, since written after a considerable lapse of time, is a coverup. When McClellan had access to his own dispatches (it is assumed that he had) for research purposes and could easily refer to the 9:10 A.M. dispatch which read: "General McClellan desires you to open your attack,"[16] why did he state otherwise?

Considering the time element, the ten o'clock receipt is acceptable. It would hardly have taken a man a full fifty minutes to ride from McClellan to the lower bridge, but since all orders were first delivered to Burnside and then relayed to Cox, ten o'clock would be a logical time for final transmittal. Confused time schedules, however, excuse neither McClellan nor Burnside.

McClellan blundered in delaying his initial orders. The seven o'clock stand-by should have been attack instructions, and they should have been delivered at the first sound of Hooker's guns, if not sooner. There can be little question that before early afternoon, giving Burnside the full benefit of the doubt as to time, Sharpsburg would have been entered, Lee's retreat route cut off and the Army of Northern Virginia caught in a gigantic vise. The combination of Confederate tenacity and aggressiveness and Federal laxity and procrastination prohibited such development and ultimately saved the day for Lee.

At seven o'clock, as McClellan had ordered, Cox moved the Ninth Corps into position on the crest of the east hill overlooking the bridge. Already casualties had been inflicted by accurate Confederate cannon fire. The guns of both sides had opened at daybreak and the enemy had hit several exposed brigades and regiments. "The whirring of the shells above us had a drowsing effect, and some of our men dozed; others munched hard bread and conversed in low tones; some went for water by detail, filling canteens from the warm, soft water of the creek."[17] (But no one had time to explore for a crossing.)

McClellan did not know how well the lower bridge was defended and that his entire left was being held off by less than 450 Confederates. When Lee's army had first taken position along the Antietam, D. R. Jones's Division, under Longstreet, was in command of the extreme right of the Confederate line, extending from the heights overlooking Sharpsburg on the Boonsboro Pike to the lower bridge. Jones's command was long and thin, six brigades only, the right of which, and the only one defending the lower bridge, was Toombs's brigade of three Georgia regiments—the 2d, 20th and 50th. Toombs was supported by two light field batteries of artillery. Four brigades formed a line about 1200 yards to the rear, facing east: G. T. Anderson with his left on the Boonsboro Pike in a line running parallel to the west boundary of the present National Cemetery, then Garnett, Draper, and Kemper to the far right behind Toombs on the Harpers Ferry Road. Evans's Brigade extended the line north of Anderson's left. The entire line consisted of less than 2500 men; Toombs had "a little over 400 . . ."[18]

Around 6:00 A.M. on the 17th, Lee had ordered Walker's Division, which had come up from Harpers Ferry the previous afternoon, to support Jones, but as McClellan was writing his orders to Burnside, Lee was pulling Walker away from his position overlooking Snavely's Ford and sending him to join Jackson on the left. Cox saw them leave; "we saw lines of troops advancing from our right upon the other side of the Antietam, and engaging the enemy between us and the East Wood."[19] This left Toombs in the precarious position of facing an entire division with only one brigade and little or no support on his immediate right. Fortunately for Toombs, several factors were in his favor. The defensive position was excellent, advance skirmishers being dug-in on the bluffs facing east. These men were veteran sharpshooters with an open target. Anyone who attempted to cross the bridge was vulnerable. There was no cover. Toombs's second advantage was McClellan's delay in pressing the Ninth Corps forward. Though the delay did not afford rapid reinforcements for the Confederates, the over-all effect was long enough for a final last minute surprise attack which set Burnside reeling. Actually, considering the defensive position, an early morning attack while Walker supported Toombs may have further delayed the taking of the bridge, but, of course, Jackson would have been denied Walker's forces. McClellan's delay was both damning and a blessing to Toombs, depending on the analyzation. Toombs's third advantage was Burnside's apparent unconcerned attitude toward proper chain of command. The lack of proper reconnaissance of the Antietam fords and the withholding of valuable Federal reserves all contributed to Toombs's benefit. Fourthly, what Burnside did not know was that a full three-fourths of the Confederate army was north of Sharpsburg. Nor did he know that at 6:30 that morning Lee had sent an urgent message to A. P. Hill at Harpers Ferry to make haste his departure, and join the army by the fastest possible route.[20] D. R. Jones's resistance would be light. At the most, the Confederate right could hold only for a few hours. Now, thanks to Sumner's and McClellan's indecision on the center, Lee had Jackson's men to fall back on. He could shift his strength just as he had done earlier in the day. But with Hill's four brigades on the way, Lee preferred not to take the risk of uncovering his left. He would hold off and wait for Hill. As the day wore on, he became increasingly assured that he had made the right decision.

And so, this is what Burnside faced. In front were 400 stalwart Georgians who would be relegated to fame on this bloody day as the brigade that held off a corps. But beyond Toombs lay more staggering ponderables for Burnside. If he was to bring about the victory McClellan had let slip from his fingers north of Sharpsburg, he would first have to eliminate D. R. Jones's Division, and do so before 2:00 P.M. At the same time, he would have to take Blackford's Ford, holding against A. P. Hill's crossing. Reaching Sharpsburg alone, though it would seriously impair Lee's withdrawal route, would not necessarily defeat Lee and bring victory. Burnside then must work in concert with another force on the Federal right. But the Ninth Corps commander did not know these things. None of them would be accomplished.

Sometime between nine and ten o'clock on the morning of September 17, Burnside, or rather Cox, directed the first assault on the bridge. McClellan had sent an aide, Gen. D. B. Sackett, Inspector-General of his army, to Burnside. Sackett was to urge the general to press forward and to stay with him until the movement was made and Sharpsburg in sight. "McClellan appears to think I am not trying my best to carry this bridge," Burnside told Sackett, "you are the third or fourth one who has been to me this morning with similar orders."[21] But Sackett stayed and so did another personal envoy from headquarters. At this late hour, for an unexplained reason, and almost simultaneously with the asault, one division, Rodman's, along with Scammon's brigade of the Kanawha Division, was sent downstream to seek the only known crossing in the vicinity—Snavely's Ford. This would have been to Toombs's extreme right, that part of the line held by Walker until it was abondoned on Lee's orders. The ford led behind Toombs and was the only route to his rear and the only means of dislodging his deadly aim at the bridge. As Rodman marched off to form the left arm of the pincer movement to the south, Col. George Crook, with the 2d Brigade of the Kanawha Division was inadvertently creating a similar movement from the north.

Sturgis's division occupied the center of Cox's advance position. Crook's Brigade was on his right and somewhat north of the bridge. The plan was to push Crook out in front and, under cover fire of the 11th Connecticut, have it dash for the bridge at an angle. Crook was a little too far to the north, however, and came over the crest of the hill in a position that prevented him from following through with the charge. The Confederates pinned him down about 450 yards upstream and there he stayed for several hours.

Crook's intended charge across the bridge had been designed to dislodge Toombs in a concerted effort with Rodman. Once Crook had gained the heights and had joined with Rodman, they would be reinforced for the drive across the fields into Sharpsburg. Crook's unintended delay caused Cox to bring Sturgis's division to the front. A new drive would be made. There seemed to be little hurry in moving the men into ready position, however. The 21st Massachusetts had received a large mail from home that morning and spent the waiting hours catching up on the latest news. The color guard from the 21st were all gathered around a hometown newspaper when a Confederate shell "descended into their midst, exploded, blowing colors and guards in all directions." The boys picked themselves up, brushed themselves off and went on as if nothing had happened.[22]

First, the 2d Maryland and the 6th New Hampshire were sent down the hill to the bridge. The 9th New Hampshire and the 48th Pennsylvania supported. The charge was a determined one, rapid and with fixed bayonets, but the concentrated fire on their necessarily narrow columns beat them back. Again and again they tried and each time the attack was repulsed before the bridge was reached. The Confederates were throwing in everything they had. A member of the 9th New Hampshire claimed the enemy artillery was using railroad iron. One piece 15 inches long whizzed by his head and "went rolling end over end down the hill."[23] No one would have believed it had they not been the targets. The 8th New York Cavalry had seen this kind of "ammunition" in Longstreet's wagons but to see it whizzing through the air was another matter. One German officer was heard to exclaim, "Mein Gott! We shall have a blacksmith's shop to come next."[24] By this time it was noon and McClellan had heard nothing from Burnside.

Nearly every tense moment in battle has a fleeting second of comical relief. The lower bridge action had several, not the least of which nearly caused panic among the charging forces. As the 9th New Hampshire was making its attempt at the bridge, a frightened sow and her litter of pigs came running up the creek bank, heading pell-mell for the ranks. Just as she reached the men she made a sharp turn catching one man between the legs, carrying him off astride her back, his musket waving frantically in the air and his lungs bursting with panic-stricken screams.[25]

Sturgis had received his orders from Burnside: "Carry the bridge at all hazards." He assigned his 2d Brigade under Col. Edward Ferrero; four crack regiments—51st New York, 51st Pennsylvania, 35th and 21st Massachusetts.

"It is General Burnside's especial request that the two 51st's take that bridge," called Ferrero to his men. "Will you do it?"

"Will you give us our whiskey, Colonel, if we make it?" shouted someone from the Pennsylvania regiment.

It was kind of a ticklish subject with Ferrero. This unit had gained quite a reputation from their drinking habits. But they would deserve their fair share if they pulled off this job.

"Yes, by God!" he said, and the boys cheered.

"Charge with the bayonet," Sturgis ordered.[26]

At this instant, Crook opened a "point blank fire" on the far end of the bridge with a "light Howitzer" he had managed to bring down hill from the lines. With double charges of canister hailing their advance, the New York and Pennsylvania boys forged steadily but quickly ahead.[27] Gen. J. F. Hartranft, who commanded the 51st Pennsylvania, described the scene:

From the crest to the bridge the slope was a cleared field, commanded at point blank range by the opposite banks. As the regiment charged across, it was subject to a close, continued and deadly fire. Along the upper side of the road was a complete post and rail fence connecting with the upper wing-wall of the bridge. This was a serious obstacle, but the regiment moved on and drove the enemy from the bridge and forced him to take shelter in the defenses beyond. Part of the command climbed over the fence and took possession of the lower wing-wall, which turned sufficiently down stream to afford some protection, and those getting to the center of the bridge were compelled to cross the bridge for shelter, and part took position behind the wall along the stream above the bridge. While the men replied to the fire of the enemy, I was at the end of the upper wing-wall and had the two panels of fence nearest the bridge torn down.

In the meantime, Col. Potter came up with his regiment, the 51st New York, and formed along the fence to the left of the bridge. The fence afforded little or no protection and the 51st New York was losing heavily. This also impelled me to arouse my regiment to another effort. The brigade commander had also sent an aide to request me to make another effort to cross. Passing through the opening in the fence with the colors and a few officers and men on to the Bridge, and they passing, I called on the regiment to follow. While thus engaged, Col. Potter came up, likewise calling to his regiment. Both regiments responded promptly, and passing rapidly over the bridge, the 51st Pennsylvania filed to the right on the roadway and the 51st New York to the left. This was about noon. I have no means to fix the exact time. Our heavy losses occurred in crossing the exposed slope and in tearing down and surmounting the fence. When the colors had reached the centre of the bridge the fire of the enemy had almost or entirely ceased. The principal loss of the 51st New York was also incurred in the few moments of its exposed position along the fence. It numbered about 75 killed and wounded. . . . Stopping and returning the enemy's fire was the most fatal act of the regiment. If we had not stopped, we would have returned with little loss and there would be no question as to who carried the bridge.

About the same time—his report says 1 o'clock—Gen. Rodman was pushing a column across the ford below the bridge, and I also remember artillery firing over our heads into the enemy's position...What effect these movements had upon the final retirement of the enemy I cannot say. We doubt they had some influence and I would not wish to detract from the merits or glory of a single comrade who shared with us in any degree in that brilliant achievement. But so far as we were concerned, it is certainly true that the 51st Pennsylvania moved upon the bridge without any promise or expectation of support.

After crossing I moved the regiments from the roadway, to leave it clear for other troops of the corps to pass. But they were so long in coming that Lieutenant-Colonel Bell became very uneasy and I asked him to go back and see about it. As he went back he met Col. Ferrero on the bridge, who ordered him to return and tell me to move my regiment to the top of the hill beyond. As he was coming back on the road, he was struck, by what I supposed was a canister shot, on the left temple and rolled down the bank to the edge of the water, where the regiment had stacked arms, the enemy then firing only with artillery and having the range of the road. In his death the regiment lost a valuable, conscientious and accomplished officer. The order to move never reached me, and this accident saved the regiment from other heavy losses.

The troops commenced crossing and a continuous stream of infantry and artillery poured over the bridge during the afternoon. All except our second division were sent forward and attacked the enemy's right flank, which if done earlier in the day, when the enemy's left and center were engaged, might have destroyed Lee's army . . .[28]

It was hours before Rodman's division had made any progress at all. Finally, he found Snavely's Ford several hundred yards from the bridge, an excellent crossing spot that could have easily been located and time saved had scouts been sent out earlier. The water was shallow, about waist-deep,[29] but the bluffs on the other side gave the men a difficult climb. Confederate pickets managed to pick off several men in mid-stream, but once on top they came face to face with the enemy planted firmly in a maze of knolls and cornfields, as perplexing a problem as any the Federals had encountered that day. "There, if anywhere," wrote a young member of the 9th New York, "I should have remembered that I was soaking wet from my waist down. So great was the excitement, however, that I have never been able to recall it."[30] Had Rodman's crossing come an hour or two earlier, he would have caught Walker's Division before it left for the Confederate right. As it was, he was facing Kemper's Brigade and some skirmishers from Toombs's.

Meanwhile, Crook was trying desperately to locate some crossing point so that he might continue his assignment. After some reconnaissance, a ford was found some distance to the right, and at about the same time as the bridge was charged, Crook got five companies of the 28th Ohio across.[31] The right arm of the attack began to develop.

Despite Toombs's excellent position, he had suffered heavily. Regiments were depleted, one by nearly 50 per cent, and his only available field officers were either killed or wounded and out of action. Members of the 35th Massachusetts claimed to have seen some of the Georgians surrender, coming down the hill "waving a dirty white rag."[32] To claim he was hard pressed would be understating the facts, for his own reports reveal the damage incurred by the continuous morning action. It was Toombs himself, however, that understated the facts when he wrote of his noon actions: "Not being able to get any re-enforcements for the defense of the . . . fords . . . I deemed it my duty to withdraw my command . . . Though the bridge and upper ford were thus left open to the enemy, he moved with such extreme caution and slowness that he lost nearly two hours in crossing and getting into action on our side . . . ."[33] "Why . . . Burnside's Bridge?" asked Kyd Douglas, "is it sarcasm?"[34] "What puzzles me," remarked one observer, "is how did Burnside keep his troops from breaking over."[35]

Toombs made his withdrawal sound so easy, almost as if it was little more than an ordinary camp drill. It was certainly no less dramatic. Toombs's two regiments had nearly exhausted their ammunition by this time. Certain final assault on the bridge was imminent. The Georgians would be lambs for the slaughter unless pulled back. D. R. Jones, by this time concentrating his attention on Toombs's defensives, ordered a quiet withdrawal to a cornfield south of Sharpsburg. Here they refilled their cartridge cases while reinforcements from other areas on the field took up position on their front.[36] Sturgis's men distinguished themselves with "brilliance" and "bravery" and "in scarcely more time than it takes to tell it," according to Cox, the bridge was theirs and the bluff was clear.[37] It was one o'clock. Six hours had passed since McClellan had alerted Burnside, three hours since Burnside had given orders to advance. The action on McClellan's extreme right had been over for several hours and his center was now spent. All attention was focused on the Ninth Corps. It was now or never. And Ferrero did not forget the whisky. He had promised and the men had earned it. Several days later, in a flashy ceremony resplendent with all the high trimmings from headquarters, Ferrero was being presented his commission to general for his singular achievements at the lower bridge, when one of the Pennsylvanians, maybe the same thirsty character who had not forgotten, shouted out, "How about that whisky?" "You'll get it," said Ferrero with a sly chuckle, and sure enough they did, by the barrel. The boys remembered this as one of the highlights of the campaign.[38]

It was now or never, too, for Lee. The bridge was lost. Burnside was across the Antietam with Sharpsburg nearly in his grasp. As Sturgis planted the Stars and Stripes on the far side of the bridge, Rodman and Crook crossed their fords and climbed onto the fields south of Sharpsburg. Suddenly, someone realized that a terrible mistake had been made. In the exchange of fire that morning and noon, Sturgis's men had used all their ammunition. The pursuit would have to be halted while the men returned to their wagons. Meantime, someone else would have to take over. Willcox's First Division, up to this point in reserve, was called up, but the confusion of men marching and countermarching, the hauling of wagons and caissons across the narrow bridge, and the hot fire of Confederate artillery and sharpshooters, delayed things for nearly two hours.[39] Two precious hours for McClellan and two precious hours for Lee. It was giving Rodman and Crook time to close in but it was also giving Lee time to bring back some of the troops he had borrowed that morning.

It was now three o'clock and Burnside, contrary to popular belief, was on the bridge himself urging the men on to the heights.[40] The bridge was slippery with blood, so slippery, local legend has it, that walking was difficult. Willcox crossed, thus placing all of the Ninth Corps, with the exception of Sturgis's division and parts of Cox's Ohio division, on the road north to Sharpsburg.

Every available Confederate soldier was put into action. All of Jones's Division, now less than 2,400, faced Willcox. Every available artillery piece was brought forward. Lee himself was on the field. His army was exerting a new strength; a strength from sheer desperation. The church spires of Sharpsburg were within Burnside's sight. The town must be held at all costs. It was already reeling under the concussion of battle. Stragglers were flooding the streets; shells were bursting through the buildings. The Army of Northern Virginia and the town of Sharpsburg became one as they braced themselves for a gallant stand.

Slowly, the blue lines moved across the fields, six brigades in all—two on the right under Willcox, Rodman's two on the left, and Crook and Scammon on the extremes. Confederate artillery was holding the men down and under cover of fences, trees, and little ravines, but still steadily they drove forward. Pvt. John Dooley of the 1st Virginia under Kemper's Brigade witnessed the approach of the Federals:

In the field below us the enemy are slowly but cautiously approaching, crouching low as they advance behind the undulating tracks in the rich meadows through which they are passing. From the numbers of their flags which are distinctly visible above the rising ground we judge them to be at least two thousand in number. As long as our little battery of two guns is served with tolerable precision the enemy, who appear to be new troops, do not dare to venture close or raise their heads. But in a few minutes the Yankee artillery, far superior to ours, dismounted one of our pieces, killed the horses; and the remaining gunner, fearing capture, hitched the only remaining horse to the other cannon and made away to the rear as hard as he could go.

We were now left to oppose the numerous masses before us with a mere picket line of musketry. There may have been other troops to our left and right but I did not see any. The Yankees, finding no batteries opposing them, approach closer and closer, cowering down as near to the ground as possible, while we keep up a pretty warm fire by file upon them as they advance. Now they are at the last elevation of rising ground and whenever a head is raised we fire. Now they rise up and make a charge for our fence. Hastily emptying our muskets into their lines, we fled back through the cornfield.[41]

Evans's Brigade straddled the Boonsboro Pike with an eye on either side of the road, prepared to flank any movement. He had with him five batteries, representing the last Confederate stronghold east of Sharpsburg on the main ridge. This offered an advantage over the Ninth Corps, but it was short lived. Pleasonton's cavalry, which had been relatively inactive throughout the battle, was now sent into action on the pike. Pleasonton crossed the middle bridge and pushed Evans back until finally the ridge was abandoned. Federal light artillery was immediately moved in and range taken on the slow withdrawal of Jones's brigades. Then Kemper's Brigade fell back into the streets of

Sharpsburg. Drayton's and Garnett's brigades, crisis near at hand, followed. Dooley talked about the withdrawal:

Oh, how I ran! or tried to run through the high corn, for my heavy belt and cartridge box and musket kept me back to *half* my speed. I was afraid of being struck in the *back,* and I frequently turned half around in running, so as to avoid if possible so disgraceful a wound. It never entered my head to throw away gun or cartridge box; but, encumbered as I was, I endeavored to keep pace with my captain, who with his long legs and unemcumbered would in a little while have far outstripped me but that he frequently turned towards the enemy, and, running backwards, managed not to come out ahead in this our anything but creditable race. The enemy having taken our position appeared to think they had performed wonders, for instead of pursuing us and shooting us down, they began to give regular *methodical* cheers, as if they had gained a game of base ball.

Scarcely had we, breathless, reached the edge of the cornfield than we met Toombs's brigade of Georgians advancing in line of battle to our relief. Hastily forming in their rear we returned to our former line which by this time a well directed volley from this little brigade of Georgians had restored again to our possession. Still, even with this brigade, we were scarcely 800 men, and how were we to repulse the thousands that still threatened us, backed as they were by a terribly efficient artillery force.[42]

And then Willcox's ammunition ran out. For the second time in less than three hours, the Federal drive was halted for this reason. The delays were to be just what Lee's doctor ordered.

Rodman, meanwhile, found the going much harder than he had anticipated. By the time he had crossed the creek, Willcox was up over the crest of the bluffs and was moving in the direction of the town. The plan had been for Rodman's division to take the ford to the south and sweep the Confederate right flank, joining the main body of the corps. Rather than coming up on the enemy's flank, Rodman found himself face to face with Toombs's revitalized troops. The action was strong and fierce and delayed Rodman from connecting with Willcox. As the minutes flew on, the gap grew larger, Rodman all the while trying to beat off the stubborn Confederate resistance on his left. For a while it looked as though it would be Sedgwick and French all over again. The confusion was nearly as great as that with Hooker in the cornfield. The enemy was behind tall "Indian" corn and stone fences, and the artillery had their range. The fire was devastating and the gap between Rodman's right and Willcox's left grew even wider. The Confederate batteries had depressed their guns and were strafing the ground, cutting down everything that was visible. "As the range grew better, the firing became more rapid, the situation desperate and exasperating to the last degree," wrote a member of the 9th New York.[43] Sharpshooters crouched low behind stone walls, waiting patiently for the blue lines to approach.

As we rose and started, all the fire that had been held back so long was loosed. In a second the air was full of the hiss of bullets and the hurtle of grape-shot. The mental strain was so great that I saw at that moment the singular affect mentioned, I think, in the life of Goethe on a similar occasion—the whole landscape for an instant turned slightly red. We heard all through the war that the army, "was eager to be led against the enemy." But when you came to hunt for this particular itch, it was always the next regiment that had it. The truth is, when bullets are whacking against tree-trunks and solid shot are cracking skulls like eggshells, the consuming passion in the breast of the average man is to get out of the way. Between the physical fear of going forward and the moral fear of turning back, there is a predicament of exceptional awkwardness from which a hidden hole in the ground would be a wonderfully welcome outlet.[44]

Sturgis's division, which by this time had received their new supply of ammunition and was standing in reserve, was ordered up along with Cox's division to fill the gap in the line. Burnside's Ninth Corps was now on the field in full, and driving hard. Sharpsburg was within its grasp. It was clear that when Sharpsburg fell, Lee would be surrounded within an hour.

Throughout the day Lee looked to the south in hopes of spotting his only reserves, A. P. Hill's Division of some 3,000 men. As the afternoon drew to a close, these men became his only hope for survival on the field. At 2:30 P.M. Hill rode into headquarters with the news that his division was on the way; they had started crossing the river at 2:00 o'clock. He brought with him one battery of artillery which was immediately pressed into action supporting Jones. (It was subsequently overrun and captured when Jones withdrew towards Sharpsburg.)

It was a long hard march for Hill's men—17 miles by the route he took—and they were being forced to travel at full speed. Hill, himself, with his battle-worn flaming-red shirt, had been with them most of the way, sabre in hand, urging them forward.[45] There was a sense of urgency in his movements, each shout of command carrying with it the fiery, impetuous sharpness his men knew so well. It was almost as if each cannon roar from Sharpsburg beckoned them on, "one step further, one step further," and the men answered with renewed vigor and speed. Those who failed, those who hid behind trees and out-houses, and there were many, knew the wrath of their commander and remembered it for years.[46] Hill was filled with rage when he saw one young lieutenant quietly slip to the side of the road and out of sight from the marching troops. With language fit only for the field, Hill raced to the officer's side, demanded his sword, and immediately broke it over the man's back.[47]

Lee had waited patiently for Hill's men to come up. It was a long and agonizing wait, for throughout the afternoon it seemed that at any minute his whole line would collapse. At about 4:00 o'clock, off in the distance, Lee saw a cloud of dust rising in the sky. He asked a young officer, whose glass was pointed in that direction, if he could determine the nature of the approaching force. The officer offered Lee his glass but the general held up his bandaged hands indicating he could not use them. Then turning to Lee, the officer said, "They are flying the Vir-ginia and Confederate flags, sir." With a great sigh of relief, Lee calm-ly said, "It is A. P. Hill from Harpers Ferry."[48] When the news of re-inforcements reached Jones's men, there was a mighty roar of happy voices. They dug in just a little harder.

The actual arrival time of Hill's Division has been confused through the years because of conflicting reports on both sides. Times range from 3:00 P.M. to 4:30 P.M. Greggs's Brigade, the first up from the river and on the field reported contact with the enemy at 3:40 P.M.,[49] probably a fairly accurate figure. At about this time, Rodman's left, manned by Scammon's brigade, was under heavy fire from the corn-field. One regiment, the 16th Connecticut, had been in the service for only three weeks. This was their first taste of blood and it was not pleasant. A confederate line advanced toward them from the corn and they broke and ran for the rear. At this moment, Rodman himself was coming to their rescue with the 4th Rhode Island. Nothing could have been more confusing to the boys from Connecticut. What had hap-pened in the Miller cornfield that morning and what was feared in any battle, was happening here. There were bluecoats in front firing at them and bluecoats to the rear firing over their heads. They were ut-terly and totally confused. The Rhode Island boys were no better off and both regiments turned to flee from the field. In the excitement,

Situation at Lower Bridge, 1:00 P.M.

Rodman was killed. With the commander fallen, the rout was complete.

Cox called a halt to the advance on the far right, sending reinforcements to plug Rodman's break. Sturgis was brought into the left but all of these, seeing the advancing blue uniforms, held their fire until it was too late. Whatever was happening was too much for them and soon the whole Federal line withdrew to the knolls behind. Lt. Col. Joseph R. Curtis, commander of the 4th Rhode Island, described this odd twist to the battle in this manner:

As the enemy showed the national flag [Stars and Stripes], and as our troops had been seen in advance on our right, moving diagonally across the front, the order to cease firing was given, and a volunteer officer to go forward to ascertain who was in our front was called for. Lieuts. George E. Curtis and George H. Watts immediately stepped forward, and placing themselves one on each side of the color-bearer, carried the flag up the hill within 20 feet of the rebels when the enemy fired, killing the corporal. Lieutenant Curtis seized the colors and returned, followed by Lieutenant Watts. The order to commence firing was then given . . .[50]

The answer to their puzzlement was simple but there was not time to sit down and figure it out. All Confederates had been lacking in uniforms and shoes, A. P. Hill's Division no exception. During their short stay at Harpers Ferry, they made good use of their time. They had stocked themselves well with just as much Federal booty as they could carry and blue uniforms, whole or any combination thereof, became the order of the day. There is no indication that the flag was an intended ruse, but it did have a devastating effect. Tall corn concealed the uniforms of the Confederates and the Federals were completely fooled.[51] The tide of blue which swept Burnside back to the Antietam was Hill's Division arriving in the nick of time. They were on the field about one hour. The historian of Greggs's Brigade described it:

The firing during this period . . . was as rapid as possible, and on our side unusually accurate. So dense was the corn that the lines sometimes approached within 30 to 40 yards of each other before opening. We had somewhat the advantage, for the enemy, descending to attack us, naturally fired too high, while we had either a level or a rise to fire upon . . . it is a fact that men fire above their own levels. And when the enemy retreated they had to pass through our ground, which enabled us to kill large numbers of them.[52]

Situation between 3:30 P.M. and 3:45 P.M.

At about the time Rodman fell, General Branch was killed.

He had just swept the enemy before him and driven them in such confusion and dismay, that all firing had ceased in his immediate front, when Generals Gregg and Archer directed his attention to a V-shaped column of the enemy that was advancing the troops on his left. He stepped forward and formed with these generals a little group, which evidently attracted the attention of some sharpshooter on the other side. For, just as he was raising his glasses to his eyes, a single shot was fired, and a bullet was sent to do its deadly work, which, striking him in the right cheek, passed out back of his left ear, and he fell dying into the arms of [one] of his staff.[53]

By 4:30 P.M. it was all over. Hill had lost 63 killed out of the approximate 2,000 men of the division he had sent in. His losses were light compared to other units, but he had performed the necessary task to save the day for Lee. The two armies each settled into defensive positions and the battle was stopped.

That night George Smalley called all his *Tribune* associates together to work out the dispatch that must be transmitted immediately in order to scoop the other New York newspapers. By candlelight they composed until late hours. At midnight Smalley rode off towards Frederick where he wired his column to New York via Baltimore: "Fierce and desperate battle between two hundred thousand men has raged since daylight, yet night closes on an uncertain field. It is the greatest fight since Waterloo . . ."[54]

Mr. Smalley's dispatch took a circuitous route. At Baltimore, the American Telegraph Company agent, acting on an intelligent hunch that the report might be of some value to Washington, wired the Frederick message to the War Department. By noon on the 18th, Smalley's account of Antietam was on Lincoln's desk at the White House replacing the absent reports from McClellan.[55]

Late that night the star *Tribune* reporter changed trains at Baltimore, switching from the box car he had taken at Frederick to one on the New York express, continuing without a wink of sleep to compose what would be hailed by the world's press as the outstanding battle account of all time. At 6:00 A.M. on the 19th, he stumbled into the composing room at the Tribune building and within two hours heard his headlines being shouted from every street corner in New York. Antietam and Sharpsburg had become household words.[56]

Situation at Lower Bridge, 4:20 P.M.

Situation at 5:30 P.M.

11

"Fatal Thursday"

The battle was over, but it was not won. Neither Lee nor McClellan would admit defeat, yet neither could lay claim to victory. Lee's Army of Northern Virginia had held off not the Army of the Potomac but George B. McClellan. Antietam would go down in history as a stalemate, a draw between the two armies, but it was clear, even as the battle progressed, that it was a fight between the men in gray and McClellan and his generals. In each of the three major phases of the battle, the Confederate army had fought against terrible odds, both numerically and tactically speaking, and in each case, when the action had died down, there were still twice as many Federals on the field as there were Confederates. At some points the odds were even greater. At the end of the day, with the exception of Lee's right, the Army of Northern Virginia was in close proximity to the same position it had held that morning. McClellan had gained that "no-man's land" between the lines, and as a result, had his army on the Sharpsburg ridge within a relatively short striking distance of the enemy. Though he had not gained the smashing victory he would claim, he had greatly improved his position. Lee had beaten off each of the Federal attacks, but McClellan clearly held the initiative. How he would use it to his advantage would remain to be seen.

Hill's attack late in the afternoon was taken by the Federals as a defeat. It had every element of surprise, but it would have been most ineffective had Rodman and Willcox rallied their men and struck back. There were enough Federals to do it—to roll Hill and Jones right back to Sharpsburg and cut off their retreat, which was what they intended

to do in the first place. General Cox saw this—many years too late.
He wrote in his memoirs:

No doubt a single strong division, marching beyond the left flank of the
Ninth Corps, would have so occupied A. P. Hill's division that our movement into Sharpsburg could not have been checked, and assisted by the
advance of Sumner and Franklin on the right, would apparently to have
made certain the complete rout of Lee.[1]

The move would have had far reaching implications, but defeat was
accepted easily and with no questions asked. No one asked Burnside
to let them renew the advance; Burnside made no appeal to McClellan;
McClellan gave no orders.

The day had been long. Battle had raged for nearly 12 hours. The
men on both sides were weary, but still alert. The Confederates below
Sharpsburg, particularly sensitive to the situation, prepared for a
countercharge should it come. But it never came. The sun set and
campfires were struck. As the sounds of battle slowly faded, screaming
shells and musket rattle were replaced with the terrible moans of the
wounded; the mournful cries of thousands who would not live to see
daybreak.

Throughout the night, informal truces were set up between the lines
so that medical attendants could bring their own back for treatment.
Barns, chickenhouses, private homes, and churches, almost any building or shelter that was not occupied, were used for surgery, embalm-
ing stations, and make-shift hospitals, where the wounded, crowded
like so many logs, waited for death.

As darkness fell, Lee called his lieutenants to his side. It was a
solemn occasion, each man humbled by battle in his own way. There
was pride in their carriage, but heads were bowed with weariness. The
campfire cast a strange, amost ghostly glow over their faces, faces lined
with the bravery, the death, the tragedy of the day. To each Lee
quietly, almost reverently, asked, "General, how is it on your part of
the line?"

Longstreet, Lee's "Old War Horse," was obviously depressed. He
had been late in arriving. On his way through Sharpsburg, he passed
a burning house and stopped to do what he could to help the unfortunate family. He seemed to carry some of their burdens with him. His

voice, only that afternoon blended harshly with his men in battle, was now soft and gentle, reflecting the despair with which he spoke. "It was as bad as it could be," he said. "My division has lost terribly. There is little better than a skirmish line left on my front." D. H. Hill echoed Longstreet's words. His division was cut to pieces. There were no troops to hold his line. Jackson admitted to the greatest odds he had ever seen. His generals were gone.

Hood was unnerved and with great emotion, said, "I have no division, General Lee." Raising his voice for the first time, Lee exclaimed, "Great God! General Hood, where is your splendid division you had this morning?" Hood replied, "They are lying on the field where you sent them. My division has been almost wiped out." After Hood had spoken, each man, one by one, suggested complete withdrawal before daybreak. There was no recourse as they saw it. A renewed attack by morning would surely bring disaster.

The silence that followed was penetrating. The faces gazed at each other and then turned to meet the eyes of a man being put to the test. The day's battle must have flitted across Lee's mind in an instant, much the same as the past is quickly recalled to a drowning man. What reinforcements were there? None. Thomas's Brigade of A. P. Hill's Division was at Harpers Ferry guarding captured supplies and could not possibly be spared. It was the only other Confederate force north of the Potomac. What had South Mountain and Harpers Ferry cost him? Nearly 3,000 men. And Sharpsburg? Maybe 10,000. Two general officers were dead; Starke and Branch, and another, G. B. Anderson, was mortally wounded. Divisions were wrecked, brigades reduced to regiment size, and regiments to companies. The 7th South Carolina had lost 140 of its 268; the 1st Texas, 182 of 226, and another could only claim 294 survivors out of 854.[2] It was a panorama of disaster. And then, slowly, softly, and firmly, Lee spoke.

"Gentlemen, we will not cross the Potomac tonight. You will go to your respective commands, strengthen your lines. Send two officers from each brigade towards the ford to collect your stragglers and get them up. If McClellan wants to fight in the morning, I will give him battle again. Go!"

There were no cheers, no smiles, no handshakes. There was no grumbling, no discontent. With shoulders erect, with confidence regained, with a renewed pride, the generals quietly departed and rode out into the night to their men.[3]

It was a restless night for both armies. "Not a soldier, I venture to say, slept half an hour," wrote Kyd Douglas. "Half of Lee's army were hunting the other half."[4] Those fortunate enough to have survived the terrible ordeal sought to comfort their friends. Many were out searching in the darkness for the remains of their companies. Others sought refuge in the solitude of prayer. "When the soldiers are seeking rest, the work of the army correspondents begins," wrote Charles Coffin of the Boston *Journal*. That night he filled his notebook with the thoughts of men far from home, waiting, wondering what the dawn would bring. They were words that could have fitted any battle, but somehow they belonged to Antietam. They still ring of the lost souls, the precious wounded bodies, the campfires which gave some warmth to troubled hearts:

Both before and after a battle, sad and solemn thoughts come to the soldier. Before the conflict they are of apprehension; after the strife there is a sense of relief; but the thinned ranks, the knowledge that the comrade who stood by your side in the morning never will stand there again, bring inexpressible sadness. The soldiers, with thoughts far away, were apprehensive that the conflict of the day was but a prelude to another struggle more fierce and bloody in the morning. The men in position and lying on their arms, ready to renew the battle at daylight . . .[5]

One lone Union veteran lay beneath the darkened sky, contemplating, trying to comprehend what this battle had really been about:

There was no tree over our heads to shut out the stars, and as I lay looking up at these orbs moving so calmly on their appointed way, I felt, as never so strongly before, how utterly absurd in the face of high Heaven is this whole game of war, relieved only from contempt and ridicule by its tragic accompaniments, and by the sublime illustrations of man's nobler qualities incidentally called forth in its service. Sent to occupy this little planet, one among ten thousand worlds revolving through infinite space, how worse than foolish these mighty efforts to make our tenancy unhappy or to drive each other out of it. Within a space of four square miles lay two thousand men, some stiff and stark, looking with visionless eyes up into the pitying heavens; some tossing on the beds of the hospital, or lying maimed and bleeding under the trees; some hugging in their sleep the deadly weapon with which, to-morrow, they may renew the work of death.[6]

After Jackson left Lee's headquarters, he retired to a small "campsite" to the west of Sharpsburg. Here beneath the trees, with no tent and only the grass for his comfort, he called his own council of war. The staff members talked and rested. About midnight, Jeb Stuart interrupted to say that the hill on the far left that he had occupied that morning, and later abandoned, was now a choice spot for the launching of a Federal offensive. He thought it should be kept in Confederate hands and suggested posting a force there even if it was small. Jackson agreed and sent Douglas off to get fifty men from Early's Division near the Dunkard Church.

On his way Douglas saw the dreadful sights of Antietam. They left an impression he would never forget; "a veritable field of blood, the dead and dying lay as thick over it as harvest sheaves." Through the cries and moans and curses, he could hear a prayer, or in the darkness he could see a body struggle to lift itself in one last desperate attempt to join the living. There was no difference between blue and gray. The voices and prayers were all the same; all beseeching the same God for deliverance from this hell. "My horse trembled under me in terror, looking at the ground, sniffing the scent of blood, stepping falteringly as a horse will over or by the side of human flesh; afraid to stand still, hesitating to go on, his animal instinct shuddering at this cruel human mystery."[7]

Douglas had seen his share of blood for the day so he moved on rapidly to deliver his message. Early was in the West Wood resting. Aside from the sounds of death, all was quiet. The lines were "within a stone's throw" of each other. Douglas spoke softly and the word was passed down the front in a whisper. Slowly the officers and men assembled, coming as ghosts through the trees to answer the call of their commander. When they had fifty men, Douglas and Early struck out for "Stuart's hill."[8]

Stuart was not the only one who knew the military importance of that hill. That afternoon, after the Confederate cavalry had moved farther south, General Franklin proposed to McClellan that all efforts should be made to place Federal artillery on that location early the next morning. McClellan, who regarded Franklin's opinions highly, agreed. The plan was good, though at that time of the day they could only guess at what Lee's conditions would be the next day. During the night, however, McClellan changed his mind. He would make no attempt once he discovered it was occupied.[9]

Jackson arrived on the scene early the next morning. With him was Colonel Stephen D. Lee, Longstreet's Chief of Artillery. He was under orders from General Lee to see if by establishing a battery on the hill the Federal right could be successfully turned. The young Lee and Jackson surveyed the blue lines. "I wish you to take fifty pieces of artillery and crush that force which is the Federal right," said Jackson. "Can you do it?" Lee knew immediately that it would be impossible, but fearing he might show a lack of nerve and courage, he said, "Yes, General, where will I get the fifty guns?"

"How many have you?" asked Jackson.

"About twelve out of the thirty I carried into action yesterday," replied Lee. "My losses in men, horses and carriages have been great."

Jackson said that between the various units on the field he was certain that they could get the equipment they wanted. "Shall I go after the guns?" Lee asked.

"No, not yet," said Jackson. And then pressing the issue, "Col. Lee, can you crush the Federal right with 50 guns?"

"General, I can try. I can do it if anyone can."

"That is not what I asked you, sir. If I give you 50 guns, can you crush the Federal right?"

Lee evaded the question again. "General, you seem to be more intent upon my giving you my technical opinion as an artillery officer, than my going after the guns and making the attempt."

"Yes, sir," Jackson said, "and I want your positive opinion, yes or no."

Lee waited, took his glasses again over the field and after an indeterminable amount of time, finally exclaimed, "General, it cannot be done with 50 guns and the troops you have near here."

Immediately Jackson said, "Let us ride back, Colonel."

If Lee was not unnerved before, he certainly was now. With considerable emotion, he said, "General, you forced me to say what I did unwillingly. If you give the fifty guns to any other artillery officer, I am ruined for life. I promise you that I will fight the guns to the last extremity, if you will only let me command them."

Jackson, benevolent in attitude and perhaps with a slight grin, said, "It is all right, Colonel, everybody knows that you are a brave officer and would fight the guns well. Go to General Lee, and tell him what has occurred since you reported to me. Describe our ride to the hill, your examination of the Federal position, and my conversation about your crushing the Federal right with fifty guns, and my forcing you to give your opinion."

Puzzed no end and with deepest misgivings, Colonel Lee did as he was told. He delivered his story to the general and stood in amazement as the color drained from his commander's face. After a heart-throbbing pause, General Lee said, "Colonel, go and join your command."[10]

It was a long time before Stephen Lee caught the significance of what had transpired, of how he had been used as a pawn in a little game between Robert E. Lee and Stonewall Jackson. In April of the following year, Jackson wrote his official report of the battle at Sharpsburg. It was then that he revealed that Lee had ordered him to place artillery on the hill in question on the afternoon of the 17th with the purpose of turning McClellan's right.[11] Jackson knew it could not be done and obviously voiced his opinion to the general. Only when he read the report did Colonel Lee realize that the incident showed "General Lee's decision and boldness in battle, and General Jackson's delicate loyalty to his commanding general, in convincing him of the inadvisability of a proposed movement, which he felt it would be hazardous to undertake."[12]

It was one of the rarely recorded conversations of Jackson during the campaign and it revealed so much of his character. Jackson was a fighting man and one known to take risks, but, as illustrated by this story, he was also a wise and prudent man. This seemed almost contrary to legend. Douglas could never quite agree with the claims that Jackson had wanted to withdraw to Virginia the night of the 17th. He could not understand such a disagreement between Jackson and Lee. Douglas could forgive his beloved Stonewall had the advice actually been given, but if Jackson did make the suggestion to Lee, "he kept his apprehensions so strictly to himself, in his words, his manners, and his actions, that no one of his staff ever suspected them."[13]

On Thursday morning, the 18th, McClellan issued specific orders "not to precipitate hostilities."[14] He was expecting reinforcements, he told his generals, and he would make no movements to the front until they came up. While the men on the lines waited for further instructions, Confederate sharpshooters opened up and during the day carried on a brisk fire with Federal pickets. Brief exchanges kept up on and off throughout the day; Lee waiting for McClellan; McClellan waiting for reinforcements.

Brig. Gen. Winfield Scott Hancock, who had moved from brigade command in Smith's division of the Sixth Corps to Richardson's position of division command when that general was wounded, was on the field at the Sunken Road with his men that afternoon when he was informed that a flag of truce from the enemy was coming toward his front. Hancock was a West Point man and a general who went by the books. If there was going to be any negotiating, it would be done with strict protocol. He immediately sent General Meagher forward. "It was then learned that no flag had been sent by the enemy, and that a misunderstanding had arisen on account of an unauthorized arrangement which had been made by the pickets of the opposing forces, ostensibly for the purpose of collecting the wounded between our lines." It was a false alarm, but Hancock gave the blame to his own men stating that they had started the whole thing. He then sent a message to General Pryor, who seemed to be acting spokesman for the Confederates, informing him that "any communication having for its object their collection must proceed from them, expressing a desire, however, that the wounded, who had been lying on the ground for thirty hours, might be removed."[15] Hancock had been riding the line, pistol in hand, chasing plunderers from his own division who were ghoulishly going through the pockets of the enemy dead. He was not letting anyone into that no man's land without proper permission; if not the Confederates, certainly not his own men.[16]

General Pryor replied to Hancock that he had no authority to initiate such communications and the negotiations broke down. Later another flag appeared, this time in the hands of a Confederate colonel. General Meagher went out to meet him. The colonel said he was there to collect the wounded under a previously arranged truce. Meagher said that it was in error, that no such truce existed, and again the Confederate went back; "in a few minutes hostilities recommenced."[17] "Subsequently a number of the enemy appeared in the corn-field in our front," wrote Hancock, "apparently for the purpose of collecting the dead, five of whom approached our picket line. At that moment several shots were delivered by their own sharpshooters, when these five men were arrested and sent to the rear as prisoners of war."[18] Nerves were tense. The slightest suspicious movement brought on rapid retaliation. While this misunderstanding existed throughout the day and evening, hundreds of wounded, who might have been saved, died with help a few yards away. It was this way all along the lines. "It was a sickening sight," observed Maj. Von Borcke. "Many wounded still remained untended in their agony in out-of-the-way spots of the woods and corn-fields."[19]

At 1:20 P.M. on the afternoon of the battle, McClellan wired Washington that he was in the midst of "the most terrible battle of the war — perhaps of history." It was urgent that he be sent reinforcements immediately. "Burnside is now attacking . . . and I hold my small reserve, consisting of Porter's corps, ready to attack the center as soon as the flank movements are developed."[20] This was one of two messages sent to the War Department during the day. The second asked for additional ammunition to be sent during the night for renewed battle the next morning. This was meager news for General Halleck and the War Department, but McClellan had said, "Thus far it looks well."[21] This small bit of encouragement would have to suffice for the time being. Gideon Welles said that McClellan's dispatches were seldom "full, clear, or satisfactory. 'Behaved splendidly,' 'performed handsomely,' but wherein or what accomplished is never told. Our anxiety is intense."[22] Meanwhile, the War Department would do everything in its power to rush the needed supplies. Two trains loaded with ammunition set out early the morning of the 18th, one direct to Frederick, the other to Hagerstown by way of Harrisburg.[23]

McClellan told Halleck that he had only Porter's "small reserves." In actuality he had much more than this on the 17th. Although one division and several brigades of another were pulled from Porter to support Burnside, they were not used to any great extent. In truth, then, Porter's entire corps was available on the 18th, some 12,800 unused men. McClellan also forgot Franklin's Sixth Corps. Only one brigade, Irwin's of Smith's 2nd Division, had been used in the battle. Irwin lost 439 men but Franklin still had nearly 12,000 available. This meant that on the morning of the 18th, McClellan had almost 25,000 fresh troops, men who had not fired a rifle on the 17th. Of the 55,956 McClellan claimed were available for battle on the 17th, he had lost 12,410. Considering that under the most critical conditions he could muster the remainder of all the battled divisions, Mc-

Clellan would have had another 18,500 or a grand total of 43,500 fit for action the morning of the 18th.[24]

This was not all. The War Department had answered McClellan's continued call for more troops by dispatching at daybreak on the 14th, the day of the battle at South Mountain, 6,000 men under Maj. Gen. Andrew A. Humphreys. Though Humphreys was untried in battle, he showed great ability in assuming quick command. His division was in Frederick by the 17th. At 3:00 P.M. that afternoon he was ordered to proceed immediately to Sharpsburg. Marching all night, he was taking position on the Federal left early the next morning.[25] Now McClellan had nearly 50,000 troops.

What are reserves for but to use in a "pinch?" Many of McClellan's contemporaries wondered this, not the least of whom was General Cox. Why was Porter not used? If A. P. Hill, McLaws, and Walker came up for Lee, why could not Couch, who had replaced Franklin in Pleasant Valley, do the same? In trying to answer these questions some years later, Cox analyzed the situation in this way:

I am convinced that McClellan's refusal to [put in reserves] on the left was the result of his rooted belief, through all the day after Sedgwick's defeat, that Lee was overwhelmingly superior in force, and was preparing to return a crushing blow upon our right flank. He was keeping something in hand to fill a gap or cover a retreat, if that wing should be driven back.[26]

But what about Lee? Confederate records are quite incomplete, making an accurate tabulation of the losses for the battle and of the number of troops the following day impossible. Next to McClellan himself, this particular aspect of the Maryland Campaign has been the most controversial. Southern figures range anywhere from 8,000 to 13,724 killed, wounded, and missing. If the figures of 35,255 given for strength on the 17th and losses of 10,291 are accepted, this would give Lee about 24,000 available on the morning of the 18th, or a little more than half that of his enemy.[27]

Why, then, did not McClellan attack on the 18th? "The fault was in the man," wrote Francis Palfrey. It was as simple as that. McClellan had the force he needed on that date, had he seen fit to use it. To Palfrey, it was "hardly worth while to state his reasons."[28]

After the battle on the 17th, McClellan rode the lines, looking, searching, saying little. "The General then led us back to the headquarters camp, where, forgetting the movements of the day for the time, we supped heartily and slept profoundly," wrote D. H. Strother of McClellan's staff. There seemed to be no conversation of major significance in the Federal camp. All thoughts were of what fate the morning might bring. It was not until the small hours of the morning that Strother learned of McClellan's plans:

I had gone to sleep, firmly convinced that we had thrashed Lee soundly, and that he would escape in the night; or otherwise, we would open the attack at daylight and finish him. Some time between midnight and morning, being awakened by the going and coming of messengers to the General's tent, I heard McClellan's voice charging some officer with the following message: "They are to hold the ground they occupy, but are not to attack without further orders." I was so much annoyed and disappointed at hearing this that I slept but little after.[29]

Strother was not alone in his thoughts. The feeling spread through the ranks like a cancerous growth; first disappointment, then bitterness. A young officer in Hooker's corps wrote:

The prize to be gained, for the country and for ourselves, was worthy of any venture, and I saw no one who did not seem anxious to make the trial. But sunrise came, hour after hour slipped by, with no orders to advance, no attack by the rebels, and gradually a bitter feeling of disappointment began to trouble us, while the conviction forced itself upon our minds that the enemy was to be permitted to escape. The battles of South Mountain and Antietam were robbed of any decisive significance. It is not for me to attempt any criticism of military measures or military men, but only to delineate truly the bitter feelings of disappointment shared by so many in our army that day. My heart almost sunk within me at the dreary prospect before us; this was to me blue Friday indeed.[30]

A respected surgeon in the Army of the Potomac, who was in a position to hear and diagnose the emotions of a fighting man, recorded in his diary on September 19:

The feeling against Gen. McClellan to-day is no longer expressed in muttered disaffection, but in loud angry execration. The soldiers cannot be reconciled to their disappointment, and to having permitted Gen. Lee to escape with his army. My own hopes that he would retrieve his lost character are all gone. I have lost all confidence in him. He can be nothing short of an imbecile, a coward, or a traitor.

I am now satisfied that this army will win no decisive battle whilst under command of General George B. McClellan. It is not a part of his programme. Gen. McClellan's aims were satisfied with clearing Maryland of the enemy, when destruction or capitulation should have been demanded. This I do not doubt will be the verdict of history. But how terrible was our loss! Nine Generals fell, killed or wounded, in their determined efforts to vindicate McClellan. All in vain.[31]

On September 29, the New York *Tribune* published this benediction to the battle from its correspondent: "Adieu to the drenched field of Antietam, with its glorious Wednesday, winning for our army a record than which nothing brighter shines through history — with its fatal Thursday, permitting the clean leisurely escape of the foe down into the valley, across the difficult ford, and up the Virginia heights."[32] The *Tribune* reporter wrote his editor that he was amazed at the "brigade, division, and regimental commanders" who were not only anti-McClellan, but were claiming the whole country was dying of McClellan. "I would write a careful, entire[ly] frank, just letter about McClellan, but I infer from the tone of the paper that you would not publish it."[33] If this paper was not interested, certainly the Chicago *Daily Tribune* was. On October 13, Joseph Medill of the Chicago paper wrote to O. M. Hatch, Illinois Secretary of State, who had been to Antietam on an inspection trip after the battle: "What devil is it that prevents the Potomac Army from advancing on the rebels? What malign influence palsies our army and wastes away these glorious days for fighting? If it is McClellan, does not the President see that he is a traitor, and is plunging the nation into the gulf of destruction?"[34] Medill was echoing the questions of thousands of thinking people all over the country.

On the afternoon of the battle, as McClellan was riding behind the lines, he met an old friend, a Massachusetts general, who told him that though his men had behaved "admirably," they were then scattered and badly dispersed. "Collect them at once," said McClellan. "We must fight tonight and fight tomorrow. This is our golden opportunity. If we cannot whip the enemy now, we may just as well all die upon the field."[35] There were those to whom McClellan's words would ring loud and clear for years to come. There were those who would never forget. Benjamin W. Crowinshield of the 1st Massachusetts, was one. In his history of the regiment, he wrote:

At Antietam, McClellan in the centre, above the Antietam Creek, on high ground, with Porter's large and efficient corps at his elbow, and all his cavalry within five hundred yards of Lee's guns, which alone connected the two wings of his army, should have seen his opportunity. He was not accustomed, as was Sheridan, to be on the ground visiting in turn all the critical positions, in contact with his generals, and almost with his enemy, ready to fight his battle as opportunity offered, taking advantage of his enemy's errors, and snatching victory from him. But he could not help seeing the chance at Antietam, for it was thundered into his ears, and must have burned his eyes. He was of the generals who fight battles in tents, on paper, at a table the day before. His enthusiasm was shown at reviews, or before the battle. The battlefield showed him nothing.[36]

"The night . . . brought with it grave responsibilities," wrote McClellan in his official report. "Whether to renew the attack on the 18th or to defer it, even with the risk of the enemy's retirement, was the question before me." For McClellan, these *were* grave responsibilities, and he revealed his reason in only a few words of the proceeding paragraphs of his report. "Nearly 200,000 men . . . were engaged in this memorable battle."[37] He had given Lee credit for 60,000 more men than he had, and as late as August 4, 1863, when this report was written, General McClellan still labored under these false figures. His report continued:

After a night of anxious deliberation, and a full and careful survey of the situation and condition of our army, the strength and position of the enemy, I concluded that the success of an attack on the 18th was not certain. I am aware of the fact that under ordinary circumstances a general is expected to risk a battle if he has a reasonable prospect of success; but at this critical juncture I should have had a narrow view of the condition of the country had I been willing to hazard another battle with less than an absolute assurance of success. At that moment—Virginia lost, Washington menaced, Maryland invaded—the national cause could afford no risks of defeat. One battle lost and almost all would have been lost. Lee's army might then have marched, as it pleased, on Washington, Baltimore, Philadelphia, or New York. It could have levied its supplies from a fertile and undevastated country, extorted tribute from wealthy and populous cities, and nowhere east of the Alleghanies was there another organized force able to arrest its march.[38]

Then McClellan became more specific with his excuses. His men were fatigued from battle; they were hungry; they were demoralized and scattered; they were out of ammunition and reinforcements had not arrived. "During the 18th, orders were given for a renewal of the attack on the 19th."[39]

McClellan says that he gave orders to attack on the 19th, but a search of official documents reveals no such directions. At 4:00 A.M. on the morning of the 19th, a message from headquarters was sent to General Sumner. "The commanding general directs you, if the enemy appears to be retiring, to mass your troops in readiness to move in any direction. The other corps commanders are directed to push forward their pickets, and if the enemy is retreating, to mass their commands."[40] Perhaps to McClellan these were attack orders. Certainly, to those unschooled in the military, and even to his subordinates, they were decidedly not.

At about the same time as McClellan gave his orders, Lee, too, had reached a decision. Late on the afternoon of the 18th, he issued orders for the evacuation of the field that night and the withdrawal to Virginia. Lee's sole purpose in remaining on the 18th was that one hope of turning McClellan's right. Now that Jackson's opinion had been verified by Stephen Lee, and it was obvious that McClellan would never renew the attack, there was nothing left to do but recross the Potomac. Longstreet, who had wanted to withdraw from Maryland as far back as September 13th, now had his views accepted. He wrote: "I took the liberty of addressing a note to the commanding general, about 2 o'clock in the afternoon, suggesting a withdrawal to the south side of the Potomac. Before my note reached him, however, he rode to my bivouac and expressed the same views."[41]

Immediately after orders were given, the wagon train was packed and started on its way to Blackford's Ford. It would take until sunset to get the cumbersome vehicles across. A brief rain shower had come up and the roads were muddy. Then as darkness fell, Lee's lines slowly dissolved into the night. There was no pursuit, and there was no element of surprise, for Federal pickets, and even troops on the lines, listened to the scuffle of feet and the jangle of harnesses throughout the night. But no orders came to give chase, and the Army of Northern Virginia withdrew from the fields of the Antietam without incident. Again they left their dead to be buried by the enemy.

Though McClellan was exerting no pressure on Lee's army, the crossing was not an easy one. The long lines of wagons threatened several times to delay the whole operation. The narrow road was jammed, and the ford was filled with cursing muledrivers, who pushed and pulled through the night to prevent catastrophy. Jackson, astride his horse, moved from bank to bank shouting orders and directions, urging the men to move on. Maj. John Harmon, Jackson's quartermaster, who had "cussed" the muleteams across the Potomac earlier in September, was again delegated this authority by the general, and, according to Douglas, was "the genius of this retreat." Harmon, "big-bodied, big-voiced, untiring, fearless of man or devil, would have ordered Jackson himself out of his way if necessary to obey Jackson's orders."[42]

Stuart assigned Fitzhugh Lee's brigade of cavalry to cover the crossing, while he took the remainder along the river to Williamsport from where he planned to later attack the Federal flank, should McClellan pursue the withdrawal. Walker was the last to leave the field and among the last to cross the Potomac. "As I rode into the river I passed General Lee, sitting on his horse in the stream, watching the crossing of the wagons and artillery," wrote Walker. "Returning my greeting, he inquired as to what was still behind. There was nothing but the wagons containing my wounded, and a battery of artillery, all of which were near at hand, and I told him so. 'Thank God!' I heard him say as I rode on."[43]

The crossing into Maryland had been a joyous one. The men sang and cheered their way across the river. Now it was different. There was little to be said. When someone would strike up the tune to "Maryland, My Maryland," he would be shouted down with "Damn My Maryland."[44] That song never again held the promise it did in early September, 1862. Maj. Walter H. Taylor wrote to his sister on September 21: "Don't let any of your friends sing 'My Maryland,' — not 'my Western Maryland' anyhow."[45] Thomas R. Cobb wrote to his wife: "I have not heard 'My Maryland' sung, whistled or played by a band, since I returned to the army. I hear that one band struck the tune not long since and the men groaned and hissed until they discontinued it."[46]

In 1893, Lafayette McLaws, in a letter to a young lady in New Jersey, wrote of the morning after the battle. The men were fatigued, exhausted from battle:

Our supplies were very limited, and no one seemed to be disposed to be cheerful. This was about sunrise when the band of my Mississippi Brigade commenced playing My Maryland. . . . the men all along the line shouted out, "Stop that! Stop that! Give us no more of that, but let us have "Old Virginny." The Band realized that it made an unfortunate selection, at once changed from "Maryland, My Maryland" to "Carry me back to Old Virginny" . . . And all along the line, the men saluted the change with shouts of welcome, and the shouts of my men, were taken up and repeated by troops of other Commands . . . and the spirits of the men rose again and there was laughter and cheering all along the lines.[47]

Two hours after sunrise on the 19th, the Confederate crossing of the Potomac was complete. Everybody was over and not a shot had been fired. General William Pendleton, with Lee's reserve artillery of ten batteries and a supporting infantry of some 600 men, had been waiting for Lee on the Virginia shore and was now in position for whatever McClellan would send. It came that morning shortly after the last of the Confederates were safely across. Pleasonton's cavalry was the first to take up the pursuit, if indeed at this point it could be called a pursuit. Porter's Fifth Corps followed. Eighteen guns of Pleasonton's horse artillery effectively dueled Pendleton for several hours until Porter was in position along the banks of the canal. Despite his advantage in artillery, Pendleton's meager infantry support provided little hope as a deterrent. Late in the afternoon he was forced to abandon several of his cannon. Under orders from Lee to hold off the enemy at least until sundown, Pendleton stayed with the action until late afternoon before gathering what he could and moving off to join the main body of the army. Pendleton was in a rather odd command position. He had infantry but hardly knew where they were or how many in each location. Throughout the day he had moved them from place to place without at any given time knowing how many men he had moved. When a Federal crossing reached the south side of the river late in the day and pushed back the front line skirmishers, Pendleton became alarmed and rode off to tell Lee that all was lost; all of his 44 guns. Lee was visibly and audibly shaken.

Jackson was thoroughly disgusted. "The news of this appalling disaster caused [Jackson] more anxiety than he had ever shown before during the war," wrote Jackson's wife in her memoirs.[48] Jackson immediately ordered A. P. Hill to turn back toward the ford.

Porter had sent the 4th Michigan across the river that evening as an "attacking party." In reality it was more a scavaging party, for they did little more than bring back what Pendleton had abandoned. The men were called back during the night and bivouaced on the canal towpath. Early the next morning, two divisions were alerted and moved across the river at 7:00 A.M. This, for all intent and purpose, was the "attacking party." Porter called it an "advance," but the attack, or advance, hardly was off the ground when it ran head-on into A. P. Hill's Division racing back under Jackson's urgent orders. Within an hour Porter had the news that his troops had met the enemy. He recalled them immediately. Hill pushed ahead and forced the Federals into the river. Most units were able to make it back to the Maryland side; all but the 118th Pennsylvania, a comparatively new regiment that had been supplied with faulty rifles. The men had not long before been issued new Enfields, "at its best a most defective weapon." Not having fired them in battle, no one had questioned their reliability. "Some of the weapons were too weak to explode the cap," wrote the regimental historian. "This defect was the first unnoticed in the excitement; cartridge after cartridge was rammed into the barrel under the belief that each had been discharged until they nearly filled the piece to the muzzle." Ramrods jammed; pieces fouled. The men were powerless to defend themselves between the river and the Confederate veterans. Porter called off the attack and salvaged the remnants of the regiment. His official report of casualities listed 363 killed or wounded for the river action, of which 269 were from the 118th Pennsylvania.[49] A. P. Hill claimed that "by their own account," the Federals lost "3,000 killed and drowned." He called it "the most terrible slaughter" the war had thus far seen:

The broad surface of the Potomac was blue with the floating bodies of our foe. [Joseph Ashbrook, a sergeant in the 118th Pennsylvania at the time of the action, commented in his later years on Gen. Hill's remarks. In Ashbrook's personal copy of Volume XIX of the *Official Records,* beside Hill's statement, he noted: "Loose writing!"] Some 200 prisoners were taken [Hill went on]. My own loss was 30 killed and 231 wounded; total 261. This was a wholesale lesson to the enemy, and taught them to know it may be dangerous sometimes to press a retreating army.[50]

Porter took the point well and did not renew the pursuit.

With the rear guard of the army safe now, Lee went into camp for several days near Martinsburg on the Opequon Creek and then at Winchester and Bunker Hill. During this move back to the Shenandoah Valley, the Confederates "broke up" several miles of the B & O Railroad between Martinsburg and Harpers Ferry, thereby rendering useless McClellan's best means of transportation should he decide to follow.[51]

McClellan, rather than following Lee into the Valley, reconcentrated his forces. The Twelfth Corps moved to Maryland Heights and the Second Corps into Harpers Ferry. The First and Ninth Corps stayed at Sharpsburg. Couch's division, Franklin's corps, and a portion of Pleasonton's cavalry moved on the 20th to Williamsport, where they quickly drove Jeb Stuart back across the river. Thus, McClellan sealed Maryland's river border from Harpers Ferry to Williamsport; sealed the Army of the Potomac in and the Army of Northern Virginia out. Within nineteen days after Lincoln had asked him to command the defenses of Washington, he had brought some semblance of order to the Federal army, fought two hotly contested battles, forced Lee to withdraw from Maryland soil, and effectively established a blockade against a Confederate re-entry. Lee's Maryland Campaign was over, and McClellan told Halleck, "Our victory was complete. The enemy is driven back into Virginia. Maryland and Pennsylvania are now safe."[52]

Southern newspaper editors were unwilling to accept defeat. They had a manner of interpreting the late news from the front to suit themselves. The Richmond *Enquirer*, for example, reported on September 22: "We have the gratification of being able to announce that the battle resulted in one of the most complete victories that has yet immortalized the Confederate arms."[53] "Judged by all the rules of warfare, it was a victory to our arms," stated the Charleston *Courier*. "If we failed to rout the enemy, it was only because the nature of the ground prevented him from running."[54]

On the other hand, the editor of the Petersburg (Virginia) *Express* approached the matter much more realistically, and perhaps by reading through the usual Southern eupherisms, one could take some consolation:

We think that General Lee has very wisely withdrawn his army from Maryland, the co-operation of whose people in his plans and purposes was indispensable for success. They have failed to respond to his noble appeal in the desired way, and the victories of Sharpsburg and Boonsborough, South Mountain, purchased with the torrents of blood, have been rendered improfitable in a material point of view.

They have, moreover, deepened the impression upon the enemy of the previous lessons which we gave him in the art of fighting, and though they may exult, in their crazy fashion, over imaginary successes heralded in the lying dispatches of McClellan and his trumpet-blowers, and no less lying correspondents and editors of the Lincoln journals, yet they will be willing enough to let Lee and his army alone on this side of the Potomac.

The recrossing of the Potomac by our forces does not at all disturb us. Under the circumstances it was a most judicious movement, and in no manner or degree prejudicial to our interests in a military point of view,—save and except the losses we sustained in the sanguinary battles in Maryland, which are to be deeply deplored.

But the enemy suffered in this respect far more than we did, and although this is no adequate consolation or compensation to us in the premises, yet it assures us that the blows which we struck lost nothing of their vigor and efficacy by the brief change which was made in the seat of war.[55]

12

"McClellan's Bodyguard"

"I am sick, tired, and disgusted with the condition of military affairs here in the East," wrote General Halleck to a friend on October 30, 1862. "There is an immobility here that exceeds all that any man can conceive of. It requires the lever of Archimedes to move this inert mass. I have tried my best, but without success."[1] On October 7, Halleck had written his wife, "Everything would now be satisfactory if I could only get General McClellan to move. He has lain still twenty days since the battle of Antietam, and I cannot persuade him to advance an inch. It puts me all out of patience."[2]

It is difficult to reconcile McClellan's excuses in not following Lee across the Potomac and into Virginia with the relative condition of the two armies. He listed fatigue from battle as one excuse, and undoubtedly he was right. A battle such as he had fought was most assuredly one which would have drained all resistance from the best of soldiers. That both armies were physically exhausted, no one can deny. Yet the Confederates were not superhuman. If anything, at this point in the campaign they were less likely to be classified human than the Northern soldiers. The war would continue for more than two years, and at no other time, until the surrender at Appomattox, would the Army of Northern Virginia be so weak as it was in September, 1862. Though McClellan's writings continued for many years after Antietam, he failed to explain how Lee's army could rally after South Mountain and Harpers Ferry, how Hill, Walker, and McLaws could arrive on the field with so much fight still in their blood, or why, after losing 10,000 men, Lee remained on the field the 18th.

McClellan claimed his men were hungry, and indeed some of them were, but he knew before he had left his camp at Rockville that the Army of Northern Virginia was literally traveling on empty stomachs. It had been days, in some cases weeks, since Lee's men had had a hot meal. They lived off the land, as meager a living as it was, and still fought gallantly. But McClellan refused to subject his men to the same conditions though a great deal was at stake. His men were demoralized and scattered, so he claimed, yet he said he had 25,000 who were not so disorganized. Had he found it possible to use these troops, it would have been, at the least, a man for man fight. Lee took a chance with odds much greater than this against him. McClellan's first official report following the battle, compiled within 24 hours of Lee's withdrawal, claimed his "aggregate present for duty" to be 93,149, odds of more than three to one.[3]

In his official report to the War Department, McClellan stated that the Potomac River at the time of the battle "was very low and presented a comparatively weak line of defense unless watched by large masses of troops."[4] Yet in his *Own Story*, he commented that in light of the condition of his men, he "did not feel authorized to cross the river with the main army, over a deep and difficult ford, in pursuit of the retreating enemy, known to be in strong force on the south bank, and thereby place the stream, which was liable at any time to rise above a fording stage, between my army and its base of supply."[5] There can be no doubt that the ford was a difficult one. There were many boulders at this point obstructing maneuverability of the wagons, and the little shower the night of the 18th might well have raised the river level some. (On the afternoon of the 17th, when A. P. Hill had crossed, the Potomac was "hip deep.")[6] But Lee got across with his entire army. Apparently McClellan forgot this.

McClellan said he was lacking in ammunition, as good as any reason for not wanting to fight, but when those trains arrived from Washington, he let them set.[7] His only serious ammunition shortage was noted in artillery. The batteries of 20-pounder Parrotts had depleted their supplies on the 17th. It would have been a serious and legitimate disadvantage had Lee been able to offer some opposition, but the Army of Northern Virginia had only six such guns to its name, only two of which were on the field at Antietam.[8] There was no serious shortage in animals. At the end of September, official figures showed 32,885 horses and mules available for duty in the Army of the Potomac, and over 3,200 baggage and supply wagons in acceptable condition.[9]

General McClellan had questioned the authorization of leaving Washington with his army. At the time he said he felt it was his duty to do so, yet while on the brink of destroying Lee and bringing the war to a close, he let that authority, which in reality was his own, hold him back. In essence, McClellan was doing exactly what he said he would do and little more.

The purpose of advancing from Washington was simply to meet the necessities of the moment by frustrating Lee's invasion of the Northern States, and, when that was accomplished, to push with the utmost rapidity the work of reorganization and supply, so that a new campaign might be promptly inaugurated with the army in condition to prosecute it to a successful termination without intermission.[10]

As if in reply to McClellan's claims, C. E. Davis of the 13th Massachusetts wrote: "To us of the Thirteenth it seemed just possible that the enemy might be equally tired and a good deal more discomfited. . . . when men are stimulated by success in battle they forget everything but pushing their good fortune to a complete triumph."[11] Another Davis, Lt. Col. George B., writing for the Military Historical Society, said, "The management of the Army of the Potomac was halting, dilatory, wanting in firm direction and, to a degree, irresolute and unskillful. An opportunity such as rarely occurs in war presented itself and was not availed of, and the Army of Northern Virginia was permitted to escape from a situation which should have gone far to compass its defeat, if not its utter discomfiture."[12] Gideon Welles's commentary was typical of high level thinking and somewhat humorous. On September 19, he wrote: "Nothing from the army, except that, instead of following up the victory, attacking and capturing the Rebels, they, after a day's armistice, are rapidly escaping over the river. McClellan says they are crossing and that Pleasanton is after them. Oh dear!"[13]

And so the days drifted by and the Army of the Potomac remained in camp while the Confederates nursed their wounds less than twenty miles away. The procedures of normal camp life continued on the banks of the Antietam through the rest of September. The burying of the dead and the disposing of unfit equipment occupied most of the soldiers' spare time. Occasionally scouting parties were sent out, mostly to round up leftover Confederate gear. On one such "foraging" expedition, a Captain Waldron of the 16th Maine discovered "ninety dead rebel cannon buried near the river, with neat headstones, bearing a name, and the regiment to which they belonged, so as to be identified by the affectionate relatives, should they be fortunate enough to make another raid into Maryland."[14]

On September 22, Abraham Lincoln said at his cabinet meeting: "The action of the army against the rebels has not been quite what I should have liked. But they have been driven out of Maryland, and Pennsylvania is no longer in danger of invasion." The President was not as satisfied as he sounded. He had wanted a victory. Antietam was certainly not that. Almost as if he expected little from his general, he said, "When the rebel army was at Frederick, I determined as soon as it should be driven out of Maryland, to issue a proclamation of emancipation such as I thought most likely to be useful."[15] For the moment, driving Lee from Maryland was victory enough. Now he would deal the death blow to Richmond; he would seal the doom of the Confederacy.

On September 23, newspapers published the following communique from the White House:

That on the first day of January in the year of our Lord, one thousand eight hundred and sixty-three, all persons held as slaves within any State, or designated part of a State, the people whereof shall then be in rebellion against the United States, shall be then, thenceforward, and forever free; and the Executive Government of the United States, including the military and naval authority thereof, will recognize and maintain the freedom of such persons, and will do no act or acts to repress such persons, or any of them, in efforts they may make for their actual freedom.[16]

In a few strokes of the pen, with the thin thread of "victory" at Sharpsburg as his guide, Lincoln changed the Civil War from a war of economics and politics to a war for the abolition of slavery, and automatically made Lee's Maryland Campaign and the Battle of Antietam one of the most decisive of the war.

But the "victory" was all McClellan's. He had saved the Union. To his wife he wrote: "I feel some little pride in having, with a beaten and demoralized army, defeated Lee so utterly and saved the North so completely. I feel that I have done all that can be asked in twice saving the country."[17] Later he wrote: "Those in whose judgment I rely tell me that I fought the battle splendidly and that it is a masterpiece of art."[18] In answer to McClellan's claims, General Michie commented:

It is difficult to analyze satisfactorily McClellan's mental constitution in accepting the judgment of his friends with regard to this battle. It does not seem possible to find any other battle ever fought in the conduct of which more errors were committed then are clearly attributable to the commander of the Army of the Potomac; and in this case, the only battle in which throughout the whole of his career as a commander it may be said that he exercised personal direction, it cannot with justice be held that he displayed those rare qualities that belong *per se* to the few men who are entitled to be called great commanders.[19]

McClellan's message to Washington after the battle stated that the victory was "complete." To Lincoln this meant only one thing; he wanted to believe that Lee was finished. He had waited for a long time for McClellan to justify the faith he had in him from the beginning. "I rejoice in this success for many public reasons," the President told Postmaster General Montgomery Blair at a cabinet meeting, "but I am also happy on account of McClellan."[20] But the days dragged by and on October 1, Lincoln came to McClellan to see for himself why the victory had not been "complete," and why the commander of his army had failed to pursue Lee. Observers said the President was in a melancholy mood, "unusualy thin and silent . . . weary and careworn."[21] McClellan reported that Lincoln congratulated him on the outcome of the battle and had agreed with his decision to rebuild his army before going into Virginia.

He more than once assured me that he was fully satisfied with my whole course from the beginning [wrote McClellan]; that the only fault he could possibly find was that I was perhaps too prone to be sure that everything was ready before acting, but that my actions were all right when I started. [Lincoln] told me as he was convinced I was the best general in the country, etc., etc.[22]

"General, you have saved the country," McClellan quoted the President. "You must remain in command and carry us through to the end." The general answered, "That will be impossible. We need time. The influences at Washington will be too strong for you, Mr. President. I will not be allowed the required time for preparation." According to McClellan, Lincoln answered him by saying, "General, I pledge myself to stand between you and harm." Years later, McClellan would say, "I honestly believe that the President meant every word he said, but that the influences at Washington, as I predicted, were too strong for him or any living man."[23]

There is one interesting aspect of Lincoln's visit which should not be ignored. Allan Pinkerton, McClellan's "secret service" expert and close friend, was with the President and the general for at least a part of the visit; this is evident in the famous photograph taken at the Pry farm. Pinkerton rode back to Washington with Lincoln and in a rather candid conversation the two men discussed the urgent issues of the day. Later in a letter to McClellan, Pinkerton corroborated everything the general had said. "He [Lincoln] spoke very freely and was very friendly when speaking of you," wrote Pinkerton. "He freely admits the importance of the battles at South Mountain and Antietam and the great strategy you displayed in the conduct of this campaign and the disposition and handling of your army on the field." Pinkerton had also had an interview with Lincoln on September 22, during which time he gave the President the latest information from the field. He wrote McClellan: "He [Lincoln] expressed himself as highly pleased and gratified with all you had done [commending your caution] and frankly admitted that you had done everything which could or ought to be expected of you."[24]

These messages undoubtedly did wonders for McClellan's soul, and the general would have believed Pinkerton, for this was his friend, the man who had told him that Lee had over 100,000 men. In light of Pinkerton's reputation during McClellan's two campaigns and other later developments, this specialized information appears completely worthless. McClellan, then, could say what he wished of Lincoln's visit. The conversations were solely between himself and the President. Sadly, not a word was recorded. The events which followed, however, failed to support the general.

Five days after Lincoln's visit to Sharpsburg on October 7, McClel-

lan received orders to "cross the Potomac and give battle to the enemy
or drive him south. Your army must move now while the roads are
good."[25] A week later, when nothing had developed, Lincoln sat down
and wrote one of his "on bended knees" letters. It would not be his
last direct correspondence with McClellan, but it would show the
signs of a man whose patience was wearing very thin. "You remember
my speaking to you of what I called your over-cautiousness," began
the President. In this first sentence, Lincoln confirmed suspicions that
McClellan perhaps had not evaluated his visit correctly. The President went on: "Are you not over-cautious when you assume that you
can not do what the enemy is constantly doing? Should you not claim
to be at least his equal in prowess, and act upon that claim?" It
seemed to Mr. Lincoln, and rightly so, that if the enemy could undertake such arduous adventures as an invasion with limited strength and
under hardships of, for all practical purposes, nonexistent supply lines,
then the Federal army, with its vastly superior means of communication and supply, could venture across the river and make some effort to
find Lee. "Exclusive of the water line, you are now nearer Richmond
than the enemy is by the route that you *can*, and he *must* take," the
President reminded General McClellan. Why could not the general
reach there before Lee, "unless you admit that he is more than your
equal on a march." Lee's route to Richmond was the arc of a circle;
McClellan's was the chord. "I would press closely to him, fight him if
a favorable opportunity should present, and, at least, try to beat him
to Richmond on the inside track. I say 'try;' if we never try, we shall
never succeed."[26]

Lee was still in the vicinity of Winchester. To Lincoln this was the
same as being just across the river. Yet here he was again suffering
the forbearance of a father telling his young son the rules of the game,
a game that the player should, by now, know and understand. McClellan "has got the slows," Lincoln told a friend.[27] Had the general forgotten the maxims of war? Perhaps he needed reminding. When the
enemy comes to you, he tenders a tremendous advantage, which should
not for one moment be permitted to escape. "We should not so operate as to merely drive him away. As we must beat him somewhere,
or fail finally, we can do it, if at all, easier near to us, than far away. If
we can not beat the enemy where he now is, we never can, he again
being within the entrenchments of Richmond." The President went

on to some length explaining to McClellan what routes to Richmond were open, how many miles distant they were, and the advantage of certain mountain passes. Then he concluded the letter by telling the general that it was all easy "if our troops march as well as the enemy; and it is unmanly to say they can not do it."[28] Lincoln was proud of this army; he had said so many times, but he saw in it something that no one else could see. One morning at Antietam, the President had gotten up early and with a close friend from Illinois walked to the high ground behind McClellan's headquarters. Gazing out over the vast expanse of the Army of the Potomac as it lay in camp, Lincoln said, "Do you know what this is?" "It is the Army of the Potomac," his friend answered in astonishment. "So it is called," said the President, "but that is a mistake; it is only McClellan's bodyguard."[29]

It would not have been unlike McClellan to completely ignore Lincoln's letter of advice, so great must have been his contempt by this time. The general was back to calling the President names again. In a portion of a letter to his wife not published in his *Own Story*, he wrote: "There never was a truer epithet applied to a certain individual than that of the 'Gorilla.' "[30] And he had never ceased blaming Secretary of War Stanton for all his troubles. On October 31, in another unpublished letter, he said that "it will afford me the great pleasure if I can in any honorable & open way be instrumental in consigning the rascal to the infamous fate he deserves. If I can crush him I will, relentlessly & without reserve."[31] To McClellan, Lincoln and Stanton were partners in crime. He could hardly be expected to heed the advice of his enemies in Washington. He did ignore the President's letter. On October 16, he acknowledged receipt by stating that he had not time at that moment to reply. The next day he wrote: "I have been unable to give Your Excellency's letter that full and respected consideration which it merits at my hands."[32] There was no further answer. Meanwhile, Lee was showing that he was still full of fight. Longstreet wrote to a friend: "We are beginning to feel like game cocks again, some begin [to] wish for the chance to convince the Yankees that Sharpsburg is but a trifle to what they could do."[33] On September 25, just eight days after the battle, Lee wrote to President Davis that from a military viewpoint he felt the best move he could make would be to advance on Hagerstown and endeavor to defeat McClellan there. "I would not hesitate to make it even with our dimished numbers, did the army exhibit its former temper and condition . . ."[34] But Lee was in no condition to stand a reverse and chose to stay put for a while. He did not hesitate for a moment, however, in letting Jeb Stuart show his prowess at McClellan's expense. At daybreak on October 10, Stuart, with 1,500 of his best cavalrymen and four guns, set out across the Potomac, rode through Chambersburg, Pennsylvania, and Emmittsburg, Maryland, and on the 12th, recrossed the Potomac at the Monocacy without a single loss; a ride of some 126 miles around the Army of the Potomac, the last 80 miles without a halt. The raid gained precious little for Lee; a few stores were burned in Chambersburg, but vital bridges assigned for destruction were unharmed and intelligence on McClellan's army was negligible.[35] Similarly, the raid did little for McClellan. If anything, it tightened his grip on his base.

Another week went by and Halleck wrote McClellan:

[The President] directs me to say that he has no change to make in his order of the 6th instant. If you have not been and are now in condition to obey it, you will be able to show such want of ability. The President does not expect impossibilities, but he is very anxious that all this good weather should not be wasted in inactivity. Telegraph when you will move and on what lines you propose to march.[36]

Still the Army of the Potomac remained in Maryland. Could it be that McClellan was blind and deaf to what his superiors wanted of him? Not likely when he told his wife, in so many words, that he knew he was stalling and that he had a reason. "I am tired of fighting against . . . disadvantage," he told Mrs. McClellan, referring to Stanton and the War Department and the constant badgering he received. "[I] feel that it is now time for my country to come to my help and remove these difficulties from my path. If my countrymen will not open their eyes and assist themselves they must pardon me if I decline longer to pursue the thankless avocation of serving them."[37] There was, in fact, a certain degree of "badgering" going on among the radical elements of Congress, but it was in Washington and not on the field. The worse they were saying was that McClellan had secretly visited Lee on the night of the 16th to check on how he would conduct the battle, and now he was under specific instructions from Lee not to pursue him across the Potomac.[38]

There are historians to this day, who, in support of McClellan, still use this "badgering" as a crutch, hobbling through page after page of claims that Washington hamstrung McClellan into inactivity. Aside from the confusion over initial orders for McClellan's command, the general's defenders continually fall back on the logistics problem. There is abundant evidence that the Federal army was well supplied. McClellan was receiving an average of 1,079 horses a week from September 1 through October 14, at the staggering cost to the government of $1,200,000. If they were being mistreated or mishandled at camp, this was no fault of the quartermaster. Every commander, from the highest to the lowest in rank, had a responsibility to see that supplies, animate or inanimate, were effectively and efficiently used.[39] As for food, clothing, tents, etc., not a single requisition from the Army of the Potomac can be cited as purposely delayed. There were occasional delays to be sure; normal military procedures dictates this. There would be soldiers without shoes and some with empty stomachs; even the most normal military redtape would dictate this also; but there would never be such deficiencies to keep an army from fighting an enemy whose requisitions were never answered. Lt. Col. Rufus Ingalls, Chief Quartermaster for the Army of the Potomac, said, "It has been my pride to know the fact that no army was ever more perfectly supplied than this has been, as a general rule." The army had returned from the Peninsula with "an abundant supply of clothing." None of it was returned to the quartermaster depot. "The army . . . marched [into Maryland] quite well supplied with all necessary clothing and transportation." Ingalls declared, with no embarrassment, that there had been suffering and it was expected, for "such commands make no effort to help themselves in the proper way, but content themselves with suffering and grumbling." Ingalls, a man with convictions and quite frank opinions, wrote: "I have frequently remarked that an army will never move if it waits until all the different commanders report that they are ready and want no more supplies."[40] He was, consciously or unconsciously, placing the shoe precisely where it fit.

Apostles of McClellan miss the point as did the general himself. It was not a matter anymore of how well the Army of the Potomac was supplied. The time had long since passed for some consideration to be given to how poorly the Confederate army had been provided. If McClellan mistrusted Washington, and if his egotism screened the truth from his generals, he could go to the private, the man who "idolized" him, the man who "worshiped" him. He knew. "While it was true that many of the Union soldiers were poorly clothed; that our shoes were badly worn, and that at times we were short of our regular rations, we were infinitely better provided in every respect than the enemy," wrote one enlisted man.[41] By now, McClellan's reasons for delay were becoming "frivolous" to his men. His excuses for doing nothing instead of making do with what he had was slowly bending Lincoln to the breaking point. If one thing failed to bring the general satisfaction from Washington, he would try another. On October 25, McClellan lamented that portions of Bragg's army would probably now join up with Lee. Halleck fired back, "I do not think we need any immediate fear of Bragg's army. You are within 20 miles of Lee's, while Bragg is distant about 400 miles."[42]

Then the general entered into a verbal duel with the President that, had it not been for the pathetic nature of Lincoln's pleading, would have been amusing. In reply to an officially authorized report on the condition of Federal cavalry ("horses are absolutely broken down from fatigue . . . sore-tongued, lameness and sore backs"), Lincoln said, "Will you pardon me for asking what the horses of your army have done since the battle of Antietam that fatigue anything?"[43] McClellan was indignant. His cavalry had been on the march constantly since Antietam, he said, making reconnaissance trips of up to 78 miles in 24 hours. They had been on scouting duty covering 150 miles of river front and had made trips of 200 miles searching for Stuart. "If any instance can be found where overworked cavalry has performed more labor than mine since the battle of Antietam, I am not conscious of it."[44]

"Of course you know the facts better than I," replied Lincoln, "still two considerations remain. Stuart's cavalry outmarched ours, having certainly done more marked service on the Peninsula, and everywhere since. Secondly, will not a movement of our army be a relief to the cavalry, compelling the enemy to concentrate, instead of 'foraging' in squads everywhere?"[45] McClellan was quick to snap back. The President had been misinformed about his cavalry. Certainly Mr. Lincoln "would not do injustice to the excellent officers and men of which it is composed." With the exception of Stuart's two raids, McClellan could not recall one instance where Confederate cavalry outshown his.

Though the Southern cavalry general had outridden General Pleasonton, there had been extra lead horses and fresh horses stolen along the way. Pleasonton had done all his work without a change of horses. "After this statement of facts has been placed before you, I feel confident you will concur with me that our cavalry is equally as efficient as that of the rebels."[46] Lincoln replied:

Most certainly I intend no injustice to any; and if I have done any, I deeply regret it. To be told after more than five weeks total inaction of the Army, and during which period we had sent to that Army every fresh horse we possibly could, amounting in the whole to 7918 that the cavalry horses were too much fatigued to move, presented a very cheerless, almost hopeless, prospect for the future; and it may have forced something of impatience into my despatches. If not recruited, and rested then, when could they ever be? I suppose the river is rising, and I am glad to believe you are crossing.[47]

McClellan had finally started to move on October 26, but it was too late. Two weeks later, on November 7, Maj. Gen. Ambrose E. Burnside, accompanied by Brig. Gen. C. P. Buckingham, Adjutant-General to Secretary of War Stanton, handed McClellan an official document from Washington. When McClellan finished reading it, he faced Burnside and with a restrained smile, said, "I turn the command over to you."[48]

Some eighty-eight years later, another president reflected on Lincoln and his dilemma and the similarities to his own problem. "Lincoln had had great and continuous trouble with McClellan," wrote Harry S. Truman, "though the policy differences in those days were the opposite of mine: Lincoln wanted McClellan to attack, and McClellan would not budge. Lincoln was patient, for that was his nature, but at long last he was compelled to relieve the Union Army's principal commander." Though President Truman gave the MacArthur difficulties "much wearisome thought," he knew that he had no choice than to relieve the nation's top field commander during the Korean War. Several years later, Mr. Truman wrote:

If there is one basic element in our constitution, it is civilian control of the military. Policies are to be made by the elected political officials, not by generals or admirals. Yet time and again General MacArthur had shown

that he was unwilling to accept the policies of the administration. By this
. . . MacArthur left me no choice — I could no longer tolerate his insubordination.[49]

Lincoln put his case this way in a conversation with John Hay, his
secretary:

After the battle of Antietam, I went up to the field to try to get him
to move & came back thinking he would move at once. But when I got
home he began to argue why he ought not to move. I preemptorily ordered
him to advance. It was 19 days before he put a man over the river.
It was 9 days longer before he got his army across and then he stopped
again, delaying on little pretexts of wanting this and that. I began to fear
he was playing fales — that he did not want to hurt the enemy. I saw
how he could intercept the enemy on the way to Richmond. I determined
to make the test. If he let them get away I would remove him. He did
so and I relieved him.[50]

William Todd of the 79th New York said that the decision "was
hailed by the men of the corps with great satisfaction."[51] The men of
the western armies felt the same. They certainly did not want McClellan there. His presence would have completely "demoralized" that
army, so great was their denunciation.[52] Of course there were those
who were sorely disappointed in McClellan's removal. "I am so mad,"
wrote one soldier, "that I can hardly write, the God-d—— abolition-
ists of the North have succeeded in their hellish work of removing
little Mac. We received information of the fact yesterday and such
a blue set of men you never saw. The boys all want to go home."[53]
"Little Mac has gone, and my heart and hopes have gone with him,"
wrote another.[54] There were demonstrations, some fantastically wild in
nature, when McClellan reviewed his troops for the last time. Some
threw down their arms and raced behind him as he turned away from
the columns. Regimental histories are full of pathetic accounts of
sadness expressed over McClellan's departure. Some thoughts, however, were more sophisticated and faced up to the realities of the
moment. "[The men] knew nothing of the neglect, not to say disobedience, of order, on his part, which had so sorely tried the much en-
during President," wrote a Vermont veteran.[55] C. B. Fairchild of the
27th New York added this comment to a soldier's diary depicting the

final hours of McClellan's command: "The soldiers at this time did not realize what Gen. McClellan might have done after the battle of Antietam, by following up the enemy more rapidly."[56] A surgeon of the 29th Massachusetts probably encompassed many feelings when he wrote:

We cannot help *loving* the *man* for he posseses those elements of character that endear him to all with whom he is connected. In spite of my desire for a change, I could not help feeling badly, when he left us. I regret the necessity of a change but I *do* think that McClellan was awful slow. He seemed to be *afraid* to risk a battle.

The doctor added that McClellan's best friends would soon forget him and support Burnside as enthusiastically.[57] "There will be no resignations on account of the removal of Gen. McClellan," wrote a correspondent for the New York *Times*. "Gen. Burnside, I can assure you, takes command of no demoralized or discontented army." Another correspondent added, "The heart of the army is sound."[58]

It must be remembered that though Lincoln's decision was inevitable, it was not made without considerable thought. He was not quick to condemn McClellan after Antietam. To the contrary. "He determined to give him one more chance," wrote Nicolay and Hay in their collective study on the President.

If McClellan, after Antietam, had destroyed the army of Lee his official position would have been impregnable. If, after Lee had recrossed the Potomac, McClellan had followed and delivered a successful battle in Virginia, nothing could afterwards have prevented his standing as the foremost man of his time. The President, in his intense anxiety for the success of the national arms, would have welcomed McClellan as his own presumtive successor if he could have won that position by successful battle.[59]

Lincoln liked McClellan personally and undoubtedly harbored many regrets at having to part with a general who had contributed so greatly to the organization of the country's military might. Lincoln must have thought back to the Peninsula Campaign when he visited McClellan's field and the general ignored him. Three days after that visit he came very close to removing McClellan from command. Only a congressional resolution praising McClellan for attaining important results with "little sacrifice of human life" stopped Lincoln.[60] The time of worrying about public opinion had now passed. Lincoln had once said that McClellan was an "admirable engineer," and then added, "but he seems to have a special talent for a stationary engine."[61] This time the engine was idle and the engineer was making little effort to raise steam, so on November 5 the President sent the following message to General Halleck: "By direction of the President, it is ordered that Major General McClellan be relieved from the command of the Army of the Potomac; and that Major General Burnside take command of that Army."[62]

On November 7, McClellan wrote one of his usual long and detailed letters to his wife. He had started the letter that afternoon and had had several interruptions. At 11:30 P.M. he had another interruption, "this time more important."

It was in the shape of Burnside, accompanied by Gen. Buckingham, the secretary's adjutant-general. They brought with them the order relieving me from the command of the Army of the Potomac, and assigning Burnside to the command. No cause is given. I am ordered to turn over the command immediately . . . Of course, I was much surprised; but as I read the order in the presense of Gen. Buckingham I am sure that not the slightest expression of feeling was visible on my face, which he watched closely. They shall not have that triumph. They have made a great mistake. Alas for my poor country! I know in my inmost heart she never had a truer servant. I have informally turned over the command to Burnside . . . Do not be at all worried — I am not. I have done the best I could for my country; to the last I have done my duty as I understand it. That I must have made many mistakes I cannot deny. I do not see any great blunders; but no one can judge of himself. Our consolation must be that we have tried to do what was right; if we have failed it was not our fault.[63]

McClellan's writings are particularly vivid on his departure from the army. According to him, many in the command and amongst the ranks were in favor of disobeying the order. Some wanted him to march on Washington and take over the government.[64] Stanton actually had fears that something like this might develop. This was why he had sent General Buckingham to deliver the orders to both Burnside and McClellan; to insure that Burnside would accept the command without backing out this time, and to make certain that McClellan's staff would not make an effort to prevent the general from being served with the order:

The Secretary had not only no confidence in McClellan's military skill [Buckingham wrote], but he very much doubted his patriotism, and even loyalty, and he expressed to me some fear that McClellan would not give up the command, and he wished, therefore, that the order should be presented by an officer of high rank, direct from the War Department, so as to carry the full weight of the President's authority.[65]

But McClellan could not have carried through a *coup d'état*. T. Harry Williams, in his *Lincoln and His Generals,* said, "Those people who feared that McClellan might be an American Cromwell need never have worried. He was not the stuff of which dictators are made."[66]

McClellan's farewell message announced simply that "an order of the President devolves upon Maj.-Gen. Burnside the command of this army." There was no call to stand behind Burnside, no mention of Lincoln or the war effort:

In parting from you I cannot express the love and gratitude I bear to you. As an army you have grown up under my care. In you I have never found doubt or coldness. The battles you have fought under my command will proudly live in our nation's history. The glory you have achieved, our mutual perils and fatigues, the graves of our comrades fallen in battle and by disease, the broken forms of those whom wounds and sickness have disabled — the strongest associations which can exist among men —unite us still by an indissoluble tie. We shall ever be comrades in supporting the Constitution of our country and the nationality of its people.[67]

Thus ended the military career of George Brinton McClellan. "Stanton is gratified," wrote Welles.[68] "Loyal men rejoiced," wrote an aid to the governor of Ohio.[69] The general would go on to be a candidate for the presidency against Lincoln on the Democratic ticket, and then would become governor of the state of New Jersey. As for Lincoln and the army, the search for total victory would give the Union Burnside at Fredericksburg, Hooker at Chancellorsville, Meade at Gettysburg, and finally Ulysses S. Grant. Before Robert E. Lee would meet Grant at Appomattox, he would lose in death James Ewell Brown Stuart, the "eyes" of his army, Thomas Jonathan Jackson, his "right arm," and Ambrose Powell Hill, one of the most gallant fighters the South gave to history.

The stakes had been high at Antietam; the toll heavy. In it the Confederacy saw a forecast for ultimate defeat; Lincoln, ultimate victory. Antietam altered the course of the war, indeed, it turned the tide of history.

Lee, in General Orders No. 116 to his army, summed up his campaign in these words:

Since your great victories around Richmond, you have defeated the enemy at Cedar Mountain, expelled him from the Rappahannock, and, after a conflict of three days, utterly repulsed him on the plains of Manassas and forced him to take shelter within the fortifications around his capital. Without halting for repose, you crossed the Potomac, stormed the heights of Harper's Ferry, made prisoners of more than 11,000 men and captured upwards of 75 pieces of artillery, all their small arms and other munitions of war. While one corps of the army was thus engaged, the other insured its success by arresting at Boonsborough the combined armies of the enemy, advancing under their favorite general to the relief of their beleagured comrades. On the field of Sharpsburg with less than one-third of his numbers, you resisted from daylight until dark the whole army of the enemy and repulsed every attack along his entire front of more than four miles in extent. The whole of the following day you stood prepared to resume the conflict on the same ground and retired the next morning without molestation across the Potomac . . . History records few examples of greater fortitude and endurance than this army has exhibited. . . .[70]

13

Epilogue

Robert E. Lee was proud of his army at Antietam; some say he considered this the finest battle he directed. He believed his men had shown their best against the greatest odds they ever encountered.[1] He had done wonders; indeed, he had done what many would have considered impossible. With an army exhausted from battle and long marches, lacking in material strength, and with only a thin thread of spirit to drive it on, Lee succeeded in bringing far greater damage to his opponent than he himself received. The outcome of the Maryland Campaign cannot be based on physical damage alone, however, any more than the question of victory or defeat at Sharpsburg can be resolved on the successful accomplishments of either army. Antietam is far more complex than this.

The Maryland Campaign began as a political and economic struggle; a fight by the Confederacy for the right to be left alone, to exist within its own boundaries. The Southern states were asking nothing more. Lee carried in his pocket this message to the people of the North. He was not invading to conquer, to occupy per se, but to demonstrate to the North and the world the determination with which his people were willing to fight for their independence.

When the Maryland Campaign ended, the Emancipation Proclamation had altered the course of the war. It was a calculated political move by Lincoln, designed as a last ditch effort to change the nature of the struggle to preserve the Union from a defensive one to an offensive one. He had said, "I would save it the shortest way under the Constitution," whether it be by freeing all the slaves, part of them, or none of them.[2] Lincoln had wanted a crushing victory. He had waited a year

325

and a half for it, trying first one general and then another. When Lee withdrew from Maryland, the President had no alternative but to interpret this as the opportunity he needed. If McClellan could or would not convert Antietam into the necessary advantage, Lincoln must.

Those early September days did not foretell of the momentous events which would follow. To the military mind of Robert E. Lee, there were clear-cut advantages in invading Northern soil. Despite warning signals from several sources, he gambled the very existence of his army on gaining another victory over the Federal army. It seems obvious now, with the benefit of historical records, that the invasion was doomed to failure before it was launched. The Army of Northern Virginia was in no condition to undertake such a monstrous task. There can be little doubt about the spirit of the Confederate soldier, but physically, Lee's army was exhausted. As he miscalculated the recuperative powers of the Federals, Lee also misjudged the capabilities of his own men and put them under an extravagant strain that all but diminished their strength and caused irreparable damage. How plain and simple fortitude replaced their inadequacies on the battlefield and during the weeks that followed Antietam is one of those marvelous chapters of history to which all Americans can point with pride.

Lee was not ignorant of his deficiencies. He wrote Jefferson Davis about them numerous times. So great was his confidence that with the exception of the night of September 14, when he considered the possibility of withdrawal, he did not once feel he would fail in Maryland. His miscalculations, however, were not intentional. If Lee ever believed he could beat the Federal army, he did so in September 1862. This very belief led him across the river, guided the daring Special Orders No. 191, and finally, in the waning hours of the campaign, directed his stand at Sharpsburg. Though he confidently thought the consequences would be in his favor, in each of the three decisions there was little hope, relatively little to gain, and so very much to lose.

Though Lee was successful in capturing Harpers Ferry and its prize of prisoners and equipment, he did so at extreme risk. Lee was never taught at West Point to divide his army in the face of the enemy. This was not in his military training. "He practiced his own theory of the art of war," one military historian has written. "Although indebted to Napoleon, he treated each problem as a concrete case, which he solved according to circumstances, and he had his greatest success when he departed furthest from established rules."[3] The army was split with full knowledge that McClellan was approaching. Then McClellan found a copy of the plans and came uncomfortably close to putting a premature end to the campaign. Douglas Southall Freeman, in his commentary on the results of the battle at Sharpsburg, says that it was not that "Lee was reckless but that McClellan was lucky."[4] McClellan found fortune beyond compare in war, but because McClellan was McClellan, his luck was minimized and Lee's fortune was enhanced. Lee made the best of the many advantages offered him; McClellan tossed away every one Lee gave him.

The mistakes in the Maryland Campaign are many. Blame for the results is shared by both Confederates and Federals. Lee placed too much confidence in his army; he expected the impossible from the people of Maryland; he overestimated his Harpers Ferry timetable; McClellan dallied on his way to meet Lee; he disregarded intelligence and advice; his command system failed him at the most crucial of moments; he failed his army by not pursuing Lee after Antietam, and this must forever remain McClellan's folly. The Army of the Potomac would be defeated under other commanders before it would at last find victory. The Army of Northern Virginia would see spirits surge and strength regained and would again come close to gaining all that the Confederacy sought. But never again quite so close as during the sixteen days of crisis in September 1862. Lord Russell and Lord Palmerston shelved their plans for intervention and recognition; the fall elections came and went and little Southern support was gained; the state of Maryland remained impassive to their Confederate neighbors; and Abraham Lincoln turned a stalemate on the battlefield into a victory for the North. Antietam was the end of McClellan. It was the forecast of disaster for the Confederacy. It was a turning point in American history.

Appendix A

LEE'S "LOST DISPATCH"

SPECIAL ORDERS,   HDQRS. ARMY OF NORTHERN VIRGINIA
No. 191   *September* 9, 1862.

I. The citizens of Fredericktown being unwilling, while overrun by members of this army, to open their stores, in order to give them confidence, and to secure to officers and men purchasing supplies for benefit of this command, all officers and men of this army are strictly prohibited from visiting Fredericktown except on business, in which cases they will bear evidence of this in writing from division commanders. The provost-marshal in Fredericktown will see that his guard rigidly enforces this order.

II. Major Taylor will proceed to Leesburg, Va. and arrange for transportation of the sick and those unable to walk to Winchester, securing the transportation of the country for this purpose. Then route between this and Culpeper Court-House east of the mountains being unsafe will no longer be traveled. Those on the way to this army already across the river will move up promptly; all others will proceed to Winchester collectively and under command of officers, at which point, being the general depot of this army, its movements will be known and instructions given by commanding officer regulating further movements.

III. The army will resume its march to-morrow, taking the Hagerstown road. General Jackson's command will form the advance, and, after passing Middletown, with such portion as he may select, take the route toward Sharpsburg, cross the Potomac at the most convenient point, and by Friday morning take possession of the Baltimore and Ohio Railroad, capture such of them as may be at Martinsburg, and intercept such as may attempt to escape from Harper's Ferry.

IV. General Longstreet's command will pursue the same road as far as Boonsborough, where it will halt, with reserve, supply, and baggage trains of the army.

V. General McLaws, with his own division and that of General R. H.

328

Anderson, will follow General Longstreet. On reaching Middletown will take the route to Harper's Ferry, and by Friday morning possess himself of the Maryland Heights and endeavor to capture the enemy at Harper's Ferry and vicinity.

VI. General Walker, with his division, after accomplishing the object in which he is now engaged, will cross the Potomac at Cheek's Ford, ascend its right bank to Lovettsville, take possession of Loudoun Heights, if practicable, by Friday morning, Key's Ford on his left, and the road between the end of the mountain and the Potomac on his right. He will, as far as practicable, co-operate with Generals McLaws and Jackson, and intercept retreat of the enemy.

VII. General D. H. Hill's division will form the rear guard of the army, pursuing the road taken by the main body. The reserve artillery, ordnance, and supply trains, & c., will precede General Hill.

VIII. General Stuart will detach a squadron of cavalry to accompany the commands of Generals Longstreet, Jackson, and McLaws, and, with the main body of the cavalry, will cover the route of the army, bringing up all stragglers that may have been left behind.

IX. The commands of Generals Jackson, McLaws, and Walker, after accomplishing the objects for which they have been detached, will join the main body of the army at Boonsborough or Hagerstown.

X. Each regiment on the march will habitually carry its axes in the regimental ordnance-wagons, for use of the men at their encampments, to procure wood &c.

By command of General R. E. Lee:
R. H. CHILTON, Assistant Adjutant-General.[1]

On the morning of September 9, 1862, Gen. Robert E. Lee dictated these special orders, orders that revealed his strategy for the next several days. Four days later, on the morning of September 13, the Federal army was aware of these same orders, and within twelve hours, by at least 10 P.M. that night, Lee knew that McClellan had discovered his plans. "The God of battles alone knows what would have occurred but for the singular accident mentioned; it is useless to speculate on this point, but certainly the loss of this battle-order constitutes one of the pivots on which turned the event of the war." So wrote Maj. Walter H. Taylor, Lee's Adjutant-General.[2] This series of events is one of the strangest of the Civil War and one of the least understood. It is impossible to clear matters completely due to the few facts available, but new interpretations do warrant a reappraisal, this being the first, perhaps, since Douglas Southall Freeman's objective comments in *Lee's Lieutenants*.[3]

On September 9, the Army of Northern Virginia had been in Frederick for three days resting its weary feet and stocking its supply wagons following the march from Second Manassas. Their welcome was wearing thin. Lee's appeal to Marylanders had failed and now the Federal army was approaching. It was time to put the second phase of the campaign into action. Since the garrison at Harpers Ferry had apparently elected to make a stand, Lee had little choice but to remove this thorn from his side. Harpers Ferry posed a serious threat to his plans. To simply ignore it would be senseless. McClellan would have 12,000 additional men with which to strike the Confederate army, whether it be in Maryland or in Pennsylvania. To post only a guarding or observing force would be equally as risky. There was no alternative in Lee's mind. He was confident that he could do the job, and quickly. If luck and Jackson's men were with him, he could surround and capture Harpers Ferry and still move on to Pennsylvania—all before McClellan could do anything about it. What he proposed to do and how he would accomplish it was probably his most daring feat.

Lee would divide his army into four wings, sending three to surround Harpers Ferry and retaining a fourth for cover and screening. This he spelled out specifically in Special Orders No. 191. On September 9, he had copies of the orders transcribed for his generals. There can be no accurate count of exactly how many copies were written. Robert H. Chilton, Lee's Assistant Adjutant-General, stated some years after the war that, although he had kept no journal, he was "certain that the order was sent to all the Major Generals . . . to all Division Comdrs. entrusted with special duties."[4] Assuming that Chilton's memory had not failed him, this would give copies to those officers mentioned in the orders, those who would participate in the forthcoming strategy, namely Jackson, Longstreet, Walker, McLaws, R. H. Anderson, Taylor, Stuart, D. H. Hill, and one for the headquarters record book; a total of nine copies. Chilton signed each one and sent them out by courier. Receipts of delivery were returned and supposedly filed. Chilton claimed that the "couriers were required to bring back envelopes or evidence of delivery . . ."[5]

Of the nine copies of Special Orders No. 191, if indeed there were nine, four cannot be accounted for. Neither McLaws, Taylor, or Stuart made any mention of having received theirs. Anderson specifically stated to D. H. Hill that he was "perfectly sure" he did not see the orders.[6] If one accepts the logic that Anderson was not entitled to one because he actually was under McLaws' command at Harpers Ferry and traveling with him, the total number of copies is reduced from nine to eight.

Of the five remaining copies, three are relatively unimportant as far as the mystery is concerned. Walker verifies that his was received and secured in a safe place.[7] Longstreet promptly destroyed his copy by tearing it into small bits and chewing it to insure absolute secrecy.[8] The copy entered into the records has no bearing on the incident which followed. G. Moxley Sorrel of Longstreet's staff claimed a copy of the order came into his "possession." "I wondered what could be done with it in event of my falling into the enemy's hands," wrote Sorrel. He makes no further comment, leaving something of a mystery about his own role in the drama. Sorrel had no cause to receive the order other than being the intermediary between the courier and Longstreet. Thought his words sound as if he knew exactly what the orders said, it must be assumed that he referred to Longstreet's copy and no other, otherwise Lee's staff was much more careless than history has theorized.[9] (At Lee's direction, a transcript of the first and second paragraphs of Special Orders No. 191 was transmitted to General Samuel Cooper, Adjutant and Inspector General of the Confederate States Army, in Richmond. Chilton signed the copy which was received at the War Department on September 16.)[10]

When Stonewall Jackson received his copy of the orders, he tucked the paper inside his coat. Before he performed his usual passion for secrecy, he sat down in his tent and transcribed himself copy number ten, a copy which he sent to his brother-in-law, Daniel Harvey Hill. General Hill received that particular copy of the orders that evening and placed them away for safe keeping, totally unaware that a copy had been designated for him by headquarters. With absolutely no indication of the events to come, the four separate contingents of Lee's army moved on to their designations on the morning of September 10.

The first Federal troops began filtering into Frederick two days later, on the morning of September 12. The 27th Indiana, which had camped at Frederick the winter before and was familiar with the ground, arrived about midmorning the next day, the 13th. Within an hour or so, Company F had settled down to rest. It had been a warm morning and uniforms were particularly uncomfortable after the showers the day before. The men quickly sought the shade of nearby trees. There is some dispute over which Confederate campsite the 27th Indiana selected—D. H. Hill's or A. P. Hill's. Since there are no Confederate records revealing such information, the matter is irrelevant. The finger of evidence points to the fact that D. H. Hill might well have occupied this spot. Regardless of which general it was, this particular field was to prove a most significant one.

Private Barton W. Mitchell and a companion, Sergeant John M. Bloss, were among the first of the 27th Indiana to drop their gear. They both flopped to the ground in anticipation of a few winks before duties began. About ten o'clock, Mitchell noticed a rather unusual piece of paper not far distant. It was wrapped around three cigars. Bloss writes: "The cigars were divided and while the needed match was being secured, I began to read the . . . document. As I read, each line became more interesting. I forgot the cigars."[11] He saw that the paper was addressed to D. H. Hill and that it was signed on the authority of R. E. Lee. Recognizing the importance of their discovery, both men took the paper to their commanding officer, Colonel Silas Colgrove. In a matter of minutes it was shown to Colonel S. E. Pittman, division headquarters adjutant. Pittman immediately recognized the signature of Robert Chilton, an old military comrade. There was no doubt in his mind that the paper was genuine.[12]

At that particular moment, General McClellan was in conference with several Frederick businessmen, probably discussing arrangements for supplies. Pittman requested immediate audience and was admitted. McClellan unfolded the paper in the presence of his guests and read it. He is reported to have thrown his arms in the air and uttered several jubilant exclamations. Here was positive confirmation of the information which had been pouring across his desk for the past week—that Jackson had crossed the Potomac, and that troops were headed for Hagerstown. And it told him more—coming directly from the enemy's hands. Could it be a Confederate hoax? Pittman assured him that it was not. In 1869, D. H. Hill wrote McClellan in an effort to clear the mystery. The general, then Governor of New Jersey, replied: "I was satisfied in regard to the genuineness of the order and made no further inquiries."[13]

All of this action that morning did not go unseen. One of McClellan's visitors happened to be in sympathy with the Confederacy. Concealing his shock, he listened intently. Upon completion of the conference, this man made immediate arrangements to ride through the lines. If he had heard correctly, the orders said that Lee would be at Boonsboro. By nightfall he had made his way to South Mountain without raising any question from Federal authorities.

Stuart had been pushed out of the Catoctin Mountains by an advance of Pleasonton's cavalry that afternoon and was now at the base of Turner's Gap in the South Mountain range. Identifying himself as a civilian from Frederick with an important message for General Lee, the stranger was taken immediately to Stuart. Within minutes, a courier was on his way to Lee in Hagerstown.

It is not known at exactly what time the courier reached Lee. Col. William Allan, faculty member of Washington College in Lexington and postwar friend of Lee's, quotes the general as saying the message reached him before daybreak on the 14th.[14] But at 10:00 P.M. on the night of the 13th, Lee sent the following message to McLaws at Maryland Heights. It was signed by Major T. M. R. Talcott: "General Lee directs me to say that, from reports reaching him, he believes the enemy is moving toward Harper's Ferry to relieve the force they have there."[15]

It seems obvious that among these reports Maj. Talcott speaks of was Stuart's message concerning his Frederick visitor. How else could Lee have known of McClellan's projected move at that hour? The only Federal activities on the 13th were aimed toward Middletown and Turner's Gap. Franklin's Sixth Corps, the Federal left wing, did not move until daybreak the next morning. Although Lee knew McClellan was a cautious man, he also knew him to be an intelligent man. With a copy of such important Confederate orders dropped into Union hands, it was quite clear that there was only one move McClellan could make, regardless of how soon it would come. Lee's belief that the "enemy" would move towards Harpers Ferry in one fashion or another was simply a matter of deduction. Though the question of Lee's knowledge of the mishap has been argued for a century, his own words prove that he did learn of the "lost dispatch" and that he had that information within at least 12 hours after discovery.

This is a reconstruction of the known circumstances surrounding the incident. But the story of Special Orders No. 191 does not end here. There are many missing links, as many unanswered questions, little substantial evidence, and dozens of theories.

First, what happened to D. H. Hill's copy? Naturally, in the early years following the Maryland Campaign, Hill was favored as the culprit. He was accused of everything from deliberately throwing the orders away in a fit of passion "because I was not pleased with its contents,"[16] to carelessly losing the paper before departure from Frederick, having left in on "the corner table in the house which had served as his headquarters."[17] The only fact his adversaries seemed to forget, if, indeed, they knew, was that Hill was a cigar smoker (He was seen smoking a cigar during the Battle of Seven Pines)—a point they could well have exploited into a very convincing argument.[18]

The whole thing seemed to be quite a surprise to General Hill. According to him, it was some time before he learned of the "accident." He claimed, as did his chief of staff, Major J. W. Ratchford, that the official copy, that which had been written at army headquarters, never arrived at his camp. To his dying day he held to this story. Hoping that a mistake had been made in the official Federal report, and that the copy found had not been directed to him, Hill conducted an exhaustive study of the matter. Finally in 1888 he wrote:

I went into Maryland under Jackson's command. I was under his command when Lee's order was issued. It was proper that I should receive that order through Jackson and not through Lee. I have now before me the order received from Jackson . . . My adjutant-general made affidavit, twenty years ago, that no order was received at our office from General Lee.[19]

Hill was correct. He did enter Maryland under Jackson's command, and was in his command when the orders were issued, and, although Special Orders No. 191 withdrew him from Jackson, Jackson's transmittal was perfectly in order.

Longstreet was in error when in *From Manassas to Appomattox* he stated that the lost copy was the one Jackson had written.[20] The copy published in McClellan's report was directed to D. H. Hill.[21] Jackson's handwritten copy was preserved by Hill as his only piece of tangible evidence and is today in the collection of Hill papers at the North Carolina Department of Archives and History.[22]

Were it not for the fact that Hill has been accused of losing another important piece of paper, an order similar in nature, during the battle of Seven Pines only a few months earlier,[23] there would be no reason to doubt his word. There is little, if any, evidence to substantiate this, however. Douglas Southall Freeman completely discounts the story as any reflection on Hill's character.[24] As far as concrete evidence on the Maryland orders is concerned then, Hill is completely innocent and has long since been vindicated of the accusations leveled at him in the late 1860's.

Delivering Hill from his accusers does not end the matter, however. Although the facts are obscure, some glaring contradictions in the Federal side of the story bear observation. For example, what time were the orders found, by whom, and in what state were they when discovered?

On two separate occasions, Sergeant Bloss told of his role in the drama. In each case, he failed to mention his companion, Private Mitchell, ignoring him, and stating that he, Bloss, was the finder. On June 26, 1886, Silas Colgrove, who had commanded the 27th Indiana as a colonel, made the statement that "the order was brought to me by First Sergeant John M. Bloss and Private B. W. Mitchell of Co. F . . . who stated that it was found by Private Mitchell near where they stacked arms."[25] But, in Bloss's own words, "I noticed," "I found," and "I picked up."[26]

To further confuse matters, Bloss claimed that the paper was loose in an envelope along with (not wrapped around) *two* cigars.[27] The most popular and acceptable story belongs to Colgrove, who wrote: "When I received the order, it was *wrapped around three* cigars, and Private Mitchell stated that it was in that condition when found by *him*."[28] This is to say nothing of Chilton's conflicting statement that couriers were required to bring back (empty) envelopes as evidence of delivery.[29] And to pile mystery on top of mystery, Bloss claimed that the paper was taken first to a Captain Koop "and together we took it to Colonel Colgrove."[30] Koop figures only in Bloss's story and no other.

All of this, according to Bloss, happened "not later than 10 o'clock [a.m., September 13]" and he admits that it could have been as much as an hour earlier.[31] Colgrove says that the 27th Indiana did not arrive at Frederick until noon of that day.[32] No clear time of discovery can be determined for as jubilant as McClellan is supposed to have been, he did not bother to inform his commander in Washington, General Halleck, until 11:00 P.M. that night. The earliest exactly noted time is 3:00 P.M., when McClellan gave Pleasonton instructions to check out the Confederate routes of withdrawal from Frederick with a view of corresponding them to the orders.[33] McClellan's actions from this point on are mysteries in themselves and are only remotely connected to the "lost dispatch."

There still remains some Confederate questions to answer. It is not known whether Chilton sent one or nine couriers to deliver the orders to the various commanders. (Chilton kept no journal.) But it stands to reason that nine copies were not entrusted to one man. If this is the case, then the man to look for is Hill's messenger.

One odd fact enters the picture here. The orders were written on September 9. All generals, with the exception of Walker and Major Taylor, were in the vicinity of Frederick. No one in Frederick left until the next morning—Jackson, the first, at about 5:00 A.M., Hill, bringing up the rear guard, was the last to leave. Both Jackson and Longstreet received their copies on the evening of the 9th. Even if Jackson's courier did not reach him until as late as 10:00 P.M., there remained at least seven hours before the troops moved. This means at least an additional six or seven hours before Hill moved—a minimum of fourteen hours for Hill's orders to be delivered. What happened to the courier? And how did he manage to obtain a receipt for the false delivery? Chilton said that all couriers were required to bring back some evidence of delivery and that failure to do so in this case would certainly have been noted, causing a duplicate copy to be written and precautionary measures taken against discovery of loss.[34] No excitement of this nature is noted in Lee's camp.

The question of courier disloyalty is one not seriously considered by most historians. It would be assumed that all couriers could be trusted, although there was no such thing as a security clearance. The theory, however, is not as ridiculous as it sounds when one reads J. W. Ratchford's report that "a spy acting as a Confederate courier was discovered near Harpers Ferry [during this campaign] and was at once hung to a limb of a tree on the road-side."[35] Hill, in his own defense, commented that "there was something wrong in the manner of transmitting it, or treachery in the persons carrying it."[36]

Whether or not it was carelessness or clever espionage may never be known. The Civil War Centennial has done little more for this subject than stimulate new interest. Hopes for the missing clue have all but vanished, leaving nothing but theories. The receipts of delivery, which may hold the only answer, still remain buried in some dusty archives, if, indeed, they exist.

Neither General Lee, the War Department, or the Confederate government ever pressed charges against D. H. Hill. Aside from Edward A. Pollard, editor of the Richmond *Examiner,* who, in his book *The Lost Cause,* published two years after the war, accused Hill of tossing the orders away, Hill himself was the only one who kept the story alive. Barton Mitchell dropped into obscurity, Bloss wrote mostly in military papers, and the participants in the Maryland Campaign seemed to regard it simply as a passing incident, fortunate or unfortunate, depending on their viewpoint. Hill, however, was determined to set the record straight. In 1868 he was editing and publishing a monthly magazine in Charlotte, North Carolina. In the February, 1868 issue of *The Land We Love,* he took issue with Mr. Pollard, and in further defense of his position, went so far as to state that since the "lost dispatch" actually misinformed McClellan on Longstreet's whereabouts, it had slowed the Federal approach to South Mountain, "saved Lee from destruction; and in the inscrutable Providence of God the loss of the dispatch prolonged the Confederate struggle for two more years."[37]

Lee, in a somewhat terse letter to Hill, dated February 21, 1868, sought to close the case once and for all. In replying to the magazine article, he wrote:

My dear Sir
    I am obliged to you for the opportunity you have afforded me of reading your article on the "Lost Dispatch." I have not read Mr. Pollards account & therefore do not know what he says; but at the time the order fell into Genl McClellans hands, I considered it a great calamity & subsequent reflection has not caused me to change my opinion.
    Your division having joined the Army after the 2nd battle of Manassas, was placed in front in its subsequent movement, & was the first to cross the Potomac. When the whole army was ready to cross, Genl Jackson was sent to the front and directed to take command of the advanced troops;

and when it became necessary to dislodge the Federal troops occupying Martinsburg & Harpers Ferry, he was by verbal instructions placed in command of the expedition. The special order of the 9th Sept: which you quote [No. 191], was intended to guide the several divisions in the general movement of the Army. In it your division was designated as the rear guard, & it was proper in my opinion that a copy of the order should have been sent to you by the Adjt Genl; and as you were by it withdrawn from Genl Jackson's command, it was also right for you to have been served with a copy from his office.

. . . When they [the orders] were issued (9th Sept.) I supposed there would have been time for their accomplishment & for the army to have reunited before Genl McClellan could cross the South Mountains. Genl Stuart who was on the line of the Monocacy with the cavalry masking our movements & watching those of the Federal army, reported that Genl McClellan had reached Rockville & was advancing very slowly with an extended front, covering the roads to Washington & to Baltimore. Early on the morning of the 14th I recd at Hagerstown a dispatch from him stating that he had fallen back to the South Mountains; that Genl McClellan was pressing forward on the roads to Boonsborough & Rohersville gaps, & that he had learned from a citizen of Maryland, that he was in possession of the order directing the movement of our troops. Nor did he seem to have been "mystified & deceived" by it; . . .

I do not know how the order was lost, nor until I saw Genl McClellans published reports after the termination of the war did I know certainly that it was the copy addressed to you. From what I have stated you will see that I do not concur with you in the opinion that its having fallen into Genl McClellan's hands was a "benefit" but on the contrary, "an injury to the Confederate arms."[38]

Appendix B

On September 4, 1862, Robert E. Lee wrote Jefferson Davis: "Should the results of the [Maryland] expedition justify it, I propose to enter Pennsylvania, unless you should deem it unadvisable upon political or other grounds."[1] Throughout his correspondence with Davis during the early part of September, Lee clearly indicated that the state of Pennsylvania was on his agenda; he told his staff that Harrisburg was "the objective point of the campaign."[2] His exact strategy, however, other than his goal of disrupting railroad traffic at Harrisburg, was not made evident until his official report in August of 1863 when he stated that he had intended to "threaten" Pennsylvania.[3] Civil War interpretation of a "threat" as opposed to an "invasion" was as contrasting as Lee in Maryland and Sherman in Georgia. Since there can be absolutely no comparison between these two armies on military grounds, it would seem then that Lee was, in a manner of speaking, on a promotion expedition. Although, through his own admission he intended to give battle to McClellan sooner or later,[4] his "invasion" of the North was, by comparison, more a mission of goodwill and influence. As evidenced by his message to the people of Maryland, he sought, through a show of might, and perhaps through a display of Southern gentility, to woo his sister state to the Confederate cause. Once the Potomac was crossed, Pennsylvania was only a few miles away, but there are no indications in any of Lee's wartime or post-war writings that he intended to ask the people of Pennsylvania to break from the Union. It would have been fruitless and Lee knew this. Jefferson Davis, however, not only expected Lee to "invade" Pennsylvania, but he anticipated an opportunity to issue what amounted to an ultimatum to its citizens.

Sometime between September 7 and 12, Davis wrote three of his generals a letter of great importance. "It is deemed proper that you should in accordance with established usage announce by proclamation to the people of ———— the motives and purposes of your presence among them at the head of an invading army . . ."[5] Directed to Lee in Maryland and to Bragg and Smith in Kentucky, the letter had three blanks to be filled in with the state name, when, and if, it was considered appropriate by the general. "The Confederate Government is waging this war solely for self-defense," the document read. "It has no design of conquest, or any other purpose than to secure peace and the abandonment by the United States of their pretensions to govern a people who have never been their subjects, and who prefer self-government to a union with them." In an eight point declaration of Confederate aims, Davis, in no uncertain terms, left full responsibility of the continuation of the war squarely on the shoulders of the people, calling on them to exercise their state "sovereignty," securing "immunity from the desolating effects of warfare on the soil of the State by [negotiating] a separate treaty of peace, which [the Confederate] Government will ever be ready to conclude on the most just and liberal basis." He made it clear that the "theater of hostilities" had shifted from the South to northern territory and that without the people's intervention, the war could "never end." They were strong words but the proclamation left no doubt just where the President of the Confederacy stood.

Several copies of the letter were made—copies other than those intended for Lee, Smith, and Bragg; one in Davis's "letter book" (See Appendix E, Document 9.), one transcribed from the "letter book" especially for the editors of the *Official Records* in 1882, a third which now rests with the Davis papers at Tulane University, and a fourth which found its way into the hands of a private collector.[6] Each copy, with the exception of that in the Davis papers, is unique in itself and sheds revealing light on Davis's invasion strategy.

The original, or "letter book" copy, undated, avoids mentioning any specific state, leaving three blanks. ("to the people of ———— . . ."— "with the people of ———— themselves rests the power . . ."—"the responsibility thus rests on the people of ———— . . .") This would indicate that Davis was giving each general some latitude in their battlefield diplomacy.

In 1882, when the War Department requested Mr. Davis to submit any correspondence with Robert E. Lee which he might still have in his possession for inclusion in the *Official Records,* the former Confederate President had this document, among others, transcribed from his "letter book." Davis himself made two alterations. He personally added "Maryland" to the first blank. Because his memory may have failed him, a probable date of September 7, 1862 was inserted. The first paragraph of the document thus read: "It is deemed proper that you should in accordance with established usage announce by proclamation to the people of Maryland the motives and purposes of your presence among them at the head of an invading Army . . ."[7] Though there was no endorsement from Lee to indicate that he had received or seen the document, the additions of "Maryland" and the date in Davis's handwriting reveal his switch from defensive warfare to a diplomatic offensive; an appeal to the emotions of an oppressed people. Lee was in Maryland by September 7. A direct proclamation from the Confederate president was in order. Twenty years later Davis intimated by his reply to the War Department request that he intended that proclamation to be made to the people of "Maryland."

A recent historical find sheds even more light on Davis's thinking. The Rodman Collection of manuscripts in the North Carolina Department of Archives and History holds a heretofore unknown copy of the Davis proclamation. Dated September 12, 1862, directed to Robert E. Lee, and with no interruption in the handwriting, it reads: "It is deemed proper that, in accordance with established usage, you should announce by proclamation to the people of the state of Pennsylvania . . ."[8]

How this copy, signed by Davis, and authenticated by historians, got into the hands of a private collector, or why Davis chose to make public the "Maryland" proclamation rather than the "Pennsylvania," will never be known. One thing seems certain, however. The Confederate president saw an opportunity in Lee's campaign to carry his cause direct to the grass roots. Commissioners of peace sent to Washington "were not received;" communications to President Lincoln "remained unanswered;" "The responsibility thus rests on the people," Davis wrote. Why he considered Pennsylvania vulnerable is not revealed. There were split loyalties throughout the Union, but a general uprising north of the Mason and Dixon was out of the question. Davis's language tends to reflect his interpretation of Lee's "threat" to Pennsylvania.

Neither Lee, Smith, or Bragg, however, waited for Davis to suggest peace overtures to the people of the Union. While Lee was urging the people of Maryland to throw off their yoke of oppression, Smith was saying to Kentuckians: "Let no one make you believe we come as invaders, to coerce your will, or to exercise control over your soil. Far from it. We come not as invaders but as liberators."[9] And Bragg was offering the same people an oportunity to free themselves from the tyranny of a "despotic ruler." "We come not as conquerors or as despoilers," he said, "but to restore to you the liberties of which you have been deprived by a cruel and relentless foe."[10] But the Confederate messages of peace and friendship fell on deaf ears and the Davis proclamation of September 7, or September 12, was forgotten for a century.

Appendix C

ARMY OF THE POTOMAC
MAJ. GEN. GEORGE B. McCLELLAN, U.S. ARMY
COMMANDING

GENERAL HEADQUARTERS
Escort — Capt. James B. McIntyre

Independent Company, Oneida (New York) Cavalry, Capt. Daniel P. Mann
4th U. S. Cavalry, Company A, Lieut. Thomas H. McCormick
4th U. S. Cavalry, Company E, Capt. James B. McIntyre

ENGINEER BATTALION
Lieut. Charles E. Cross
Provost Guard — Maj. William H. Wood

2d U. S. Cavalry, Companies E, F, H, and K, Capt. George A. Gordon
8th U. S. Infantry, Companies A, D, F, and G, Capt. Royal T. Frank
19th U. S. Infantry, Company G, Capt. Edmund L. Smith
19th U. S. Infantry, Company H, Capt. Henry S. Welton

HEADQUARTERS GUARD — Maj. Granville O. Haller
93d New York, Lieut. Col. Benjamin C. Butler

QUARTERMASTER'S GUARD
1st U. S. Cavalry, Companies B, C, H, and I, Capt. Marcus A. Reno

FIRST ARMY CORPS — Maj. Gen. Joseph Hooker, wounded 9/17
Brig. Gen. George G. Meade

343

Escort: 2d New York Cavalry, Companies A, B, I, and K, Capt. John E. Naylor

FIRST DIVISION — Brig. Gen. Rufus King, relieved 9/14
Brig. Gen. John P. Hatch, wounded 9/14
Brig. Gen. Abner Doubleday

FIRST BRIGADE: Col. Walter Phelps, Jr.
22d New York, Lieut. Col. John McKie, Jr.
24th New York, Capt. John D. O'Brian, wounded 9/17
30th New York, Col. William M. Searing
Capt. John H. Campbell
84th New York (14th Militia), Maj. William H. de Bevoise
2d U. S. Sharpshooters, Col. Henry A. V. Post, wounded 9/17

SECOND BRIGADE: Brig. Gen. Abner Doubleday
Col. William P. Wainwright, wounded 9/14
Lieut. Col. J. William Hofmann

7th Indiana, Maj. Ira G. Grover
76th New York, Col. William P. Wainwright
Capt. John W. Young
95th New York, Maj. Edward Pye
56th Pennsylvania, Lieut. Col. J. William Hofmann
Capt. Frederick Williams

THIRD BRIGADE: Brig. Gen. Marsena R. Patrick
21st New York, Col. William F. Rogers
23d New York, Col. Henry C. Hoffman
35th New York, Col. Newton B. Lord
80th New York (20th Militia), Lieut. Col. Theodore B. Gates

FOURTH BRIGADE: Brig. Gen. John Gibbon
19th Indiana, Col. Solomon Meredith, ill from fall on 8/28;
relinquished command 9/16
Lieut. Col. Alois O. Bachman, killed 9/17
Capt. William W. Dudley
2d Wisconsin, Col. Lucius Fairchild, wounded 9/14
Lieut. Col. Thomas S. Allen, wounded 9/17
Capt. George B. Ely

6th Wisconsin, Lieut. Col. Edward S. Bragg, wounded 9/17
    Maj. Rufus R. Dawes
7th Wisconsin, Capt. John B. Callis

ARTILLERY: Capt. J. Albert Monroe
 New Hampshire Light, First Battery, Lieut. Frederick M. Edgell
1st Rhode Island Light, Battery D, Capt. J. Albert Monroe
1st New York Light, Battery L, Capt. John A. Reynolds
4th United States, Battery B, Capt. Joseph B. Campbell, wounded 9/17
    Lieut. James Stewart

SECOND DIVISION — Brig. Gen. James B. Ricketts

FIRST BRIGADE: Brig. Gen. Abram Duryea
 97th New York, Maj. Charles Northrup
    Capt. R. S. Eggleston
104th New York, Maj. Lewis C. Skinner
105th New York, Col. Howard Carroll, mortally wounded 9/17
107th Pennsylvania, Capt. James Mac Thomson

SECOND BRIGADE: Col. William A. Christian, wounded 9/17
    Col. Peter Lyle, wounded 9/17
26th New York, Lieut. Col. Richard H. Richardson
94th New York, Lieut. Col. Calvin Littlefield
88th Pennsylvania, Lieut. Col. George W. Gile, wounded 9/17
    Capt. Henry R. Myers
90th Pennsylvania, Col. Peter Lyle
    Lieut. Col. William A. Leech

THIRD BRIGADE: Brig. Gen. George L. Hartsuff, wounded 9/17
    Col. Richard Coulter
16th Maine, Col. Asa W. Wildes, joined 2d Div. 9/9;
    detached as railroad guard 9/12
12th Massachusetts, Maj. Elisha Burbank, mortally wounded 9/17
    Capt. Benjamin F. Cook
13th Massachusetts, Maj. J. Parker Gould
83d New York (9th Militia), Lieut. Col. William Atterbury
11th Pennsylvania, Col. Richard Coulter
    Capt. David M. Cook

346

ARTILLERY:
1st Pennsylvania Light, Battery F, Capt. Ezra W. Matthews
Pennsylvania Light, Battery C, Capt. James Thompson

THIRD DIVISION — Brig. Gen. George G. Meade
Brig. Gen. Truman Seymour

FIRST BRIGADE: Brig. Gen. Truman Seymour
Col. R. Biddle Roberts
1st Pennsylvania Reserves, Col. R. Biddle Roberts
Capt. William C. Talley
2d Pennsylvania Reserves, Capt. James N. Byrnes
5th Pennsylvania Reserves, Col. Joseph W. Fisher
6th Pennsylvania Reserves, Col. William Sinclair
13th Pennsylvania Reserves (1st Rifles),
Col. Hugh W. McNeil, killed 9/16
Capt. Dennis McGee

SECOND BRIGADE: Col. Henry C. Bolinger, wounded 9/14
Col. Albert L. Magilton
3d Pennsylvania Reserves, Lieut. Col. John Clark
4th Pennsylvania Reserves, Maj. John Nyce
7th Pennsylvania Reserves, Maj. Chauncey A. Lyman
8th Pennsylvania Reserves, Maj. Silas M. Baily

THIRD BRIGADE: Col. Thomas F. Gallagher, wounded 9/14
Lieut. Col. Robert Anderson
9th Pennsylvania Reserves, Lieut. Col. Robert Anderson
Capt. Samuel B. Dick
10th Pennsylvania Reserves, Lieut. Col. Adoniram J. Warner,
wounded 9/17
Capt. Jonathan P. Smith
11th Pennsylvania Reserves, Lieut. Col. Samuel M. Jackson
12th Pennsylvania Reserves, Capt. Richard Gustin

ARTILLERY:
1st Pennsylvania Light, Battery A, Lieut. John G. Simpson
1st Pennsylvania Light, Battery B, Capt. James H. Cooper
1st Pennsylvania Light, Battery G, Lieut. Frank P. Amsden,
detached at Washington 9/16
5th United States, Battery C, Capt. Dunbar R. Ransom

SECOND ARMY CORPS — Maj. Gen. Edwin V. Sumner
Escort: 6th New York Cavalry, Company D, Capt. Henry W. Lyon
6th New York Cavalry, Company K, Capt. Riley Johnson

FIRST DIVISION — Maj. Gen. Israel B. Richardson, mortally wounded 9/17
Brig. Gen. John C. Caldwell, temporary, senior brigadier
Brig. Gen. Winfield S. Hancock, assigned 9/17
from Sixth Corps

FIRST BRIGADE: Brig. Gen. John C. Caldwell
5th New Hampshire, Col. Edward E. Cross, wounded 9/17
7th New York, Capt. Charles Brestel
61st New York) Col. Francis C. Barlow, wounded 9/17
64th New York (Lieut. Col. Nelson A. Miles
81st Pennsylvania, Maj. H. Boyd McKeen

SECOND BRIGADE: Brig. Gen. Thomas F. Meagher, wounded 9/17
Col. John Burke
29th Massachusetts, Lieut. Col. Joseph H. Barnes
63d New York, Col. John Burke
Lieut. Col. Henry Fowler, wounded 9/17
Maj. Richard C. Bentley, wounded 9/17
Capt. Joseph O'Neill
69th New York, Lieut. Col. James Kelly, wounded 9/17
Maj. James Cavanagh
88th New York, Lieut. Col. Patrick Kelly

THIRD BRIGADE: Col. John R. Brooke
2d Delaware, Capt. David L. Stricker
52d New York, Col. Paul Frank
57th New York, Lieut. Col. Philip J. Parisen, killed 9/17
Maj. Alford B. Chapman
66th New York, Capt. Julius Wehle
53d Pennsylvania, Lieut. Col. Richards McMichael

ARTILLERY:
1st New York Light, Battery B, Capt. Rufus D. Pettit
4th United States, Batteries A and C, Lieut. Evan Thomas

SECOND DIVISION — Maj. Gen. John Sedgwick, wounded 9/17
Brig. Gen. Oliver O. Howard

FIRST BRIGADE: Brig. Gen. Willis A. Gorman
15th Massachusetts, Lieut. Col. John W. Kimball
1st Minnesota, Col. Alfred Sully
34th New York, Col. James A. Suiter
82d New York (2d Militia), Col. Henry W. Hudson
Massachusetts Sharpshooters, 1st Company, Capt. John Saunders,
attached to 15th Massachusetts
Minnesota Sharpshooters, 2d Company, Capt. William F. Russell,
attached to 1st Minnesota

SECOND BRIGADE: Brig. Gen. Oliver O. Howard
Col. Joshua T. Owen
Col. DeWitt C. Baxter
69th Pennsylvania, Col Joshua T. Owen
71st Pennsylvania, Col. Isaac J. Wistar, wounded 9/17
Lieut. Richard P. Smith
Capt. Enoch E. Lewis
72d Pennsylvania, Col. DeWitt C. Baxter
106th Pennsylvania, Col. Turner G. Morehead

THIRD BRIGADE: Brig. Gen. Napoleon J. T. Dana, wounded 9/17
Col. Norman J. Hall
19th Massachusetts, Col. Edward W. Hinks, wounded 9/17
Lieut. Col. Arthur F. Devereux
Capt. H. G. O. Weymouth
20th Massachusetts, Col. William R. Lee
7th Michigan, Col. Norman J. Hall
Capt. Charles J. Hunt
42d New York, Lieut. Col. George N. Bomford, wounded 9/17
Maj. James E. Mallon
59th New York, Col. William L. Tidball

ARTILLERY:
1st Rhode Island Light, Battery A, Capt. John A. Tompkins
1st United States Battery I, Lieut. George A. Woodruff

THIRD DIVISION — Brig. Gen. William H. French

FIRST BRIGADE: Brig. Gen. Nathan Kimball
14th Indiana, Col. William Harrow
8th Ohio, Lieut. Col. Franklin Sawyer
132d Pennsylvania, Col. Richard A. Oakford, killed 9/17
                  Lieut. Col. Vincent M. Wilcox
7th West Virginia, Col. Joseph Snider

SECOND BRIGADE: Col. Dwight Morris
14th Connecticut, Lieut. Col. Sanford H. Perkins
108th New York, Col. Oliver H. Palmer
130th Pennsylvania, Col. Henry I. Zinn

THIRD BRIGADE: Brig. Gen. Max Weber, wounded 9/17
              Col. John W. Andrews
1st Delaware, Col. John W. Andrews
              Lieut. Col. Oliver Hopkinson, wounded 9/17
5th Maryland, Maj. Leopold Blumenberg, wounded 9/17
              Capt. E. F. M. Faehtz
4th New York, Lieut. Col. John D. McGregor

UNATTACHED ARTILLERY
1st New York Light, Battery G, Capt. John D. Frank
1st Rhode Island Light, Battery B, Capt. John G. Hazard
1st Rhode Island Light, Battery G, Capt. Charles D. Owen

FOURTH ARMY CORPS

FIRST DIVISION — Maj. Gen. Darius N. Couch, arrived Antietam morning
              9/18, attached to Sixth Corps as Third Division, 9/26

FIRST BRIGADE: Brig. Gen. Charles Devens, Jr.
7th Massachusetts, Col. David A. Russell
10th Massachusetts, Col. Henry L. Eustis
36th New York, Col. William H. Browne
2d Rhode Island, Col. Frank Wheaton

SECOND BRIGADE: Brig. Gen. Albion P. Howe
62d New York, Col. David J. Nevin

93d Pennsylvania, Col. James M. McCarter
98th Pennsylvania, Col. John F. Ballier
102d Pennsylvania, Col. Thomas A. Rowley
139th Pennsylvania, Col. Frank H. Collier, joined 9/17

THIRD BRIGADE: Brig. Gen. John Cochrane
65th New York, Col. Alexander Shaler
67th New York, Col. Julius W. Adams
122d New York, Col. Silas Titus
23d Pennsylvania, Col. Thomas H. Neill
61st Pennsylvania, Col. George C. Spear
82d Pennsylvania, Col. David H. Williams

ARTILLERY:
1st Pensylvania Light, Battery C, Capt. Jeremiah McCarthy
1st Pennsylvania Light, Battery D, Capt. Michael Hall
2d United States, Battery G, Lieut. John H. Butler
   New York Light, 3d Battery, Capt. William Stuart, assigned 9/15
                              from Sixth Corps Artillery Battallion

FIFTH ARMY CORPS — Maj. Gen. Fitz-John Porter
Escort: 1st Maine Cavalry (detachment), Capt. George J. Summat

FIRST DIVISION — Maj. Gen. George W. Morell

FIRST BRIGADE: Col. James Barnes
2d   Maine, Col. Charles W. Roberts
18th Massachusetts, Lieut. Col. Joseph Hayes
22d Massachusetts, Lieut. Col. William S. Tilton
1st Michigan, Capt. Emory W. Belton
13th New York, Col. Elisha G. Marshall
25th New York, Col. Charles A. Johnson
118th Pennsylvania, Col. Charles M. Prevost, wounded 9/20
     Massachusetts Sharpshooters, 2d Co., Capt. Lewis E. Wentworth

SECOND BRIGADE: Brig. Gen. Charles Griffin
2d   District of Columbia, Col. Charles M. Alexander
9th Massachusetts, Col. Patrick R. Guiney
32d Massachusetts, Col. Francis J. Parker
4th Michigan, Col. Jonathan W. Childs

14th New York, Col. James McQuade
62d Pennsylvania, Col. Jacob B. Sweitzer

THIRD BRIGADE: Col. T. B. W. Stockton
20th Maine, Col. Adelbert Ames
16th Michigan, Lieut. Col. Norval E. Welch
12th New York, Capt. William Huson
17th New York, Lieut. Col. Nelson B. Bartram
44th New York, Maj. Freeman Conner
83d Pennsylvania, Capt. Orpheus S. Woodward
Michigan Sharpshooters, Brady's Co., Lieut. Jonas H. Titus, Jr.

ARTILLERY:
Massachusetts Light, Battery C, Capt. Augustus P. Martin
1st Rhode Island Light, Battery C, Capt. Richard Waterman
5th United States, Battery D, Lieut. Charles E. Hazlett

SHARPSHOOTERS:
1st United States, Capt. John B. Isler

SECOND DIVISION — Brig. Gen. George Sykes

FIRST BRIGADE: Lieut. Col. Robert C. Buchanan
3d United States, Capt. John D. Wilkins
4th United States, Capt. Hiram Dryer
12th United States, First Battalion, Capt. Matthew M. Blunt
12th United States, Second Battalion, Capt. Thomas M. Anderson
14th United States, First Battalion, Capt. W. Harvey Brown
14th United States, Second Battalion, Capt. David B. McKibbin

SECOND BRIGADE: Maj. Charles S. Lovell
1st and 6th United States, Capt. Levi C. Bootes
2d and 10th United States, Capt. John S. Poland
11th United States, Capt. DeL. Floyd-Jones
17th United States, Maj. George L. Andrews

THIRD BRIGADE: Col. Gouverneur K. Warren
5th New York, Capt. Cleveland Winslow
10th New York, Lieut. Col. John W. Marshall

ARTILLERY:
1st United States, Batteries E and G, Lieut. Alanson M. Randol
5th United States, Battery I, Capt. Stephen H. Weed
5th United States, Battery K, Lieut. William E. Van Reed

THIRD DIVISION — Brig. Gen. Andrew A. Humphreys,
                    arrived Antietam morning 9/18

FIRST BRIGADE: Brig. Gen. Erastus B. Tyler
 91st Pennsylvania, Col. Edgar M. Gregory
126th Pennsylvania, Col. James G. Elder
129th Pennsylvania, Col. Jacob G. Frick
134th Pennsylvania, Col. Matthew S. Quay

SECOND BRIGADE: Col. Peter H. Allabach
123d Pennsylvania, Col. John B. Clark
131st Pennsylvania, Lieut. Col. William B. Shaut
133d Pennsylvania, Col. Franklin B. Speakman
155th Pennsylvania, Col. Edward J. Allen

ARTILLERY: Capt. Lucius N. Robinson
1st New York Light, Battery C., Capt. Almont Barnes
1st Ohio Light, Battery L, Capt. Lucius N. Robinson

ARTILLERY RESERVE — Lieut. Col. William Hays
1st Battallion New York Light, Battery A, Lieut. Bernhard Wever
1st Battallion New York Light, Battery B, Lieut. Alfred von Kleiser
1st Battallion New York Light, Battery C, Capt. Robert Langner
1st Battallion New York Light, Battery D, Capt. Charles Kusserow
                New York Light, Fifth Battery, Capt. Elijah D. Taft
1st United States, Battery K, Capt. William M. Graham
4th United States, Battery G, Lieut. Marcus P. Miller

SIXTH ARMY CORPS — Maj. Gen. William B. Franklin
Escort: 6th Pennsylvania Cavalry, Companies B and G,
                Capt. Henry P. Muirheid

FIRST DIVISION — Maj. Gen. Henry W. Slocum

FIRST BRIGADE: Col. Alfred T. A. Torbert
1st New Jersey, Lieut. Col. Mark W. Collet
2d New Jersey, Col. Samuel L. Buck
3d New Jersey, Col. Henry W. Brown
4th New Jersey, Col. William B. Hatch

SECOND BRIGADE: Col. Joseph J. Bartlett
5th Maine, Col. Nathaniel J. Jackson
16th New York, Lieut. Col. Joel J. Seaver
27th New York, Lieut. Col. Alexander D. Adams
96th Pennsylvania, Col. Henry L. Cake

THIRD BRIGADE: Brig. Gen. John Newton
18th New York, Lieut. Col. George R. Myers
31st New York, Lieut. Col. Francis E. Pinto
32d New York, Col. Roderick Matheson, killed 9/14
               Maj. George F. Lemon, mortally wounded 9/14
95th Pennsylvania, Col. Gustavus W. Town
121st New York, Col. Richard Franchet

ARTILLERY: Capt. Emory Upton
Maryland Light, Battery A, Capt. John W. Wolcott
Massachusetts Light, Battery A, Capt. Josiah Porter
New Jersey Light, Battery A, Capt. William Hexamer
2d United States, Battery D, Lieut. Edward B. Williston

SECOND DIVISION — Maj. Gen. William F. Smith

FIRST BRIGADE: Brig. Gen. Winfield S. Hancock, assigned to command of
        1st Div., Second Corps, 9/17
        Col. Amasa Cobb
6th Maine, Col. Hiram Burnham
43d New York, Maj. John Wilson
49th Pennsylvania, Lieut. Col. William Brisbane
137th Pennsylvania, Col. Henry M. Bossert
5th Wisconsin, Col. Amasa Cobb

SECOND BRIGADE: Brig. Gen. W. T. H. Brooks
2d Vermont, Maj. James H. Walbridge
3d Vermont, Col. Breed N. Hyde

4th Vermont, Lieut. Col. Charles B. Stoughton
5th Vermont, Col. Lewis A. Grant
6th Vermont, Maj. Oscar L. Tuttle

THIRD BRIGADE: Col. William H. Irwin
 7th Maine, Maj. Thomas W. Hyde
20th New York, Col. Ernest von Vegesack
33d New York, Lieut. Col. Joseph W. Corning
49th New York, Lieut. Col. William C. Alberger
                    Maj. George W. Johnson
77th New York, Capt. Nathan S. Babcock

ARTILLERY: Capt. Romeyn B. Ayres
    Maryland Light, Battery B, Lieut. Theodore J. Vanneman
    New York Light, 1st Battery, Capt. Andrew Cowan
5th United States, Battery F, Lieut. Leonard Martin

            NINTH ARMY CORPS — Maj. Gen. Jesse L. Reno, killed 9/14
                            Maj. Gen. Ambrose E. Burnside
                            Brig. Gen. Jacob D. Cox
        Escort: 1st Maine Cavalry, Company G, Capt. Zebulon B. Blethen

FIRST DIVISION — Brig. Gen. Orlando B. Willcox

FIRST BRIGADE: Col. Benjamin C. Christ
28th Massachusetts, Capt. Andrew P. Caraher
17th Michigan, Col. William H. Withington
79th New York, Lieut. Col. David Morrison
50th Pennsylvania, Maj. Edward Overton, wounded 9/17
                    Capt. William H. Diehl

SECOND BRIGADE: Col. Thomas Welsh
 8th Michigan, Lt. Col. Frank Graves,
                    regiment transferred from 1st Brigade 9/16
                    Maj. Ralph Ely
46th New York, Lieut. Col. Joseph Gerhardt
45th Pennsylvania, Lieut. Col. John I. Curtin
100th Pennsylvania, Lieut. Col. David A. Leckey

ARTILLERY:
Massachusetts Light, Eighth Battery, Capt. Asa M. Cook
2d United States, Battery E, Lieut. Samuel N. Benjamin

SECOND DIVISION — Brig. Gen. Samuel D. Sturgis

FIRST BRIGADE: Brig. Gen. James Nagle
2d Maryland, Lieut. Col. J. Eugene Duryea
6th New Hampshire, Col. Simon G. Griffin
9th New Hampshire, Col. Enoch Q. Fellows
48th Pennsylvania, Lieut. Col. Joshua K. Sigfried

SECOND BRIGADE: Brig. Gen. Edward Ferrero
21st Massachusetts, Col. William S. Clark
35th Massachusetts, Col. Edward A. Wild, wounded 9/17
                Lieut. Col. Sumner Carruth, wounded 9/17
51st New York, Col. Robert B. Potter
51st Pennsylvania, Col. John F. Hartranft

ARTILLERY:
Pennsylvania Light, Battery D, Capt. George W. Durell
4th United States, Battery E, Capt. Joseph C. Clark, Jr., wounded 9/17

THIRD DIVISION — Brig. Gen. Isaac P. Rodman, mortally wounded 9/17
              Col. Edward Harland

FIRST BRIGADE: Col. Harrison S. Fairchild
9th New York, Lieut. Col. Edgar A. Kimball
89th New York, Maj. Edward Jardine
103d New York, Maj. Benjamin Ringold
Hawkins (New York) Zouaves, attached to 9th New York

SECOND BRIGADE: Col. Edward Harland
8th Connecticut, Lieut. Col. Hiram Appelman, wounded 9/17
11th Connecticut, Col. Henry W. Kingsbury, mortally wounded 9/17
              Maj. John E. Ward
16th Connecticut, Col. Francis Beach, assigned 9/16
4th Rhode Island, Col. William H. P. Steere, wounded 9/17
              Lieut. Col. Joseph R. Curtis

ARTILLERY:
5th United States, Battery A, Lieut. Charles P. Muhlenberg
    Battery of Dalgren Boat Howitzers, attached to 9th New York

KANAWHA DIVISION — Brig. Gen. Jacob D. Cox
                    Col. Eliakim P. Scammon

FIRST BRIGADE: Col. Eliakim P. Scammon
                Col. Hugh Ewing
12th Ohio, Col. Carr B. White
23d Ohio, Lieut. Col. Rutherford B. Hayes, wounded 9/14
              Maj. James M. Comly
30th Ohio, Col. Hugh Ewing
          Lieut. Col. Theodore Jones, wounded and captured 9/17
          Maj. George H. Hildt
          Ohio Light Artillery, First Battery, Capt. James R. McMullin
          Gilmore's Co., West Virginia Cavalry, Lieut. James Abraham
          Harrison's Co., West Virginia Cavalry, Lieut. Dennis Delaney

SECOND BRIGADE: Col. George Crook
11th Ohio, Lieut. Col. Augustus H. Coleman, killed 9/17
              Maj. Lyman J. Jackson
28th Ohio, Lieut. Col. Gottfried Becker
36th Ohio, Lieut. Col. Melvin Clarke, killed 9/17
              Capt. H. F. Devol
          Schambeck's Co., Chicago Dragoons, Capt. Frederick Schambeck
          Kentucky Light Artillery, Simmond's Battery, Capt. Seth J. Simmonds

UNATTACHED:
6th New York Cavalry (eight companies), Col. Thomas C. Devin
          Ohio Cavalry, Third Independent Co., Lieut. Jonas Seamen
3d U. S. Artillery, Batteries L and M, Capt. John Edwards, Jr.
2d New York Artillery, Battery L, Capt. Jacob Roemer

TWELFTH ARMY CORPS — Maj. Gen. Joseph K. F. Mansfield,
                    mortally wounded 9/17
                  Brig. Gen. Alpheus S. Williams
    Escort: 1st Michigan Cavalry, Company L, Capt. Melvin Brewer

FIRST DIVISION — Brig. Gen. Alpheus S. Williams
Brig. Gen. Samuel W. Crawford,
wounded 9/17
Brig. Gen. George H. Gordon

FIRST BRIGADE: Brig. Gen. Samuel W. Crawford, wounded 9/17
Col. Joseph F. Knipe
5th Connecticut, Capt. Henry W. Daboll, detached at Frederick 9/15
10th Maine, Col. George L. Beal, wounded 9/17
28th New York, Capt. William H. H. Mapes
46th Pennsylvania, Col. Joseph F. Knipe
Lieut. Col. James L. Selfridge
124th Pennsylvania, Col. Joseph W. Hawley, wounded 9/17
Maj. Isaac L. Haldeman
125th Pennsylvania, Col. Jacob Higgins
128th Pennsylvania, Col. Samuel Croasdale, killed 9/17
Lieut. Col. William H. Hammersly, wounded 9/17
Maj. Joel B. Wanner

THIRD BRIGADE: Brig. Gen. George H. Gordon
Col. Thomas H. Ruger
27th Indiana, Col. Silas Colgrove
2d Massachusetts, Col. George L. Andrews
13th New Jersey, Col. Ezra A. Carman
107th New York, Col. R. B. Van Valkenburgh
3d Wisconsin, Col. Thomas H. Ruger
Zouaves d'Afrique, Pennsylvania, no offiers present; attached
to 2d Massachusetts

SECOND DIVISION — Brig. Gen. George S. Greene

FIRST BRIGADE: Lieut. Col. Hector Tyndale, wounded 9/17
Maj. Orrin J. Crane
5th Ohio, Maj. John Collins
7th Ohio, Maj. Orrin J. Crane
Capt. Frederick A. Seymour
66th Ohio, Lieut. Col. Eugene Powell, wounded 9/17
28th Pennsylvania, Maj. Ario Pardee, Jr.
29th Ohio, Lieut. Theron S. Winship, detached 9/9

SECOND BRIGADE: Col. Henry J. Stainrook
  3d Maryland, Lieut. Col. Joseph M. Sudsburg
102d New York, Lieut. Col. James C. Lane
111th Pennsylvania, Maj. Thomas M. Walker
109th New York, Capt. George E. Seymour, detached 9/13

THIRD BRIGADE: Col. William B. Goodrich, killed 9/17
                    Lieut. Col. Jonanthan Austin
  3d Delaware, Maj. Arthur Maginnis, wounded 9/17
                Capt. W. J. McKaig
      Purnell Legion, Maryland, Lieut. Col. Benjamin L. Simpson
60th New York, Lieut. Col. Charles R. Brundage
78th New York, Lieut. Col. Jonanthan Austin
                Capt. Henry R. Stagg

ARTILLERY: Capt. Clermont L. Best
    Maine Light, 4th Battery, Capt. O'Neil W. Robinson
    Maine Light, 6th Battery, Capt. Freeman McGilvery
1st New York Light, Battery M, Capt. George W. Cothran
    New York Light, 10th Battery, Capt. John T. Bruen
    Pennsylvania Light, Battery E, Capt. Joseph M. Knap
    Pennsylvania Light, Battery F, Capt. Robert B. Hampton
4th United States, Battery F. Lieut. Edward D. Muhlenberg

CAVALRY DIVISION — Brig. Gen. Alfred Pleasonton

FIRST BRIGADE: Maj. Charles J. Whiting
5th United States, Capt. Joseph H. McArthur
6th United States, Capt. William P. Sanders

SECOND BRIGADE: Col. John F. Farnsworth
8th Illinois, Maj. William H. Medill
  3d Indiana, Maj. George H. Chapman
1st Massachusetts, Col. Robert Williams
                Capt. Casper Crownenshield
8th Pennsylvania, Lieut. Col. A. E. Griffiths
                Capt. Peter Keenan

THIRD BRIGADE: Col. Richard H. Rush

4th Pennsylvania, Col. James H. Childs, killed 9/17
          Lieut. Col. James K. Kerr
6th Pennsylvania, Lieut. Col. C. Ross Smith

FOURTH BRIGADE: Col. Andrew T. McReynolds
1st New York, Maj. Alonzo W. Adams
12th Pennsylvania, Maj. James A. Congdon

FIFTH BRIGADE: Col. Benjamin F. Davis
8th New York, Col. Benjamin F. Davis
3d Pennsylvania, Lieut. Col. Samuel W. Owen

ARTILLERY:
2d United States, Battery A, Capt. John C. Tidball
2d United States, Batteries B and L, Capt. James M. Robertson
2d United States, Batteries M, Lieut. Peter C. Hains
3d United States, Batteries C and G, Capt. Horatio G. Gibson

UNATTACHED:
15th Pennsylvania Cavalry (detachment), Col. William J. Palmer
1st Maine Cavalry, Col. Samuel Allen, detached at Frederick

ARMY OF NORTHERN VIRGINIA
GEN. ROBERT E. LEE, C. S. ARMY
COMMANDING

LONGSTREET'S CORPS — Maj. Gen. James Longstreet

McLAWS' DIVISION — Maj. Gen. Lafayette McLaws

KERSHAW'S BRIGADE: Brig. Gen. J. B. Kershaw
2d South Carolina, Col. John D. Kennedy, wounded 9/17
          Maj. Franklin Gaillard
3d South Carolina, Col. James D. Nance
7th South Carolina, Col. D. Wyatt Aiken, wounded 9/17
          Capt. John S. Hard
8th South Carolina, Lieut. Col. A. J. Hoole

COBB'S BRIGADE: Brig. Gen. Howell Cobb, temporarily absent from
            command
            Lieut. Col. C. C. Sanders
            Lieut. Col. Wiliam MacRae
16th Georgia, Lieut. Col. Henry P. Thomas
24th Georgia, Maj. R. E. McMillan
15th North Carolina, Lieut. Col. William MacRae
      Cobb's (Georgia) Legion, Lieut. Col. L. J. Glenn

SEMMES'S BRIGADE: Brig. Gen. Paul J. Semmes
10th Georgia, Maj. William C. Holt, wounded 9/14
            Capt. P. H. Loud
53d Georgia, Lieut. Col. Thomas Sloan, wounded 9/17
            Capt. S. W. Marshborne
15th Virginia, Capt. Edward M. Morrison, wounded 9/17
            Capt. Edward J. Willis
32d Virginia, Col. E. B. Montague

BARKSDALE'S BRIGADE: Brig. Gen. William Barksdale
13th Mississippi, Lieut. Col. Kennon McElroy
17th Mississippi, Lieut. Col. John C. Fiser
18th Mississippi, Maj. J. C. Campbell
            Lieut. Col. William H. Luse
21st Mississippi, Capt. John Sims
            Col. Benjamin G. Humphreys

ARTILLERY: Col. Henry C. Cabell
        Maj. S. P. Hamilton
Manly's (North Carolina) Battery, Capt. B. C. Manly
Pulaski (Georgia) Artillery, Capt. J. P. W. Read
Richmond (Fayette) Artillery, Capt. M. C. Macon
Troup (Georgia) Artillery, Capt. H. H. Carlton
Richmond Howitzers (1st Company), Capt. E. S. McCarthy

ANDERSON'S DIVISION — Maj. Gen. Richard H. Anderson, wounded 9/17
            Brig. Gen. Roger A. Pryor

WILCOX'S BRIGADE: Col. Alfred Cumming
            Maj. H. A. Herbert
            Capt. J. M. Crow

8th Alabama, Maj. H. A. Herbert
9th Alabama, Maj. J. H. J. Williams, wounded 9/17
    Capt. J. M. Crow
    Capt. A. C. Chisolm
10th Alabama, Capt. G. C. Wheatly, killed 9/17
11th Alabama, Maj. John C. C. Sanders

MAHONE'S BRIGADE: Col. William A. Parkham
 6th Virginia, Capt. John R. Ludlow
12th Virginia, Capt. J. R. Llewellyn
16th Virginia, Maj. F. D. Holliday
41st Virginia,
61st Virginia,

FEATHERSTON'S BRIGADE: Col. Carnot Posey
12th Mississippi, Col. W. H. Taylor
16th Mississippi, Capt. A.A M. Feltus
19th Mississippi, Col. N. W. Harris, wounded 9-/17
 2d Mississippi Battalion, Maj. William S. Wilson, wounded 9/17

ARMISTEAD'S BRIGADE: Brig. Gen. Lewis A. Armistead, wounded
       Col. J. G. Hodges
 9th Virginia, Capt. W. J. Richardson
    Capt. Joseph J. Phillips
14th Virginia, Col. J. G. Hodges
38th Virginia, Col. Edward C. Edmonds
53d Virginia, Capt. W. G. Pollard, killed 9/17
    Capt. Harwood
57th Virginia,

PRYOR'S BRIGADE: Brig. Gen. Roger A. Pryor
     Col. John C. Hately, wounded 9/17
14th Alabama, Maj. J. A. Broome
 2d Florida, Col. W. D. Ballantine, wounded 9/17
    Lieut. Geiger
 8th Florida, Lieut. Col. George A. Coppens, killed 9/17
    Capt. Richard A. Walker, killed 9/17
    Capt. W. Baya
 3d Virginia, Col. Joseph Mayo, wounded 9/17
    Lieut. Col. A. D. Callcote

5th Florida, Col. John C. Hately, wounded 9/17
          Lieut. Col. Thomas B. Lamar, wounded 9/17
          Maj. Benjamin F. Davis

WRIGHT'S BRIGADE: Brig. Gen. Ambrose R. Wright, wounded 9/17
          Col. Robert Jones, wounded 9/17
          Col. William Gibson
44th Alabama, Lieut. Col. Charles A. Derby, killed 9/17
          Maj. W. F. Perry
 3d Georgia, Capt. R. B. Nisbit, wounded 9/17
          Capt. John T. Jones
22d Georgia, Col. Robert Jones, wounded 9/17
          Lieut. Col. L. D. Lallerstedt, wounded 9/17
48th Georgia, Col. William Gibson

ARTILLERY: Capt. Cary F. Grimes, killed 9/17
          Maj. John S. Saunders
Donaldsonville (Louisiana) Artillery (Maurin's Battery),
          Capt. Victor Maurin
Huger's (Virginia) Battery, Capt. Frank Huger
Moorman's (Virginia) Battery, Capt. Marcellus N. Moorman
Thompson's (Grimes's) (Virginia) Battery, Capt. Cary F. Grimes

JONES'S DIVISION — Brig. Gen. David R. Jones

TOOMBS'S BRIGADE: Brig. Gen. Robert Toombs
          Col. Henry L. Benning
 2d Georgia, Lieut. Col. William R. Holmes, killed 9/17
          Maj. Skidmore Harris, wounded 9/17
          Capt. A. McLewis
15th Georgia, Col. W. T. Millican, killed 9/17
17th Georgia, Capt. J. A. McGregor
20th Georgia, Col. J. B. Cumming

DRAYTON'S BRIGADE: Brig. Gen. Thomas F. Drayton
50th Georgia, Lieut. Col. F. Kearse
51st Georgia,
15th South Carolina, Col. W. D. DeSaussure
 3d South Carolina Battalion, Maj. George S. James

PICKETT'S BRIGADE: Brig. Gen. Richard B. Garnett
8th Virginia, Col. Eppa Hunton
18th Virginia Maj. Gorege C. Cabell
19th Virginia, Col. J. B. Strange, killed 9/14
          Lieut. W. N. Wood
          Capt. J. L. Cochran
28th Virginia, Capt. W. L. Wingfield
56th Virginia, Col. William D. Stuart
          Capt. John B. McPhail

KEMPER'S BRIGADE: Brig. Gen. James L. Kemper
1st Virginia, Capt. George F. Newman
          Col. W. H. Palmer
7th Virginia, Maj. Arthur Herbert
          Capt. Philip S. Ashby
11th Virginia, Maj. Adam Clement
17th Virginia, Col. M. D. Corse, wounded 9/17
24th Virginia, Col. W. R. Perry

JENKINS'S BRIGADE: Col. Joseph Walker
1st South Carolina (Volunteers), Lieut. Col. D. Livingston,
          wounded 9/17
2d South Carolina Rifles, Lieut. Col. R. A. Thompson
5th South Carolina, Capt. T. C. Beckham
6th South Carolina, Lieut. Col. J. M. Steedman
          Capt. E. B. Cantey, wounded 9/17
4th South Carolina Battalion, Lieut. W. F. Field
Palmetto (South Carolina) Sharpshooters, Capt. A. H. Foster,
          wounded 9/17
          Capt. F. W. Kirkpatrick

ANDERSON'S BRIGADE: Col. George T. Anderson
1st Georgia (Regulars), Col. W. J. Magill, wounded 9/17
          Capt. R. A. Wayne
7th Georgia, Col. G. H. Carmichael
8th Georgia, Col. John R. Towers
9th Georgia, Lieut. Col. John C. L. Munger
11th Georgia, Maj. F. H. Little

ARTILLERY:
Wise (Virginia) Artillery (J. S. Brown's Battery)

WALKER'S DIVISION — Brig. Gen. John G. Walker

WALKER'S BRIGADE: Col. Van H. Manning, wounded 9/17
　　　　　　　　　　Col. E. D. Hall
3d　Arkansas, Capt. John W. Reedy
27th North Carolina, Col. J. R. Cooke
46th North Carolina, Col. E. D. Hall
　　　　　　　　　　　Lieut. Col. William A. Jackson
48th North Carolina, Col. R. C. Hill
　　　　　　　　　　　Lieut. Col. S. H. Walkup
30th Virginia, Lieut. Col. Robert S. Chew, wounded 9/17
　　French's (Virginia) Battery, Capt. Thomas B. French

RANSOM'S BRIGADE: Brig. Gen. Robert Ransom, Jr.
24th North Carolina, Lieut. Col. John L. Harris
25th North Carolina, Col. H. M. Rutledge
35th North Carolina, Col. Mathew W. Ransom
49th North Carolina, Lieut. Col. Lee M. McAfee
　　Branch's Field Artillery (Virginia), Capt. James R. Branch

HOOD'S DIVISION — Brig. Gen. John B. Hood

HOOD'S BRIGADE: Col. William T. Wofford
18th Georgia, Lieut. Col. S. Z. Ruff
1st　Texas, Lieut. Col. P. A. Work
4th　Texas, Lieut. Col. B. F. Carter
5th　Texas, Capt. I. N. M. Turner
　　Hampton (South Carolina) Legion, Lieut. Col. M. W. Gary

LAW'S BRIGADE: Col. Evander McIver Law
4th Alabama, Lieut. Col. O. K. McLemore, mortally wounded 9/17
　　　　　　　　Capt. H. L. Scruggs, wounded 9/17
　　　　　　　　Capt. W. M. Robbins
2d　Mississippi, Col. J. M. Stone, wounded 9/17
　　　　　　　　Lieut. Moody
11th Mississippi, Col. P. F. Liddle, killed 9/16
　　　　　　　　Lieut. Col. S. Butler, killed 9/17
　　　　　　　　Maj. T. S. Evans, killed 9/17
6th North Carolina, Maj. Robert F. Webb, wounded 9/17

ARTILLERY: Maj. B. W. Frobel
German Artillery (South Carolina), Capt. W. K. Bachman
Palmetto Artillery (South Carolina), Capt. H. R. Garden
Rowan Artillery (North Carolina), Capt. James Reilly

EVANS'S (Independent) BRIGADE: Brig. Gen. Nathan G. Evans
Col. P. F. Stevens
17th South Carolina, Col. F. W. McMaster
18th South Carolina, Col. W. H. Wallace
22d South Carolina, Lieut. Col. T. C. Watkins, killed 9/14
Maj. M. Hilton
23d South Carolina, Capt. S. A. Durham
Lieut. E. R. White
Holcombe (South Carolina) Legion, Col. P. F. Stevens
Macbeth (South Carolina) Artillery, Capt. R. Boyce

ARTILLERY

WASHINGTON (LOUISIANA) ARTILLERY: Col. J. B. Walton
1st Company, Capt. C. W. Squires
2d Company, Capt. J. B. Richardson
3d Company, Capt. M. B. Miller
4th Company, Capt. B. F. Eshleman

LEE'S BATTALION: Col. S. D. Lee
Ashland (Virginia) Artillery, Capt. P. Woolfolk, Jr.
Bedford (Virginia) Artillery, Capt. T. C. Jordan
Brooks (South Carolina) Artillery, Lieut. William Elliott
Eubank's (Virginia) Battery, Capt. J. L. Eubank
Madison (Louisiana) Light Artillery, Capt. G. V. Moody
Parker's (Virginia) Battery, Capt. W. W. Parker

JACKSON'S CORPS — Maj. Gen. Thomas J. Jackson

EWELL'S DIVISION — Brig. Gen. A. R. Lawton, wounded 9/17
Brig. Gen. Jubal A. Early

LAWTON'S BRIGADE: Col. Marcellus Douglas, killed 9/17
Col. John H. Lamar
Maj. J. H. Lowe

13th Georgia, Capt. D. A. Kidd
26th Georgia,
31st Georgia, Lieut. Col. J. T. Crowder, killed 9/17
        Maj. J. H. Lowe
38th Georgia, Capt. W. H. Battey, killed 9/17
        Capt. Peter Brennan
        Capt. John W. McCurdy
60th Georgia, Maj. W. B. Jones
61st Georgia, Col. John H. Lamar
        Maj. A. P. McRae, killed 9/17
        Capt. Van Valkenberg

EARLY'S BRIGADE: Brig. Gen. Jubal A. Early
        Col. William Smith, wounded 9/17
13th Virginia, Capt. F. V. Winston
25th Virginia, Capt. R. D. Lilley
31st Virginia,
44th Virginia, Capt. D. W. Anderson
49th Virginia, Col. William Smith, wounded 9/17
        Lieut. Col. J. C. Gibson
52d   Virginia, Col. M. G. Harman
58th Virginia,

TRIMBLE'S BRIGADE: Col. James A. Walker, wounded 9/17
15th Alabama, Capt. I. B. Feagin
12th Georgia, Capt. Rodgers, wounded 9/17
        Capt. Carson
21st Georgia, Maj. Thomas C. Glover, wounded 9/17
        Capt. J. C. Nisbit
21st North Carolina, Capt. F. P. Miller, killed 9/17
  1st North Carolina Battalion, attached to 21st North Carolina

HAYS'S BRIGADE: Col. H. B. Strong
        Brig. Gen. Harry T. Hays, joined 9/16
  5th Louisiana, Col. Henry Forno
  6th Louisiana, Col. H. B. Strong, killed 9/17
  7th Louisiana,
  8th Louisiana, Lieut. Col. Trevanion D. Lewis
14th Louisiana,

ARTILLERY: Maj. A. R. Courtney
Johnson's (Virginia) Battery, Capt. John R. Johnson, at Antietam

Louisiana Guard Artillery (D'Aquin's Battery), Capt. L. E. D'Aquin,
at Antietam
First Maryland Battery (Dement's Battery), Capt. W. F. Dement, at
Harpers Ferry
Staunton (Virginia) Artillery (Balthis's Battery), Lieut. A. W. Garber,
at Harpers Ferry
Chesapeake (Maryland) Artillery (Brown's Battery), at Harpers Ferry

Courtney (Virginia) Artillery (Latimer's Battery), at Harpers Ferry

HILL'S LIGHT DIVISION — Maj. Gen. Ambrose P. Hill

BRANCH'S BRIGADE: Brig. Gen. L. O'Brien Branch, killed 9/17
Col. James H. Lane
7th North Carolina, Col. E. G. Haywood
18th North Carolina, Lieut. Col. Thomas J. Purdie
28th North Carolina, Col. James H. Lane
Maj. W. J. Montgomery
33d North Carolina, Lieut. Col. R. F. Hoke
37th North Carolina, Capt. W. G. Morris

GREGG'S BRIGADE: Brig. Gen. Maxcy Gregg, wounded 9/17
1st South Carolina (Provisional Army), Col. D. H. Hamilton
Maj. E. McCrady, Jr.
1st South Carolina Rifles, Lieut. Col. James M. Perrin
12th South Carolina, Col. Dixon Barnes, killed 9/17
Lieut. Col. C. Jones
Maj. W. H. McCorkle
13th South Carolina, Col. O. E. Edwards
14th South Carolina, Lieut. Col. W. D. Simpson

FIELD'S BRIGADE: Col. John M. Brockenbrough
40th Virginia, Lieut. Col. Fleet W. Cox
47th Virginia, Lieut. Col. John W. Lyell
55th Virginia, Maj. Charles N. Lawson
22d Virginia Battalion, Maj. E. P. Tayloe

ARCHER'S BRIGADE: Brig. Gen. James J. Archer
Col. Peter Turney

19th Georgia, Maj. J. H. Neal
        Capt. F. M. Johnston
1st Tennessee (Provisional Army), Col. Peter Turney
7th Tennessee, Maj. S. G. Shepard
        Lieut. G. A. Howard
14th Tennessee, Col. William McComb, wounded 9/17
        Lieut. Col. J.W. Lockert
5th Alabama Battalion, Capt. Charles M. Hooper
        Capt. T. W. Flynn

PENDER'S BRIGADE: Brig. Gen. William D. Pender
        Col. R. H. Brewer
16th North Carolina, Lieut. Col. W. A. Stowe
22d North Carolina, Maj. C. C. Cole
34th North Carolina, Lieut. Col. J. L. McDowell
38th North Carolina,

THOMAS'S BRIGADE: Col. Edward L. Thomas,
        retained at Harpers Ferry on 9/17
14th Georgia, Col. R. W. Folsom
35th Georgia,
45th Georgia, Maj. W. L. Grice
49th Georgia, Lieut. Col. S. M. Manning

ARTILLERY: Maj. R. Lindsay Walker
Crenshaw's (Virginia) Battery, Capt. W. G. Crenshaw
Fredericksburg (Virginia) Artillery (Braxton's Battery),
    Capt. Carter M. Braxton
Pee Dee (South Carolina) Artillery (McIntosh's Battery),
    Capt. D. G. McIntosh
Purcell (Virginia) Artillery (Pegram's Battery), Capt. W. G. Pegram
Letcher (Virginia) Artillery (Davidson's Battery),
    retained at Harpers Ferry 9/17

JACKSON'S DIVISION — Brig. Gen. John R. Jones, wounded 9/17
        Brig. Gen. W. E. Starke, killed 9/17
        Col. Arnold J. Grigsby

WINDER'S BRIGADE: Col. Arnold J. Grigsby
        Lieut. Col. R. D. Gardner, wounded 9/17
        Maj. H. J. Williams

2d Virginia, Capt. R. T. Colston
4th Virginia, Lieut. Col. R. D. Gardner
5th Virginia, Maj. H. J. Williams
           Capt. E. L. Custis, wounded 9/17
27th Virginia, Capt. F. C. Wilson
33d Virginia, Capt. J. B. Golladay, wounded 9/17
           Lieut. Walton

TALIAFERRO'S BRIGADE: Col. E. T. H. Warren
                   Col. James W. Jackson, wounded 9/17
                   Col. James L. Sheffield
47th Alabama, Col. James W. Jackson
           Maj. J. M. Campbell
48th Alabama, Col. J. L. Sheffield
23d Virginia,
10th Virginia,
37th Virginia, Lieut. Col. John F. Terry

JONES'S BRIGADE: Col. Bradley T. Johnson
               Capt. J. E. Penn, wounded 9/17
               Capt. A. C. Page, wounded 9/17
               Capt. R. W. Withers
21st Virginia, Capt. A. C. Page, wounded 9/17
42d Virginia, Capt. R. W. Withers
           Capt. D. W. Garrett
48th Virginia, Capt. John H. Candler
1st Virginia Battalion, Lieut. C. A. Davidson

STARKE'S BRIGADE: Brig. Gen. William E. Starke, killed 9/17
               Col. Jesse M. Williams, wounded 9/17
               Col. Leroy A. Stafford, wounded 9/17
               Col. Edmund Pendleton
1st Louisiana, Lieut. Col. M. Nolan, wounded 9/17
            Capt. W. E. Moore
2d Louisiana, Col. Jesse M. Williams, wounded 9/17
9th Louisiana, Col. Leroy A. Stafford, wounded 9/17
            Lieut. Col. W. R. Peck
10th Louisiana, Capt. H. D. Monier
15th Louisiana, Col. Edmund Pendleton
1st Louisiana Battalion (Coppen's Zouaves)

ARTILLERY: Maj. L. M. Shumaker

Alleghany (Virginia) Artillery (Carpenter's Battery),
     Capt. Joseph Carpenter
Brockenbrough's (Maryland) Battery, Capt. J. B. Brockenbrough
Danville (Virginia) Artillery (Wooding's Battery), Capt. G. W. Wooding
Lee (Virginia) Battery (Raine's Battery), Capt. Charles J. Raine
Rockbridge (Virginia) Artillery (Poague's Battery), Capt. W. P. Poague
Hampden (Virginia) Artillery (Caskie's Battery)

HILL'S DIVISION — Maj. Gen. Daniel H. Hill

RIPLEY'S BRIGADE: Brig. Gen. Roswell S. Ripley, wounded 9/17
                 Col. George Doles
   4th Georgia, Col. George Doles
                 Maj. Robert Smith, killed 9/17
                 Capt. W. H. Willis
   44th Georgia, Capt. John C. Key
   1st North Carolina, Lieut. Col. H. A. Brown
   3d North Carolina, Col. William L. DeRosset, wounded 9/17
                 Maj. S. D. Thruston, wounded 9/17

RODES'S BRIGADE: Brig. Gen. Robert E. Rodes
   3d Alabama, Col. Cullum A. Battle
   5th Alabama, Maj. E. L. Hobson
   6th Alabama, Col. John B. Gordon, wounded 9/17
                Lieut. Col. J. N. Lightfoot, wounded 9/17
   12th Alabama, Col. B. B. Gayle, killed 9/14
                Lieut. Col. S. B. Pickens
                Capt. Tucker, killed 9/17
                Capt. Maroney, wounded 9/17
                Capt. A. Proskauer, wounded 9/17
   26th Alabama, Col. E. A. O'Neal, wounded 9/17

GARLAND'S BRIGADE: Brig. Gen. Samuel Garland, killed 9/14
                   Col. D. K. McRae, wounded 9/17
   5th North Carolina, Col. D. K. McRae, wounded 9/17
                   Capt. T. M. Garrett
   12th North Carolina, Capt. S. Snow
   13th North Carolina, Lieut. Col. Thomas Ruffin, Jr., wounded 9/14
                   Capt. J. H. Hyam
   20th North Carolina, Col. Alfred Iverson
   23d North Carolina, Col. D. H. Christie

ANDERSON'S BRIGADE: Brig. Gen. George B. Anderson,
                      mortally wounded 9/17
                      Col. C. C. Tew, killed 9/17
                      Col. R. T. Bennett
2d North Carolina, Col. C. C. Tew, killed 9/17
                      Maj. John Howard, wounded 9/17
                      Capt. George M. Roberts
4th North Carolina, Col. Bryan Grimes
                      Capt. W. T. Marsh, killed 9/17
                      Capt. E. A. Osborne, wounded 9/17
                      Capt. D. P. Latham, killed 9/17
14th North Carolina, Col. R. T. Bennett
                      Lieut. Col. W. A. Johnson, wounded 9/17
                      Maj. A. J. Griffith
30th North Carolina, Col. F. M. Parker, wounded 9/17
                      Maj. W. W. Sillers

COLQUITT'S BRIGADE: Brig. Gen. Alfred H. Colquitt
13th Alabama, Col. B. D. Fry, wounded 9/17
              Maj. A. S. Reaves, wounded 9/17
  6th Georgia, Lieut. Col. J. M. Newton, killed 9/17
              Maj. P. Tracy, killed 9/17
              Lieut. E. P. Burnett
23d Georgia, Col. W. P. Barclay, killed 9/17
              Lieut. Col. E. F. Best, wounded 9/17
              Maj. J. H. Huggins, wounded 9/17
27th Georgia, Col. L. B. Smith, killed 9/17
              Lieut. Col. C. T. Zachry, wounded 9/17
              Capt. W. H. Rentfro
28th Georgia, Maj. T. Graybill, wounded 9/14
              Capt. N. J. Garrison, wounded 9/17
              Capt. R. A. Warthen
              Lieut. John W. Fuller

ARTILLERY: Maj. C. F. Pierson
Hardaway's Alabama Battery, Capt. R. A. Hardaway
                            Lieut. John W. Tullis
Jeff Davis (Alabama) Artillery, Capt. J. W. Bondurant
Jones's (Virginia) Battery, Capt. William B. Jones
King William (Virginia) Artillery, Capt. T. H. Carter

RESERVE ARTILLERY — Brig. Gen. William N. Pendleton

CUTTS'S BATTALION: Lieut. Col. A. S. Cutts, under D. H. Hill 9/17
Blackshears' (Georgia) Battery, Capt. J. A. Blackshears
Irwin (Georgia) Artillery (Lane's Battery), Capt. John Lane
Lloyd's (North Carolina) Battery
Patterson's (Georgia) Battery, Capt. G. M. Patterson
Ross's (Georgia) Battery, Capt. H. M. Ross

JONES'S BATTALION: Maj. Hilary P. Jones, under D. H. Hill 9/17
Morris (Virginia) Artillery (R. C. M. Page's Battery)
Orange (Virginia) Artillery (Peyton's Battery), Capt. Jefferson Peyton
Turner's (Virginia) Battery, Capt. W. H. Turner
Wimbish's (Virginia) Battery, Capt. Abram Wimbish

BROWN'S BATTALION (1ST VIRGINIA ARTILLERY):
                 Col. J. Thompson Brown, guarding Potomac fords
Powhatan Artillery (Dance's Battery), Capt. Willis J. Dance
Richmond Howitzers, 2d Company, Capt. D. Watson
                        3d Company, Capt. B. H. Smith, Jr.
Salem Artillery (Hupp's Battery), Capt. A. Hupp
Williamsburg Artillery (Coke's Battery), Capt. John A. Coke

NELSON'S BATTALION: Maj. William Nelson, guarding Potomac fords
Amherst (Virginia) Artillery (Kirkpatrick's Battery)
                      Capt. T. J. Kirkpatrick
Fluvanna (Virginia) Artillery (Ancell's Battery), Capt. John J. Ancell
Huckstep's (Virginia) Battery, Capt. Charles T. Huckstep
Johnson's (Virginia) Battery, Capt. Marmaduke Johnson
Milledge (Georgia) Battery, Capt. John Milledge

MISCELLANEOUS:
Cutshaw's (Virginia) Battery, Capt. W. E. Cutshaw
Magruder Artillery, Capt. T. J. Page, Jr.
Dixie (Virginia) Artillery (Chapman's Battery), Capt. G. B. Chapman
Rice's (Virginia) Battery, Capt. W. H. Rice

CAVALRY — Maj. Gen. James E. B. Stuart

HAMPTON'S BRIGADE: Brig. Gen. Wade Hampton

1st North Carolina, Col. L. S. Baker
2d North Carolina, Col. M. C. Butler
    Cobb's (Georgia) Legion, Lieut. Col. P. M. B. Young
                         Maj. W. G. Deloney
10th Virginia Cavalry,
    Jeff Davis Legion (Mississippi), Lieut. Col. W. T. Martin

LEE'S BRIGADE: Brig. Gen. Fitzhugh Lee
1st Virginia, Lieut. Col. L. Tiernan Brien
3d Virginia, Lieut. Col. John T. Thornton, killed 9/17
    Capt. Thomas H. Owen
4th Virginia, Col. Williams C. Wickham
5th Virginia, Col. T. L. Rosser
9th Virginia, Col. W. H. F. Lee

ROBERTSON'S BRIGADE: Brig. Gen. Beverly H. Robertson, transferred
                    Col. Thomas T. Munford
2d Virginia, Col. Thomas T. Munford
           Lieut. Col. Richard A. Burke
6th Virginia,
7th Virginia, Capt. S. B. Myers
12th Virginia, Col. A. W. Harman
17th Virginia Battalion

HORSE ARTILLERY — Capt. John Pelham
Chew's (Virginia) Battery, Capt. R. P. Chew
Hart's (South Carolina) Battery, Capt. J. F. Hart
Pelham's (Virginia) Battery, Capt. John Pelham

Appendix D

ARMY OF THE POTOMAC

BATTLES OF SOUTH MOUNTAIN AND CRAMPTON'S PASS
SEPTEMBER 14, 1862

	Killed	Wounded	Missing	Aggregate
First Corps				
1st Division	62	395	42	499
2d Division	9	26	0	35
3d Division	99	299	1	399
Total	170	720	43	933
Ninth Corps	1 (Reno)			
1st Division	65	285	0	350
2d Division	10	117	30	157
3d Division	2	8	0	10
4th Division	80	260	0	340
Total	158	670	30	858
Sixth Corps				
1st Division	114	397	2	513
2d Division	1	19	0	20
Total	115	416	2	533
Cavalry Brigade	0	1	0	1
Grand Total	443	1,807	75	2,325

BATTLE OF ANTIETAM, SEPTEMBER 17, 1862
INCLUDING REPORTS FROM SEPTEMBER 16

	Killed	Wounded	Missing	Aggregate
First Corps				
1st Division	98	669	95	862

374

2d Division	153	898	137	1,188
3d Division	97	449	23	569
Total	348	2,016	255	2,619

Second Corps

1st Division	212	900	24	1,136
2d Division	355	1,579	321	2,255
3d Division	293	1,322	203	1,818
Total	860	3,801	548	5,209

Fifth Corps

1st Division	0	0	0	0
2d Division	13	94	1	108
Artillery Reserve	8	13	1	22
Total	21	107	2	130

Sixth Corps

1st Division	5	58	2	65
2d Division	65	277	31	373
Total	70	355	33	438

Ninth Corps

1st Division	46	284	7	337
2d Division	128	522	20	670
3d Division	220	783	70	1,073
4th Division	38	152	23	213
Total	432	1,741	120	2,293

Twelfth Corps

1st Division	160	862	54	1,076
2d Division	113	507	30	650
Artillery	1	15	1	17
Total	274	1,384	85	1,743

Couch's Division	0	9	0	9
Pleasonton's cavalry	5	23	0	28
Grand Total	2,010	9,416	1,043	12,469

ACTION AT SHEPHERDSTOWN, VA., SEPTEMBER 19-20, 1862

	Killed	Wounded	Missing	Aggregate
Fifth Corps				
Morell's Division	70	148	128	346

ARMY OF NORTHERN VIRGINIA

TOTAL KILLED AND WOUNDED FROM SOUTH MOUNTAIN,
SEPTEMBER 14, 1862, THROUGH SHEPHERDSTOWN, VA.,
SEPTEMBER 20, 1862

	Killed	Wounded	Aggregate
Jackson's Corps			
Jackson's Division			
Winder's Birgade	11	77	88
Taliaferro's Brigade	30	146	176
Starke's Brigade	70	212	282
Ewell's Division			
Lawton's Brigade	86	347	433
Early's Brigade	12	167	179
Hays's Brigade	41	216	257
Trimble's Brigade	22	124	146
D. H. Hill's Division			
Garland's Brigade	86	440	526
G. B. Anderson's Brigade	75	299	374
Ripley's Brigade	54	294	348
Colquitt's Brigade	53	291	344
Rodes's Brigade	70	409	479
A. P. Hill's Division	113	818	931
Officers	2	2	4
Total	725	3,842	4,567
Longstreet's Corps			
D. R. Jones's Division			
Kemper's Brigade	11	88	99
Garnett's Brigade	25	157	182
Toombs's Brigade	16	123	139
Jenkins' Brigade	25	183	208
Walker's Division			
Ransom's Brigade	43	144	187
Walker's Brigade	134	691	825
Hood's Division			
Anderson's Brigade	8	79	87
Law's Brigade	50	377	427
Wofford's Brigade	83	453	536

McLaws' Division

Drayton's Brigade	56	188	244
Barksdale's Brigade	35	266	301
Kershaw's Brigade	53	294	347
Semmes's Brigade	52	252	304
Cobb's Brigade	70	439	509

Anderson's Division

Wright's Brigade	16	187	203
Armistead's Brigade	5	30	35
Wilcox's Brigade	37	184	221
Pryor's Brigade	24	158	182
Featherston's Brigade	44	260	304
Mahone's Brigade	8	68	76
Total	795	4,621	5,416
Evans's Independent Brigade	47	262	309
Grand Total	1,567	8,725	10,292

Appendix E

DOCUMENT No. 1

Letter from Robert E. Lee to Jefferson Davis on invasion intentions:

HEADQUARTERS ALEXANDRIA AND LEESBURG ROAD,
Near Dranesville, September 3, 1862.

His Excellency President DAVIS,
Richmond, Va.:

Mr. PRESIDENT: The present seems to be the most propitious time since the commencement of the war for the Confederate Army to enter Maryland. The two grand armies of the United States that have been operating in Virginia, though now united, are much weakened and demoralized. Their new levies, of which I understand 60,000 men have already been posted in Washington, are not yet organized, and will take some time to prepare for the field. If it is ever desired to give material aid to Maryland and afford her an opportunity of throwing off the oppression to which she is now subject, this would seem the most favorable.

After the enemy had disappeared from the vicinity of Fairfax Court-House, and taken the road to Alexandria and Washington, I did not think it would be advantageous to follow him farther. I had no intention of attacking him in his fortifications, and am not prepared to invest them. If I possessed the necessary munitions, I should be unable to supply provisions for the troops. I therefore determined, while threatening the approaches to Washington, to draw the troops into Loudoun, where forage and some provisions can be obtained, menace their possession of the Shenandoah Valley, and if practicable, to cross into Maryland. The purpose, if discovered, will have the effect of carrying the enemy north of the Potomac, and if prevented, will not result in much evil.

The army is not properly equipped for an invasion of an enemy's territory. It lacks much of the material of war, is feeble in transportation, the animals being much reduced, and the men are poorly provided with clothes, and in thousands of instances are destitute of shoes. Still, we cannot afford to be idle, and though weaker than our opponents in men and military equipments, must endeavor to harass if we cannot destroy them. I am aware that the movement is attended with much risk, yet I do not consider success impossible, and shall endeavor to guard it from loss. As long as the army of the enemy are employed on this frontier I have no fears for the safety of Richmond, yet I earnestly recommend that advantage be taken of this period of comparative safety to place its defence, both by land and water, in the most perfect condition. A respectable force can be collected to defend its approaches by land, and the steamer *Richmond* I hope is now ready to clear the river of hostile vessels.

Should General [Braxton] Bragg find it impracticable to operate to advantage on his present frontier, his army, after leaving sufficient garrisons, could be advantageously employed in opposing the overwhelming numbers which it seems to be the intention of the enemy now to concentrate in Virginia.

I have already been told by prisoners that some of [General Don Carlos] Buell's cavalry have been joined to General Pope's army, and have reason to believe that the whole of McClellan's, the larger portions of Burnside's and Cox's, and a portion of [General David] Hunter's, are united to it.

What occasions me most concern is the fear of getting out of ammunition. I beg you will instruct the Ordnance Department to spare no pains in manufacturing a sufficient amount of the best kind, and to be particular in preparing that for the artillery, to provide three times as much of the long-range ammunition as of that for smooth-bore or short range guns. The points to which I desire the ammunition to be forwarded will be made known to the Department in time. If the Quartermaster's Department can furnish any shoes, it would be the greatest relief. We have entered upon September, and the nights are becoming cool.

I have the honor to be, with high respect, your obedient servant,

R. E. LEE
General.[1]

DOCUMENT NO. 2

Order from Secretary of War Edwin M. Stanton to Maj. Gen. Henry W. Halleck concerning organization of an army to pursue Lee (original in Lincoln's handwriting; referred to in preceding text as the order authorizing McClellan to take to the field):

WASHINGTON, D. C., *September* 3, 1862.
Ordered, that the General-in-Chief, Major-General Halleck, immediately commence, and proceed with all possible dispatch, to organize an army for active operations, from all the material within and coming within his control, independent of the forces he may deem necessary for the defence of Washington, when such active army shall take the field.

By order of the President:

EDWIN M. STANTON,
Secretary of War[2]

DOCUMENT NO. 3

Order from General Halleck to General McClellan to organize a "movable army" for the field:

WASHINGTON, *September* 3, 1862.
Major-General McCLELLAN, *Commanding, &c.:*
There is every probability that the enemy, baffled in his intended capture of Washington, will cross the Potomac, and make a raid into Maryland or Pennsylvania. A movable army must be immediately organized to meet him again in the field. You will, therefore, report the approximate force of each corps of the three armies now in the vicinity of Washington, which can be prepared in the next two days to take the field, and have them supplied and ready for that service.

H. W. HALLECK,
General-in-Chief.[3]

DOCUMENT NO. 4

Lee's General Orders, No. 102, defining preparations for invasion (equipment, supplies, stragglers):

GENERAL ORDERS,   HDQRS. ARMY OF NORTHERN VIRGINIA,
No. 102.   *Leesburg, Va., September* 4, 1862.
I. It is ordered and earnestly enjoined upon all commanders to reduce their transportation to a mere sufficiency to transport cooking utensils and the absolute necessaries of a regiment. All animals not actually employed for artillery, cavalry, or draught purposes will be left in charge of Lieutenant-Colonel Corley, chief quartermaster Army of Northern Virginia, to be recruited, the use of public animals, captured or otherwise, except for this service, being positively prohibited. Division, brigade, and regimental com-

manders, and officers in charge of artillery battalions, will give special attention to this matter. Batteries will select the best horses for use, turning over all others. Those batteries with horses too much reduced for service will be, men and horses, temporarily transferred by General [W. N.] Pendleton [Chief of Artillery] to other batteries, the guns and unserviceable horses being sent to the rear, the ammunition being turned in to reserve ordnance train. All cannoneers are positively prohibited from riding on the ammunition chests or guns.

II. This army is about to engage in most important operations, where any excesses committed will exasperate the people, lead to disastrous results, and enlist the populace on the side of the Federal forces in hostility to our own. Quartermasters and commissaries will make all arrangements for purchase of supplies needed by our army, to be issued to the respective commands upon proper requisitions, thereby removing all excuse for depredations.

III. A provost guard, under direction of Brig. Gen. L. A. Armistead, will follow in rear of the army, arrest stragglers, and punish summarily all depredators, and keep the men with their commands. Commanders of brigades will cause rear guards to be placed under charge of efficient officers in rear of their brigades, to prevent the men from leaving the ranks, right, left, front, or rear, this officer being held by brigade commanders to a strict accountability for proper performance of this duty.

IV. Stragglers are usually those who desert their comrades in peril. Such characters are better absent from the army on such momentous occasions as those about to be entered upon. They will, as bringing discredit upon our cause, as useless members of the service and as especially deserving odium, come under the special attention of the provost-marshal, and be considered as unworthy members of an army which has immortalized itself in the recent glorious and successful engagements against the enemy, and will be brought before a military commission to receive the punishment due to their misconduct. The gallant soldiers who have so nobly sustained our cause by heroism in battle will assist the commanding general in securing success by aiding their officers in checking the desire for straggling among their comrades.

By order of General R. E. Lee:

R. H. CHILTON
Assistant Adjutant-General.[4]

DOCUMENT NO. 5

Lee's General Orders, No. 103, (part II only) telling his men of other

Confederate victories and urging them to strive for victory in Maryland:

GENERAL ORDERS,   HDQRS. ARMY OF NORTHERN VIRGINIA,
No. 103.   *September* 6, 1862.
II. The general commanding takes pleasure in announcing to the brave soldiers of the Army of Northern Virginia the signal success of their comrades in arms in the West. The Confederate forces, under the command of Maj. Gen. E. Kirby Smith, defeated on August 30 the Federal forces commanded by General Nelson, capturing General Nelson and his staff, 3,000 prisoners, and all his artillery, small-arms, wagons, &c. This great victory is simultaneous with your own at Manassas. Soldiers, press onward! Let each man feel the responsibility now resting on him to pursue vigorously the success vouchsafed to us by Heaven. Let the armies of the East and the West vie with each other in discipline, bravery, and activity, and our brethren of our sister States will soon be released from tyranny, and our independence be established upon a sure and abiding basis.
By command of General R. E. Lee:

R. H. CHILTON,
Assistant Adjutant-General.[5]

DOCUMENT NO. 6

Letter from Lee to Davis discussing discipline in the army and measures to control it:

HEADQUARTERS,
Two Miles from Fredericktown, Md., September 7, 1862.
His Excellency President DAVIS,
Richmond, Va.:
Mr. President:
I find that the discipline of the army, which, from the manner of its organization, the necessity of bringing it into immediate service, its constant occupation and hard duty, was naturally defective, has not been improved by the forced marches and hard service it has lately undergone. I need not say to you that the material of which it is composed is the best in the world, and, if properly disciplined and instructed, would be able successfully to resist any force that could be brought against it. Nothing can surpass the gallantry and intelligence of the main body, but there are individuals who, from their backwardness in duty, tardiness of movement, and neglect of orders, do it no credit. These, if possible, should be removed from its rolls if they cannot be improved by correction.

Owing to the constitution of our court-martial, great delay and difficulty occur in correcting daily evils. We require more promptness and certainty of punishment. One of the greatest evils, from which many minor ones proceed, is the habit of straggling from the ranks. The higher officers feel as I do, and I believe have done all in their power to stop it. It has become a habit difficult to correct. With some, the sick and feeble, it results from necessity, but with the greater number from design. These latter do not wish to be with their regiments, nor to share in their hardships and glories. They are the cowards of the army, desert their comrades in times of danger, and fill the houses of the charitable and hospitable in the march. I know of no better way of correcting this great evil than by the appointment of a military commission of men known to the country, and having its confidence and support, to accompany the army constantly, with a provost-marshal and guard to execute promptly its decisions.

If, in addition, a proper inspector-general, with sufficient rank and standing, with assistants, could be appointed to see to the execution of orders, and to fix the responsibility of acts, great benefits and saving to the service would be secured. I know there is no law for carrying out these suggestions, but beg to call your attention to the subject, and ask, if this plan does not meet with your approval, that, in your better judgement, you will devise some other, for I assure you some remedy is necessary, especially now, when the army is in a State whose citizens it is our purpose to conciliate and bring with us. Every outrage upon their feelings and property should be checked.

I am, with high respect, your obedient servant,

R. E. LEE,
General.[6]

DOCUMENT NO. 7

Letter from Davis to Generals Lee, Bragg, and E. K. Smith containing proclamation of Confederate "motives and purposes" of invasion; one of three versions. (See Appendix B for commentary.):

RICHMOND, VA., *September* 7 [?], 1862.
SIRS: It is deemed proper that you should, in accordance with established usage announce by proclamation to the people of ——— the motives and purposes of your presence among them at the head of an invading army, and you are instructed in such proclamation to make known,

1st. That the Confederate Government is waging this war solely for self-defence, that it has no design of conquest or any other purpose than to secure peace and the abandonment by the United States of their pretensions to govern a people who have never been their subjects and who prefer self-government to a Union with them.

2nd. That this Government at the very moment of its inauguration, sent commissioners to Washington to treat for a peaceful adjustment of all differences, but that these commissioners were not received nor even allowed to communicate the object of their mission, and that on a subsequent occasion a communication from the President of the Confederacy to President Lincoln remained without answer, although a reply was promised by General Scott into whose hands the communication was delivered.

3rd. That among the pretexts urged for continuance of the War is the assertion that the Confederate Government desires to deprive the United States of the free navigation of the Western Rivers although the truth is that the Confederate Congress by public act, prior to the commencement of the War, enacted that "the peaceful navigation of the Mississippi River is hereby declared free to the citizens of any of the States upon its boundaries, or upon the borders of its navigable tributaries" — a declaration to which this Government has always been and still is ready to adhere.

4th. That now at a juncture when our arms have been successful, we restrict ourselves to the same just and moderate demand, that we made at the darkest period of our reverses, the simple demand that the people of the United States should cease to war upon us and permit us to pursue our own path to happiness, while they in peace pursue theirs.

5th. That we are debarred from the renewal of formal proposals for peace by having no reason to expect that they would be received with the respect mutually due by nations in their intercourse, whether in peace or in war.

6th. That under these circumstances we are driven to protect our own country by transferring the seat of war to that of an enemy who pursues us with a relentless and apparently aimless hostility; That our fields have been laid waste, our people killed, many homes made desolate, and that rapine and murder have ravaged our frontiers, that the sacred right of self defence demands that if such a war is to continue its consequences shall fall on those who persist in their refusal to make peace.

7th. That the Confederate army therefore comes to occupy the territory of their enemies and to make it the theater of hostilities. That with the people of ——— themselves rests the power to put an end to this invasion of their homes, for if unable to prevail on the Government of the United States to conclude a general peace, their own State Government in the exercise of its sovereignty can secure immunity from the desolating effects of warfare on the soil of the State by a separate treaty of peace which this Government will ever be ready to conclude on the most just and liberal basis.

8th.   That the responsibility thus rests on the people of ——— of continuing an unjust and oppressive warfare upon the Confederate States, a warfare which can never end in any other manner than that now proposed. With them is the option of preserving the blessings of peace, by the simple abandonment of the design of subjugating a people over whom no right of dominion has been ever conferred either by God or man.

JEFFERSON DAVIS.[7]

DOCUMENT NO. 8

Letter from Lee to Davis suggesting a Confederate proposal to the United States government for the recognition of Southern independence (Lee had not received the Davis proclamation when the following letter was written.):

HEADQUARTERS,
Near Fredericktown, Md., September 8, 1862.

His Excellency JEFFERSON DAVIS
President of the Confederate States, Richmond, Va.:

Mr. PRESIDENT: The present position of affairs, in my opinion, places it in the power of the Government of the Confederate States to propose with propriety to that of the United States the recognition of our independence. For more than a year both sections of the country have been devastated by hostilities which have brought sorrow and suffering upon thousands of homes, without advancing the objects which our enemies proposed to themselves in beginning the contest. Such a proposition, coming from us at this time, could in no way be regarded as suing for peace; but, being made when it is in our power to inflict injury upon our adversary, would show conclusively to the world that our sole object is the establishment of our independence and the attainment of an honorable peace. The rejection of this offer would prove to the country that the responsibility of the continuance of the war does not rest upon us, but that the party in power in the United States elect to prosecute it for purposes of their own. The proposal of peace would enable the people of the United States to determine at their coming elections whether they will support those who favor a prolongation of the war, or those who wish to bring it to a termination, which can but be productive of good to both parties without affecting the honor of either.

I have the honor to be, with high respect, your obedient servant,

R. E. LEE,
General.[8]

DOCUMENT NO. 9

Lee's proclamation to the people of Maryland, delivered in Frederick, September 8, 1862. The Davis proclamation had not yet arrived at Lee's headquarters when the following was issued:

HEADQUARTERS ARMY OF NORTHERN VIRGINIA,
Near Fredericktown, Md., September 8, 1862.

To the People of Maryland:

It is right that you should know the purpose that brought the army under my command within the limits of your State, so far as that purpose concerns yourselves. The people of the Confederate States have longed watched with the deepest sympathy the wrongs and outrages that have been inflicted upon the citizens of a commonwealth allied to the States of the South by the strongest social, political, and commercial ties. They have seen with profound indignation their sister State deprived of every right and reduced to the condition of a conquered province. Under the pretense of supporting the Constitution, but in violation of its most valuable provisions, your citizens have been arrested and imprisoned upon no charge and contrary to all forms of law. The faithful and manly protest against this outrage made by the venerable and illustrious Marylander, to whom in better days no citizen appealed for right in vain, was treated with scorn and contempt; the government of your chief city has been usurped by armed strangers; your legislature has been dissolved by the unlawful arrest of its members; freedom of the press and of speech has been suppressed; words have been declared offenses by an arbitrary decree of the Federal Executive, and citizens ordered to be tried by a military commission for what they may dare to speak. Believing that the people of Maryland possessed a spirit too lofty to submit to such a government, the people of the South have long wished to aid you in throwing off this foreign yoke, to enable you again to enjoy the inalienable rights of freemen, and restore independence and sovereignty to your State. In obedience to this wish, our army has come among you, and is prepared to assist you with the power of its arms in regaining the rights of which you have been despoiled.

This, citizens of Maryland, is our mission, so far as you are concerned. No constraint upon your free will is intended; no intimidation will be allowed within the limits of this army, at least. Marylanders shall once more enjoy their ancient freedom of thought and speech. We know no enemies among you, and will protect all, of every opinion. It is for you to decide your destiny freely and without constraint. This army will respect your choice, whatever it may be; and while the Southern people will rejoice to

welcome you to your natural position among them, they will only welcome
you when you come of your own free will.

R. E. LEE,

General, Commanding.[9]

DOCUMENT NO. 10

The best estimated time of the discovery of Lee's "lost dispatch" is 10:00
a.m., September 13, 1862, this in the words of one of the two men who
made the discovery, Sgt. John Bloss.[10] The next pinpointed reference to the
Confederate order is in the following message from McClellan to his chief
of cavalry:

HEADQUARTERS, ARMY OF THE POTOMAC,

Frederick, September 13, 1862 — 3 *p.m.*

Brigadier-General PLEASONTON:

GENERAL: The following order of march of the enemy is dated September 9.* General McClellan desires you to ascertain whether this order
of march has thus far been followed by the enemy. As the pass through the
Blue Ridge may be disputed by two columns [Hill and Longstreet], he desires you to approach it with great caution.

I am, general, very respectfully, your obedient servant,

R. B. MARCY,

Chief of Staff.

*Footnote: For order (here omitted), see paragraphs III to X, inclusive,
Vol. XIX, Part II, pp. 603, 604.[11] [This footnote refers to the copy of
Special Orders No. 191 directed to D. H. Hill reprinted in the *Official
Records.* The "two columns" reference in the above communication
clearly indicates that though McClellan had been informed of Longstreet's
movement to Hagerstown, he was accepting little of his intelligence. There
is little doubt that the "two columns," in McClellan's mind, were D. H.
Hill and Longstreet at Boonsboro as was indicated by Lee's orders.]

DOCUMENT NO. 11

McClellan's dispatch to Gen. William B. Franklin on the extreme left wing
of the Federal advance is one of the most interesting of the campaign.
Assuming that it was noon, at the latest, before the "lost orders" were
presented to McClellan, a total of six hours elapsed before the following
was written. This communication and its appendage plays a vital role in
the interpretation of both McClellan's and Franklin's actions:

HEADQUARTERS ARMY OF THE POTOMAC
Camp near Frederick, September 13, 1862 — 6.20 p.m.

Maj. Gen. W. B. FRANKLIN,
Commanding Sixth Corps:

GENERAL: I have now full information as to movements and intentions of the enemy. Jackson has crossed the Upper Potomac to capture the garrison at Martinsburg and cut off Miles' retreat toward the west. A division on the south side of the Potomac was to carry Loudoun Heights and cut off his retreat in that direction. McLaws, with his own command, and the division of R. H. Anderson, was to move to Boonsborough and Rohrersville to carry the Maryland Heights. The signal officers inform me that he is now in Pleasant Valley. The firing shows that Miles still holds out. Longstreet was to move to Boonsborough and there halt with the reserve corps, D. H. Hill to form the rear guard, Stuart's cavalry to bring up stragglers, &c. We have cleared out all the cavalry this side of the mountains and north of us.

The last I heard from Pleasonton he occupied Middletown, after several sharp skirmishes. A division of Burnside's command started several hours ago to support him. The whole of Burnside's command, including Hooker's corps, march this evening and early to-morrow morning, followed by the corps of Sumner and Banks and Sykes' division, upon Boonsborough, to carry that position. Couch has been ordered to concentrate his division and join you as rapidly as possible. Without waiting for the whole of that division to join, you will move at daybreak in the morning, by Jefferson and Burkittsville, upon the road to Rohrersville. I have reliable information that the mountain pass by this road is practicable for artillery and wagons. If this pass is not occupied by the enemy in force, seize it as soon as practicable, and debouch upon Rohrersville, in order to cut off the retreat of or destroy McLaws' command. If you find this pass held by the enemy in large force, make all your dispositions for the attack, and commence it about half an hour after you hear severe firing at the pass on the Hagerstown pike, where the main body will attack. Having gained the pass, your duty will be first to cut off, destroy, or capture McLaws' command and relieve Colonel Miles. If you effect this, you will order him to join you at once with all his disposable troops, first destroying the bridges over the Potomac, if not already done, and, leaving a sufficient garrison to prevent the enemy from passing the ford, you will then return by Rohrersville on the direct route to Boonsborough if the main column has not succeeded in its attack. If it has succeeded, take the road by Rohrersville to Sharpsburg and Williamsport, in order either to cut off the retreat of Hill and Longstreet toward the Potomac, or prevent the repassage of

Jackson. My general idea is to cut the enemy in two and beat him in detail. I believe I have sufficiently explained my intentions. I ask of you, at this important moment, all your intellect and the utmost activity that a general can exercise.

GEO. B. McCLELLAN,
Major-General, Commanding.[12]

[Supplemental volumes of the *Official Records* were published for the specific purpose of making public certain documents not received by the editors in time for inclusion in previously designated areas, i.e., dates, battles, campaigns. Volume LI, Part I offers what the editors indicate as an appendage to the above McClellan dispatch to Franklin. An editorial note states: "For portion of this [the following] communication here omitted, see Vol. XIX, Part I, p. 45 [the preceding]." For some unknown reason, McClellan failed to include this in his official report to the Secretary of War. The date and time of dispatch are listed the same as the preceding. It is herein reproduced as it appears in the *Official Records*. Research does not reveal whether it is a part of the first message or a postscript, nor can any explanation be found for McClellan's deletion of these important words from his report.]

HEADQUARTERS ARMY OF THE POTOMAC
Camp near Frederick, September 13, 1862 — 6.20 *p.m.*
Maj. Gen. W. B. FRANKLIN,
Commanding Sixth Corps:
   GENERAL:
*   *   *   *   *   *   *

Knowing my views and intentions, you are fully authorized to change any of the details of this order as circumstances may change, provided the purpose is carried out; that purpose being to attack the enemy in detail and beat him. General Smith's dispatch of 4 p.m. with your comments is received. If, with a full knowledge of all the circumstances, you consider it preferable to crush the enemy at Petersville before undertaking the movement I have directed, you are at liberty to do so, but you will readily perceive that no slight advantage should for a moment interfere with the decisive results I propose to gain. I cannot too strongly impress upon you the absolute necessity of informing me every hour during the day of your movements, and frequently during the night. Force your colonels to prevent straggling, and bring every available man into action. I think the force you have is, with good management, sufficient for the end in view. If you differ widely from me, and being on the spot you know better than I do the circumstances of the case, inform me at once, and I will do my

best to re-enforce you. Inform me at the same time how many more troops
you think you should have. Until 5 a.m. to-morrow general headquarters
will be at this place. At that hour they will move upon the main road to
Hagerstown.

I am, general, very respectfully, your obedient servant,

GEO. B. McCLELLAN,
Major-General, Commanding.[13]

DOCUMENT NO. 12

The following communication from Lee to McLaws would seem to support
the fact that Lee knew by 10 p.m. on September 13 that McClellan had a
copy of Special Orders No. 191 in his hands:

HEADQUARTERS ARMY OF NORTHERN VIRGINIA,
September 13, 1862 — 10 *p.m.*

General LAFAYETTE McLAWS,
Commanding, &c.:

GENERAL: General Lee directs me to say that, from reports reaching
him, he believes the enemy is moving toward Harper's Ferry to relieve the
force they have there. You will see, therefore, the necessity of expediting
your operations as much as possible. As soon as they are completed, he
desires you, unless you receive orders from General Jackson, to move your
force as rapidly as possible to Sharpsburg. General Longstreet will move
down to-morrow and take position on Beaver Creek, this side of Boonsborough. General Stuart has been requested to keep you informed of
the movements of the enemy.

Very respectfully, your obedient servant,

T. M. R. TALCOTT
Major and Aide-de-Camp.[14]

DOCUMENT NO. 13

At 11 p.m. on the night of September 13, nearly twelve hours following
the discovery of the "lost orders," McClellan informed army headquarters
in Washington:

FREDERICK CITY, MD., *September* 13, 1862 — 11 *p.m.*
(Received 1 p.m., September 14.)

Maj. Gen. H. W. HALLECK,
General-in-Chief:

An order from General R. E. Lee, addressed to General D. H. Hill, which has accidentally come into my hands this evening — the authenticity of which is unquestionable — discloses some of the plans of the enemy, and shows most conclusively that the main rebel army is now before us, including Longstreet's, Jackson's, the two Hills', McLaws', Walker's, R. H. Anderson's, and Hood's commands. That army was ordered to march on the 10th, and to attack and capture our forces at Harper's Ferry and Martinsburg yesterday, by surrounding them with such a heavy force that they conceived it impossible they could escape. They were also ordered to take possession of the Batimore and Ohio Railroad; afterward to concentrate again at Boonsborough or Hagerstown. That this was the plan of campaign on the 9th is confirmed by the fact that heavy firing has been heard in the direction of Harper's Ferry this afternoon, and the columns took the roads specified in the order. It may, therefore, in my judgement, be regarded as certain that this rebel army, which I have good reasons for believing amounts to 120,000 men or more, and know to be commanded by Lee in person, intended to attempt penetrating Pennsylvania. The officers told their friends here that they were going to Harrisburg and Philadelphia. My advance has pushed forward to-day, and overtaken the enemy on the Middletown and Harper's Ferry roads, and several slight engagements have taken place, in which our troops have driven the enemy from their position. A train of wagons, about three-quarters of a mile long, was destroyed to-day by the rebels in their flight. We took over 50 prisoners. This army marches forward early to-morrow morning, and will make forced marches, to endeavor to relieve Colonel Miles, but I fear, unless he makes a stout resistance, we may be too late. A report came in just this moment that Miles was attacked to-day and repulsed the enemy, but I do not know what credit to attach to the statement. I shall do everything in my power to save Miles if he still holds out. Portions of Burnside's and Franklin's corps moved forward this evening. I have received your dispatch of 10 a.m. You will perceive, from what I have stated, that there is but little probability of the enemy being in much force south of the Potomac. I do not, by any means, wish to be understood as undervaluing the importance of holding Washington. It is of great consequence, but upon the success of this army the fate of the nation depends. It was for this reason that I said everything else should be made subordinate to placing this army in proper condition to meet the large rebel force in our front. Unless General Lee has changed his plans, I expect a severe general engagement to-morrow. I feel confident that there is now no rebel force immediately threatening Washington or Baltimore, but that I have the mass of their troops to contend with, and they outnumber me when united.

GEO. B. McCLELLAN,
Major-General.[15]

DOCUMENT NO. 14

One hour after his message to Gen. Halleck, McClellan sent the following to the White House:

HEADQUARTERS, *Frederick, September* 13, 1862 — 12 *m.*
(Received 2.35 a.m., September 14.)
To the PRESIDENT:
I have the whole rebel force in front of me, but am confident, and no time shall be lost. I have a difficult task to perform, but with God's blessing will accomplish it. I think Lee has made a gross mistake, and that he will be severely punished for it. The army is in motion as rapidly as possible. I hope for a great success if the plans of the rebels remain unchanged. We have possession of Catoctin. I have all the plans of the rebels, and will catch them in their own trap if my men are equal to the emergency. I now feel that I can count on them as of old. All forces of Pennsylvania should be placed to co-operate at Chambersburg. My respects to Mrs. Lincoln. Received most enthusiastically by the ladies. Will send you trophies. All well, and with God's blessing will accomplish it.

GEO. B. McCLELLAN.[16]

DOCUMENT NO. 15

McClellan's "victory" message to Halleck following the Battle of South Mountain:

HEADQUARTERS ARMY OF THE POTOMAC,
Three mile beyond Middletown, Md., Sept. 14, 1862 — 9.40 *p.m.*
(Received 1 a.m., 15th.)
Major-General HALLECK,
General-in-Chief:
After a very severe engagement, the corps of Hooker and Reno have carried the heights commanding the Hagerstown road. The troops behaved magnificently. They never fought better. Franklin has been hotly engaged on the extreme left. I do not yet know the result, except that the firing indicated progress on his part. The action continued until after

dark, and terminated leaving us in possession of the entire crest. It has been a glorious victory. I cannot yet tell whether the enemy will retreat during the night or appear in increased force in the morning. I am hurrying up everything from the rear, to be prepared for any eventuality. I regret to add that the gallant and able General Reno is killed.

GEO. B. McCLELLAN,
Major-General, Commanding.[17]

DOCUMENT NO. 16

Evidence of Lee's decision to withdraw his army from Maryland before facing McClellan at Sharpsburg is illustrated in the following message to McLaws dated late on the day of the Battle of South Mountain:

HEADQUARTERS ARMY OF NORTHERN VIRGINIA,
September 14, 1862 — 8 *p.m.*

Major-General McLAWS,
  Commanding, &c.:
  GENERAL: The day has gone against us and this army will go by Sharpsburg and cross the river. It is necessary for you to abandon your position tonight. Send your trains not required on the road to cross the river. Your troops you must have well in hand to unite with this command, which will retire by Sharpsburg. Send forward officers to explore the way, ascertain the best crossing of the Potomac, and if you can find any between you and Shepherdstown leave Shepherdstown Ford for this command. Send an officer to report to me on the Sharpsburg road, where you are and what crossing you will take. You will of course bring Anderson's division with you.
  I am, sir, respectfully, your obedient servant,

R. H. CHILTON,
Assistant Adjutant-General.[18]

DOCUMENT NO. 17

Jackson's message to headquarters which may have changed Lee's mind about withdrawal into Virginia:

NEAR HALLTOWN,
September 14, 1862 — 8.15 p.m.

  COLONEL: Through God's blessing, the advance, which commenced this evening, has been successful thus far, and I look to Him for complete

success to-morrow. The advance has been directed to be resumed at dawn
to-morrow morning. I am thankful that our loss has been small. Your
dispatch respecting the movements of the enemy and the importance of
concentration has been received. Can you not connect the headquarters of
the army, by signal, with General McLaws?

T. J. JACKSON,
Major-General[19]

Col. R. H. CHILTON.

DOCUMENT NO. 18

The first of a series of correspondence between the British Prime Minister,
the Viscount Palmerston, and the Foreign Minister, Lord John Russell,
which, along with the Maryland Campaign of 1862, climaxed the question
of foreign intervention on the behalf of the Confederacy:

94 Piccadilly: September 14, 1862
My dear Russell, The detailed account given in the *Observer* to-day of
the battles of August 29 and 30 between the Confederates and the Federals
show that the latter got a very complete smashing; and it seems not altogether unlikely that still greater disasters await them, and that even
Washington or Baltimore may fall into the hands of the Confederates.
If this should happen, would it not be time for us to consider whether in
such a state of things England and France might not address the contending parties and recommend an arrangement upon the basis of separation?
Yours sincerely,

PALMERSTON.[20]

DOCUMENT NO. 19

Jackson's message to Lee following the surrender of Harpers Ferry:

NEAR 8 A.M., September 15, 1862.
GENERAL: Through God's blessing, Harper's Ferry and its garrison
are to be surrendered. As Hill's troops have borne the heaviest part in the
engagement, he will be left in command until the prisoners and public
property shall be disposed of, unless you direct otherwise. The other
forces can move off this evening as soon as they get their rations. To
what point shall they move? I write at this time in order that you may be
apprised of the condition of things. You may expect to hear from me

again to-day after I get more information respecting the number of prisoners, &c.

Respectfully,

T. J. JACKSON,
Major-General.[21]

General R. E. LEE.

DOCUMENT NO. 20

Lincoln's message to McClellan following South Mountain:

WAR DEPARTMENT,
Washington, September 15, 1862 — 2.45 *p.m.*

Major-General McCLELLAN:

Your dispatch of to-day received. God bless you and all with you. Destroy the rebel army if possible.

A. LINCOLN.[22]

DOCUMENT NO. 21

McClellan to Halleck on Lee's reaction to the Battle of South Mountain:

HEADQUARTERS ARMY OF THE POTOMAC,
Bolivar, Md., September 15, 1862 — 8 *a.m.*

Maj. Gen. H. W. HALLECK,
General-in-Chief:

I have just learned from General Hooker, in the advance, who states that the information is perfectly reliable that the enemy is making for Shepherdstown in a perfect panic; and General Lee last night stated publicly that he must admit they had been shockingly whipped. I am hurrying everything forward to endeavor to press their retreat to the utmost.

GEO. B. McCLELLAN,
Major-General.[23]

DOCUMENT NO. 22

Lee's message to his reserve artillery commander, Brig. Gen. Pendleton, early on the morning of battle clearly indicates that though he intended to give McClellan a fight, he kept one eye on a possible escape route into Virginia:

SHARPSBURG,
September 17, 1862 — 4.30 *a.m.*

Brigadier-General Pendleton,
          Commanding Artillery:

  GENERAL: I desire you to keep some artillery guarding each of the fords at Williamsport, Falling Waters and Shepherdstown, and have some infantry with it, if possible.
  Very respectfully, yours,

R. E. LEE,
General.[24]

DOCUMENT NO. 23

McClellan's only message to Washington concerning the battle:

HEADQUARTERS ARMY OF THE POTOMAC,
September 17, 1862 — 1.20 *p.m.* (Received 5 p.m.)

Maj. Gen. H. W. HALLECK,
          General-in-Chief:

  Please take military possession of the Chambersburg and Hagerstown Railroad, that our ammunition and supplies may be hurried up without delay. We are in the midst of the most terrible battle of the war — perhaps of history. Thus far it looks well, but I have great odds against me. Hurry up all the troops possible. Our loss has been terrific, but we have gained much ground. I have thrown the mass of the army on the left flank. Burnside is now attacking the right, and I hold my small reserve, consisting of Porter's (Fifth) corps, ready to attack the center as soon as the flank movements are developed. I hope that God will give us a glorious victory.

GEO. B. McCLELLAN,
Major-General, Commanding.[25]

DOCUMENT NO. 24

Lord Russell's reply to Prime Minister Palmerston's letter of the 14th:

Gotha: September 17, 1862
  My dear Palmerston, Whether the Federal army is destroyed or not, it is clear that it is driven back to Washington, and has made no progress in subduing the insurgent States. Such being the case, I agree with you that the time is come for offering mediation to the United States Government,

with a view to the recognition of the Independence of the Confederates. I agree further, that, in case of failure, we ought ourselves to recognise the Southern States as an independent State. For the purpose of taking so important a step, I think we must have a meeting of the Cabinet. The 23rd or 30th would suit me for the meeting.

We ought then, if we agree on such a step, to propose it first to France, and then, on the part of England and France, to Russia and other powers, as a measure decided upon by us.

We ought to make ourselves safe in Canada, not by sending more troops there, but by concentrating those we have in a few defensible posts befor the winter sets in.

J. RUSSELL.[26]

DOCUMENT NO. 25

On the morning after the Battle of Antietam, McClellan sent the following message to Gen. Halleck:

HEADQUARTERS,
Keedysville, Md., September 18, 1862 — 8 *a.m.*
Maj. Gen. H. W. HALLECK,
General-in-Chief, U. S. Army:
The battle of yesterday continued for fourteen hours, and until after dark. We held all we gained, except a portion of the extreme left; that was obliged to abandon a part of what it had gained. Our losses very heavy, especially in general officers. The battle will probably be renewed to-day. Send all the troops you can by the most expeditious route.

GEO. B. McCLELLAN,
Major-General, Commanding.[27]

DOCUMENT NO. 26

McClellan's report to Halleck on Lee's withdrawal from the field:

HEADQUARTERS ARMY OF THE POTOMAC,
September 19, 1862 — 8.30 *a.m.* (Received 11 a.m.)
Maj. Gen. H. W. HALLECK,
General-in-Chief:
But little occurred yesterday except skirmishing, being fully occupied in replenishing ammunition, taking care of wounded, &c. Last night the enemy abandoned his position, leaving his dead and wounded in the field.

We are again in pursuit. I do not yet know whether he is falling back to an interior position or crossing the river. We may safely claim a complete victory.

GEO. B. McCLELLAN,
Major-General.[28]

DOCUMENT NO. 27

McClellan claims a complete victory:

HEADQUARTERS ARMY OF THE POTOMAC,
September 19, 1862 — 10.30 a.m. (Received 11 a.m.)
Maj. Gen. H. W. HALLECK,
General-in-Chief:
Pleasonton is driving the enemy across the river. Our victory was complete. The enemy is driven back into Virginia. Maryland and Pennsylvania are now safe.

GEO. B. McCLELLAN,
Major-General.[29]

DOCUMENT NO. 28

First of a long series of excuses McClellan offered Halleck for not pursuing the Confederate army (paragraph one only):

McCLELLAN'S HEADQUARTERS,
Near the Potomac, September 22, 1862 — 12 *noon.*
Major-General HALLECK,
General-in-Chief:
When I was assigned to the command of this army in Washington, it was suffering under the disheartening influence of defeat. It had been greatly reduced by casualties in General Pope's campaign, and its efficiency had been much impaired. The sanguinary battles fought by these troops at South Mountain and Antietam Creek have resulted in a loss to us of 10 general officers and many regimental and company officers, besides a large number of enlisted men. The army corps have been badly cut up and scattered by the overwhelming numbers brought against them in the battle of the 17th instant, and the entire army has been greatly exhausted by unavoidable overwork, hunger, and want of sleep and rest. When the enemy recrossed the Potomac the means of transportation at my disposal was inadequate to furnish a single day's supply of subsistence in

advance. Under these circumstances I did not feel authorized to cross the river in pursuit of the retreating enemy, and thereby place that stream — which is liable at any time to rise above a fording stage — between this army and its base of supply. As soon as the exigencies of the service will admit of it, this army should be reorganized. It is absolutely necessary, to secure its efficiency, that the old skeleton regiments should be filled up at once, and officers appointed to supply the numerous existing vacancies. There are instances where captains are commanding regiments, and companies without a single commissioned officer.

GEO. B. McCLELLAN,
Major-General.[30]

DOCUMENT NO. 29

A continuation of the Palmerston-Russell correspondence; the news of Antietam had not yet arrived in England:

Broadlands: September 23, 1862

My dear Russell, Your plan of proceedings about the mediation between the Federals and Confederates seems to be excellent. Of course, the offer would be made to both the contending parties at the same time; for, though the offer would be as sure to be accepted by the Southerns as was the proposal of the Prince of Wales by the Danish Princess, yet, in the one case as in the other, there are certain forms which it is decent and proper to go through.

A question would occur whether, if the two parties were to accept the mediation, the fact of our mediating would not of itself be tantamount to an acknowledgement of the Confederate as an independent State.

Might it not be well to ask Russia to join England and France in the offer of mediation? She might probably decline, but we should have paid her a compliment and have shown confidence in her.

We should be better without her in the mediation, because she would be too favourable to the North; but on the other hand her participation in the offer might render the North the more willing to accept it.

The after communication to the other European powers would be quite right, although they would be too many for mediation.

As to the time of making the offer, if France and Russia agree, — and France, we know, is quite ready, and only waiting for our concurrence — events may be taking place which might render it desirable that the offer should be made before the middle of October.

It is evident that a great conflict is taking place to the north-west of

Washington, and its issue must have a great effect on the state of affairs. If the Federals sustain a great defeat, they may be at once ready for mediation, and the iron should be struck while it is hot. If, on the other hand, they should have the best of it, we may wait awhile and see what may follow.

Yours sincerely,

PALMERSTON[31]

DOCUMENT NO. 30

Palmerston to Russell on October 2nd, after news of Antietam had reached London. Though there is still interest in mediation, the results of the Maryland Campaign has caused some serious reservations:

October 2,

My dear Russell, There is no doubt that the offer of Mediation upon the basis of Separation would be accepted by the South. Why should it not be accepted? It would give the South in principle the points for which they are fighting. The refusal, if refusal there was, would come from the North, who would be unwilling to give up the principle for which they have been fighting so long as they had a reasonable expectation that by going on fighting they could carry their point. The condition of things therefore which would be favourable to an offer of mediation would be great success of the South against the North. That state of things seemed ten days ago to be approaching. Its advance has been lately checked, but we do not yet know the real course of recent events, and still less can we foresee what is about to follow. Ten days or a fortnight more may throw a clearer light upon future prospects.

As regards possible resentment on the part of the Northerns following upon an acknowledgment of the Independence of the South, it is quite true that we should have less to care about that resentment in the spring when communication with Canada was open, and when our naval force could more easily operate upon the American coast, than in winter when we are cut off from Canada and the American coast is not so safe.

But if the acknowledgment were made at one and the same time by England, France and some other Powers, the Yankees would probably not seek a quarrel with us alone, and would not like one against a European Confederation. Such a quarrel would render certain and permanent that Southern Independence the acknowledgment of which would have caused it.

The first communication to be made by England and France to the contending parties might be, not an absolute offer of mediation but a friendly suggestion whether the time was not come when it might be well for the two parties to consider whether the war, however long continued, could lead to any other result than separation; and whether it might not therefore be best to avoid the great evils which must necessarily flow from a prolongation of hostilities by at once coming to an agreement to treat upon that principle of separation which must apparently be the inevitable result of the contest, however long it may last.

The best thing would be that the two parties should settle details by direct negotiation with each other, though perhaps with the rancorous hatred now existing between them this might be difficult. But their quarrels in negotiation would do us no harm if they did not lead to a renewal of war. An armistice, if not accompanied by a cessation of blockades, would be all in favour of the North, especially if New Orleans remained in the hands of the North.

The whole matter is full of difficulty, and can only be cleared up by some more decided events between the contending armies.

PALMERSTON.[32]

DOCUMENT NO. 31

Nearly three weeks following Antietam, Halleck sent the following telegram to McClellan:

WASHINGTON, D. C., *October* 6, 1862.

Major-General McCLELLAN:

I am instructed to telegraph you as follows: The President directs that you cross the Potomac and give battle to the enemy or drive him south. Your army must move now while the roads are good. If you cross the river between the enemy and Washington, and cover the latter by your operation, you can be re-enforced with 30,000 men. If you move up the Valley of the Shenandoah, not more than 12,000 or 15,000 can be sent to you. The President advises the interior line, between Washington and the enemy, but does not order it. He is very desirous that your army move as soon as possible. You will immediately report what line you adopt and when you intend to cross the river; also to what point the re-enforcements are to be sent. It is necessary that the plan of your operations be positively determined on before orders are given for building bridges and repairing railroads.

I am directed to add that the Secretary of War and the General-in-Chief fully concur with the President in these instructions.

H. W. HALLECK,
General-in-Chief.[33]

DOCUMENT NO. 32

The Executive Order removing McClellan from command:

EXECUTIVE MANSION,
Washington, November 5, 1862.

By direction of the President, it is ordered that Major-General McClellan be relieved from the command of the Army of the Potomac, and that Major-General Burnside take command of that army. Also that Major-General Hunter take command of the corps in said army which is now commanded by General Burnside. That Major-General Fitz John Porter be relieved from the command of the corps he now commands in said army, and that Major-General Hooker take command of said corps.

The General-in-Chief is authorized, in [his] discretion, to issue an order substantially as the above, forthwith, or so soon as he may deem proper.

A. LINCOLN.[34]

DOCUMENT NO. 33

Halleck's direct order to McClellan, the order which ended his military career:

HEADQUARTERS OF THE ARMY,
Washington, November 5, 1862.

Major-General McCLELLAN, *Commanding, &c.*:

GENERAL: On receipt of the order of the President, sent herewith, you will immediately turn over your command to Major-General Burnside, and repair to Trenton, N. J., reporting, on your arrival at that place, by telegraph, for further orders.

Very respectfully, your obedient servant,

H. W. HALLECK,
General-in-Chief.[35]

Notes

<small>CHAPTER</small> 1

1. *War of the Rebellion: A Compilation of the Official Records of the Union and Confederate Armies* (70 vols. in 127 and index, Washington, 1880-1901), Series I, Volume II, p. 753. (Hereafter cited as *O.R.* All references are from Series I unless otherwise identified. Volume XIX, the most frequently cited, has two parts, thus *O.R.*, XIX, I, p. 100 signifies page 100 of the first part of Volume XIX, Series I.)
2. *O.R.*, V, p. 42; McClellan, George B., *McClellan's Own Story* (New York, 1887), p. 67. (Hereafter cited as *M.O.S.*)
3. *M.O.S.*, p. 67fn.
4. *Ibid.*, p. 136.
5. Rhodes, James Ford, *History of the United States* (7 vols., New York, 1893-1906), III, p. 493.
6. *M.O.S.*, p. 68.
7. Nicolay, John G., and John Hay, *Abraham Lincoln: A History* (10 vols., New York, 1890), IV, p. 444.
8. *Battles and Leaders of the Civil War* (4 vols., New York, 1956), II, pp. 112, 113. (Hereafter cited as *B.&L.*)
9. *M.O.S.*, pp. 82, 85.
10. *Ibid.*, p. 84.
11. *Ibid.*, pp. 82, 83.
12. *M.O.S.*, p. 85.
13. *Ibid.*, pp. 84-86.
14. *Ibid.*, p. 173.
15. *Ibid.*, p. 83.
16. *Ibid.*, p. 72.
17. Johnston, Joseph E., *Narrative of Military Operations* (New York, 1874), p. 81.
18. *O.R.*, XI, III, p. 3.
19. *Ibid.*, V, pp. 884, 886.
20. *Ibid.*, p. 9.
21. *Harper's Weekly*, August 24, 1861.
22. Williams, Kenneth P., *Lincoln Finds a General* (5 vols., New York, 1949-1959), I, p. 130. (All references cited from Vol. I.)
23. *M.O.S.*, pp. 87, 176.
24. *Ibid.*, p. 168.
25. *Lincoln and the Civil War in the Diaries and Letters of John Hay*, Tyler Dennett, ed. (New York, 1939), p. 27. (Hereafter cited as Dennett.)

26. *The Collected Works of Abraham Lincoln*, Roy P. Basler, ed. (8 vols. and index, New Brunswick, N. J., 1953), V, pp. 50, 51. (Hereafter cited as *Collected Works*. All references cited from Vol. V.)

27. Nicolay and Hay, *op. cit.*, IV, p. 468.

28. *Collected Works*, pp. 34, 35.

29. *Ibid*, pp. 111, 112.

30. *Diary of a Union Lady*, Harold Earl Hammond, ed. (New York, 1962), p. 98.

31. *M.O.S.*, p. 150.

32. *Ibid.*, p. 153.

33. *Collected Works*, pp. 120-124.

34. *M.O.S.*, p. 195.

35. *Ibid.*, p. 196.

36. *Ibid.*

37. *Collected Works*, pp. 149, 150.

38. New York *Tribune*, March 13, 14, 1862; *O.R.*, V, p. 52.

39. *Collected Works*, p. 155.

40. McClellan, George B., *Report on the Organization and Campaigns of the Army of the Potomac* (New York, 1864), p. 129. (Hereafter cited as *McClellan's Report.*)

41. *O.R.*, XI, III, pp. 60, 61.

42. *McClellan's Report*, p. 160.

43. *Collected Works*, pp. 184, 185.

44. Williams, T. Harry, *McClellan, Sherman and Grant* (New Brunswick, N. J., 1962), pp. 24, 25.

45. *M.O.S.*, p. 310.

46. *Ibid.*, p. 150.

47. Myers, William Starr, *General George Brinton McClellan, A Study in Personality* (New York, 1934), p. 399.

48. McClure, Alexander K., *Abraham Lincoln and Men of War-Times* (Philadelphia, 1892), p. 216.

49. Michie, Peter S., *General McClellan* (New York, 1915), p. 241.

50. *Collected Works*, p. 182.

51. *M.O.S.*, p. 308.

52. *O.R.*, XI, III, pp. 479-484.

53. *Ibid.*, p. 456.

54. *Colected Works*, p. 185.

55. *M.O.S.*, pp. 398, 408.

56. Williams, T. Harry, *Lincoln and His Generals* (New York, 1952), pp. 106, 107.

57. George B. McClellan Papers, Library of Congress, Manuscript Division, McClellan to S. L. M. Barlow, March 16, 1862. (Hereafter cited as McClellan Papers.)

58. *O.R.*, IX, p. 392.

59. *M.O.S.*, p. 389.

60. *Collected Works*, pp. 272, 273.

61. Freeman, Douglas Southall, *R. E. Lee, A Biography* (4 vols., New York, 1934-1935), II, pp. 77, 78fn. (All references cited from Vol. II.)

62. *B.&L.*, II, p. 404.

63. *M.O.S.*, p. 392.
64. *Collected Works*, p. 286.
65. McClellan Papers, McClellan to Stanton, June 26, 1862.
66. *O.R.*, XI, III, p. 266.
67. *M.O.S.*, p. 425.
68. George Gordon Meade, *The Life and Letters of George Gordon Meade* (2 vols., New York, 1913), I, p. 345. (All references cited from Vol. I.)
69. *Collected Works*, pp. 289, 290.
70. *M.O.S.*, p. 425.
71. *O.R.*, XI, III, p. 281.
72. *Collected Works*, p. 301.
73. *Ibid.*, p. 303, 306.
74. *M.O.S.*, p. 485.
75. Thomas, Benjamin P. and Harold M. Hyman, *Stanton: The Life and Times of Lincoln's Secretary of War* (New York, 1962), p. 211.
76. *McClellan's Report*, p. 295.
77. *M.O.S.*, p. 496.
78. *O.R.*, XI, I, p. 82.
79. *M.O.S.*, p. 512.
80. *Ibid.*, p. 513.
81. *Ibid.*, p. 530.
82. Welles, Gideon, *Diary of Gideon Welles* (3 vols., Boston, 1911), I, p. 104. (Hereafter cited as *Welles' Diary*. All references cited from Vol. I.)
83. *M.O.S.*, p. 532.
84. *O.R.*, XI, I, p. 103.
85. *B.&L.*, II, p. 549.

CHAPTER 2

1. *O.R.*, XIX, II, p. 590.
2. Alexander, E. P., *Military Memoirs of a Confederate*, T. Harry Williams, ed. (Bloomington, Ind., 1962), p. 220.
3. *O.R.*, XIX, II, p. 590.
4. *Ibid.*
5. Carman, Ezra A., *History of the Civil War, Maryland Campaign, September, 1862* (Library of Congress, Manuscript Division), Chap. I, p. 1; Chap. II, p. 10.
6. *O.R.*, XIX, II, pp. 590, 591.
7. *Ibid.*, p. 591.
8. William Allan Papers, Southern Historical Collection, University of North Carolina Library, Chapel Hill, N. C., Col. William Allan of the faculty of Washington College, Lexington, Virginia, Conversations with Robert E. Lee, Febraury 15, 1868. (Hereafter cited as Allan Papers.)
9. *O.R.*, XIX, II, p. 592.
10. Richmond *Examiner*, July 21, 1862.
11. Nevins, Allan, *The War for the Union* (2 vols., New York, 1959-1960), II, *War Becomes Revolution*, 1862-1863, pp. 216, 217. (All references cited from Vol. II.)

12. Vandiver, Frank E., *Basic History of the Confederacy* (Princeton, N. J., 1962), p.70.
13. *Jefferson Davis, Constitutionalist,* Dunbar Rowland, ed. (10 vols., Jackson, Miss., 1923), V, pp. 338, 339. (Hereafter cited as Rowland.)
14. Richmond *Dispatch,* August 11, 1862.
15. *Ibid.,* September 10, 1862.
16. Charleston *Mercury,* September 6, 1862.
17. Richmond *Examiner,* September 8, 1862.
18. Henderson, G. F. R., Col., *Stonewall Jackson and the American Civil War* (New York, 1961), p. 493.
19. Allan Papers, April 15, 1868.
20. *M.O.S.,* p. 535.
21. *Ibid.,* p. 534.
22. *Ibid.,* p. 535.
23. *Ibid.,* p. 566.
24. McClellan Papers, McClellan to his wife, September 2, 1862.
25. *B.&L.,* II, p. 551.
26. *M.O.S.,* p. 549.
27. *Welles' Diary,* p. 113.
28. Dennett, *op. cit.,* p. 47.
29. Gorham, George C., *Life and Public Services of Edwin M. Stanton* (2 vols., Boston, 1899), II, pp. 38, 39.
30. *Welles' Diary,* pp. 94, 102.
31. Welles, Gideon, *Lincoln and Seward* (New York, 1874), pp. 193, 194.
32. *Welles' Diary,* p. 104.
33. Hendrick, Burton J., *Lincoln's War Cabinet* (Boston, 1946), p. 316; *Welles' Diary,* p. 105; Chase, Salmon P., *Diary and Correspondence, In American Historical Association, Annual Report for 1902* (2 vols., Washington, 1903), II, p. 65.(Al references cited from Vol. II.)
34. *Welles' Diary,* p. 112.
35. Chase, *op. cit.,* pp. 76, 77.
36. *Report of the Joint Committee on the Conduct of the War,* 37th Congress, 3d Session (3 vols., Washington, 1863), I, Part I, Army of the Potomac, pp. 451, 453.
37. *M.O.S.,* p. 567.
38. *Welles' Diary,* p. 124.
39. *O.R.,* XIX, II, p. 169.
40. *Ibid.*
41. Williams, T. Harry, *Lincoln and His Generals,* p. 165.
42. *M.O.S.,* p. 551; Douglas, Henry Kyd, *I Rode With Stonewall* (Chapel Hill, N. C., 1940), p. 177.
43. *O.R.,* XIX, II, pp. 189, 212, 216.
44. *Ibid.,* XIX, I, p. 25.
45. *Ibid.,* XIX, II, p. 545.
46. Chase, *op. cit.,* p. 65.
47. *M.O.S.,* p. 566.
48. Cox, Jacob Dolson, *Military Reminiscences of the Civil War* (2 vols., New York, 1900), I, p. 245. (All references cited from Vol. I.)
49. *B.&L.,* II, p. 490.

50. *Ibid.,* pp. 550, 551fn.
51. Cox, *op. cit.,* p. 243.
52. *M.O.S.,* p. 91.
53. *Ibid.,* p. 567.
54. *B.&L.,* II, p. 550fn.
55. Francis Chaning Barlow Papers, Massachusetts Historical Society, Boston, Mass., Barlow to his family, September 6, 1862.
56. *M.O.S.,* p. 567.
57. McClellan Papers, McClellan to Col. E. D. Townsend, July 5, 1861.
58. Meade, *op. cit.,* p. 307.
59. Nicolay and Hay, *op. cit.,* VI, p. 28.
60. Dyer, Frederick H., *A Compendium of the War of the Rebellion* (3 vols., New York, 1959), I, p. 284. (All references cited from Vol. I.)
61. *M.O.S.,* p. 553.
62. *B.&L.,* II, p. 542.
63. Dyer, *op. cit.,* pp. 339, 340.
64. *M.O.S.,* p. 550.
65. *Ibid.,* p. 551.
66. Starr, Louis M., *Bohemian Brigade* (New York, 1954), p. 135.

CHAPTER 3

1. *O.R.,* XIX, II, pp. 590, 591.
2. *B.&L.,* II, p. 663.
3. [Cooke, John Esten], *The Life of Stonewall Jackson,* by a Virginian (Richmond, 1863), p. 195.
4. Richmond *Dispatch,* September 8, 1862.
5. *O.R.,* XIX, II, p. 591.
6. *Ibid.*
7. Freeman, Douglas Southall, *Lee's Lieutenants* (3 vols., New York, 1942-1944), II, p. 720. (All references cited from Vol. II.)
8. Longstreet, James, *From Manassas to Appomattox* (Philadelphia, 1896), p. 192; Sorrel, G. Moxley, Brig. Gen., C. S. A., *Recollections of a Confederate Staff Officer,* Bell Irvin Wiley, ed. (Jackson, Tenn., 1958), pp. 96, 97.
9. Douglas, *op. cit.,* p. 148.
10. Sorrel, *op. cit.,* p. 97.
11. Hood, John Bell, *Advance and Retreat,* Richard N. Current, ed. (Bloomington, Ind., 1959), p. 38.
12. Eliot, Ellsworth, Jr., *West Point in the Confederacy* (New York, 1941), p. 244.
13. *Century Magazine,* Vol. 70, No. 2, p. 258fn.
14. Cooke, *op. cit.,* p. 341.
15. *B.&L.,* II, p. 620fn.
16. Owen, William Miller, *In Camp and Battle with the Washington Artillery of New Orleans* (Boston, 1885), p. 130.
17. *Southern Historical Society Papers* (52 vols., Richmond, 1876-1959), X, p. 507. (Hereafter cited as *S.H.S.P.*)

18. *Berry Benson's Civil War Book*, Susan Williams Benson, ed. (Athens, Ga., 1962), p. 25. (Hereafter cited as Benson.)

19. *O.R.*, XIX, II, p. 606.

20. Cooke, *op. cit.*, p. 341.

21. *O.R.*, XIX, II, p. 590.

22. Charleston *Courier*, September 3, 1862.

23. Wiley, Bell Irvin, *The Life of Johnny Reb* (Indianapolis, 1943), p. 120.

24. Taylor, Richard, *Destruction and Reconstruction: Personal Experiences of the Late War* (New York, 1879), p. 36.

25. Freeman, *Lee's Lieutenants*, p. 150.

26. Longstreet, Helen Dortch, *In the Path of Lee's "Old War Horse"* (Atlanta, 1917), p. 22.

27. Richmond *Dispatch*, October 9, 1862.

28. *B.&L.*, II, p. 607.

29. *Histories of the Several Regiments and Battalions from North Carolina in the Great War*, 1861-1865, Walter Clark, ed. (5 vols., Raleigh and Greensboro, 1901), II, pp. 293, 296. (Hereafter cited as *North Carolina Regiments.*)

30. Walcott, Charles F., *History of the Twenty-First Regiment Massachusetts Volunteers in the War for the Preservation of the Union, 1861-1865* (Boston, 1882), p. 192.

31. Joseph Clay Stiles Papers, Henry E. Huntington Library, San Marino, Calif., Stiles to his daughter, September 30, 1862.

32. *O.R.*, XIX, II, p. 606.

33. *Ibid.*, p. 597.

34. *Ibid.*, pp. 592, 593.

35. Walcott, *op. cit.*, p. 188.

36. Longstreet, James, *op. cit.*, p. 199.

37. *Confederate Military History*, Clement A. Evans, ed. (12 vols., New York, 1962), III, p. 336. (Hereafter cited as *C.M.H.*); Von Borcke, Heros, *Memoirs of the Confederate War for Independence* (2 vols., New York, 1938), I, p. 185. (All references cited from Vol. I.)

38. Jed Hotchkiss Diary, Library of Congress, Manuscript Division, Transcript Book VI, p. 83, September 5, 1862. (Hereafter cited as Hotchkiss Diary. All references cited from Book VI.)

39. Von Borcke, *op. cit.*, p. 185.

40. *B.&L.*, I, p. 238fn.

41. Hotchkiss Diary, p. 83.

42. Ankrum, Freeman, Rev., *Maryland and Pennsylvania Historical Sketches* (West Newton, Pa., 1947), p. 111.

43. *O.R.*, XIX, II, p. 596.

44. The story of Keedysville's duplicity cannot be documented. It is one of the many Antietam legends handed down through the years. The older families of this small community will, to this day, claim it factual.

45. Owen, *op. cit.*, p. 130.

46. Douglas, *op. cit.*, p. 148.

47. Owen, *op. cit.*, pp. 130, 131.

48. Von Borcke, *op. cit.*, pp. 185-187.

49. Dabney, Robert L., *Life and Campaigns of Lieut.-Gen. Thomas J. Jackson* (New York, 1866), p. 149.
50. Douglas, *op. cit.*, p. 149.
51. *Ibid.*, pp. 149, 181.
52. Carman, *op. cit.*, Chap. 3, p. 7.
53. Douglas, *op. cit.*, pp. 149, 150.
54. Jackson, Mary Anna (Mrs. Thomas Jonathan Jackson), *Memoirs of Stonewall Jackson* (Louisville, 1895), p. 332.
55. *Ibid.*, p. 346.
56. *The Wartime Papers of R. E. Lee*, Clifford Dowdey and Louis H. Manarin, eds. (Boston, 1961), p. 296.
57. *O.R.*, XIX, II, p. 596.
58. *C.M.H.*, II, pp. 90, 91.
59. *O.R.*, XIX, II, pp. 601, 602.
60. *Ibid.*, p. 596.
61. Nevins, *op. cit.*, p. 217.
62. Carman, *op. cit.*, Chap. 3, p. 21.
63. Hill, D. H. [Jr.], *A History of North Carolina in the War Between the States* (2 vols., Raleigh, 1926), II, p. 339.
64. Richmond *Dispatch*, September 15, 1862.
65. *S.H.S.P.*, XII, pp. 503, 504.
66. Lee, Fitzhugh, *General Lee* (New York, 1894), p. 200.
67. *The Rebellion Record: A Diary of American Events*, Frank Moore, ed. (11 vols., New York, 1862-1871), V, Doc. 202, p. 606. (Hereafter cited as *Rebellion Record*. All references cited from Vol. V.)
68. *Ibid.*, p. 606.
69. Owen, *op. cit.*, p. 131.
70. *O.R.*, XIX, II, p. 602.
71. *Rebellion Record*, Doc. 202, p. 607.
72. Reminiscences of George W. Shreve in the Stuart Horse Artillery, Virginia State Library, Richmond, Va.
73. Von Borcke, *op. cit.*, p. 189.
74. Manakee, Harold R., *Maryland in the Civil War* (Baltimore, 1961), p. 67.
75. New York *Tribune*, September 13, 1862.
76. *Rebellion Record*, Doc. 202, p. 606.
77. Edward S. Bragg Papers, State Historical Society of Wisconsin, Madison, Wisc., Bragg to his wife, September 21, 1862. (Hereafter cited as Bragg Papers.)
78. *S.H.S.P.*, X, p. 511.
79. *Ibid.*, pp. 508, 509.
80. *Ibid.*, XXXI, p. 40.
81. Letter of James Gillette of the 71st New York State Militia, later of the 4th Maryland Volunteers, dated September 13, 1862. From the collection of Mrs. Amy G. Bassett, Bluff Head-Huletts Landing, New York.
82. *Harper's Weekly*, September 27, 1862.
83. Von Borcke, *op. cit.*, pp. 193-197.
84. Richmond *Dispatch*, September 9, 11, 13, 1862.
85. *Ibid.*, September 17, 1862.

CHAPTER 4

1. *B.&L.*, II, p. 605.
2. *Ibid.*, pp. 605, 606.
3. *Ibid.*, p. 604.
4. *Ibid.*
5. *O.R.*, XIX, I, p. 43.
6. Longstreet, James, *op. cit.*, pp. 201, 202.
7. *B.&L.*, II, p. 663.
8. *Ibid.*
9. *Ibid.*
10. Robert L. Dabney Papers, Union Theological Seminary Library, Richmond, Va., Letter from D. H. Hill to Dabney, July 21, 1864.
11. Longstreet, James, *op. cit.*, p. 213.
12. *B.&L.*, II, p. 607.
13. See Illustrations.
14. *S.H.S.P.*, VII, p. 437.
15. Douglas, *op. cit.*, pp. 151, 155.
16. Ankrum, *op. cit.*, p. 65.
17. Douglas, *op. cit.*, pp. 151, 152.
18. *Welles' Diary*, p. 65.
19. Sandburg, Carl, *Abraham Lincoln, The War Years* (4 vols., New York, 1939), I, p. 233.
20. *O.R.*, XIX, II, pp. 254, 255.
21. Quoted in the Richmond *Dispatch*, September 16, 1862.
22. Small, A. R., Major, *The Sixteenth Maine Regiment* (Portland, 1886), pp. 33, 38.
23. *Ibid.*
24. *Ibid.*, pp. 34, 35, 39.
25. *O.R.*, XIX, I, pp. 25, 26, 42.
26. Allan Papers, February 15, 1868.
27. *O.R.*, XIX, II, p. 179.
28. *Ibid.*, p. 195.
29. *Ibid.*, p. 200.
30. *Ibid.*, p. 198.
31. *Ibid.*, p. 201.
32. Richmond *Dispatch*, September 17, 1862.
33. New York *Tribune*, September 8, 1862.
34. Cincinnati *Daily Gazette*, June 27, 1861.
35. *New York Times*, December 4, 1861.
36. New York *Tribune*, September 8, 1862.
37. *O.R.*, XIX, II, p. 219.
38. Pinkerton, Allan, *The Spy of the Rebellion* (New York, 1883), p. 567.
39. Cox, *op. cit.*, p. 250.
40. *Report of the Joint Committee on the Conduct of the War*, 38th Congress, 2d Session (Washington, 1865), p. 74.
41. *O.R.*, XIX, II, p. 195.
42. New York *Herald*, September 9, 1862.
43. *O.R.*, XIX, I, p. 67.

44. *Ibid.*, XIX, II, pp. 452, 453.
45. *Ibid.*, p. 254.
46. *Ibid.*
47. McClure, *op. cit.*, p. 182.
48. *O.R.*, XIX, II, p. 255.
49. *Ibid.*, p. 269.
50. *Ibid.*, p. 270.
51. *Ibid.*, XXI, I, p. 89.
52. *Ibid.*, XI, II, p. 277.
53. *The Land We Love* (6 vols., Charlotte, N. C., 1866-1869), IV, p. 276. (All references cited from Vol. IV.)
54. Small, *op. cit.*, pp. 33, 34.
55. Livermore, Thomas L., *Days and Events, 1860-1866* (Boston, 1920), pp. 113, 114.
56. *History of the One Hundred and Twenty-fourth Regiment Pennsylvania Volunteers*, Robert M. Green, comp. (Philadelphia, 1907), p. 120. (Hereafter cited as *124th Pennsylvania.*)
57. Noyes, George F., *The Bivouac and the Battle-Field* (New York, 1863), p. 160; Hyde, Thomas W., *Following the Greek Cross or, Memories of the Sixth Army Corps* (Boston, 1895), p. 90.
58. Hough, Franklin B., *History of Duryee's Brigade* (Albany, N. Y., 1864), p. 110.
59. *M.O.S.*, p. 571.
60. *O.R.*, XIX, II, pp. 226, 227.
61. *124th Pennsylvania*, p. 119.
62. *Ibid.*, p. 120.
63. Quint, Alonzo H., *The Potomac and the Rapidan* (Boston, 1864), p. 81; Story of camp followers at Boonsboro from the private letter collection of Dr. Francis A. Lord.
64. *O.R.*, XIX, I, pp. 42, 43.
65. *B.&L.*, II, p. 603.
66. Gibbon, John, *Personal Recollections of the Civil War* (New York, 1928), p. 73.
67. *O.R.*, XIX, II, p. 281.
68. *Ibid.*
69. *Ibid.*, p. 211.
70. Daniel Harvey Hill Papers, Virginia State Library, Richmond, Va., George B. McClellan to Hill, February 1, 1869. (Hereafter cited as Hill Papers.)
71. *O.R.*, XIX, II, p. 282.

CHAPTER 5

1. Douglas, *op. cit.*, p. 151.
2. *Ibid.*
3. *Ibid.*, p. 152.
4. *Ibid.*, p. 153.
5. *Ibid.*, *O.R.*, XIX, II, p. 249.
6. Douglas, *op. cit.*, p. 153 .

7. *Ibid.;* pp. 153, 154.
8. *North Carolina Regiments*, IV, p. 165.
9. *Ibid.;* Douglas, *op. cit.*, p. 158.
10. *B.&L.*, II, p. 617.
11. *Rebellion Record*, Doc. 120, p. 444; *Campaigns in Virginia, Maryland and Pennsylvania, 1862-1863*, Military Historical Society of Massachusetts (14 vols., Boston, 1881-1905), III, pp. 41, 42. (Hereafter cited as *Campaign in Virginia.* All references cited from Vol. III.)
12. *Rebellion Record*, Doc. 120, p. 444.
13. *The Official Atlas of the Civil War* (New York, 1958), Plate 42, Map 1.
14. *O.R.*, XIX, I, p. 852.
15. *Ibid.*, p. 853.
16. *Ibid.*, p. 863.
17. *Ibid.*
18. *Ibid.*, pp. 567-570.
19. *Ibid.*, p. 863.
20. *Ibid.*, p. 854.
21. *S.H.S.P.*, XIV, pp. 103, 108.
22. *O.R.*, XIX, I, pp. 866, 867.
23. *Ibid.*, p. 854.
24. *B.&L.*, II, p. 606.
25. *O.R.*, XIX, I, pp. 912, 913.
26. *North Carolina Regiments*, III, p. 67.
27. *O.R.*, XIX, I, p. 913.
28. *B.&L.*, II, p. 608.
29. *O.R.*, XIX, I, p. 764.
30. *Ibid.*, p. 913.
31. *M.O.S.*, p. 550.
32. *O.R.*, XIX, II, p. 181.
33. *Ibid.*, p. 182.
34. *Ibid.*, p. 181.
35. *Ibid.*, p. 189.
36. *Ibid.*, p. 207.
37. *Ibid.*
38. *Ibid.*, XIX, I, p. 767.
39. *M.O.S.*, p. 558.
40. *Ibid.*, p. 559.
41. *O.R.*, XIX, I, pp. 549-803.
42. *Ibid.*, p. 519.
43. *Ibid.*, p. 583.
44. *B.&L.*, II, p. 613.
45. Cullum, George Washington, *Biographical Register of the Officers and Graduates of the United States Military Academy* (3 vols., New York, 1879), II, p. 385.
46. Norton, Henry, *History of the Eighth New York Volunteer Cavalry* (Norwich, N. Y., 1889), p. 18.
47. *Military Essays and Recollections*, Military Order of the Loyal Legion of the United States, Illinois Commandery (4 vols., Chicago, 1891-1907), II,

"March of the Cavalry from Harper's Ferry, September 14, 1862," William M. Luff, p. 38. (Hereafter cited as Luff.)

48. *O.R.*, XIX, I, p. 583; *B.&L.*, II, p. 613.
49. *B.&L.*, II, p. 613.
50. Pettengill, Samuel B., *The College Cavaliers* (Chicago, 1883), p. 81.
51. *O.R.*,XIX, I, pp. 720-723.
52. Norton, *op. cit.*, p. 27.
53. *O.R.*, XIX, I, pp. 583, 584.
54. *Ibid.*, p. 630.
55. *Ibid.*, p. 584.
56. *Ibid.*
57. Luff, *op. cit.*, p. 39.
58. *O.R.*, XIX, I, p. 584.
59. *Ibid.*, pp. 770, 771.
60. *Ibid.*, p. 753.
61. *Ibid.*, p. 629.
62. *Ibid.*, p. 559.
63. *Ibid.*, p. 685.
64. *Ibid.*, pp. 584, 685.
65. Corliss, Augustus W., *History of the Seventh Squadron, Rhode Island Cavalry* (Yarmouth, Maine, 1879), p. 10.
66. Luff, *op. cit.*, p. 40.
67. *O.R.*, XIX, I, pp. 558, 559.
68. Newcomer, Christopher A., *Three Years in the Saddle in the Shenandoah Valley* (Baltimore, 1895), p. 43.
69. Luff, *op. cit.*, p. 39.
70. *Personal Narratives of Events in the War of the Rebellion*, Rhode Island Soldiers and Sailors Historical Society (Providence, 1889), Series IV, No. 2, p. 33. (Hereafter cited as *Personal Narratives* (Rhode Island Soldiers).
71. *O.R.*, XIX, I, p. 954.
72. *Ibid.*, p. 818.
73. Pettengill, *op. cit.*, *pp.* 78, 79.
74. Norton, *op. cit.*, p. 28.
75. *Ibid.*
76. *Ibid.*
77. Luff, *op. cit.*, p. 41.
78. *Ibid.*
79. Norton, *op. cit.*, p. 29.
80. Luff, *op. cit.*, p. 41.
81. Norton, *op. cit.*, p. 30.
82. *O.R.*, XIX, I, p. 765.
83. Luff, *op. cit.*, p. 41.
84. *Ibid.*
85. *Ibid.*, p. 42.
86. *O.R.*, XIX, I, p. 720.
87. *Ibid.*
88. *Ibid.*
89. *Ibid.*, pp. 721, 723.

[90.] *M.O.S.*, p. 560.
[91.] *Ibid.*, pp. 559-561.
[92.] *O.R.*, XIX, II, p. 607.
[93.] *Ibid.*, XIX, I, p. 958.
[94.] *B.&L.*, II, pp. 604-611.
[95.] *Ibid.*, p. 609.
[96.] *O.R.*, XIX, II, p. 607.
[97.] *Ibid.*, XIX, I, p. 958.
[98.] *B.&L.*, II, p. 609.
[99.] *Ibid.*
[100.] *O.R.*, XIX, I, p. 958.
[101.] *B.&L.*, II, p. 615.
[102.] *Ibid.*, p. 610.
[103.] *O.R.*, XIX, I, p. 980.
[104.] Douglas, *op. cit.*, pp. 159, 160.
[105.] *O.R.*, XIX, I, p. 951.

CHAPTER 6

[1.] Freeman, *Lee's Lieutenants*, p. 166.
[2.] *O.R.*, XIX, II, p. 605.
[3.] *Ibid.*, p. 287.
[4.] *Ibid.*, LI, I, p. 800.
[5.] Williams, Kenneth P., *op. cit.*, p. 371.
[6.] *O.R.*, XIX, I, p. 145.
[7.] *Ibid.*, p. 42.
[8.] *Ibid.*, LI, I, p. 827.
[9.] *Ibid.*, p. 829.
[10.] *Ibid.*, XIX, I, p. 45.
[11.] Ballard, Colin R., Brig. Gen., *The Military Genius of Abraham Lincoln* (New York, 1952), p. 125.
[12.] Palfrey, Francis Winthrop, *The Army in the Civil War, The Antietam and Fredericksburg* (New York, 1881), pp. 29, 30.
[13.] *O.R.*, XIX, I, p. 45.
[14.] *Ibid.*, LI, I, pp. 826, 827.
[15.] Palfrey, *op. cit.*, p. 30.
[16.] Carman, *op. cit.*, Chap. V, p. 12.
[17.] Cox, *op. cit.*, pp. 267, 273, 277.
[18.] Robert E. Lee Papers, Library of Congress, Manuscript Division, Letterbook IV, November 29, 1866 to September 12, 1870 (hereafter cited as Lee's Letterbook); Freeman, *Lee's Lieutenants*, p. 722.
[19.] *O.R.*, XIX, II, p. 607.
[20.] *B.&L.*, II, p. 666.
[21.] Owen, *op. cit.*, p. 136.
[22.] Alexander, *op. cit.*, pp. 228, 229.
[23.] *O.R.*, XIX, I, p. 941.
[24.] *Ibid.*, p. 1022.

25. *Ibid.*, p. 1052.
26. *Ibid.*, p. 817.
27. Hill Papers, Thomas L. Rosser to Hill, July 10, 1883.
28. *O.R.*, XIX, I, p. 1052.
29. *Ibid.*, p. 817.
30. *Ibid.*
31. James E. B. Stuart Papers, Henry E. Huntington Library, San Marino, Calif.
32. *B&L.*, II, p. 561.
33. *O.R.*, XIX, I, pp. 1019, 1020.
34. *Ibid.*, p. 1031.
35. *B.&L.*, II, pp. 564, 565.
36. *Ibid.*, p. 566.
37. *O.R.*, XIX, I, p. 46.
38. *Ibid.*, p. 209.
39. *Ibid.*, p. 816.
40. *Ibid.*, pp. 209, 816, 817.
41. *Ibid.*, p. 48.
42. *Ibid.*, p. 461; *B&L.*, II, p. 586.
43. *B&L.*, II, p. 587.
44. *Ibid.*, p. 566.
45. *Ibid.*, pp. 566, 570.
46. *O.R.*, XIX, I, p. 443.
47. *B.&L.*, II, p. 586; *O.R.*, XIX, I, p. 458.
48. *B.&L.*, II, pp. 587, 588.
49. Alexander, *op. cit.*, pp. 231, 232.
50. *O.R.*, XIX, I, p. 885.
51. Alexander, *op. cit.*, p. 232.
52. *O.R.*, XIX, I, pp. 894, 895, 899, 905, 907; *B.&L.*, II, p. 577.
53. Polley, J. B., *Hood's Texas Brigade* (Washington, 1910), p. 114; Hood, *op. cit.*, p. 39.
54. *B.&L.*, II, p. 569.
55. Parker, Thomas H., *History of the 51st Regiment of Pennsylvania Volunteers* (Philadelphia, 1869), pp. 226, 227.
56. *O.R.*, XIX, I, p. 214.
57. *B.&L.*, II, pp. 573, 574.
58. *Ibid.*, p. 573.
59. *Ibid.*, p. 574.
60. *O.R.*, XIX, I, p. 894.
61. *Ibid.*, p. 1034.
62. *Ibid.*, p. 1035.
63. *Ibid.*, p. 242.
64. *Ibid.*, p. 222.
65. Eisenschiml, Otto, and Ralph Newman, *The Civil War* (2 vols., New York, 1956), I, *The American Iliad, As Told by Those Who Lived It*, p. 254. (All references cited from Vol. I.)
66. *O.R.*, XIX, I, p. 380.
67. Eisenschiml and Newman, *op. cit.*, p. 254.
68. *O.R.*, XIX, I, p. 47.

CHAPTER 7

1. Sorrel, *op. cit.*, pp. 101, 102.
2. Noyes, *op. cit.*, pp. 186, 187.
3. *B.&L.*, II, p. 558.
4. *O.R.*, XIX, I, p. 268.
5. *B.&L.*, II, p. 558.
6. *History of the Ninth Regiment New Hampshire Volunteers in the War of the Rebellion*, Edward O. Lord, ed. (Concord, 1895), pp. 88-90. (Hereafter cited as Lord, Edward O.)
7. Walcott, *op. cit.*, p. 193.
8. *Ibid.*
9. Washburn, George H., *A Complete Military Record of the 108th Regiment New York Volunteers* (Rochester, 1894), p. 20.
10. Walcott, *op. cit.*, pp. 194, 194fn.
11. *O.R.*, XIX, II, pp. 294, 295.
12. Richmond *Dispatch*, September 22, 1862.
13. *O.R.*, XIX, II, p. 295.
14. *M.O.S.*, p. 583.
15. *Collected Works*, p. 426.
16. *Ibid.*, pp. 425, 426.
17. *Ibid.*, p. 427.
18. *Welles' Diary*, p. 130.
19. *O.R.*, XIX, II, p. 607.
20. *Ibid.*, LI, II, pp. 618, 619.
21. *B.&L.*, II, p. 627.
22. *O.R.*, XIX, I, p. 951.
23. Thomas, Henry W., *History of the Doles-Cook Brigade* (Atlanta, 1903), pp. 68, 69.
24. *O.R.*, XIX, I, p. 888.
25. Carman, *op. cit.*, Chap. IX, p. 5.
26. *O.R.*, XIX, I, p. 142.
27. Alexander, *op. cit.*, p. 232.
28. Carman, *op. cit.*, Chap. IX, p. 5.
29. *O.R.*, XIX, I, p. 142; Carman, *op. cit.*, Chap. IX, p. 5.
30. Carman, *op. cit.*, Chap. IX, p. 6.
31. Luff, *op. cit.*, p. 43.
32. *Ibid.*, p. 45.
33. *Ibid.*, p. 44.
34. Norton, *op. cit.*, p. 32.
35. *Ibid.*, p. 142.
36. *Ibid.*, p. 33.
37. Pettengill, *op. cit.*, p. 85.
38. Carman, *op. cit.*, Chap. IX, p. 6.
39. *O.R.*, XIX, I, p. 830.
40. Carman, *op. cit.*, Chap. IX, p. 6.
41. *O.R.*, XIX, II, p. 305.
42. *Ibid.*, XIX, I, pp. 758, 759.
43. *Ibid.*, p. 911.

44. *Ibid.*, pp. 911, 912.
45. *Ibid.*, p. 802.
46. *Personal Narratives* (Rhode Island Soldiers), p. 37.
47. Luff, *op. cit.*, p. 46.
48. Pettengill, *op. cit.*, p. 88.
49. Luff, *op. cit.*, p. 48.
50. Ropes, John Codman, *The Story of the Civil War* (2 vols., New York, 1898), II, p. 351.
51. *Ibid.*, p. 349.
52. *Ibid.*, p. 352.
53. Taylor, Walter H., *Four Years With General Lee*, James I. Robertson, Jr., ed. (Bloomington, Ind., 1962), p. 73.
54. *Letter of The Secretary of War, Transmitting Report on the Organization of the Army of the Potomac* (Washington, 1864), p. 214. (Hereafter cited as *Letter of The Secretary of War . . .*)
55. *O.R.*, XIX, I, p. 28.
56. McClellan, H. B., *I Rode with Jeb Stuart*, Burke Davis, ed. (Bloomington, Ind., 1958), pp. 124-126.
57. *O.R.*, XIX, I, p. 743.
58. *Ibid.*, p. 539.
59. *Ibid.*, p. 955.
60. *Ibid.*, p. 539.
61. *Ibid.*, p. 540.
62. *Ibid.*, pp. 541, 553.
63. Douglas, *op. cit.*, p. 162.
64. *O.R.*, XIX, I, p. 980.
65. *B.&L.*, II, p. 627.
66. *O.R.*, XIX, I, p. 955.
67. *Ibid.*, p. 980.
68. Blackford, W. W., Lieut. Col., C. S. A., *War Years with Jeb Stuart* (New York, 1946), p. 146.
69. Carman, *op. cit.*, Chap. VI, p. 70.
70. *O.R.*, XIX, I, p. 951.
71. Douglas, *op. cit.*, p. 163.
72. Blackford, *op. cit.*, p. 145.
73. Owen, *op. cit.*, p. 139.
74. *O.R.*, XIX, I, p. 53.
75. *M.O.S.*, p. 586.
76. *O.R.*, LI, I, p. 836.
77. *Ibid.*, XIX, I, p. 53.
78. S. L. M. Barlow Papers, Henry E. Huntington Library, San Marino, Calif., McClellan to his wife, September 16, 1862 (7 a.m.).
79. *O.R.*, XIX, II, p. 307.
80. *M.O.S.*, p. 588.
81. *B.&L.*, II, p. 675.
82. *M.O.S.*, p. 588.
83. Poague, William Thomas, *Gunner With Stonewall*, Monroe F. Cockrell, ed. (Jackson, Tenn., 1957), pp. 44, 45.
84. *O.R.*, XIX, I, p. 508.
85. Starr, *op. cit.*, p. 140.

CHAPTER 8

1. *B.&L.*, II, p. 660.
2. Sorrel, *op. cit.*, pp. 103, 104.
3. Livermore, *op. cit.*, pp. 129, 130.
4. *B.&L.*, II, p. 660.
5. Hood, *op. cit.*, p. 42; Longstreet, James, *op. cit.*, p. 237; *O.R.*, XIX, I, p. 149.
6. Poague, *op. cit.*, pp. 45, 46.
7. Starr, *op. cit.*, p. 140.
8. *O.R.*, XIX, II, p. 610.
9. *Letter of The Secretary of War* . . ., p. 214; Taylor, Walter H., *op. cit.*, p. 73.
10. *124th Pennsylvania*, p. 211.
11. *Pennsylvania at Antietam*, Report of the Antietam Battlefield Memorial Commission of Pennsylvania (Harrisburg, 1906), p. 141.
12. Officially recorded sunrise for September 17, 1862 at Sharpsburg, Maryland has been provided by Mr. R. L. Duncombe, Director, Nautical Alamanac Office, United States Naval Observatory, Washington, D. C.
13. Weather conditions for the day of battle are from the Register of Meteorological Observations, under the direction of the Smithsonian Institution, and provided through the National Weather Records Center, Asheville, North Carolina, William H. Hoggard, Deputy Director, Weather Bureau, United States Department of Commerce. Actual reports for Sharpsburg, Maryland were unavailable. Figures quoted are from a Frederick, Maryland station, approximately twenty air miles distance from the battlefield. J. Howard Beckenbaugh, U. S. Government Weather Bureau Agent in Boonsboro, Maryland, and grand-nephew of Henry Kyd Douglas, has assured the author that conditions between Sharpsburg and Frederick would not normally vary more than five degrees.
14. Henderson, *op. cit.*, pp. 518, 519.
15. *O.R.*, XIX, I, p. 218.
16. *Confederate Veteran* (40 vols., 1893-1932), XXII, p. 66.
17. Swinton, William, *Campaigns of the Army of the Potomac* (New York, 1882), p. 211.
18. Worsham, John H., *One of Jackson's Foot Cavalry* (New York, 1912), p. 144; *O.R.*, XIX, I, p. 956.
19. *O.R.*, XIX, I, p. 244.
20. *Ibid.*, p. 218.
21. Richardson, Albert D., *The Secret Service* (Hartford, Conn., 1865), p. 284.
22. Henderson, *op. cit.*, p. 527.
23. Andrews, J. Cutler, *The North Reports the Civil War* (Pittsburgh, Pa., 1955), pp. 277, 278.
24. Starr, *op. cit.*, p. 141.
25. *O.R.*, XIX, I, p. 1033.
26. *124th Pennsylvania*, p. 271; *North Carolina Regiments*, V, p. 76.
27. *The History of the Fighting Fourteenth* (New York, 1911), p. 49fn.
28. Palfrey, *op. cit.*, p. 76.
29. Lyman C. Holford Diary, Library of Congress, Manuscript Division, p. 114.

30. *North Carolina Regiments*, V, p. 76.
31. Dawes, Rufus R., *Service with the Sixth Wisconsin Volunteers* (Marietta, Ohio, 1890), pp. 90-92.
32. *O.R.*, XIX, I, p. 968.
33. *Ibid.*, p. 923.
34. *Ibid.*, p. 218.
35. New York *Tribune*, September 20, 1862.
36. *124th Pennsylvania*, pp. 120, 121.
37. *Ibid.*, p. 285.
38. *Welles' Diary*, p. 140.
39. Diary of J. R. Boulware, Asst. Surgeon, 6th South Carolina Volunteer Regiment, Jenkins' Brigade, C. S. A., Virginia State Library, Richmond, Va., entry for September 17, 1862.
40. Richardson, *op. cit.*, p. 284.
41. Andrews, *op. cit.*, p. 215.
42. *Harper's Weekly*, February 1868, p. 282.
43. Coffin, Charles Carlton, *The Boys of '61* (Boston, 1896), p. 149.
44. *O.R.*, XIX, I, p. 275.
45. Palfrey, *op. cit.*, p. 82.
46. *C.M.H.*, III, p. 351.
47. *B.&L.*, II, pp. 676, 677.
48. Palfrey, *op. cit.*, p. 82.
49. W. F. Smith Papers, Personal collection of Walter Wilgus, Falls Church, Virginia. A copy of a paper entitled "Three Personal Incidents in the Battle of Sharpsburg or Antietam, fought September 17, 1862," by Gen. S. D. Lee; sent to Smith by Lee. (Hereafter cited Lee, S. D.)
50. Douglas, *op. cit.*, p. 171.
51. Long, A. L., *Memoirs of Robert E. Lee* (New York, 1887), p. 222.
52. *Report of the Joint Committee on the Conduct of the War*, 37th Congress, I, Part I, p. 368.
53. *O.R.*, XIX, I, pp. 486, 488.
54. *Ibid.*, p. 320; Palfrey, *op. cit.*, pp. 83, 84.
55. *O.R.*, XIX, I, p. 316.
56. Ward, Joseph R. C., *History of the One Hundred and Sixth Regiment Pennsylvania Volunteers* (Philadelphia, 1906), pp. 102, 103.
57. *O.R.*, XIX, I, pp. 858, 874.
58. *Ibid.*, pp. 861, 871.
59. *B.&L.*, II, pp. 676-678.
60. *Ibid.*, p. 678; Von Borcke, *op. cit.*, p. 234.
61. *O.R.*, XIX, I, pp. 970, 971.
62. *Ibid.*, pp. 316, 492.
63. *Ibid.*, p. 874.
64. *Ibid.*, p. 309.
65. *Ibid.*, p. 866.
66. *Ibid.*, p. 308.
67. *Ibid.*, pp. 510fn, 866.
68. *Ibid.*, p. 313.
69. *Ibid.*, pp. 306, 318; Palfrey, *op. cit.*, p. 87.
70. Palfrey, *op. cit.*, p. 87.

71. *Ibid.,* pp. 89, 90.
72. *North Carolina Regiments,* V, p. 77.
73. *Ibid.,* p. 78.
74. *Harper's New Monthly Magazine,* August 1894, pp. 428, 429.

CHAPTER 9

1. Gordon, John B., Gen., *Reminiscences of the Civil War* (New York, 1904), p. 84.
2. Longstreet, James., *op. cit.,* p. 254.
3. *O.R.,* XIX, I, p. 1023.
4. *Ibid.,* p. 334.
5. Longstreet, James, *op. cit.,* p. 248.
6. *Pennsylvania at Antietam,* p. 190.
7. Gordon, *op. cit.,* pp. 84-87; *Personal Recollections of the War of the Rebellion,* Military Order of the Loyal Legion of the United States, New York Commandery, 3rd Series (New York, 1907), Galwey, Thomas F. DeBurgh, "At the Battle of Antietam with the Eighth Ohio Infantry," p. 77. (Hereafter cited as Galwey.)
8. Eisenschiml and Newman, *op. cit.,* pp. 262, 263.
9. Gordon, *op. cit.,* p. 88.
10. Galwey, *op. cit.,* p. 79.
11. *O.R.,* XIX, I, p. 331.
12. *Ibid.,* p. 332.
13. *Ibid.,* p. 327.
14. *Ibid.,* p. 1037.
15. *Ibid.,* p. 299.
16. *Ibid.,* p. 329.
17. *Ibid.,* p. 327.
18. *Ibid.,* p. 1037.
19. *Ibid.,* p. 335.
20. *Ibid.,* p. 327.
21. Livermore, *op. cit.,* p. 146.
22. *O.R.,* XIX, I, p. 293.
23. Livermore, *op. cit.,* p. 133.
24. *O.R.,* XIX, I, p. 294.
25. *Ibid.*
26. *Ibid.,* p. 295; *A Virginia Yankee in the Civil War, The Diaries of David Hunter Strother,* Cecil D. Eby, Jr., ed. (Chapel Hill, N. C., 1961), p. 113; Hitchcock, Frederick L., *War From the Inside,* (Philadelphia, 1904), pp. 63, 64.
27. *O.R.,* XIX, I, p. 285.
28. *Ibid.,* p. 301.
29. *Souvenir of Excursion to Battlefield by the Society of the Fourteenth Connecticut Regiment* (Washington, 1893), pp. 51, 56, 57.
30. Livermore, *op. cit.,* p. 136.
31. This relic of the Battle of Antietam is in the possession of Dr. Francis A. Lord, Civil War collector and recognized authority on ammunition of this period.

32. Reilly, Oliver T., *The Battlefield of Antietam* (Sharpsburg, Md., 1906).
33. Livermore, *op. cit.*, p. 138; *124th Pennsylvania*, p. 118.
34. Gordon, *op. cit.*, p. 90.
35. *O.R.*, XIX, I, pp. 1037, 1038.
36. *Ibid.*, pp. 285, 286.
37. *Ibid.*, p. 1024.
38. Livermore, *op. cit.*, p. 141.
39. *O.R.*, XIX, I, p. 291.
40. Longstreet, James, *op. cit.*, p. 250.
41. Sorrel, *op. cit.*, pp. 106, 107.
42. *Ibid.*
43. Longstreet, James, *op. cit.*, p. 251.
44. Alexander, *op. cit.*, p. 263.
45. Longstreet, James, *op. cit.*, p. 250.
46. *O.R.*, XIX, I, p. 850.
47. *Ibid.*, p. 286.
48. *Ibid.*, p. 956.
49. Livermore, *op. cit.*, pp. 143, 144.
50. *Ibid.*, pp. 140, 149.
51. *Harper's New Monthly Magazine*, February 1868, p. 282.
52. The "little old lady" has never been identified, but the story remains to this day as the most popular of a number of origins for the term "Bloody Lane."
53. *B.&L.*, II, p. 670.
54. Alexander, *op. cit.*, p. 262.
55. *O.R.*, XIX, I, p. 377.
56. Michie, *op. cit.*, p. 422.
57. *O.R.*, XIX, I, pp. 343, 344.

CHAPTER 10

1. *B.&L.*, II, p. 631.
2. Manton Marble Papers, Library of Congress, Manuscript Division, Fitz John Porter to Marble, September 30, 1862.
3. Cox, *op. cit.*, p. 376.
4. S. H. Gay Prapers, Columbia University Library, New York, S. D. Richardson to Gay, September 27, 1862. (Hereafter cited as Gay Papers.)
5. Daniel Reed Larned Papers, Library of Congress, Manuscript Division, Larned to his sister, October 9, 1862.
6. *B.&L.*, II, p. 631.
7. *O.R.*, XIX, I, p. 30.
8. *Ibid.*, p. 55.
9. *Ibid.*, p. 63.
10. Douglas, *op. cit.*, p. 172.
11. *O.R.*, XIX, I, p. 63.
12. *Ibid.*, pp. 63, 424.
13. *Ibid.*, p. 63.
14. *Ibid.*, p. 31, 419.
15. *O.R.*, LI, I, p. 844.
16. *Ibid.*

17. *History of the Thirty-Fifth Regiment Massachusetts Volunteers, 1862-1865* (Boston, 1884), p. 44. (Hereafter cited as *35th Massachusetts*.)
18. *O.R.*, XIX, I, pp. 886, 889, 890, 897, 909.
19. *B.&L.*, II, p. 648.
20. *O.R.*, XIX, I, p. 981.
21. *M.O.S.*, p. 609.
22. Walcott, *op. cit.*, p. 199.
23. Lord, Edward O., *op. cit.*, p. 125.
24. Moore, Frank, *The Civil War in Song and Story* (New York, 1889), p. 467.
25. Lord, Edward O., *op. cit.*, p. 129.
26. Parker, *op. cit.*, p. 232.
27. *B.&L.*, II, p. 652.
28. Hagerstown (Md.) *Herald and Torch Light*, October 13, 1887.
29. *B.&L.*, II, p. 661.
30. *Ibid.*
31. *Ibid.*, p. 651.
32. *35th Massachusetts*, p. 42.
33. *O.R.*, XIX, I, pp. 890, 891.
34. Douglas, *op. cit.*, p. 172.
35. *Ibid.*
36. *O.R.*, XIX, I, pp. 890, 891.
37. *B.&L.*, II, p. 652.
38. Parker, *op. cit.*, p. 232.
39. Palfrey, *op. cit.*, p. 112.
40. *B.&L.*, II, p. 653.
41. *John Dooley, Confederate Soldier*, Joseph T. Durkin, ed. (Washington, 1945), pp. 45-48.
42. *Ibid.*
43. *B.&L.*, II, p. 661.
44. *Ibid.*, pp. 661, 662.
45. Alexander, *op. cit.*, p. 266.
46. Douglas, *op. cit.*, p. 173; *S.H.S.P.*, XIX, p. 181.
47. *S.H.S.P.*, XIX, p. 181.
48. *North Carolina Regiments*, III, p. 575.
49. *O.R.*, XIX, I, p. 988.
50. *Ibid.*, p. 456.
51. *Ibid.*
52. Caldwell, James F. J., *The History of a Brigade of South Carolinians Known First as "Greggs' " and Subsequently as "McGowan's Brigade"* (Philadelphia, 1866), p. 46.
53. *North Carolina Regiments*, II, p. 537.
54. Richardson, *op. cit.*, p. 286; New York *Tribune*, September 20, 1862.
55. Starr, *op. cit.*, p. 145.
56. Richardson, *op. cit.*, p. 286.

CHAPTER 11

1. Cox, *op. cit.*, p. 350. ,
2. *O.R.*, XIX, I, pp. 866, 929, 933.

3. Lee, S. D.
4. Douglas, *op. cit.*, p. 174.
5. *B.&L.*, II, pp. 684, 685.
6. Noyes, *op. cit.*, p. 207.
7. Douglas, *op. cit.*, p. 175.
8. *Ibid.*, pp. 175, 176.
9. *B.&L.*, II, p. 597.
10. Lee, S. D.
11. *O.R.*, XIX, I, p. 956, 957.
12. Lee, S. D.
13. Douglas, *op. cit.*, p. 179.
14. *O.R.*, XIX, I, p. 280.
15. *Ibid.*
16. W. F. Smith Papers, Personal collection of Walter Wilgus, Falls Church, Virginia. A letter of Capt. G. E. Pingree; no date.
17. *O.R.*, XIX, I, p. 281.
18. *Ibid.*
19. Von Borcke, *op. cit.*, p. 237.
20. *O.R.*, XIX, II, p. 312.
21. *Ibid.*
22. *Welles' Diary*, p. 140.
23. *O.R.*, XIX, II, pp. 313, 314, 327.
24. *Ibid.*, XIX, I, pp. 67, 189-200.
25. *Ibid.*, pp. 368-372.
26. Cox., *op. cit.*, pp. 350, 351.
27. *O.R.*, XIX, I, pp. 810-813; Alexander, *op. cit.*, pp. 273, 274.
28. Palfrey, *op. cit.*, p. 127.
29. *Harper's New Monthly Magazine*, February, 1868, pp. 284, 285.
30. Noyes, *op. cit.*, pp. 211-213.
31. Castleman, Alfred L., *The Army of the Potomac: Behind the Scene* (Milwaukee, 1863), pp. 229, 230, 234-236.
32. New York *Tribune*, September 29, 1862.
33. Gay Papers, Richardson to Gay, October 22, 1862.
34. O. M. Hatch Papers, Illinois State Historical Library, Springfield, Ill., Joseph Medill, Chicago *Daily Tribune*, to Hatch, October 13, 1862.
35. New York *Tribune*, September 29, 1862.
36. Crowinshield, Benjamin W., *A History of the First Regiment of Massachusetts Cavalry Volunteers* (Boston, 1891), pp. 38, 39.
37. *O.R.*, XIX, I, p. 65.
38. *Ibid.*
39. *Ibid.*, pp. 66, 67.
40. *Ibid.*, LI, I, pp. 849, 850.
41. *Ibid.*, XIX, I, p. 841.
42. Douglas, *op. cit.*, p. 180.
43. *B.&L.*, II, p. 682.
44. Freeman, *R. E. Lee*, p. 406.
45. *Ibid.*, p. 409.
46. Coulter, E. Merton, *A History of the South* (10 vols., Baton Rouge, La., 1950), VII, *The Confederate States of America, 1861-1865*, pp. 355fn, 356fn.

47. Simon Gratz Autograph Collection, The Historical Society of Pennsylvania, Philadelphia, Lafayette McLaws to Miss Lida Perry, Woodbury, N. J., March 28, 1893.
48. Jackson, *op. cit.*, p. 358.
49. *History of the Corn Exchange Regiment, 118th Pennsylvania Volunteers* (Philadelphia, 1888), p. 61; *O.R.*, XIX, I, p. 204.
50. *O.R.*, XIX, I, p. 982. The Ashbrook copy of this particular volume is in the private collection of John Divine, Waterford, Virginia.
51. *O.R.*, XIX, I, p. 152.
52. *Ibid.*, XIX, II, p. 330.
53. Richmond Enquirer, September 22, 1862.
54. *Rebellion Record*, Doc. 122, p. 475. (Charleston *Courier* account written September 17, 1862.)
55. Petersburg *Express*, September 23, 1862.

CHAPTER 12

1. *O.R.*, Series III, II, p. 703.
2. Ambrose, Stephen E., *Halleck: Lincoln's Chief of Staff* (Baton Rouge, La., 1962), p. 86.
3. *O.R.*, XIX, II, p. 336.
4. *Ibid.*, XIX, I, p. 82.
5. *M.O.S.*, p. 623.
6. Benson, *op. cit.*, p. 27.
7. *O.R.*, XIX, II, p. 341.
8. Wise, Jennings Cropper, *The Long Arm of Lee* (New York, 1959), pp. 284-286; Poague, *op. cit.*, p. 52; *O.R.*, XIX, I, pp. 836, 837.
9. *O.R.*, XIX, I, p. 95.
10. *M.O.S.*, p. 553.
11. Davis, Charles E., Jr., *Three Years in the Army: The Story of the Thirteenth Massachusetts Volunteers* (Boston, 1894), pp. 142, 143.
12. *Campaigns in Virginia*, pp. 41, 42.
13. *Welles' Diary*, p. 140.
14. Small, *op. cit.*, p. 36.
15. Nicolay and Hay, *op. cit.*, VI, p. 159.
16. *Ibid.*, p. 168.
17. *M.O.S.*, p. 613.
18. *Ibid.*, p. 612.
19. Michie, *op. cit.*, pp. 428, 429.
20. McClellan Papers, Montgomery Blair to McClellan, September 19, 1862.
21. Richardson, *op. cit.*, p. 291.
22. *M.O.S.*, pp. 627, 655.
23. *Reminiscences of Abraham Lincoln by Distinguished Men of his Time*, Allen Thorndike Rice, ed. (New York, 1888), p. xxxix-xl.
24. Allan Pinkerton Papers, Library of Congress, Manuscript Division.
25. *O.R.*, XIX, I, p. 72.
26. *Collected Works*, pp. 460, 461.
27. Smith, William E., *The Francis Preston Blair Family in Politics* (2 vols., New York, 1933), II, pp. 144, 145.

28. *Collected Works,* p. 461.
29. Nicolay and Hay, *op. cit.,* VI, p. 175.
30. McClellan Papers, McClellan to his wife, October —, 1862. (See *M.O.S.,* p. 658.)
31. *Ibid.,* Letter dated October 31, 1862.
32. *O.R.,* XIX, I, p. 16.
33. James Longstreet Papers, Duke University Library, Durham, N. C., Letter to Gen. Joseph E. Johnston, October 5, 1862.
34. *O.R.,* XIX, II, p. 627.
35. Steele, Matthew Forney, *American Campaigns* (2 vols., Washington, 1951), I, pp. 139, 140.
36. *O.R.,* XIX, I, p. 81.
37. *M.O.S.,* p. 613.
38. Rhodes, *op. cit.,* IV, pp. 184, 185.
39. Alexander Stewart Webb Papers, Yale University Library, Historical Manuscript Division, New Haven, Conn., Montgomery Meigs to Edwin M. Stanton, October 14, 1862.
40. *O.R.,* XIX, II, pp. 492, 493.
41. Todd, William, *The Seventy-Ninth Highlanders New York Volunteers in the War of the Rebellion* (Albany, 1886), p. 245.
42. *O.R.,* XIX, I, p. 85.
43. *Ibid.,* XIX, II, pp. 485, 486; *Collected Works,* p. 474.
44. *O.R.,* XIX, II, p. 485.
45. *Collected Works,* p. 477.
46. *O.R.,* XIX, II, pp. 490, 491.
47. *Collected Works,* p. 479.
48. *M.O.S.,* p. 652.
49. Truman, Harry S., *Memoirs by Harry S. Truman* (2 vols., New York, 1956), II, *Years of Trial and Hope, 1946-1952,* pp. 442, 444.
50. Dennett, *op. cit.,* p. 51.
51. Todd, *op. cit.,* p. 245.
52. Dennett, *op. cit.,* pp. 218, 218.
53. Letter of George W. Salter, Brown University Library, Providence, R. I., Salter to James M. Wilson, November 9, 1862.
54. Bragg Papers, Bragg to his wife, November 16, 1862.
55. Benedict, G. G., *Vermont in the Civil War* (2 vols., Burlington, 1866-1888), I, p. 335.
56. Fairchild, C. B., *History of the 27the Regiment New York Volunteers* (Binghamton, 1888), p. 111.
57. Robert Edwin Jameson Papers, Library of Congress, Manuscript Division, Jameson to his mother, November 16, 1862.
58. *The New York Times,* November 13, 1862.
59. Nicolay and Hay, *op. cit.,* VI, p. 188.
60. *The Congressional Globe: Containing the Debates and Proceedings of the Second Session of the Thirty-Seventh Congress* (Washington, 1862), Vol. 32, Part 3, May 6 - June 23, 1862, p. 2041.
61. Arnold, Isaac N., *The Life of Abraham Lincoln* (Chicago, 1885), p. 300.
62. *Collected Works,* p. 485.
63. *M.O.S.,* p. 660.

64. *Ibid.*, p. 652.
65. Comte de Paris (Louis Phillippe Albert d'Orleans), *History of the Civil War in America* (4 vols., Philadelphia, 1875-1888), II, p. 555 (footnote quotes a letter from Gen. Buckingham to Chicago *Tribune*, September 4, 1875).
66. Williams, T. Harry, *Lincoln and His Generals*, p. 172.
67. *M.O.S.*, p. 653.
68. *Welles' Diary*, p. 182.
69. Diary of William T. Coggeshall, Military Secretary to Gov. Dennison of Ohio, Illinois State Historical Library, Diary entry of November 11, 1862.
70. *O.R.*, XIX, II, pp. 644, 645.

EPILOGUE

1. *S.H.S.P.*, XXXI, p. 38.
2. *Collected Works*, p. 388.
3. Bradford, Gamaliel, Jr., *Lee the American* (Boston, 1912), p. 189.
4. Freeman, *R. E. Lee*, p. 411.

APPENDIX A

1. *O.R.*, XIX, II, pp. 603, 604.
2. Taylor, Walter, H., *op. cit.*, p. 67.
3. Freeman, *Lee's Lieutenants*, pp. 715-723.
4. Rowland, *op. cit.*, VII, pp. 412, 413.
5. *Ibid.*
6. *The Land We Love*, p. 275.
7. *B.&L.*, II, p. 607.
8. Longstreet, James, *op. cit.*, p. 213.
9. Sorrel, *op. cit.*, p. 99.
10. Army of Northern Virginia, Orders and Circulars, 1861-65, National Archives Record Group 109, Entry 68, National Archives.
11. *War Talks in Kansas*, Military Order of the Loyal Legion of the United States, Kansas Commandery (Kansas City, Mo., 1906), I, "Antietam and the Lost Dispatch," Capt. John M. Bloss, p. 250. (Hereafter cited as Bloss.)
12. *B.&L.*, II, p. 603.
13. Hill Papers, McClellan to Hill, February 1, 1869.
14. Allan Papers, February 15, 1868.
15. *O.R.*, XIX, II, p. 607.
16. Pollard, Edward A., *The Lost Cause: A New Southern History of the War of the Confederates* (New York, 1867), p. 314.
17. *S.H.S.P.*, XIII, pp. 420-423.
18. Macrae, David, *The Americans at Home* (2 vols., New York, 1952), I, pp. 249, 250.
19. *B.&L.*, II, p. 570.
20. Longstreet, James, *op. cit.*, p. 213.
21. *O.R.*, XIX, I, pp. 42, 43.

22. North Carolina Department of Archives and History, Raleigh, N. C.
23. Ross, Fitzgerald, *Cities and Camps of the Confederate States,* Richard B. Harwell, Ed. (Urbana, Ill., 1958), p. 44.
24. Freeman, *Lee's Lieutenants,* p. 723.
25. *B.&L.,* II, p. 603.
26. Bloss, *op. cit.,* p. 205.
27. *Ibid.*
28. *B.&L.,* II, p. 603.
29. Rowland, *op. cit.,* VII, p. 413.
30. Bloss, *op. cit.,* p. 205.
31. *Ibid.*
32. *B.&L.,* II, p. 603.
33. *O.R.,* LI, I, p. 829.
34. Rowland, *op. cit.,* VII, p. 829.
35. Bridges, Hal, *Lee's Maverick General, Daniel Harvey Hill* (New York, 1961), p. 98.
36. *The Land We Love,* p. 275.
37. *Ibid.,* pp. 277, 278.
38. Lee's Letterbook.

Appendix B

1. *O.R.,* XIX, II, p. 592.
2. *B.&L.,* II, p. 605.
3. *O.R.,* XIX, I, p. 145.
4. Allan Papers, February 15, 1868.
5. Rowland, *op. cit.,* V, pp. 338, 339.
6. *The North Carolina Historical Review* (Raleigh, N. C.), Vol. XLI, No. 2, April, 1964, "A Proclamation: 'To The People Of ——————,' " Louis Manarin, pp. 246 - 251. (Hereafter cited as Manarin.)
7. *O.R.,* XIX, II, pp. 598, 599; Manarin, *op. cit.*
8. Manarin, *op. cit.*
9. Parks, John Howard, *General Edmund Kirby Smith, C.S.A.,* (Baton Rouge, La., 1954), p. 219.
10. *O.R.,* XVI, II, pp. 822, 823.

Appendix C

The organizational tables for both armies have been taken from several sources. The basic charts were drafted by the Antietam Battlefield Commission in the late 1800's and never revised. The present tables are the result of research based on official records and hundreds of personal reminiscences. Confederate organization is based on the best available sources.

APPENDIX D

The casualty reports are transcribed directly from official records and must be accepted as approximate figures. Confederate records are incomplete and, in many cases, totally inaccurate.

APPENDIX E

1. *O.R.*, XIX, II, pp. 590, 591.
2. *Ibid.*, p. 169.
3. *Ibid.*
4. *Ibid.*, pp. 592, 593.
5. *Ibid.*, p. 596.
6. *Ibid.*, pp. 597, 598.
7. Rowland, *op. cit.*, V, pp. 338, 339.
8. *O.R.*, XIX, II, p. 600.
9. *Ibid.*, pp. 601, 602.
10. Bloss, *op. cit.*, p. 205.
11. *O.R.*, LI, I, p. 829.
12. *Ibid.*, XIX, I, p. 45.
13. *Ibid.*, LI, I, pp. 826, 827.
14. *Ibid.*, XIX, II, p. 607.
15. *Ibid.*, pp. 281, 282.
16. *Ibid.*, p. 281.
17. *Ibid.*, p. 289.
18. *Ibid.*, LI, II, pp. 618, 619.
19. *Ibid.*, XIX, I, p. 951.
20. Lord Russell Papers, Public Record Office, London, England, Ref. P. R .O. 30/22-14. (Hereafter cited as Russell Papers.)
21. *O.R.*, XIX, I, p. 951.
22. *Ibid.*, p. 53.
23. *Ibid.*, XIX, II, p. 294.
24. *Ibid.*, p. 610.
25. *Ibid.*, p. 312.
26. Lord Russell Papers.
27. *O.R.*, XIX, II, p. 322.
28. *Ibid.*, p. 330.
29. *Ibid.*
30. *Ibid.*, pp. 342, 343.
31. Lord Russell Papers.
32. *Ibid.*
33. *O.R.*, XIX, I, p. 72.
34. *Ibid.*, p. 545.
35. *Ibid.*

Bibliography

Basic research for this manuscript is primarily from the orders, reports, and dispatches found in *War of the Rebellion: A Compilation of the Official Records of the Union and Confederate Armies*. Volume XIX, Parts I and II of this work covers the Maryland Campaign of 1862. Federal references such as General McClellan's *Report on the Organization and Campaigns of the Army of the Potomac* and the *Report of the Joint Committee on the Conduct of the War* are used to reflect the attitude of Northern military and political leaders. *The Collected Works of Abraham Lincoln* provides the answers to much of General McClellan's correspondence with the President. Southern attitudes are found primarily in private letters and diaries and in the newspapers of the two political centers, Richmond and Charleston. Henry Kyd Douglas (*I Rode With Stonewall*) is used throughout the manuscript as a general spokesman for the Army of Northern Virginia.

Many of the references cited herewith are contemporary publications edited and revised during the Civil War Centennnial years:

Primary Sources

Basler, Roy P., ed., *The Collected Works of Abraham Lincoln,* Vol. V, New Brunswick, New Jersey, 1953.

The Congressional Globe: Containing the Debates and Proceedings of the Second Session of the Thirty-Seventh Congress, Vol. XXXII, Washington, 1862.

Dyer, Frederick H., *A Compendium of the War of the Rebellion,* Vol. I, New York, 1959.

Letter of The Secretary of War, Transmitting Report on the Organization of the Army of the Potomac, Washington, 1864.

McClellan, George B., *Report on the Organization and Campaigns of the Army of the Potomac,* New York, 1864.

The Official Atlas of the Civil War, New York, 1958.

Report of the Joint Committee on the Conduct of the War, 37th Congress, 3d Session, Washington, 1863; 38th Congress, 2d Session, Washington, 1865.

War of the Rebellion: A Compilation of the Official Records of the Union and Confederate Armies, Series I, Vols. II, V, IX, XI, XVI, XIX, XXI, LI; Series III, Vol. II, Washington 1880-1901.

Manuscripts, Letters, Diaries, and Documents

William Allan Papers, Southern Historical Collection, University of North Carolina Library.

Orders and Circulars, Army of Northern Virginia, National Archives.

Francis Chaning Barlow Papers, Massachusetts Historical Society.

S. L. M. Barlow Papers, Henry E. Huntington Library.

J. R. Boulware Diary, Virginia State Library.

Edward S. Bragg Papers, State Historical Society of Wisconsin.

Ezra A. Carman Manuscript and Papers, Library of Congress.

William T. Coggeshall Diary, Illinois State Historical Library.

Robert L. Dabney Papers, Union Theological Seminary Library.

S. H. Gay Papers, Columbia University Library.

James Gillette Letters, Mrs. Amy G. Bassett, Private Collection.

Simon Gratz Autograph Collection, Historical Society of Pennsylvania.

O. M. Hatch Papers, Illinois State Historical Library.

Daniel Harvey Hill Papers, North Carolina Department of Archives and History.

Daniel Harvey Hill Papers, Virginia State Library.

Lyman C. Holford Diary, Library of Congress.

Jed Hotchkiss Diary, Library of Congress.

Robert Edwin Jameson Papers, Library of Congress.

Daniel Reed Larned Papers, Library of Congress.

Robert E. Lee Papers, Library of Congress.

James Longstreet Papers, Duke University Library.

Francis A. Lord Private Collection.

Manton Marble Papers, Library of Congress.

George B. McClellan Papers, Library of Congress.

Allan Pinkerton Papers, Library of Congress.

Lord Russell Papers, Public Record Office, London, England.

George W. Shreve Manuscript, Virginia State Library.

George W. Salter Papers, Brown University Library.

W. F. Smith Papers, Walter Wilgus, Private Collection.

Joseph Clay Stiles Papers, Henry E. Huntington Library.

J. E. B. Stuart Papers, Henry E. Huntington Library.

Alexander Stewart Webb Papers, Yale University Library.

Military and Political Biographical Studies

Ambrose, Stephen E., *Halleck: Lincoln's Chief of Staff*, Baton Rouge, Louisiana, 1962.
Arnold, Isaac N., *The Life of Abraham Lincoln*, Chicago, 1885.
Bradford, Gamaliel, Jr., *Lee the American*, Boston, 1912.
Bridges, Hal, *Lee's Maverick General, Daniel Harvey Hill*, New York, 1961.
Cooke, John Esten, *The Life of Stonewall Jackson*, Richmond, 1863.
Dabney, Robert L., *Life and Campaigns of Lieut.-Gen. Thomas J. Jackson*, New York, 1866.
Freeman, Douglas Southall, *R. E. Lee, A Biography*, Vol. II, New York, 1934-1935.
Gorham, George C., *Life and Public Services of Edwin M. Stanton*, Vol. II, Boston, 1899.
Henderson, G. F. R., Col. *Stonewall Jackson and the American Civil War*, New York, 1961.
Lee, Fitzhugh, *General Lee*, New York, 1894.
Michie, Peter S., *General McClellan*, New York, 1915.
Myers, William Starr, *General George Brinton McClellan, A Study in Personality*, New York, 1934.
Parks, John Howard, *General Edmund Kirby Smith, C. S. A.*, Baton Rouge, Louisiana, 1954.
Thomas, Benjamin P. and Hyman, Harold M., *Stanton: The Life and Times of Lincoln's Secretary of War*, New York, 1962.

Personal Reminiscences and Unit Histories

Alexander, E. P., *Military Memoirs of a Confederate*, T. Harry Williams, ed., Bloomington, Indiana, 1962.
Benedict, G. G., *Vermont in the Civil War*, Vol. I, Burlington, Vermont, 1866-1888.
Benson, Susan Williams, ed., *Berry Benson's Civil War Book*, Athens, Georgia, 1962.
Blackford, W. W., Lieut. Col., *War Years with Jeb Stuart*, New York, 1946.
Caldwell, James F. J., *The History of a Brigade of South Carolinians Known First as "Greggs'" and Subsequently as "McGowan's" Brigade*, Philadelphia, 1866.
Castleman, Alfred L., *The Army of the Potomac: Behind the Scene*, Milwaukee, 1863.

Clark, Walter, ed., *Histories of the Several Regiments and Battalions from North Carolina in the Great War, 1861-1865,* Vols. II, III, IV, V, Raleigh and Greensboro, North Carolina, 1901.

Corliss, Augustus, W., *History of the Seventh Squadron, Rhode Island Cavalry,* Yarmouth, Maine, 1879.

Cox, Jacob Dolson, *Military Reminiscences of the Civil War,* Vol. I, New York, 1900.

Crowinshield, Benjamin W., *A History of the First Regiment of Massachusetts Cavalry Volunteers,* Boston, 1891.

Davis, Charles E., Jr., *Three Years in the Army: The Story of the Thirteenth Massachusetts Volunteers,* Boston, 1894.

Dawes, Rufus R., *Service with the Sixth Wisconsin,* Marietta, Ohio, 1890.

Douglas, Henry Kyd, *I Rode with Stonewall,* Chapel Hill, North Carolina, 1940.

Durkin, Joseph T., ed., *John Dooley, Confederate Soldier,* Washington, D. C., 1945.

Eby, Cecil D., Jr., ed., *A Virginia Yankee in the Civil War, the Diaries of David Hunter Strother,* Chapel Hill, North Carolina, 1961.

Fairchild, C. B., *History of the 27th Regiment New York Volunteers,* Binghamton, N. Y., 1888.

Gibbon, John, *Personal Recollections of the Civil War,* New York, 1928.

Gordon, John B., Gen., *Reminiscences of the Civil War,* New York, 1904.

Green, Robert M., comp., *History of the One Hundred and Twenty-Fourth Regiment Pennsylvania Volunteers,* Philadelphia, 1907.

Hammond, Harold Earl, ed., *Diary of a Union Lady,* New York, 1962.

The History of the Corn Exchange Regiment 118th Pennsylvania Volunteers, Philadelphia, 1888.

History of the Fighting Fourteenth, New York, 1911.

History of the Thirty-Fifth Regiment Massachusetts Volunteers, 1862-1865, Boston, 1884.

Hitchcock, Frederick, L., *War From the Inside,* Philadelphia, 1904.

Hood, John Bell, *Advance and Retreat,* Richard N. Current, ed., Bloomington, Indiana, 1959.

Hough, Franklin B., *History of Duryee's Brigade,* Albany, New York, 1864.

Hyde, Thomas W., *Following the Greek Cross or Memories of the Sixth Army Corps,* Boston, 1895.

Jackson, Mary Anna, *Memoirs of Stonewall Jackson,* Louisville, 1895.

Johnson, Joseph E., *Narrative of Military Operations,* New York, 1874.

Livermore, Thomas L., *Days and Events, 1860-1865,* Boston, 1920.

Longstreet, James, *From Manassas to Appomattox,* Philadelphia, 1896.

Lord, Edward O., ed., *History of the Ninth Regiment New Hampshire Volunteers in the War of the Rebellion,* Concord, N. H., 1895.

McClellan, George B., *McClellan's Own Story,* New York, 1887.

McClellan, H. B., *I Rode With Jeb Stuart,* Burke Davis, ed., Bloomington, Indiana, 1958.

Meade, George Gordon, ed., *The Life and Letters of George Gordon Meade,* Vol. I, New York, 1913.

Military Order of the Loyal Legion of the United States, Illinois Commandery, *Military Essays and Recollections,* Vol. II, Chicago, 1891-1907.

Military Order of the Loyal Legion of the United States, New York Commandery, *Personal Recollections of the War of the Rebellion,* 3d Series, New York, 1907.

Military Order of the Loyal Legion of the United States, Kansas Commandery, *War Talks in Kansas,* Vol. I, Kansas City, Missouri, 1906.

Newcomer, Christopher A., *Three Years in the Saddle in the Shenandoah Valley,* Baltimore, 1895.

Norton, Henry, *History of the Eighth New York Volunteer Cavalry,* Norwich, New York, 1889.

Noyes, George F., *The Bivouac and the Battle-Field,* New York, 1863.

Owen, William Miller, *In Camp and Battle with the Washington Artillery of New Orleans,* Boston, 1885.

Parker, Thomas H., *History of the 51st Regiment of Pennsylvania Volunteers,* Philadelphia, 1869.

Pennsylvania at Antietam, Report of the Antietam Battlefield Memorial Commission of Pennsylvania, Harrisburg, 1906.

Pettengill, Samuel B., *The College Cavaliers,* Chicago, 1883.

Poague, William Thomas, *Gunner With Stonewall,* Monroe F. Cockrell, ed., Jackson, Tennessee, 1957.

Polley, J. B., *Hood's Texas Brigade,* Washington, 1910.

Quint, Alonzo H., *The Potomac and the Rapidan,* Boston, 1864.

Personal Narratives of Events in the War of the Rebellion, Rhode Island Soldiers and Sailors Historical Society, Series IV, Providence, 1889.

Small, A. R., Maj., *The Sixteenth Maine Regiment,* Portland, 1886.

Sorrel, G. Moxley, Brig. Gen., C.S.A., *Recollections of a Confederate Staff Officer,* Bell Irvin Wiley, ed., Jackson, Tennessee, 1958.

Souvenir of Excursion to Battlefield by the Society of the Fourteenth Connecticut Regiment, Washington, D. C., 1893.

Taylor, Walter H., *Four Years With General Lee,* James I. Robertson, Jr., ed., Bloomington, Indiana, 1962.

Thomas, Henry W., *History of the Doles-Cook Brigade,* Atlanta, 1903.

Todd, William, *The Seventy-Ninth Highlanders New York Volunteers in the War of the Rebellion,* Albany, 1886.

Von Borcke, Heros, *Memoirs of the Confederate War for Independence,* Vol. I, New York, 1938.

Walcott, Charles F., *History of the Twenty-First Regiment Massachusetts Volunteers in the War for the Preservation of the Union, 1861-1865,* Boston, 1882.

Ward, Joseph R. C., *History of the One Hundred and Sixth Regiment Pennsylvania Volunteers,* Philadelphia, 1906.

Washburn, George H., *A Complete Miltiary Record of the 108th Regiment New York Volunteers,* Rochester, 1894.

Welles, Gideon, *Diary of Gideon Welles,* Vol. I, Boston, 1911.

Worsham, John O., *One of Jackson's Foot Cavalry,* New York, 1912.

General Studies

American Historical Association, *Annual Report for 1902,* Vol. II, Washington, 1903.

Andrews, J. Cutler, *The North Reports the Civil War,* Pittsburgh, 1955.

Ankrum, Freeman, Rev., *Maryland and Pennsylvania Historical Sketches,* West Newton, Pennsylvania, 1947.

Ballard, Colin, R., Brig. Gen., *The Military Genius of Abraham Lincoln,* New York, 1952.

Battles and Leaders of the Civil War, Vols. I, II, New York, 1956.

Coffin, Charles Carlton, *The Boys of '61,* Boston, 1896.

Comte de Paris, *History of the Civil War in America,* Vol. II, Philadelphia, 1875-1888.

Coulter, E. Merton, *A History of the South: The Confederate States of America,* Vol. VII, Baton Rouge, Louisiana, 1950.

Cullum, George Washington, *Biographical Register of the Officers and Graduates of the United States Military Academy,* Vol. II, New York, 1879.

Dennett, Tyler, ed., *Lincoln and the Civil War in the Diaries and Letters of John Hay,* New York, 1939.

Dowdey, Clifford, and Manarin, Louis H., eds., *The Wartime Papers of R. E. Lee,* Boston, 1961.

Eisenschiml, Otto, and Newman, Ralph, *The Civil War: The American Iliad, As Told by Those Who Lived It,* Vol. I, New York, 1956.

Eliot, Ellsworth, Jr., *West Point in the Confederacy,* New York, 1941.

Evans, Clement A., ed., *Confederate Military History,* Vols. II, III, New York, 1962.

Freeman, Douglas Southall, *Lee's Lieutenants*, Vol. II, New York, 1942-1944.

Hendrick, Burton J., *Lincoln's War Cabinet*, Boston, 1946.

Hill, D. H., [Jr.], *A History of North Carolina in the War Between the States*, Vol. II, Raleigh, 1926.

Long, A. L., *Memoirs of Robert E. Lee*, New York, 1887.

Longstreet, Helen Dortch, *In the Path of Lee's "Old War Horse,"* Atlanta, 1917.

Manakee, Harold R., *Maryland in the Civil War*, Baltimore, 1961.

Macrae, David, *The Americans at Home*, Vol. I, New York, 1952.

McClure, A. K., *Abraham Lincoln and Men of War-Times*, Philadelphia, 1892.

Military Historical Society of Massachusetts, *Campaigns in Virginia, Maryland and Pennsylvania, 1862-1863*, Vol. III, Boston, 1881-1905.

Moore, Frank, *The Civil War in Song and Story*, New York, 1889.

Moore, Frank, ed., *The Rebellion Record: A Diary of American Events*, Vol. V, New York, 1862-1871.

Nevins, Allan, *The War for the Union: War Becomes Revolution, 1862-1863*, Vol. II, New York, 1959-1960.

Nicolay, John G., and Hay, John, *Abraham Lincoln: A History*, Vols. IV, VI, New York, 1890.

Palfrey, Francis Winthrop, *The Army in the Civil War, The Antietam and Fredericksburg*, New York, 1881.

Pinkerton, Allan, *The Spy of the Rebellion*, New York, 1883.

Pollard, Edward A., *The Lost Cause: A New Southern History of the War of the Confederates*, New York, 1867.

Reilly, Oliver T., *The Battlefield of Antietam*, Sharpsburg, Maryland, 1906.

Rhodes, James Ford, *History of the United States*, Vol. III, New York, 1893-1906.

Rice, Allen Thorndike, ed., *Reminiscences of Abraham Lincoln by Distinguished Men of his Time*, New York, 1888.

Richardson, Albert D., *The Secret Service*, Hartford Connecticut, 1865.

Ropes, John Codman, *The Story of the Civil War*, Vol. II, New York, 1898.

Ross, Fitzgerald, *Cities and Camps of the Confederate States*, Richard B. Harwell, ed., Urbana, Illinois, 1958.

Rowland, Dunbar, ed., *Jefferson Davis, Constitutionalist*, Vols. V, VII, Jackson, Mississippi, 1923.

Sandburg, Carl, *Abraham Lincoln, The War Years*, Vol. I, New York, 1939.

Smith, William E., *The Francis Preston Blair Family in Politics*, Vol. II, New York, 1933 .

Starr, Louis M., *Bohemian Brigade*, New York, 1954.

Steele, Matthew Forney, *American Campaigns*, Vol. I, Washington, 1951.

Swinton, William, *Campaigns of the Army of the Potomac*, New York, 1882.

Taylor, Richard, *Destruction and Reconstruction: Personal Experiences of the Late War*, New York, 1879.

Truman, Harry S., *Memoirs by Harry S. Truman: Years of Trial and Hope, 1946-1952*, Vol. II, New York, 1956.

Vandiver, Frank E., *Basic History of the Confederacy*, Princeton, New Jersey, 1962.

Welles, Gideon, *Lincoln and Seward*, New York, 1874.

Wiley, Bell Irvin, *The Life of Johnny Reb*, Indianapolis, Indiana, 1943.

Williams, Kenneth P., *Lincoln Finds a General*, Vol. I, New York, 1949-1959.

Williams, T. Harry, *Lincoln and His Generals*, New York, 1952.

——————— ———————, *McClellan, Sherman and Grant*, New Brunswick, New Jersey, 1962.

Wise, Jennings Cropper, *The Long Arm of Lee*, New York, 1959.

Newspapers and Periodicals

Charleston *Courier*, September 3, 1862.

Charleston *Mercury*, September 6, 1862.

Cincinnati *Gazette*, June 27, 1861.

Hagerstown [Md.] *Herald and Torch Light*, October 13, 1887.

New York *Herald*, September 9, 1862.

The New York Times, December 4, 1861; November 13, 1862.

New York *Tribune*, March 13, 14, 1862; September 8, 13, 20, 29, 1862.

Petersburg [Va.] *Express*, September 23, 1862.

Richmond *Dispatch*, August 11, 1862; September 8, 9, 10, 11, 13, 15, 16, 17, 22, 1862; October 9, 1862.

Richmond *Enquirer*, September 22, 1862.

Richmond *Examiner*, July 21, 1862; September 8, 1862.

Century Magazine, Vol. 70, No. 2.

Confederate Veteran, Vol. XXII.

Harper's New Monthly Magazine, February 1868; August 1894.

Harper's Weekly, August 1861; September 1862; February 1868.

The Land We Love, Vol. IV.

The North Carolina Historical Review, Vol. XLI, No. 2, April 1964.

Southern Historical Society Papers, Vols. X, XIII, XIV, XIX, XXXI.

INDEX